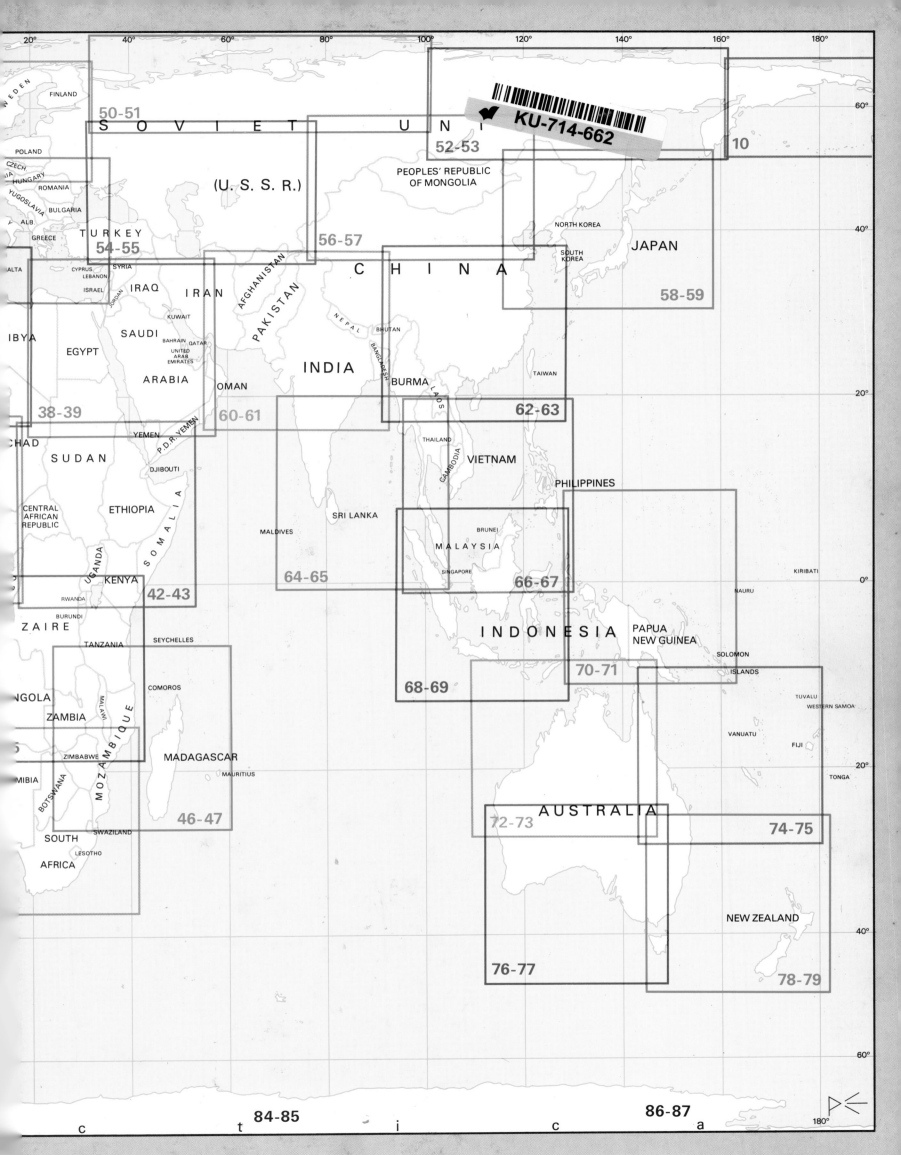

TOPOGRAPHIC MAPS

PETERS

ATLAS

OF THE

WORLD

Longman

Cartography:
Kümmerly + Frey, Bern (graticules, coastlines, borders, seas, rivers and lakes)
Oxford Cartographers (topographic and thematic maps)

Longman Group UK Limited,
Longman House, Burnt Mill, Harlow,
Essex CM20 2JE, England
And Associated Companies throughout the world.

First published 1989
Reprinted 1990
Peters, Arno
    Peters atlas of the world.
    1. World — Maps, atlases
    I. Title
    912

ISBN 0-582-03501-5

Photography: Clyde Surveys Ltd, Oxford Litho Plates Ltd
Scanning: Rapidagraphics Ltd, London
Typesetting: Oxford University Press, Getset (BTS) Ltd
Machine Proofing: Colourproof (UK) Ltd
Printing: Neue Stalling, Oldenburg
Binding: Neue Stalling, Oldenburg

FOREWORD

In 1493 – one year after Columbus's first voyage to America – the Pope apportioned the non-European world among the most powerful nations of his own continent. By the time Mercator completed his Atlas 100 years later, European domination had spread across the world, and Mercator's Atlas was the embodiment of Europe's geographical conception of the world in an age of colonialism.

Since then thousands of atlases have been published. They differ in many respects from Mercator's, but all adhere to the principle of a Eurocentric view of the world. The country and continent of origin are represented at a larger scale than the non-European countries. If, together with the age of colonialism, the view of the world that underpinned it is to come to an end, we need a new geography - one that is based on the equal status of all peoples.

This Atlas represents all countries and continents at the same scale. Their actual size and their position in the world can thus be taken directly from the map. This equal presentation is the expression of the consciousness that is gradually replacing our conventional ways of thinking about the world.

The use of a single scale for all topographic maps; the principle of fidelity of area; and a new, universally applicable presentation of relief; together, these now make possible a fundamental change in our conception of the world. All 246 thematic maps are also equal-area world maps. The comprehensive presentation in these thematic maps of man, nature and society is based on the same principle of equality as that underlying the topographic maps.

This Atlas, therefore, offers a way of understanding the background to, and causes of, the North-South divide as well as the tensions between East and West – so often the outcome of the gulf which separates rich and poor. In so doing, it throws new light on the profound changes of our times.

Arno Peters

CONTENTS

THE WORLD IN 43 MAPS AT THE SAME SCALE

THE AMERICAS

EUROPE

AFRICA

ASIA

AUSTRALASIA

ANTARCTICA

THE ARCTIC

NATURE, MAN AND SOCIETY IN 246 THEMATIC WORLD MAPS

CARTOGRAPHIC INTRODUCTION

It may come as a shock to realise that all of the atlases we have known until now present a distorted picture of the world. The nature of this distortion, and the reason for it, are now so obvious that it seems hardly possible to have overlooked them for over 400 years. The distortion caused by attempting to represent the spherical earth on flat paper is more or less unavoidable, but the distortion caused by the use of inconsistent scales, which has acquired the unquestioned sanction of habit, is not.

We have come to accept as "natural" a representation of the world that devotes disproportionate space to large-scale maps of areas perceived as important, while consigning other areas to small-scale general maps. And it is because our image of the world has become thus conditioned, that we have for so long failed to recognise the distortion for what it is — the equivalent of peering at Europe and North America through a magnifying glass and then surveying the rest of the world through the wrong end of a telescope.

There is nothing "natural" about such a view of the world. It is the remnant of a way of thinking born even before the age of colonialism and fired by that age. Few thinking people today would subscribe to a world-view of this kind. Yet, until now, no atlas has existed which provided the undistorted picture of the world which seems so long overdue.

A single scale
All topographic maps in this atlas are at the same scale: each double-page map shows one-sixtieth of the earth's surface. This means that all the topographic maps can be directly compared with one another. Among the many surprises this unique feature offers may be, for some users, the relative sizes of Great Britain (page 32) and the island of Madagascar (page 47); or, perhaps, the areas respectively covered by Europe (pages 32–33) and North Africa (pages 36–37). For most people it will soon become apparent that their hazy and long-held notions of the sizes of different countries and regions are, in a lot of cases, quite drastically wrong.

But what do we mean by scale? The scale indicator that appears on reference maps only shows distance scale. It enables the user to calculate the factor needed to multiply distances so as to compare them with those on other maps. This is a complex and somewhat tedious exercise that the great majority of users understandably neglect to carry out. Moreover, the number of different scales in our atlases is surprisingly high, in general between twenty and fifty. The concept of relative scale must become increasingly vague in the user's mind. What is generally not mentioned is that, because it is impossible to transfer the curved surface of the globe correctly to a flat plane, the scale indicator on a map is only valid for a single part of the map, such as a line of latitude.

Distance is only one aspect of the scale. Area has also to be considered. Whereas there can be no maps with absolute fidelity of distance, there can be maps with fidelity of area. The maps in this atlas preserve fidelity of area, a feature never previously achieved in an atlas. In the Peters Atlas all topographic maps have equal area scale: 1 square centimetre on the map equals 6,000 square kilometres in reality.

But there is a price to pay for the introduction of this innovation. This atlas is unsuitable for some purposes. A world atlas like this one is not designed to guide the motorist, or to replace the inexpensive detailed road map; nor is it intended as an aid for local geography. It offers, instead, a comprehensive global view.

A single symbology
This equality of scale offers further advantages besides direct comparability. The basis of any map compilation is the simplification of reality, which cartographers call "generalisation". This transfer of the real character of the earth's surface into a system of lines and symbols, which can be graphically represented, has to be adapted to the scale employed. Thus a river or road with all its turns and windings on a scale of 1:100,000 can be drawn nearer to reality, (that is, with more detail) than on a scale of 1:1,000,000. Symbols also vary for different scales. Thus the same symbol can mean a town with 50–100,000 inhabitants on one scale, but a city with 1–5 million inhabitants on another. The same elevation may be differently coloured on maps of different scale. All such difficulties vanish in this atlas, which by way of its single scale has only one level of generalisation and a single set of symbols.

Topographic map colours
The green/brown colouring of most current atlases represents the topographic relief of the region; green stands for low-lying areas, brown for mountainous country, with different shades of the two colours for different elevations. Since, however, both colours (as also the blue of the sea and the white of snow-covered mountains) are borrowed from nature, the user of the atlas may be forgiven for assuming the green parts on the map to represent areas with vegetation and the brown parts to be the barren land. Although this is broadly true in Europe it may not be so elsewhere. For example, in North Africa the lower areas, even those below sea level, are usually deserts, and it is only above a certain height in the mountains that vegetation begins. The green/brown colouring is thus unsuitable for representing relief in a genuine world atlas. So in this Atlas green represents vegetation, brown barren land, and a mixture of the two colours represents thin or scattered vegetation. Global vegetation data were obtained from 1985–86 satellite photography with the help of the Remote Sensing Unit at the Department of Geography of Bristol University. The resolution of this imagery down to individual units of 20 square kilometres, and its conversion to the Peters base maps by the Remote Sensing Unit, makes this the most up-to-date statement available of the distribution of world vegetation.

Topographic map relief
To give the impression of relief the Peters Atlas has combined two techniques: shading by hand, which has developed to an advanced art in recent years, and the technique less often used because of its high cost — that of making relief models of the terrain and then photographing them. Although model photography is unsurpassed in its three-dimensional effect, it presents two difficulties. Because the light source has to come primarily from one

direction, relief features running directly along the line of the light source are under-represented. At the same time, relief features running at 90 degrees to the light source and close to it sometimes lose detail, becoming either uniformly light or shadowed. To overcome both of these in the Peters Atlas, the relief features on the model photograph have been enhanced by hand. At the same time, more intense shading has been added to the highest mountains, so that the relative height of the mountains on any map can be judged at a glance. The addition of spot heights for selected peaks and other points on the map lends accuracy to this technique.

The Peters Projection
Anyone who has ever tried to peel an orange and press the peel into a continuous flat piece without tearing will have grasped the fundamental impossibility that lies at the heart of all cartographic endeavour: that fidelity of shape, distance and angle are of necessity lost in flattening the surface of a sphere. On the other hand it is possible to retain three other qualities: fidelity of area, fidelity of axis and fidelity of position. Fidelity of area makes it possible to compare various parts of a map directly with one another, and fidelity of axis and position guarantee correct relationships of north-south and east-west axes by way of rectangular grid.

In 1973 Arno Peters published his world map, which unites in a single flat map all three achievable qualities − fidelity of area, fidelity of axis and fidelity of position. In this way the real comparative sizes of all countries in the world are clearly visible. For this Atlas Arno Peters has generalised the projection principle upon which his World Map was based, so that now each regional map represents the maximum possible freedom from distortion. Since map distortions through a projection decrease in proportion as the area represented becomes smaller, the forty-three topographical maps in this Atlas are considerably closer to reality than in the Peters World Map. In particular these individual maps correct the distortions which are unavoidable on the Peters World Map in the equatorial and polar regions. An indication of how this has been applied can be seen from the shapes of the page areas on the Map Finder (front endpaper). In the North they are long and thin while towards the Equator they are nearly square. The degree of departure from the normal page proportion is a guide to the amount of shape correction applied to the regional maps.

The eight polar maps on pages 80−95 have the same scale as all the other topographical maps. They also have fidelity of area, and represent one-sixtieth of the Earth's surface on each double page. Thus the size of the countries and continents shown on them can be directly compared with all the other 35 topographical maps. The fidelity of position and axis which is necessarily lost on polar maps is also not present on these maps.

The thematic maps
The second part of this Atlas directs attention to the whole earth. The author has collected data for 246 individual world thematic maps under 45 subject headings. Each of these subject headings is given a double page spread, but if more than one topic is covered under any subject, separate maps are given. Thus under the subject heading "Life Expectancy" only one topic is covered so the double spread comprises a single map, whereas the subject heading "Domestic Animals" requires sixteen topics and therefore displays sixteen individual maps. The principle of one topic per map also enables all the maps to be represented by simple grades of colour, with, usually, a single hue chosen for each topic. Within this hue the range from light to dark colour represents low to high values of the topic. In this way all the thematic maps can be understood at a glance, without the necessity for complicated symbols or explanations.

The graticule
The traditional zero meridian running through Greenwich was adopted worldwide in 1884, when Britain was the strongest European colonial power and ruled over a quarter of the world. After the ending of colonialism and with the closure of Greenwich Observatory, there is no reason other than custom for retaining this zero meridian. The International Dateline, which is dependent upon the zero meridian, also needs correction, since over its whole length it has been partially diverted where it cuts an inhabited area. The retention of the division into 360 degrees is also, it can be argued, an anomaly in the age of worldwide decimalisation.

Arno Peters has therefore proposed a new decimal grid in which the zero meridian and the International Date Line would become a single line placed in the middle of the Bering Strait, and the earth is divided into 100 decimal degrees east-west and north-south. While for practical reasons the Greenwich system is retained throughout the bulk of the Atlas, the new decimal grid is shown on pages 230−231.

The Index
Someone consulting an index in search of a district, town or river has until now had to memorise, besides the page number, at least two grid figures, two letters, or a letter and a number. There can be few users of an atlas who have not experienced the irritation of forgetting at least one item in this unwieldy string of digits by the time the relevant map has been located, and the time-consuming exercise of turning back to the index to recall this information. In the Peters Atlas there is, apart from the page number, only a single letter, which can easily be remembered. This innovatory and simple indexing system is explained on page 188.

Computer cartography
Computer cartography now makes it possible to keep maps up to date with the latest results of worldwide research. At the same time, however, pure automation can rob the map of its best characteristics − the handcrafted workmanship of the cartographer.

The Peters Atlas combines both of these approaches. The base maps have been recentred from the world projection using Europe's most modern Scitex computer installation in Berne, with geographic data from the Erdgenössische Technische Hochschule. Satellite data for vegetation has been tailored by computer to fit these bases. The rest of the cartography for the topographic and thematic maps has remained in the hands of traditional cartographic craftsmen in Oxford. The Peters Atlas therefore reconciles these two approaches. We have used as much mechanisation as necessary and as much handcraft as possible.

Terry Hardaker

Chief Cartographer
Oxford Cartographers

ACKNOWLEDGEMENTS

Contributors and Consultants
Dr. E. C. Barrett
Professor Ulrich Bleil
Michael Benckert
Wolfgang Behr
Professor Heinz Bosse
Professor Walter Buchholz
Dr. Nicola Bradbear
Carol Claxton
Professor Heinrich Dathe
Hellmuth Färber
Jean Fernand-Laurent
Kurt Ficker
Professor Fritz Fischer
Karlheinz Gieseler
Professor Manfred Görlach
Professor Ulrich Grosse
Arnulf Hader
Max Hann
Dirk Hansohm
Dr. Günther Heidmann
Professor Wolf Herre
Karl-Heinz Ingenhaag
Dr. Andreas Kaiser
Professor Gunther Krause
Dr. Manfred Kummer
Daniel Lloyd
Konrad G. Lohse
Wolfgang Mache
Dr. Udo Moll
Georg Möller
Dr. Aribert Peters
Birgit Peters
Werner Peters
Thomas Plümer
D. H. Reichstein
Hellmut Schlien
Professor Hermann Schulz
Professor Axel Sell
Eduard Spescha
Jürgen Wendler
Professor Adolf Witte
Professor Karl Wohlmuth
Siegfried Zademack
Madeleine Zeller

Cartographic Editor
Terry Hardaker

Editorial Coordination
Penny Watson

Computer Programmer
H. Morelli

Topographic Map Compilation
Katharine Armitage
Claire Carlton
John Hall
Hazel Hand
Sheila Hodson
Christine Johnston
Jean Kelly
Tanya Lillington
Angela Morrison
Kay Roberts
Fiona Sutcliffe

Editorial Checking
Ann Leleu
Georg Möller

Technical Coordination
John Dawson
John Wilders

Draughting
Gerhard Engel
Bob Hawkins
Ben Hill
Sally Horn
Robert Hundley
Jeff Jones
David Lewis
Sue Lovell
Colin McCarthy
Michael Oakley
Piet Summerfield

Estimating
Peter Langran
John Williams

Terrain Modelling
David Angus

Terrain Colouring
Terry Hardaker

Indexing
Barbara Croucher
Duncan Croucher
Betty Döppl
Petra Faltermeier
Karin Geier
Franz Huber
Ingrid Kampfhenkel
Hermann Lechner
Lothar Meier
Anton Sommer
Iris Sommer
Margret Suhr

THE WORLD IN 43 MAPS AT THE SAME SCALE
EACH MAP SHOWS ONE-SIXTIETH OF THE EARTH'S SURFACE.

The colours used on the maps simulate those found in nature.

Water (Lakes, Seas, Oceans)

Ice Shelf

Vegetation (Plains)

Barren Land (Plains)

Continental Ice (Plains)

Vegetation (Hills)

Barren Land (Hills)

Continental Ice (Hills)

Vegetation (Mountains)

Barren Land (Mountains)

Continental Ice (Mountains)

Spot Heights:

- •1236   1236 Metres above Sea Level
- •-25   25 Metres below Sea Level

Communications:

- ——— Railway
- ——— Road
- ═══ Motorway
- = = = Motorway in Tunnel
- 〜〜 River
- ⊢⊢⊢ Canal

Boundaries:

- - - - International Boundary
- 〜〜 International Boundary on River
- - — - Disputed International Boundary
- ······· State Boundary

On each double page the 1000 largest and most important cities and towns are shown; if the double page shows sea as well as land, there are proportionately fewer:

- ○ fewer than 100,000 inhabitants
- ⊙ 100,000 – 1,000,000 inhabitants
- ■ 1,000,000 – 5,000,000 inhabitants
- ⬗ over 5,000,000 inhabitants

Adjoining map indicator:

 25   Map of adjoining area is on page 25.

Other physical features:

- ⊥ Waterfall
- Swamp, Marsh
- Salt Lake
- Coral Reef

Other man-made features:

- ∴ Archaeological Site
- ⊓⊓⊓ Great Wall of China

Latitude and Longitude:

- 25°E   25 degrees Longitude East
- 50°W   50 degrees Longitude West
- 30°N   30 degrees Latitude North
- 60°S   60 degrees Latitude South
- - - - Tropics

Type styles:

- *Mato Grosso*   Physical Features
- Kolhapur   Cities and towns (capital cities underlined)
- **BELGIUM**   Countries
- T E X A S   States
- *INDIAN OCEAN*   Oceans, Seas

⊳⊂ Peters Projection (fidelity of area, axis and position)

160°W 155°W 150°W 145°W 140°W 135°W 130°W

O C E A N

Cape Barrow
Barrow
Wainwright

B E A U F O R T   S E A

Cape Dalhousie

Prudhoe Bay
Deadhorse
Kaktovik
Herschel
Mackenzie Bay
Tuktoyaktuk

70°N

Colville
Mount Chamberlin 2749 2286
NORTHWEST

Misheguk Mountain 1289
Brooks Range
2438
Anaktuvuk Pass 2319
Arctic Village
Old Crow
1981
Aklavik
Inuvik
TERRITORIES

Noatak
Baird Mountains
Endicott Mountains
Wiseman
Porcupine
Fort McPherson
Arctic Red River

Kotzebue
Noorvik
Kobuk
Fort Yukon
Eagle Plain
Mackenzie

65°N

A L A S K A
1372
Hughes
Circle
Clinton Creek
1874
Wernecke Mts.

Koyuk
(U.S.A.)
Tanana
Manley Hot Springs
Eagle Summit 1611
Yukon
2499
Mount Campbell
Y U K O N
Keno Hill 2088
2975
Keele Peak

Galena
Ruby
Nenana
Fairbanks
Dawson
Barlow
Mayo
Stewart

Kaltag
Yukon
1291
McGrath
Richardson
Big Delta
Sixtymile
T E R R I T O R Y
Pelly Crossing
Stewart Crossing
Macmillan

Unalakleet
1374
Delta Junction
Mount Kimball 3155
Northway Junction
2399
Little Salmon
Faro
Ross River

Kuskokwim Mts.
Mount McKinley 6194
Cantwell
Tanacross
Tok
Stewart
C A N A D A
Pelly
Carmacks

Holy Cross
Talkeetna
Paxson
Slana
Snag
Koidern
Braeburn

Stony River
Range
Glennallen
Gulkana
Mount Blackburn 4996
Burwash Landing
Haines Junction
Whitehorse

Aniak
Lime Village
Mount Torbert 3479
Willow
Palmer
Copper Center
Chitina
Wrangell Mts.
2213
Johnsons Crossing
Jakes Corner
Teslin

Kuskokwim
Anchorage
Mount Witherspoon 3666
Valdez
5011
Mount Logan 5964 4785
Carcross
Lake Atlin
Morley River

Bethel
Kwethluk
Port Alsworth
3108
Kenai Peninsula
Seward
Cordova
St. Elias Mountains
Skagway
BRITISH 2301

60°N

Kwigillingok
Iliamna Lake
Yakutat
Haines
Mount Fairweather 4670
COLUMBIA
Cassiar

Goodnews Bay
Togiak
Dillingham
3882
Alexander
Juneau
Dease Lake

Bristol Bay
Naknek
King Salmon
G u l f
o f
A l a s k a
Archipelago
Coast
Mount Ratz 3136
Telegraph Creek

Ugashik
Kodiak
Kodiak
Stikine
3049
Sitka
Baranof Island
Wrangell
Mount Pattullo 2739

Alaska Peninsula
Chignik
Mount Veniaminof 2507
P A C I F I C
Mountains
Prince of Wales Island
Stewart

55°N

Squaw Harbor
(U.S.A.)
O C E A N
Ketchikan
Dixon Entrance
Prince Rupert

Queen Charlotte Islands

Hecate Strait

160°W 155°W 150°W 145°W 140°W 135°W 130°W

0   100   200   300   miles
Average linear scale : 1 inch ≈ 125 miles 1cm ≈ 80 km
0   100   200   300   400   500   Km

a b c d e f g h i j k l m

90

90°W 85°W 80°W 75°W 70°W 65°W

80°N

Nansen Sound

Axel Heiberg Island   Eureka   Agassiz
Ice Cap

Islands   Ellesmere

Norwegian   Bay   Island

Graham Island   Bjorne
Peninsula   Sydney
Ice Cap •1328   North Lincoln Land   Smith Bay

Table
Island   Jones   Sound   Grise Fjord

Devon   Island   •1887   Baffin

290   Dundas Harbour

Strait   Cape
Clarence   Bay   75°N

merset Island   Lancaster   Sound

Prince Regent Inlet   Admiralty
Inlet   •1189   Bylot Island
•2134

•549   Arctic Bay   Pond Inlet

Brodeur
Peninsula   Borden
Peninsula   Eclipse Sound

Gulf   Baffin   Buchan Gulf

244 •   B   •1554   Clyde

of   Bernier Bay   518

572   •

othia   Boothia   Fury and Hecla Strait   Baffin   Barnes
Ice Cap •1250   70°N

nsula
ay   •558   Jens Munk
Island   Henry Kater Pen.

E   Simpson
Peninsula   Rowley
Island   Foley   Home
Bay

229   Pelly
Bay   Committee
Bay   Wales
Island   Melville   Island   Penny
Ice Cap
•2591   Kivitoo   Davis Strait

Broughton Island

Rae Isthmus   Peninsula   Nunatak   •2134   Cape
Dyer

503   Repulse Bay   381 •   Koukdjuak   Nettiling
Lake   Pagnirtung   Exeter Sound

Lyon Inlet   Foxe Basin   Region   Cumberland Peninsula   Hoare
Bay

Wager Bay   Vansittart
Island   Nabukjuak   Kigisa   Cumberland

Southampton •625   Foxe Channel   Foxe Peninsula   Amadjuak
Lake   Hall   •1148   65°N

watin   Island   •411   Sound

RIES   Chesterfield Inlet   Roes Welcome Sound   Coral Harbour   Cape Dorset   Iqaluit
(Frobisher Bay)   Peninsula

Chesterfield
Inlet   Bell
Peninsula   Salisbury
Island   Meta Incognita Peninsula   Labrador

Rankin Inlet   Fisher
Strait   Evans
Strait   305 •   Big
Island   Frobisher Bay

Whale Cove   Nottingham
Island   Lake
Harbour   Harper Island

D   Coats
Island   •540   A   Salluit   Purtuniq

Mansel
Island   Ivujivik   •661   Resolution
Island

skimo Point   Kangiqsujuaq

gion   Akulivik   Cape Hopes
Advance   Sea

Hudson   Ungava   Akpatok
Island   Port
Burwell   Cape
Chidley

Povungnituk   60°N

pe   Ottawa Islands   1   Ungava   ATLANTIC OCEAN

churchill   Bay   Peninsula   390 •   Bay

•1621   Ramah

Inukjuak   NEWFOUNDLAND

Nelson   aux Feuilles   Kangiqsualujjuaq

York Factory   Kuujjuaq

196 •   Lac Minto   Koksoak   Nutak

Shamattawa   •472   Labrador   •1076

Fort Severn   Lac à
l'Eau-Claire   QUEBEC   Fraser

ONTARIO   241   •451   Nain

Seven   Belcher
Islands   876 •   Hopedale

Winisk   Cape
Henrietta Maria   Kuujjuarapik   Lac
Bienville   Caniapiscau   55°N

n o p q r s t u v w x y z

16   17

110°W · 105°W · 100°W · 95°W · 90°W · 55°N

CANADA

SASKATCHEWAN · **MANITOBA** · **ONTARIO**

Centre · Beaver · Meadow Lake · .747 · Lac La-Ronge · .365 · Flin Flon · Wabowden · .178 · Gods Lake · Bearskin Lake · Big Trout Lake

North Saskatchewan · North Battleford · Prince Albert · Melfort · Tisdale · Hudson Bay · .823 · The Pas · Moose-Lake · Norway House · Sandy Lake · North Caribou Lake · .396 · Wunnummin Lake

Adanac · Biggar · Saskatoon · Saskatchewan · Swan River · Cedar Lake · .217 · Island Lake · Pipangikum Lake · Lake St. Joseph

Kindersley · Rosetown · Central Butte · Davidson · .490 · Wynyard · Yorkton · Dauphin · Lake Winnipegosis · Lake Winnipeg · Berens River · .305 · Red Lake · .359 · Cat Lake · Albany

.789 · Saskatchewan · Swift Current · Moose Jaw · Regina · Indian Head · Melville · Winnipegosis · Lake Manitoba · .710 · Riverton · Pinawa · Kenora · Dryden · Lake Seul · Sioux Lookout · Lake St. Joseph

South · Maple Creek · Shaunavon · Assiniboia · Milestone · Weyburn · .678 · Neepawa · Winnipeg Beach · Pinawa · Winnipeg · Trans · English River · .500

.082 · Gladmar · Estevan · .500 · Virden · Brandon · Portage la Prairie · Winnipeg · Middleboro · Fort Frances · Rainy Lake · Canada Highway · Thunder Bay · 50°N

.1000 · Westhope · Morden · Red River · International Falls · Atikokan · Grand Marais · 646

Havre · Malta · Glasgow · Wolf Point · Culbertson · Kenmare · Stanley · Rugby · Langdon · Devils Lake · Grafton · Thief River Falls · Upper Red Lake · English River

MONTANA · **NORTH DAKOTA** · **MINNESOTA** · Lake Superior

Lewiston · Jordan · Glendive · .1108 · Williston · Minot · .300 · Grand Forks · Crookston · Bemidji · Hibbing · Virginia · Duluth · Apostle Islands

Harlowtown · Roundup · Miles City · Sidney · Sakakawea Reservoir · Carrington · Valley City · Moorhead · Fergus Falls · Grand Rapids · Cloquet · Superior · Ashland · Ironwood

Billings · Hardin · Forsyth · Baker · Belfield · Dickinson · Bismarck · Jamestown · Fargo · .381 · Lake Mille · Rhinelander

Granite Peak 3917 · Ashland · Broadus · .1076 · Bowman · Lemmon · Frederick · .500 · Sisseton · Alexandria · Little Falls · Pine City · Merrill

WYOMING · Sheridan · Cloud Peak 4016 · Buffalo · Sundance · Spearfish · Buffalo · Bison · .840 · Mobridge · Selby · Aberdeen · Ortonville · Willmar · St. Cloud · Rice Lake · Ladysmith

Grey Bull · Gillette · Newcastle · 2184 · Rapid City · Lake Oahe · Gettysburg · .619 · Montevideo · Minneapolis-St. Paul · Red Wing · Chippewa Falls · Wausau · 45°N

SOUTH DAKOTA · Black Hills · Cheyenne · Hot Springs · Pierre · Huron · Watertown · Marshall · New Ulm · Faribault · Eau Claire · Marshfield · **WISCONSIN**

Cody · Worland · Kaycee · 4202 Gannett Peak · Lander · Casper 1561 · Douglas · Lusk · Chadron · White River · .416 · Mitchell · Chamberlain · Brookings · Worthington · Fairmont · Albert Lea · Austin · Mankato · Rochester · Tomah · La Crosse

UNITED · Alcova · Muddy Gap · Niobrara · Valentine · Yankton · Missouri · Big Sioux · Sioux Falls · Spencer · Estherville · Mason City · Decorah · Portage · Madison · .436 · Janesville

Eden · Rawlins · Rock Springs · Thedford · 700 · Bassett · O'Neill · Sioux City · Storm Lake · Fort Dodge · Webster City · Dubuque · Rockford

Scottsbluff · Alliance · Norfolk · Randolph · Denison · Ames · **IOWA** · Cedar Rapids · Iowa City · Rochelle

Chugwater · **NEBRASKA** · Columbus · Omaha · Des Moines · Newton · Davenport · Moline · Princeton

Cheyenne 1848 · Sidney · North Platte · Grand Island · Platte · Council Bluffs · Creston · Burlington · Galesburg

TATES · Walden · Fort Collins · Greeley · Sterling · Imperial · Kearney · Hastings · Lincoln · Nebraska City · Shenandoah · Peoria · Bloomington

Steamboat Springs · Boulder 1655 · Fort Morgan · McCook · Republican · .500 · Beatrice · Bethany · Kirksville · .300 · Keokuk · **ILLINOIS** · 40°N

Craig · Rifle · Glenwood Springs · **Denver** 1608 · Limon · Norton · Concordia · St. Joseph · Chillicothe · Quincy · Macon · Jacksonville · Springfield

Mack · Grand Junction · **COLORADO** · Burlington · Oakley · Junction City · Manhattan · Topeka · Atchison · Leavenworth · Hannibal · Litchfield · Alton

Montrose · Mt. Elbert 4399 · Colorado Springs 1833 · Kit Carson · Hays · Salina · **Kansas City** · Independence · Marshall · Columbia · .307 · Springfield

San Juan Mountains · Pikes Peak 4300 · Canon City · 1000 · **KANSAS** · Ottawa · Sedalia · Jefferson City · **St. Louis** · Vandalia

Monticello · Blanding · Pueblo 1431 · La Junta · Lamar · Garden City · Hutchinson · Emporia · Clinton · Nevada · Lake Ozark · Rolla · Sullivan · Mount Vernon

Durango · Walsenburg · Dodge City · Pratt · Wichita · El Dorado · Fort Scott · **MISSOURI** · Lebanon · Perryville · .540 · Cape Girardeau

Mexican Water · Farmington · Trinidad · Springfield · Liberal · Cimarron · Bucklin · Arkansas City · Independence · Joplin · Bolivar · Springfield · Cabool · Cairo

NEW · Chinle · Wheeler Peak 4009 · Raton · Boise City · Guymon · Beaver · Alva · Bartlesville · Ponca City · Miami · Aurora · Neosho · Branson · .411 · Poplar Bluff

Los Alamos · Santa Fe 2132 · Las Vegas · Wagon Mound · Clayton · Dalhart · Perryton · Woodward · Enid · Tulsa · Oologah Lake · Fayetteville · Ozark Plateau · Hardy

MEXICO · Gallup · Houck · Grants · Albuquerque 1509 · Santa Rosa · .1516 · Tucumcari · **TEXAS** · Canadian · **OKLAHOMA** · Guthrie · Oklahoma City · Henryetta · Muskogee · Fort Smith · Clarksville · Newport · West Memphis

Belen · Vaughn · Pecos · Hereford · Amarillo · Shamrock · Clinton · Hobart · Chickasha · Shawnee · McAlester · **ARKANSAS** · Brinkley · Memphis

Low · Holbrook · Winslow · Rio Grande · Clovis · Tulia · Altus · Lawton · Ada · 722 · Little Rock · Pine Bluff · Dyersburg · Jonesboro

35°N

110°W · 105°W · 100°W · 95°W · 90°W

0 · 100 · 200 · 300 miles · Average linear scale: 1 inch ≈ 125 miles 1 cm ≈ 80 km · 0 · 100 · 200 · 300 · 400 · 500 Km

a b c d 12 e f g h i j k l m

95°W — 90°W — 85°W — 80°W — 75°W

MANITOBA

55°N

50°N

45°N

40°N

35°N

ONTARIO

CANADA

QUÉBEC

Hudson Bay

James Bay

Belcher Islands

Great Whale

Cape Henrietta Maria

Point Louis XIV

Akimiki Island

Hannah Bay

Winisk
Fort Severn
Shamattawa
Bearskin Lake
Big Trout Lake
Winisk Lake
Wunnummin Lake
Attawapiskat Lake
Lake River
Fort Albany
Moosonee
Fort Rupert
Kuujjuarapik
Chisasibi
La Radisson
Kanaaupscow
Sakami
Eastmain
Eastmain

Gods Lake
Island Lake
Sandy Lake 276
North Caribou Lake .396
Cat Lake
Fort Hope 268
Ogoki
Attawapiskat
Albany
Abitibi
Missinaibi
Kesagami Lake
Lake Evans 232

Pinawa .317
Kenora
Dryden
Trans Canada Highway
Sioux Lookout
Armstrong
Nakina
Longlac
Geraldton
Hearst
Fraserdale
Cochrane
Matagami
Chibougamau 556
Chapais

Red Lake .359
Lac Seul
Lake St. Joseph
358 .500
Nipigon
Longlac
Kapuskasing
Lake Abitibi
Monts Deloge 533
Noranda
Senneterre
Val-d'Or

Middleboro
Lake of the Woods
English River
Nipigon
Manitouwadge
Marathon
Schreiber
White River
Wawa
Timmins
390
New Liskeard 693
Kirkland Lake
Témiscaming
Cabonga Reservoir

Thief River Falls
International Falls
Fort Frances
Rainy Lake
Atikokan
Thunder Bay
Isle Royale
Grand Marais 646
Copper Harbor
Houghton .603
Chapleau 640
Blind River
Espanola
Sudbury
Sturgeon Falls .196
North Bay
Mont Laurier
Maniwaki
Buckingham
Hull
Ste-Agathe-des-Monts

Upper Red Lake
Lower Red Lake
358
Virginia
Lake Superior
Marquette
Seney
Sault Ste. Marie .665
Little Current
Manitoulin Island
Georgian Bay
Parry Sound
Pembroke
Bancroft 419
Ottawa

Hibbing
Grand Rapids 436.
Duluth
Superior
Ashland
Apostle Islands
Ironwood .573
Iron Mountain
Mackinaw City
Petoskey
Alpena
Tobermory
Owen Sound
Huntsville
609

Bemidji
471
Cloquet
.454
Rice Lake
Ladysmith
Rhinelander
Escanaba
Manitoulin 322
Orillia
Midland .573
Barrie
Peterborough
Cornwall

Fergus Falls
Brainerd 381.
Mille Lacs
Pine City
St. Cloud
Chippewa Falls
Wausau
Merrill
Menominee
Marinette
Sturgeon Bay
Grayling
Port Elgin
Lake Huron
Simcoe
637.

MINNESOTA
Alexandria
Willmar
Minneapolis-St. Paul
River Falls
Eau Claire
Marshfield
Stevens Point
Green Bay
Goderich
Kitchener-Waterloo
Hamilton .200
St. Catharines
Rochester
Syracuse
NEW YORK
Adirondack Mountains

15

Minnesota
Marshall
New Ulm
Faribault
.510
Red Wing
WISCONSIN
Appleton
Oshkosh
Manitowoc
Sheboygan
Luddington
Bay City
Saginaw
Flint .385
Sarnia
London
Toronto
Oshawa
Belleville
Kingston
Waterton

Mankato
Rochester
Winona
Tomah
La Crosse
Fond du Lac 369
Muskegon
Midland
MICHIGAN
Lansing
Ann Arbor
St. Thomas
Lake Ontario
Utica
Schenectady

Worthington
Estherville
Spencer
Albert Lea
Austin
Decorah
Mason City .300
Madison
494
Portage .223
Milwaukee
Racine
Grand Rapids
Kalamazoo
Détroit
Windsor
Niagara Falls
Buffalo
Seneca Lake
770
Elmira
Binghampton
Catskill Mountains

Storm Lake
Fort Dodge
Webster City
Janesville .436
Beloit
Kenosha
Chicago
Battle Creek
Jackson
Erie
Meadville .424
Dansville
Ithaca
Kingsto
Newburgh

IOWA
Denison
Ames .290
Cedar Rapids
Freeport
Rockford
Elgin
De Kalb
Rochelle
Gary
South Bend
Toledo
Sandusky
775
Olean
Kane
Mansfield
Williamsport
Scranton
Paterson
Newark

Omaha
Council Bluffs
Shenandoah
Des Moines
Newton
Iowa City
Davenport
Moline
Princeton
Morris
Joliet
Napoleon
Ashtabula
Lake Erie
Cleveland
Youngstown
Clearfield
PENNSYLVANIA
Allentown
Elizabeth

St. Joseph
Atchison
Knoxville
Oskaloosa
Ottumwa
Burlington
Galesburg
236.
Kankakee
Fort Wayne
Findlay
Lima
Canton
Mansfield
Johnstown
Altoona
Harrisburg
705
Reading
Trenton

Bethany
Kirksville
Keokuk
Peoria
Wabash
Kokomo
Kenton
Pittsburgh
Greensburg 956
Cumberland
Lancaster
Wilmington
NEW JERSEY

Leavenworth
367.
300.
Quincy
Beardstown
Bloomington
Lafayette
Rantoul
Danville
Muncie
Springfield
Newark
Wheeling .424
Fairmont
Clarksburg
Hagerstown
MARYLAND
Philadelphia

Kansas City
Topeka
ILLINOIS
Macon
Hannibal
307.
Jacksonville
Decatur
Champaign
Anderson
Dayton
Columbus
Cambridge
Parkersburg
Bickle Knob 1222
Baltimore
Washington DC

St. Joseph
Chillicothe
Marshall
Columbia
INDIANA
Indianapolis
Richmond
Washington Court House
Chillicothe
Athens
Marietta
Clarksburg
Elkins
Arlington
Alexandria
Annapolis
DELAWARE

Independence
Sedalia
Jefferson City
322
Terre Haute
Bloomington
Cincinnati
Hillsboro
412.
Portsmouth
WEST VIRGINIA
Spruce Knob 1478
1234
Culpeper
Fredericksburg
Cape May

Emporia
Fort Scott
Clinton
MISSOURI
Vandalia
Effingham
Bedford
Maysville
Huntington
Charleston
Richwood
VIRGINIA
Lexington
Park
Salisbury

Lake Ozark
Sullivan
Festus
Mt. Vernon
Jasper
Louisville
Morehead
Williamson
Beckley
Bluefield
Roanoke
Williamsburg
Hampton
23

Nevada
Lebanon
Rolla
Perryville
West Frankfort
Owensboro
Elizabethtown
Berea
Pikeville
Williamson
Spruce Knob
Lynchburg
Richmond
Chesapeake Bay

300.
Bolivar
Springfield
540
Cape Girardeau
Cairo
Central City
Hazard
Wytheville
Marion
Martinsville
Danville
Petersburg
Newport News

Independence
Miami
Bartlesville
Joplin
Aurora
510
Cabool
Poplar Bluff
Paducah
KENTUCKY
Bowling Green
Lake Cumberland
Somerset
Mount Rogers 1743
784
Mount Airy
Winston Salem
Greensboro
Roanoke Rapids
Ahoskie
Elizabeth City

Tulsa
Vinita
Neosho
Branson
Marshall
Jonesboro
Blytheville
Clarksville
Nashville
Murfreesboro
High Knob
Oak Ridge 2025
Clingmans Dome 2037
Asheville
Hickory
Kannapolis
Durham
Raleigh
Rocky Mount
Greenville
Cape Hatteras

McAlester
Henryetta
Muskogee
Fort Smith
Poteau
ARKANSAS
Fayetteville
Ozark Plateau
Hardy
TENNESSEE
Jackson
Dyersburg
Columbia
Lawrenceburg
1079
Chattanooga
Cleveland
Henderson
NORTH CAROLINA
Charlotte
Rockingham
Fayetteville
New Bern
Pamlico Sound

Little Rock
Conway
West Memphis
Memphis .100
Savannah
Fayetteville
Huntsville
Knoxville
Newport
Blue Ridge Parkway
Appalachian Mountains
Spartanburg
Greenville
Goldsboro
Greenville
Morehead City

Brinkley
Florence
95°W — 90°W — 85°W — 80°W — 75°W

This map shows 1/60 of the earth's surface. Area scale : 1 □ inch on the map ≙ 15,000 □ miles on the ground 1 □ cm on the map ≙ 6000 □ km on the ground

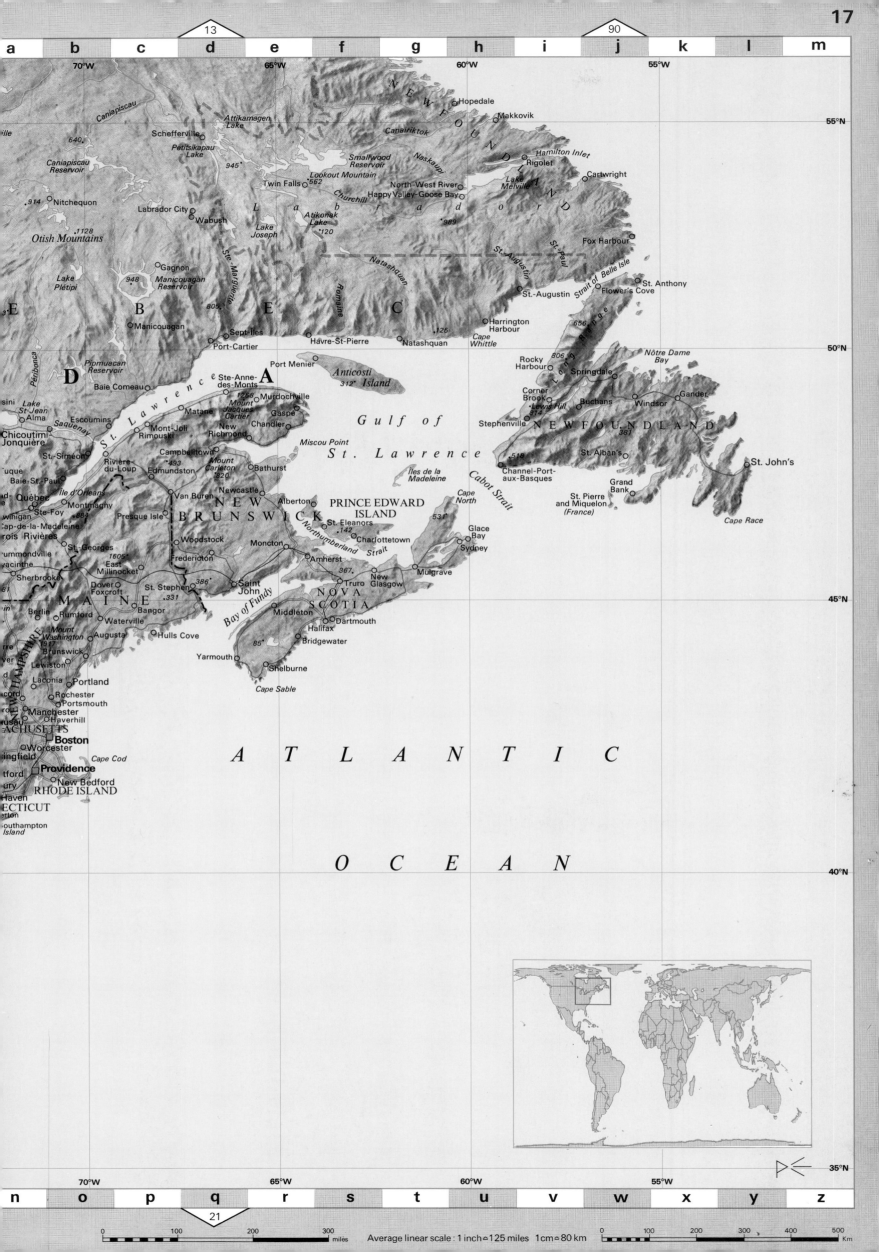

70°W   65°W   60°W   55°W

55°N

Hopedale
Makkovik

N E W F O U N D L A N D

Caniapiscau
Attikamagen
Lake
Canairiktok
Scheferville
Petitsikapau
Lake
Smallwood
Reservoir
Naskaupi
Hamilton Inlet
Rigolet
Lake
Melville
Cartwright
640.
945.
Lookout Mountain
Twin Falls 562
North-West River
Happy Valley-Goose Bay
L a b r a d o r
.914   Nitchequon
Caniapiscau
Reservoir
Churchill
.989
Labrador City
Wabush
Atikonak
Lake
.120
.1128
Fox Harbour
Otish Mountains
Lake
Joseph
Natashquan
St.-Augustin
St.-Paul
.3E   Strait of Belle Isle
Gagnon
St.-Augustin   St. Anthony
948   Manicouagan
Reservoir
E   B   E   C
Harrington
Harbour
656.
805.
Flower's Cove
Lake
Plétipi
Péribonca
Sept-Îles
Port-Cartier
Havre-St-Pierre
Natashquan
.125
Cape
Whittle
50°N
Pipmuacan
Reservoir
Port Menier
Anticosti
Island
312.
Rocky
Harbour
806.
Nôtre Dame
Bay
sini
Lake
St-Jean
Alma
Baie Comeau
Ste-Anne-
des-Monts
Murdochville
A
L o n g   R a n g e
Springdale
Gulf   of
St. Lawrence
Corner
Brook
Lewis Hill
874.
Buchans
Windsor
Gander
Chicoutimi
Jonquière
Saguenay
Escoumins
Matane
Mont-Joli
Rimouski
Mount
Jacques
Cartier
1268.
Gaspé
Chandler
New
Richmond
N E W F O U N D L A N D
Stephenville
381.
St-Siméon
Miscou Point
.518
St. Alban's
Rivière-
du-Loup
Campbelltown
.493
Mount
Carleton
.820
Bathurst
Newcastle
Îles de la
Madeleine
Cabot Strait
Channel-Port-
aux-Basques
St. John's
uque
Baie-St-Paul
Île d'Orléans
Edmundston
Van Buren
N E W
Alberton
PRINCE EDWARD
ISLAND
Cape
North
Grand
Bank
d.   Québec
Ste-Foy   .884
Montmagny
Presque Isle
B R U N S W I C K
St. Eleanors
.142
531.
Glace
Bay
St. Pierre
and Miquelon
(France)
Cape Race
winigan
Cap-de-la-Madeleine
rois Rivières
Woodstock
Moncton
Charlottetown
Sydney
ummondville
yacinthe
St-Georges
1605.
East
Millinocket
Fredericton
Amherst
Northumberland   Strait
367.
Mulgrave
Sherbrooke
Dover
Foxcroft
St. Stephen
.386
Saint
John
Truro
New
Glasgow
45°N
el
M A I N E
Bangor
.331
N O V A
S C O T I A
Berlin   Rumford
Waterville
Bay   of   Fundy
Middleton
Dartmouth
rre
ver
Mount
Washington
1917.
Augusta
Hulls Cove
Halifax
Bridgewater
Brunswick
85.
Lewiston
Yarmouth
Shelburne
Laconia
Portland
Cape Sable
cord
Rochester
Portsmouth
ro
Manchester
Haverhill
usau
ACHUSETTS
Boston
Worcester
ngfield
Cape Cod
A   T   L   A   N   T   I   C
tford
ury
Providence
New Bedford
RHODE ISLAND
Haven
ECTICUT
rton
outhampton
Island
O   C   E   A   N
40°N

70°W   65°W   60°W   55°W
n o p q r s t u v w x y z
21

35°N

0   100   200   300   miles   Average linear scale : 1 inch ≃ 125 miles   1cm ≃ 80 km   0   100   200   300   400   500
                                                                                                                                    Km

These islands lie approximately 4000 kilometres to the west of here, in the Pacific Ocean.

This map shows 1/60 of the earth's surface. Area scale : 1 ☐ inch on the map ≏ 15,000 ☐ miles on the ground 1 ☐ cm on the map ≏ 6000 ☐ km on the ground

a   b   c   d   e   f   g   h   i   j   k   l   m

15   16

Oklahoma City   Henryetta   95°W   Clarksville   Newport   West   Memphis   Jackson   TENNESSEE   Lawrenceburg   Fayetteville   Cleveland   85°W   Asheville   NORTH   Charle
35°N   Ada   McAlester   Poteau   Fort   Smith   Conway   100.   Memphis   Savannah   Florence   879.   Chattanooga   Hendersonville   Rock   Spartanburg   Rockin
OKLAHOMA   Little Rock   Corinth   246.   Huntsville   Dalton   Greenville   Anderson   Clinton Camden   SOU
722.   Arkadelphia   Pine Bluff   Clarksdale   Tupelo   Decatur   Cullman   Gadsden   Gainesville   Athens   Columbia   CAROLI
Fort   Worth   Irving   Garland   Red River   UNITED   STATES   Winona   Columbus   152.   Bessemer   Birmingham   734.   Atlanta   GEORGIA   Augusta   Ogeechee   Walterboro
Sherman   Paris   El Dorado   67°   Providence   Lake   MISSISSIPPI   425.   Macon   Dublin   Statesboro   Savannah
Dallas   Sulphur Springs   Minden   Monroe   Tuscaloosa   Opelika   Columbus   Warner   Robins   Flint
Arlington   Marshall   Natchitoches   Jackson   Meridian   149°   Selma   Montgomery   Dawson   Tifton   Jesup
TEXAS   233.   Tyler   Shreveport   113.   Vicksburg   ALABAMA   Greenville   Eufaula   Albany   Waycross   Brunswick
Waco   Nacogdoches   Lufkin   Toledo   Bend   Reservoir   Alexandria   Brookhaven   Laurel   Andalusia   Thomasville   Valdosta   Fernandina Bea
Temple   Jasper   McComb   Hattiesburg   Dothan   Marianna   Chattahoochee   Jacksonville
Killeen   Huntsville   LOUISIANA   Hammond   Mobile   Crestview   Live Oak   Lake City
Austin   Bryan   Baton Rouge   Biloxi   Fort Walton Beach   Pensacola   Tallahassee   Perry   St. Augustine
New   Braunfels   Colorado   Beaumont   Lake Charles   Slidell   Gulfport   Pascagoula   Panama   City   Apalachee   Bay   Chiefland   Gainesville   Lake   George
30°N   Houston   Lafayette   New Iberia   New Orleans   Cape San Blas   Ocala   Palatka   Daytona
Gonzales   Baytown   Houma   Mississippi   Delta   Crystal River   Leesburg   Altamonte   Springs   Titusville   Cape   Cana
Galveston   Texas City   Winter   Garden   Orlando   Melb
Victoria   Lake Jackson   Tampa   Lakeland   Avon   Park
Three   Rivers   50.   Largo   Brandon
Corpus Christi   St. Petersburg   Bradenton   FLORIDA
Kingsville   Sarasota   Lake   Okeechobee   Paho
La   Madre   Port Charlotte
McAllen   Laguna   Cape Coral   Fort Myers   Fort   Lauderdale
Harlingen   Brownsville   Matamoros   Naples   Cape   Romano   Everglades
25°N   Laguna   Madre   Cape   Sable   Florida   Bay   Key   Larg
19   La Carbonera   Key   West

Gulf   of

Mexico

Ciudad Madero   La Habana   Matanzas
Tampico   Güines   Colón
Pánuco   Pinar del Río   Cienfuegos
Laguna de   Tamiahua   Desterrada   Pérez   Peninsula de   Guanahacabibes   Yucatan   Channel   Isla de Pinos   Trin
Potrero del Llano   Arenas   Río Lagartos   Cape Catoche   Chiquilá
Tuxpan   Nuevo   Dzilam de Bravo   Tizimin   Puerto Juárez   Cancun
Poza   Rica   Papantla   Progreso   Motul   Izamal   Espita   Puerto Morelos
Huachinango   Triangulos   Mérida   Maxcanú   Valladolid   Cozumel
20°N   Martínez   de la Torre   Arcas   Calkiní   Ticul   Tekax   Tulum   Little Cayman
Teziutlán   Tlapacoyan   Bahía   de   Bolonchén de Bejón   100.   Peto   Cayman I
Perote   Jalapa   1427.   Campeche   Yucatán   B. de la Ascensión   Georgetown   (U.K.)
Citlaltépetl Orizaba   Sihochac   Felipe   Carrillo   B.del   Grand   Cayman
Puebla   Orizaba   Champotón   Chunhuhub   Puerto   Espiritu Santo
Córdoba   Alvarado   Campeche   Peninsula   Golfo
Tehuacán   Tierra   Blanca   Tlacotalpan   Ciudad   del Carmen   Laguna de   Términos   310.   C A R I
Acatlán   San Andrés   Tuxtla   1875.   Frontera   Mamantel   Hondo   Golfo
Huspanapan   Tuxtepec   Comalcalco   Villahermosa   Altamira   Chetumal   de
Huajuapan   de León   Acayucan   Coatzacoalcos   Balancán   BELIZE   Honduras
Coixtlahuaca   Minatitlán   Maculspana   Belize
Nochixtlan   Morelos   Palenque   Tenosique   Belmopan   Turneffe Islands
Tlaxiaco   Oaxaca   Paso Real   Chichón   3224.   Flores   1122.
1546.   Mitla   Istmo de   San Cristóbal   las Casas
Miahuatlán   Matías Romero   Tuxtla   Gutiérrez   de Corzo   Roatán   Guanaja
Pinotepa   Nacional   Juchitán   Tehuantepec   2127.   Chiapa   Comitán   Islas de la Bahía   Utila
Jachatengo   Arriaga   Tonalá   Angostura-   Reservoir   Puerto   Cortés   Tela   La Ceiba   Trujillo
Puerto   Escondido   Salina   Cruz   Pijijiapan   Amatenango   GUATEMALA   Puerto   Barrios   San   Pedro   Sula   HONDURAS
Puerto   Angel   Golfo de   Tehuantepec   Huixtla   3220.   Lago de Isabal   Puerto   Lempira
15°N   95°W   Mar   Muerto   Motagua   90°W   85°W   Cape Gracias á Dios

MEXICO

n   o   p   q   r   s   t   u   v   w   x   y   z

22

Page 21

Column labels (top): a b c d e f g h i j k l m
Column labels (bottom): n o p q r s t u v w x y z

Top markers: 17
Bottom markers: 23

Longitude: 75°W, 70°W, 65°W
Latitude: 35°N, 30°N, 25°N, 20°N, 15°N

ATLANTIC OCEAN

Sargasso Sea

BAHAMAS

- Goldsboro
- New Bern
- Morehead City
- Fayetteville
- Jacksonville
- berton
- INA
- Wilmington
- Myrtle Beach
- town

- Grand Bahama Island
- Great Abaco Island
- Nicholls Town
- **Nassau**
- New Providence
- Eleuthera
- Andros Islands
- Behring Point
- Cat
- San Salvador
- Rum Cay
- Great Exuma Island
- Long Island
- Crooked Island
- Acklins
- Mayaguana Island
- Grand Caicos
- *Turks and Caicos Islands (U.K.)*
- Great Inagua Island

Great Bahama Bank

CUBA
- Morón
- Ciego de Avila
- Nuevitas
- Camagüey
- Victoria de las Tunas
- Banes
- Holguín
- Bayamo
- Palma Soriano
- Baracoa
- Niquero
- Manzanillo
- 2005
- Santiago de Cuba
- Guantánamo

HAITI
- Port-de-Paix
- Cap-Haïtien
- Gonaïves
- St-Marc
- **Port-au-Prince**
- Anse d'Hainault
- Les Cayes
- Jacmel

DOMINICAN REPUBLIC
- Puerto Plata
- Mao
- Santiago
- La Vega
- San Francisco de Macoris
- 3175
- San Juan
- Barahona
- La Romana
- **Santo Domingo de Guzmán**

JAMAICA
- Montego Bay
- Spanish Town
- May Pen
- **Kingston**

Antilles

CARIBBEAN SEA

Puerto Rico (U.S.A.)
- Bayamón
- Mayagüez
- 1338
- San Juan
- Carolina
- Caguas
- Ponce

Virgin Islands
- St. Croix (U.S.A.)

- Anguilla
- St. Martin
- Philipsburg
- *Netherlands Antilles*
- Codrington
- Barbuda

ANTIGUA AND BARBUDA
- **Basseterre**
- **St KITTS NEVIS (U.K.)**
- **St. John's**
- Antigua
- *Montserrat (U.K.)*
- Plymouth

Leeward Islands

Guadeloupe (France)
- Basse-Terre
- Pointe-à-Pitre

DOMINICA
- **Roseau**

Average linear scale : 1 inch ≈ 125 miles   1cm ≈ 80 km

miles: 0 100 200 300
Km: 0 100 200 300 400 500

90°W · 85°W · 80°W

MEXICO

Amatenango

15°N
Tapachula

Huixtla
Huehuetenango
Quezaltenango
Lago de Izabal
Puerto Barrios
Puerto Cortés
Tela
La Ceiba
Trujillo
Patuca

GUATEMALA
Rio Motagua
Santa Rosa
San Pedro Sula

HONDURAS

Puerto Lempira

Mazatenango
Antigua
3752 *1502*
Guatemala
Juticalpa
2435
Coco
Cabo Gracias á Dios

Escuintla
Santa Ana
2386
San Salvador
La Paz
2310
Tegucigalpa
2438 · Isabella
Cordillera

Cayos Miskitos
Puerto Cabezas

Ahuachapan
Sonsonate
Zacatecoluca
San Miguel
Nacaome
Matagalpa

EL SALVADOR
Golfo de Fonseca
Estelí

NICARAGUA

Prinzapolca

Providencia (Col.)

Chinandega
León
1745
Managua
Lago de Managua
Escondido
Rama
Bluefields

San Andrés (Col.)

Granada
Lago de Nicaragua
1133

Mosquito Coast / Moskitoküste

Rivas
San Carlos
San Juan del Norte

San Juan

Barrano
Bara

Cabo Santa Elena
Liberia
2020

COSTA

Cartagena
Arjona
Carmer

10°N
Puntarenas
Peninsula de Nicoya
Alajuela Heredia
San José
3432
Turrialba
3820 Chirripó
Limón

Punta Manzanillo

Lorica

Golfo de Nicoya
RICA
Colón
Panamá Canal
Ailigandi

Golfo del Darien

Almirante
Golfo de los Mosquitos
Balboa
Panamá
2621

Monteria
Necoclí

Puerto Cortés
3475
David
2826
Penonomé
PANAMA
La Palma
El Real

Caucasia
Chigorodó
Zara

Puerto Armuelles
Golfo de Chiriqui
Santiago
Archipiélago de las Perlas
Rey
Golfo de Panamá
Riosucio

Atrato

3959
Yarumal

Coiba
Peninsula de Azuero
1400
Pedasi

Cupica
4083
Bello
Medellín
1541

PACIFIC

Quibdó

2140
Manizales
Cartago
4424
Armenia
Per

Cabo Corrientes

San Juan
4250
Tulua
Palmira

OCEAN

Malpelo (Col.)

Buenaventura
Cali

Santander
Nev. de Huila 5750
Neiva

Gorgona

Guapi
Popayán
4886
Garzon

Patía
El Bordo

Mocoa

5°N

Darwin
Wolf

Tumaco
Cabo Manglares

San Lorenzo
Túquerres
Pasto

Esmeraldas
Esmeraldas
4764
Ipiales
Tulcán
San Gabriel
Puerto Asis

Pinta
Marchena
Genovesa

Punta Galera
Rosa Zárate
4930
Ibarra
Cayambe
5790
Quito
4794 · 2819

0° Equator

1707
San Salvador
Santa Cruz
Fernandina
Islas Galápagos (Ecuador)
San Cristóbal

Bahía de Caráquez
Machachi
5896
Cotopaxi
Baeza
Coca

Napo

Manta
Latacunga
5263
Ambato
Tena
Cabo Pantoja

Isabela
Puerto Villamil
Portoviejo
ECUADOR
Chimborazo
6310

Santa Maria
Española

Riobamba

Alausí
5230
Macas

Guayaquil
Babahoyo
Daule
Pastaza

La Puntilla
Salinas
Cuenca
Azogues

90°W · 85°W · 80°W

This map shows 1/60 of the earth's surface. Area scale : 1 □ inch on the map ≙ 15,000 □ miles on the ground 1 □ cm on the map ≙ 6000 □ km on the ground

21

70°W 65°W 60°W 15°N

EAN SEA

DOMINICA **Roseau**

Martinique-Passage

Martinique
(Frankreich)
Fort-de-France

St.-Lucia-Passage

Castries
SAINT LUCIA

St.-Vincent-Passage **BARBADOS**

SAINT **Bridgetown**
VINCENT **Kingstown**
AND
GRENADINES

Lesser Antilles

ATLANTIC

Saint George's GRENADA

*Cabo
Gallinas* *Aruba*

Curaćao
(Neth.)

Bonaire (Neth.)
Willemstad *Peninsula de*
Paraguaná **Windward Islands**

Tobago
Scarborough

Blanquilla
(Ven.)

Peninsula de *820*
Guajira Punto Fijo

Riohacha

Golfo de
Venezuela Puerto Cumarebo

Islas
Los Roques
(Ven.)

Margarita La Asunción

Port TRINIDAD
of Spain AND
TOBAGO

ta Maicao

Coro

Tortuga

Carúpano

Güiria *940*
Gulf of
Paria *Trinidad*
(Serpents
Mouth) San Fernando

Boca
de la Serpiente

ristóbal Colón *5800*

San
Rafael Churuguara

Tocuyo Maiquetía *2765*
Cabo Codera

Cumaná

Puerto La Cruz

Boca Grande

San
Cabello Felipe **Caracas**

Maracay La Victoria Barcelona

Caripito

OCEAN

upar Maracaibo La *1900*
Concepción Cabimas

Carora

Valencia San Juan
do los Morros Piritu

2660

Unare

Maturín

dupar Machiques *Lago*
de
Maracaibo *3652* Barquisimeto

3750

Acarigua El Sombrero

Anaco

Cantaura
Zaraza

Tucupita

Orinoco
Delta

ós Catatumbo

I Banco San Carlos
del Zulia

Mérida *5007*

Cordillera de Mérida

Boconó

Guanare

El Baúl

Valle de
la Pascua

El Tigre

Guanipa

Tigre

Mariano

Grande
Barrancas *Amacuro*
Delta

Boca Grande

San José de Amacuro

Ocaña Casigua Barinas

Guárico

Calabozo

Pariaguán

Ciudad Guayana
792 Upata

Hossororo

Cúcuta San Cristóbal

Bruzual

Apure *Coledes*

San Fernando
de Apure

Suata

Boca del
Pao

Orinoco

Ciudad Bolívar

Serranía de Imataca

amanga Pamplona *4100*

El Canton

Mantecal

Arauca *Capanaparo*

Caicara de
Orinoco

Maripa

El Callao

Marlborough

Barrancabermeja

Málaga *5493*

Arauca

Santa María

Meta

La Urbana *1863*

VENEZUELA

1839 Las
Trincheras

La Paragua

Suddie

Cuyuni

Georgetown

Socorro

Cravo Norte

La Venturosa

Casanare

Puerto Carreño

100. Sabana de
Cardona

El Dorado

Peters
Mine Bartica

New Amsterdam

Rockstone Linden

Totness

Sogamoso

Trinidad

Yopal

Puerto
Nuevo

Puerto
Ayacucho

2285 Angel Falls
2100 *2950*
La Escalera
1890

Mazaruni

Tumatumari

Nieuw
Nickerie

Apoera

unja Orocué

Meta *2030*

San Juan
El Oso

Arabelo

Puricama

Cavanayen

2040

Apoteri

GUYANA

Kabalebo
Reservoir

5°N

Villavicencio

Puerto
Lopez

San José
de Ocuné

Vichada

Sucuaro

Ventuari

Mesa del
Cerro Jaua

Gran
Sabana

2810
Roraima

Pakaraima Mountains

Santa Elena
de Uairen

1240 Depósito

Maturuca

Uaricoera

Karanambo

Lethem

Juliana Top
1230

882

Oronoque

SURINAM

1026

Puerto
Limón

Pavon

Santa
Rosa

Guaviare Arrecifal

Inírida

San Fernando
de Atabapo

Santa Barbara

2579

Orinoco

Serra Parima

Serra

Highlands

2396

La Esmeralda

Uaricoera

Boa
Vista

Rupununi

Dadanawa

Isherton

Papai

Ariari

San José
del Guaviare

Victorino

San José

Casiquiare

Boca
Mavaca

Serra do Apiaú

Kanuku Mts.

New

OMBIA

Guayabero

Calamar

Morichal

Guainía

San Yanaro

El Mango

Catrimani

Caracarai

Biloku

Kamoa Mts.

Serra Acaraí

Buenos
Aires

Miraflores

Mesa de
Yambí

Uainambi San Carlos

Vista Alegre

Serra Tapirapecó

Serra Curupira
1047

Caracarai

Rio Branco

734

Cuñaré Macuje

Mitú Jibóia

Cucui

Padauiri

Demini

São José
do Anauá

Anauá

Maloca

Vaupés

3014
Picoda
Neblina

Araça

erto
uitoto

Iuareté

Içana

Rio Negro

Uaupés

Catrimani

ermo

Lérida

Taracuá

Uaupés

Amazonas

Culuni

São José Tapurucuara

Calanaque

100

BRAZIL

100

Santa
María

Nhamundá Oriximiná

La Chorrera

Caqueta

La Pedrera *100*

Vila Bittencourt

Barcelos

Tupanacca

Moura

Jaupari

Paru de Oeste

Trombetas

Faro

El Encanto

Arica

6an
Cristóbal

Puerto
Miraña

Marcelino

Maraã

Japurá

Solimões

Foz do Mamoriá

Fonte Boa

Tonantins

Unini

Jaú

Airão

Santo
Antonio

Rio Negro

Urucará

Uatumã

Parintins

Amazonas

Santa Clotilde

65°W 60°W

0°

26

25 26

miles
0 100 200 300

Average linear scale : 1 inch ≙ 125 miles 1cm ≙ 80 km

Km
0 100 200 300 400 500

a   b   c   d   e   f   g   h   i   j   k   l   m

85°W   80°W   75°W

Patia

Tumaco

El Bordo

Cabo Manglares

Florencia

Buenos Aires

San Lorenzo

Túquerres

Pasto

Mocoa

Esmeraldas

Tulcán

Ipiales

4764

C O L O M B I

Cuñar

Punta Galera

Puerto Asís

Puerto Huitoto

Ibarra

4930

San Gabriel

Rosa Zárate

Otavalo

Cayambe

Macuj

Cuaran

La Tagua

0°   Equator

Quito

2815

5843

Aguarico

La Ch

Bahía de Caráquez

Machachi

Cotopaxi

5896

Baeza

Coca

Napo

Cabo Pantoja

Puerto Leguizamo

Palermo

Manta

Latacunga

Tena

Arara

Portoviejo

Chimborazo

6310

Ambato

Curaray

Arica

Santa Maria

Putumayo

El Enc

Jipijapa

E C U A D O R

Ríobamba

San Cris

5230

Guayaquil

Babahoyo

Montalvo

La Puntilla

Salinas

Alausí

Macas

Pastaza

Marsella

Santa Clotilde

Golfo de Puná

Guayaquil

Cuenca

4138

Azogues

Vargas Guerra

Andoas

Corrientes

Tigre

P A C I F I C

Machala

Santa Isabel

Mazán

Zarumilla

Sargento Lores

Iquitos

Tumbes

Zorritos

Loja

Zamora

3810

Morona

Puerto Pardo

Santiago

Tam

Máncora

Cariamanga

Borja

Concordia

Nauta

Sar

Talara

Las Lomas

Sta. Maria de Nieva

Bagazán

Cabo Pariñas

Sullana

Orellana

Barranca

P

Marañón

Requena

5°S

Paita

Chulucanas

San Ignacio

3139

Jeberos

Bretaña

Piura

Huancabamba

C

Piura

Punta Aguja

4153

Jaén

3779

Bagua

Mayo

Yurimaguas

Santa Isabel

Neuva Alejandria

Bayóvar

Olmos

3840

Rioja

Dos de Mayo

Pacaya

Ucayali

Rod

O C E A N

517

4193

Chachapoyas

Moyobamba

Lobos de Tierra

Santa Cruz

Ferreñafe

Bambamarca

Tarapoto

Saposoa

Orellana

Bo

Lambayeque

Cajamarca

Balsas

Juanjuí

.609

Chiclayo

Bolívar

Contamaná

Cruzeiro do Sul

Pacasmayo

San Pedro de Lloc

4333

Cajabamba

4487

Tiruntán

Chicama

Otuzco

E

Pucallpa

Trujillo

3947

Santiago de Chuco

Tayabamba

Tocache Nuevo

Viru

Huacrachuco

Aguaytia

Masisea

Tau

Santa

5755

Caraz

Aguaytía

Tingo María

Puerto Inca

Chimbote

6768

Huascaran

Llata

L

Juru

Casma

Huaraz

4996

La Unión

Huánuco

Ambo

Puerto Portillo

Huarmey

Chiquián

Cajatambo

Yerupaja

6634

5748

Oxapampa

Bolognesi

10°S

Pativilca

Cerro de Pasco

R

Atalaya

Urubamba

Pues Varade

Huacho

Huaral

La Merced

Tambo

Chancay

La Oroya

Satipo

Camisea

Matucana

Jauja

5334

Puerto Rico

Fitz

Callao

Lima

Huancayo

Yauyos

Pampas

Huancavelica

Huanta

Quillabamba

Pur

San Vicente de Cañete

5237

Huamanrazo

Ayacucho

Purusillo

6246 Ur

Castrovirreyna

Chincheros

Huancapi

U

Chincha Alta

Pisco

Pampas

Andahuaylas

Al

Islas de Chincha

5350

Chalhuanca

Ica

1725

Palpa

Puquio

6185

Ica

Nazca

Coracora

Chuqui

15°S

San Juán

Lampalla

5522

Chala

Caravelí

Ocoña

Atico

Ocoña

Camaná

Mo

85°W   80°W   75°W

n   o   p   q   r   s   t   u   v   w   x   y   z

This map shows 1/60 of the earth's surface. Area scale : 1 □ inch on the map ≃ 15,000 □ miles on the ground 1 □ cm on the map ≃ 6000 □ km on the ground

a b c d e f g h i j k l m

23

70°W 65°W 60°W 55°W

VENEZUELA

GUYANA

Uainambi Biloku
Mitú Jibóia San Carlos El Mango Kamoa Mts. Serra Acaraí
Vista Alegre Cucúi 734
Iuarete Pico de Neblina 3014 Caracarai
Taracuá Içana São José do Anauá Paru de Oeste
Lérida Uaupés Demini Anauá
La Pedrera 360 Catrimani
Vila Bittencourt Calanaque Tupánacca Oriximiná Óbidos
Puerto Miraña Marcelino Barcelos Santa Maria Faro
Santa Clara Maraã Moura Airão Santarém
Foz do Mamoriá Fonte Boa Santo Antônio Urucará Parintins Belterra
Puerto San Agustin Tontantins Alvarães Badajós-See Manacapuru Itacoatiara Tupinambarama
Santo Antônio de Içá Tefé Piorini-See Badajós Manaus Maués 100
Caballococha Leticia São Paulo de Olivença Renascença Codajás Anamã Nova Olinda do Norte Mucajá Brasilia Legal
Benjamin Constant Boca do Mutúm Concórdia Coari Arumã Diamantina Borba Maués Laranjal Itaituba
Caxias 100 Carauari Itaboca Prato do Igapo-Açu Novo Aripuanã Terra Preta San Luis de Tapajós
Jutai Liberdade Jaburu Piranhas Manicoré Canumã Lajinha Santa Helena
Três Bocas Tapauá Boca do Acará Jacareacanga Creporizinho Posto Curuá
Soledade Santos Dumont Aliança Castanhal Sucunduri Sauré
Eirunepé Envira Mamoriá Pirapetinga Prainha Nova Barra do São Manuel Manuelzinho
Feijó Boca do Moaco Manjuriã Humaitá Jatuarana Samaumá Recreio
Manuel Urbano Foz do Pauini Boca do Curequeté Calama Jacaretinga Arapari
Santa Rosa Sena Madureira Pôrto Alegre Boca do Acre Bom Jardim Pôrto Velho Jamari Caratianas Tabajara Gêlo Cachimbo
Rio Branco Macapá Manoa Abunã Jaciparaná Iracema Aripuanã Pôrto do Cajueiro
Canamaria Taquaras Ariquemes Aarão Pôrto Atlântico
Xapuri Villa Bella Antuerpia Jarú Rondônia Fontanillas Pouso Alegre Carmem
Iñapari Brasileia Puerto Rico Guajará Mirim Presidente Hermes Acampamento de Indios Pôrto dos Gauchos Marape Lucas
Iberia Cobija Porvenir Riberalta Pimenta Bueno Juruena Uiariri
Las Piedras Fortaleza Costa Marques José Bonifácio Vilhena Ponta da Pedra
Providencia Madre de Dios Puerto Maldonado Cavinas Fortaleza Santo Antônio Pimenteiras Diamantino
Puerto Heath Madidi San Joaquin Mategua Puerto Alegre Santa Isabél Rosario Oeste
Quince Mill Astillero Lago Rogaguado San Luis El Carmen La Esperanza Campo dos Parecis 702
Macusani Ixiamas Lago Rogagua Magdalena R.Blanco Planalto de Mato Grosso
Sandia Santa Ana El Cerro Perseverancia Várzea Grande Cuiabá
Ayaviri Reyes San Borja San Ignacio Trinidad La Noria Tapirapua Jaciara
Azángaro Huancané Apolo Rapulo Apere Loreto Mato Grosso Cáceres Poconé
Juliaca Puerto Acosta Santa Ana Llanos de Mojos BOLIVIA Salinas Pôrto Esperidião
Puno Achacachi Ascensión Concepción San Ignacio Descalvados São Lorenço
La Paz Viacha Puerto Marquez Concepción San Javier San Matias
Mazo Cruz Guaqui Chuluman Todos Santos Puerto Villarroel San Ignacio Pôrto Jofre
Moquegua Calacoto Corocoro Sicasica Cochabamba Portachuelo Montero Laguna Concepción Laguna Uberaba Pedro Gomes
Tarata Charaña Umala Quillacollo Totora Comarapa San José de Chiquitos Amolar
Arica Oruro Aiquile Valle Grande Santa Cruz Robore Santa Corazón

B R A Z I L

B O L I V I A

Serra do Cachimbo
Serra dos Apiacás
Serra do Tombador
Serra dos Caiabis
Serra Formosa
Serra do Norte
Serra dos Pacaas Novos
Serra dos Parecis
Serra de Huanchaca
Serra Aguapei
Serra de Santiago
Cordillera Oriental
Llanos de Chiquitos
Lago Titicaca

Average linear scale : 1 inch ≈ 125 miles 1cm ≈ 80 km

0 100 200 300 miles
0 100 200 300 400 500 Km

n o p q r s t u v w x y z

28

26

a b c d e f g h i j k l m

23

60°W   55°W   50°W

Caura · *V E N E Z U E L A*

2100 · 2950 · Mayupa · 1890 · La Escalera · Maruaruni · Rockstone · New Amsterdam · Totness · **Paramaribo** · Mana

Nieuw Nickerie · Groningen · Sinnamary

Puricama · Cavanayen · Tumatumari · Linden · Paranam · Moengo · St. Laurent

Gran Sabana · Roraima 2810 · *Pakaraima* · 2040 · Apoera · Brokopondo · Kourou

5°N

Arabelo · Santa Elena de Uairen · Maturuca · 1240 · *Guyana* · Apatou · **Cayenne**

Cerro Jaua · Mexia del · Paragua · Caroni · *Guyana Mountains* · Prof. van Blommestein Lake · Aurora · Montsinery · Kaw

Catisimiña · *Serra* · *Pacaraima* · Depósito · *Essequibo* · Apoteri · Karanambo · 694 · Grand Santi · Régina

S U R I N A M · **FRENCH**

Serra Parima · Uraricoera · Lethem · *Kanuku Mts.* · Dadanawa · Juliana Top 1230 · 1026 · Bakrakondre · Patience · 710 · St. Georges · Oiapoque

GUIANA · Saul · *Cabo Orange*

Uraricoera · Boa Vista · *Taçutu* · *Rupununi* · *Serra do Apiau* · 1047 · Isherton · Oronoque · Papai · *Tapanahoni* · Intelewa · 882 · 658 · Ouaqui · *Orangegebergte* · Kawatop · Vila Velha

Caracarai · Biloku · *Serra Acarai* · *New* · Maloca Velha · 680 · Pôrto Poet · *Serra Tumucumaque* · 635 · Lorenço · *Serra Lombarda* · Camopi · *Oyapock* · Cunani · Calçoene

Serra Tapirapecó · São José do Anauá · *Anauá* · *Kamoa Mts.* 734 · Meriruma · *Araguari* · Terezinha · Amapá · *Maracá* · *Cabo Norte*

Serra Parima · Catrimani · Maloca · Malaripó · Serra do Navio · Aporema · Ferreira Gomes

0°

Calanaque · *Rio Branco* · *Demini* · Catrimani · 315 · Acampamento · *Jari* · Pôrto Grande · Janaucú · Macapá

Padauiri · *Araça* · Arere · *Paru* · Barraca da Boca · Monte Dourado · 228 · Boca do Jari · Pôrto Santana · Caviana · *Queimada* · *Canal do Norte* · *Mexiana*

Barcelos · Tupanacca · *Morro Grande* 629 · Ramos · 305 · Almeirim · *Grande de Gurupá* · *Canal do Sul* · Afuá · Chaves · *M a r a j ó* · Souré

Cuiuni · Unini · Moura · Santa Maria · *Nhamunda* · Oriximiná · Óbidos · Mulata · Prainha · Pôrto de Moz · Anajás · Cachoeira do Arari · *Pará* · Breves · Abaetetuba · Moju

Tefê · *Lago Badajós* · *Jauapari* · *Uatumã* · Urucará · Faro · Alenquer · Santarém · Monte Alegre · Curua-Uná · *Amazonas* · Victoria · Portel · Cametá · Mocajuba

Piorini · *Lago Piorini* · Badajós · Anama · Santo Antônio · 100 · *Tupinambarama* · Parintins · Belterra · Pacoval · *Xingu* · Belo Monte · Baião · Pindobal

5°S

Urucu · Coari · Codajás · *Rio* · *Negro* · Manacapuru · *Amazonas* · Itacoatiara · *Ilha* · Maués · Brasília Legal · Caima · Altamira · 229 · *Tueré* · Tucuruí · Gur

Coari · Itaboca · *Purus* · Diamantina · Nova Olinda do Norte · Mucajá · Itaituba · Rurópolis · *Iriri* · Pôrto Alegre · Lontra · *Bacajá* · *Tocantins* · Jacundá

Jaburu · Piranhas · *Rio Madeira* · Borba · *Canumã* · Terra Preta · Novo Aripuanã · *Maués* · Laranjal · San Luis de Tapajós · Sem-Tripa · Jatobá · *Serra dos Carajás* 399 · São Félix

Tapauá · Arumã · Manicoré · Canumã · Jacareacanga · Santa Helena · Lajinha · *Tapajós* · Paga-Conta · Forte Veneza · José Rodrigues · *Itacaiúnas* · Marabá · São de A

Boca do Acara · Castanhal · *Prêto do Igapó-Açu* · *Aripuanã* · Sucunduri · Sauré · *Jamanxim* · **B R A Z** · Posto Curuá · Araras · São Sebastião · Carajás · Toca

Alliança · Pirapetinga · *Sucurundi* · Creporizinho · Cajueiro · *Curua* · São Félix do Xingu · Xinguara · Babac

Lábrea · Humaitá · Prainha Nova · Barra do São Manuel · Manuelzinho · Jojoca · *Xingu* · Posto Cocraimore · Tucumã · Gorotiré · *Fresco* · Araguaina

100 · Calama · Jatuarana · Samaumá · 500 · *Iriri* · Garimpo Cumaru · Redenção

Pôrto Velho · Jamari · *Jiparaná* · Tabajara · Jacaretinga · *Juruena* · *Teles* · *Pires* · Recreio · Arapari · *Serra do Cachimbo* · Conceição do Araguaia · Guara

Jaciparaná · Caratianas · *Theodore Roosevelt* · *Aripuanã* · Gêlo · Cachimbo · Santana do Araguaia · Araguacema

Ariquemes · Iracema · Aarão · Aripuanã · *Serra dos Apiacás* · Plara-Açu · Campo Alegre · Barreira do Campo · Miracema do Norte

10°S

Serra dos Pacaás Novos · Antuerpia · Jarú · Rondônia · 242 · *Serra do Norte* · *Arinos* · Pôrto do Cajueiro · *Xingu* · São José do Xingu · Santa Teresinha · Paraíso do Norte de Goiás · Cristalandia

800 · Presidente Hermes · Pimenta Bueno · Acampamento de Indios · Fontanillas · Pôrto do Atlântico · *Serra* · *do* · Posto Alto Manissaua · Campo de Diauarum · Pôrto Alegre · Fátima

Fortaleza · *Serra dos* · José Bonifácio · Pousa Alegre · Pôrto dos Gauchos · *Serra do Tombador* · *Caiabis* · Pôrto dos Meinacos · São Félix · Gurupi

Costa Marques · *Parecis* · Juruena · Uriariti · Marape · *Serra Formosa* · *Tamitatoela* · Xingu · *Serra do Roncador* · Alvorada

San Joaquin · Mategua · *Baures* · *Itonamas* · *Guaporé* · Vilhena · Ponta da Pedra · Lucas · Pôrto Artur · Carmem · *Culiene* · Garapu · *Ilha* · *do* · São Miguel do Araguaia · 186 · Araguaçu · Peixe

Magdalena · *Lago de San Luis* · **BOLIVIA** · El Carmen · Puerto Alegre · *San Martin* · Pimenteiras · Santa Isabél · *Campo* · *dos Parecis* · *Teles Pires* · *Planalto de Mato Grosso* · 635 · *Serra do Roncador* · *Bananal* · Bandeirante · Porangatu · *Serra Dourada* · Alto Para

60°W   55°W   50°W

n o p q r s t u v w x y z

28

25

This map shows 1/60 of the earth's surface   Area scale : 1 □ inch on the map ≏ 15,000 □ miles on the ground   1 □ cm on the map ≏ 6000 □ km on the ground

a b c d e f g h i j k l m

45°W　　　　40°W　　　　35°W

5°N

A T L A N T I C

O C E A N

Equator　0°

Atol
das Rocas

Fernando
de Noronha

 Hinópolis
Bragança
apanema　Viseu
Miguel
amá
Turiaçu
Maracaçumé
Alcântara
matará
São José
do Ribamar
Baía de
São Marcos
gominas
Pinheiro
upi
São Luís
Rosário
Tutóia
Camocim
Acaraú
Cócalzinho
Arari
Urbano
Santos
Parnaíba
Parnaíba
Itapipoca
camento
Santa
Inês
Itapicuru
Mirim
Piracuruca
Tianguá
Sobral
Fortaleza
Mecejana
Serra do Tiracambu
Bacabal
Chapadinha
Ipu
1066
Açude
Araras
Maranguape
Caponga
landia
Coroatá
Piripiri
União
Nova
Russas
Canindé
Aracati
Codó
Campo
Major
Quixadá
Aracati
Pedreiras
Caxias
Serra dos Alpercatas
Timón
Teresina
Crateús
Russas
Macau
Cabo São Roque
5°S
ratriz
Presidente
Dutra
Itapicuru
Serra do Valentim
Poti
Senador
Pompeu
Açude
Orós
Jaguaribe
Mossoró
Ceará-
Mirim
Grajaú
Barra
do Cordas
São Pedro
do Piaui
Palmeirais
Tauá
Apodi
Jaguaribe
Açu
Lajes
Natal
I
L
Colinas
Amarante
Iguatu
Icó
Pau de
Ferros
Currais
Novos
Canguaretama
640
Serra do Itapicuru
Pastos
Bons
Serra da Batista
Valença
do Piauí
Campos
Sales
Juazeiro
do Norte
Caicó
Guarabira
Mamanguape
São Raimundo
das Mangabeiras
Boa Esperança
Reservoir
Floriano
Oeiras
506
Chapada do Araripe
Cajázeiras
Pombal
Patos
Soledade
João Pessoa
na
Balsas
Parnaíba
Uruçui
Picos
Jaicós
Formosa
Ouricuri
Itaporanga
São José
do Egito
Campina
Grande
Timbaúbà
Goiána
Ribeiro
Gonçalves
495
Salgueiro
Serra
Talhada
Paraíba
Limoeiro
Olinda
Tasso
Fragoso
Canto do
Buriti
Paulistana
Parnamirim
1102
Gravatá
Recife
Cristino
Castro
São João
do Piaui
Cabrobó
Arcoverde
Pesqueira
Catende
Caruarú
Jáboatão
Santa
Filomena
Casa
Nova
Rajada
Belem de São
Francisco
Aguas
Belas
Garanhuns
Palmares
Barreiros
Alto
Parnaíba
Caracol
São Raimundo
Nonato
Chorracho
Paulo
Alfonso
Palmeira
los Indios
União dos Palmares
Rio Largo
Pausa
Petrolina
Juàzeiro
Santana
do Ipanema
Maceió
Lizarda
Gilbués
Serra de Piaui
Remanso
Canudos
Vasa
Barris
Arapiraca
São Miguel
dos Campos
10°S
Curimatá
Pilão Arcado
Sobradinho
Reservoir
Senhor do
Bonfim
Jeremoabo
Propriá
Penedo
Corrente
Xique-Xique
Queimadas
Cipó
Itabaiana
884
Formosa do
Rio Preto
Barra
Jacobina
Gavião
Estancia
Dianópolis
Pirajiba
Ibotirama
Irece
Serrinha
Conde
aguatinga
Barreiras
Boqueirão
Ibitunane
1275
Mundo Novo
Feira de
Santana
Alagoinhas
Aracaju
Roda Velha
Seabra
Rui
Barbosa
Itaberaba
Santo Amaro
Camaçari
Campos
Belos
Santana
Correntina
Santa Maria
da Vitória
Iramaia
Contendas
do Sincorá
Cachoeira
Cruz das Almas
Candeias
Santo Antônio
de Jesus
Nazaré
Salvador
Posse
Caetité
Brumado
Jequié
Gandu
Contas
Valença

45°W　　　　40°W　　　　35°W

0　100　200　300 miles
Average linear scale : 1 inch ≈ 125 miles　1cm ≈ 80 km
0　100　200　300　400　500 Km

a   b   c   d   e   f   g   h   i   j   k   l   m

Abancay
Chalhuanca
Auzangate 6394
Urcos
Macusani
70°W
5852
Sandia
Carros de Bala
Ixiamas
Reyes
Lago Rogagua
65°W
Santa Ana
El Carmen
Puerto Alegre
Guaporé
Ponta da Pedra
Campo dos Parecis
Diamantino
5211
Santo Tomás
Sicuani
5443
Palomani
5999
Apolo
San Borja
San Ignacio
Trinidad
Rio Blanco
La Esperanza
Perseverancia
Serra de Huanchaca
60°W
702
Tapirapua
Rosa Oest
15°S
Yauri
Ayaviri
Huancané
Llanos de Mojos
Loreto
Ascensión
La Noria
1095
Mato Grosso
Várzea Grande

PERU
Cotahuasi
Coropuna 6425
Chuquibamba
Ocoña
Ampato 6310
Chachani 6075
Chivay
5641
Juliaca
Puno
Lago Titicaca
Illampu 6485
Ancohuma 6388
Achacachi
Coroico
Santa Ana
Puerto Marquez
Rio Beni
Rio Mamoré
Rio Grande
Concepción
San Javier
San Ignacio
Salinas
1150
Serra Aquapei
San Matías
1283
Pôrto Esperidião
Cáceres
Poconé
Cuiabá
Pocone
Descalvados

5822
Arequipa
2304
Tambo
5593
Juli
5781
5213
Guaqui
Calacoto
La Paz 3577
Viacha
Illmani 6402
Chuluman
Todos Santos
BOLIVIA
Puerto Villarroel
Montero
El Cerro
Portachuelo
Santa Cruz
Laguna Concepción
San José de Chiquitos
Santo Corazón
Lagoa Uberaba
Pôrto Jofre
Grand

Mollendo
Camaná
Moquegua
Tarata
Tacna
Arica
Putre
Guallatiri 6060
Sajama 6542
Charana
Desaquadero
Umala
Sicasica
Quillacollo
Cochabamba
Oruro
5383
Corque
Uncía
2558
Totora
3200
Comarapa
Aiquile
Cordillera
Llanos de Chiquitos
Banados del Izozog
Roboré
Santa Ana
Fortín Max Paredes
Puerto Suárez
Corumbá
Pantanal
Aquidauana
Aqui

Cuya
Nama
Sabaya 5869
Lago de Coipasa
Altiplano
Lago de Poopó
Challapata 5023
Rio Mulatos
3976
2790
Sucre
Tarabuco
Potosí
Lagunillas
Azurduy
Charagua
Camiri
Yuti
Fortín Ravelo
777
Palacios
Chaco
Bahia Negra
Guaicurus
Iquique
20°S
Pisagua
Huara 5995
Sillajnuay 5995
5218
Salar de Uyuni
Cord. de Chichas
5950
Vitichi
Macharetí
Villa Montes
998
Fortín Gral. Eugenio Garay
Boreal
Fortín Madrejón
Fuerte Olimpo
Bonito

PACIFIC
Pintados
Collahuasi 5320
5739
Lagunas
1590
Loa
Ollague
6045
5865
Quillagua
1825
Conchi
Chuquicamata
Tocopilla
Maria Elena
2293
Calama
Tocorpuri 5833
Licancabur 5921
Alota
San Pablo 5695
Mojo
Villazón
La Quiaca
5029
Tupiza
Tarija
Yacuiba
Fortín Hernandarias
Dr. Pedro P. Peña
Mariscal Estigarribia
Filadelfia
R. Verde
Fortín Garrapatal
PARAGUAY
Pôrto Murtinho
Puerto Sastre
Bella Vista
Puerto Piñasco
Por Po

San Pedro de Atacama
Carmen Alto
6050
Abra Pampa
Rosario
Humahuaca
San Ramón de la Nueva Orán
Bermejo
Tartagal
San Pedro
Fortín Juan de Zalazar
Mejillones
Antofagasta
Varillas
Caleta el Cobre
Augusta Victoria
Salar de Atacama
5890
Pular 6225
5594
Catua
Salinas Grandes
Chani 6200
San Antonio de los Cobres
San Salvador de Jujuy
San Pedro
Libertador Gral. San Martín
Juan Sola
Los Blancos
Embarcación
Fortín General Diaz
Pozo Colorado Monte
Ingeniero Guillermo Nueva Juárez
Concepción
Lima
San Pedro
Yp

OCEAN
Los Vientos
Socompa 6031
Socompá
Llullaillaco 6723
Salar Punta Negra
Salar de Arizaro
Salar de Pocitos
Cachi 6720
Salta
General Güemes
Las Lajitas
Teuco
Las Lomitas
Pozo del Tigre
Benjamín Aceval
Concepción
Esta

25°S
Paposo
Taltal
Santa Catalina
5700
Antofalla 6440
Salar de Antofalla 5070
Mojones 5990
Colorados 6049
Antofagasta de la Sierra
Cachi
Cafayate
Metán
Joaquín V. González
Monte Quemado
Castelli
Tres Isletas
Villa Hayes
Clorinda
Asunción
Coro Ovie

Diego de Almagro
Chañaral
El Salvador
Nevada 6400
Santa María
San Miguel de Tucumán
Monteros
Rosario de la Frontera
Pampa de los Guanacos
Presidencia Roque Sáenz Peña
Pirané
Paraguari
Laguna Vera
Villa

Caldera
Inca de Oro
Ojos del Salado 6808
4920
Concepción
Monteros
Hondo Reservoir
Termes de Rio Hondo
La Banda
Charata
Presidencia de la Plaza
Formosa
Resistencia
Corrientes
Tebicuary
San Juan Bauti
Enca

Copiapó
Copiapo 6080
Pissis 6558
Gonete 6872
Fiambalá
Belén
Andalgalá
Santiago del Estero
Suncho Corral
Villa Angela
Empredrado
Bella Vista
Santo Tomé
Caaz

Castilla
Carrizal Bajo
5830
Tinogasta
Salar de Pipanaco
Catamarca
Frias
Villa San Martín
Añatuya
Bandera
Reconquista
Goya
Mercedes

Huasco
Vallenar
Cabo Bascuñan
Domeyko
Jagüé
Mejicana 6250
Chilecito
Recreo
Pinto
Tostado
Villa Guillermina
Bella Vista
Apósto

La Higuera
La Serena
30°S
Coquimbo
Ovalle
5830
Toro 5380
Villa Unión
La Rioja
Chumbicha
Chepes
Villa Ojo de Aqua
Vera
Curuzú Cuatiá
Uruguaiana
Yapeyú

Maitencillo
Combarbala
Olivares 6262
San José de Jáchal
Chamical
Cruz del Eje
Dean Funes
Morteros
San Justo
La Paz
Esquina
Concordia
Salto
Chajari
Artigas

Illapel
Salamanca
5510
5620
San Juan
San Agustín de Valle Fértil
Patquía
Laguna Chiquita
Córdoba
Rafaela
Esperanza
Santa Fé
Paraná
Diamante
Villaguay
Concepción del Uruguay
Paysandú

Chincolco
San Felipe
Mercedario 6770
Aconcagua 6960
Mendoza
San Martín
Chepes
Salsacate
Alta Gracia
Villa Dolores
Quines
2880
Oliva
Río Tercero
Villa Maria
Victoria
Gualeguay
Gualeguaychu
URI

Valparaíso
Santiago
Tupungato 6800
La Calera
5830
Pampa de las Salinas
San Juan
Villa Media Agua
Santa Rosa del Conlara
San Luis
1599
Río Cuarto
La Carlota
Cañada de Gómez
Rosario
Gualeguay
Mercedes
Dura

San Antonio
San Bernardo
Tunuyán
La Paz
Vicuña Mackenna
Vanado Tuerto
San Nicolas
Pergamino
Zárate
Carmelo
Cardona
Florida
Martínez
C. del Sacramento

Rancagua
5290
Justo Daract
Mercedes
Jupin
Lincoln
Chacabuco
Chivilcoy
Lobos
Buenos Aires
La Plata
Monte

Santa Cruz
San Fernando
5160
4660
San Rafael
Diamante
Salado
General Alvear
Buena Esperanza
Huinca Renancó
General Villegas
Magdalena
Rio d

Constitución
70°W
Atuel
65°W
Union
60°W

This map shows 1/60 of the earth's surface. Area scale : 1 □ inch on the map ≈ 15,000 □ miles on the ground   1 □ cm on the map ≈ 6000 □ km on the ground

80°W 75°W 70°W 65°W

Islas Juan Fernández
(Chile)

Isla
Alejandro
Selkirk

Isla
Robinson
Crusoe

Valparaíso

Santiago

San Martín
San Luis
1599

Río
Cuarto

La Ca

San Bernardo
Tupungato
6800

Tunuyán

Desaguadero

Mercedes

Vicuña
Macken

San Antonio
5830

La Paz

Justo
Daract

Laboula

P A C I F I C

Rafael

Rancagua

5290

Santa
Cruz

5160

San Rafael

Diamante

Buena
Esperanza

Huinca
Renanc

San Fernando

Curicó
4860

4090

35°S

Constitución

Maule

Talca
4020

Malargüe
3810

General
Alvear

Sierra del Nevado

Atuel

Unión

Eduardo
Castex

Riv

Talcahuano

Concepción

Punta Lavapié

Chillán

Los Angeles

4800

Barrancas

3680

Algarroho
del Aguila

Santa
Isabel

Banados
del
Atuel

Chacharramendi

Victorica

Santa
Rosa

General
Acha

O C E A N

4115

Colorado

Lebú

Victoria

Bío Bío

Las
Lajas

Chos Malal

2200

Cerros
Colorados
Reservoir

Catriel

Puelches

Villa Iri

Temuco
3124

Curacautín

Zapala

Plaza
Huincul

Neuquén

Chelforó

Río Col

Villarrica

Cutral-Có

General
Roca

Choele
Choel

40°S

Valdivia

Neuquén

Picún
Leufú

Limay

Ezequil Ramos
Mexia Reservoir

Colo

3740
Junín
de los
Andes

San Martín
de los Andes

Paso Limay

Sierra
Colorada

General
Conesa

Río Negro

Lago de Ranco

Osorno

Lago
Nahuel
Huapi

Los
Menucos

Valcheta

San Antonio
Oeste

Vie

Lago
Llanquihue

2660

San Carlos
de Bariloche

Maquinchao

Meseta de Somuncura

Golfo
San Matías

Puerto
Montt

Ingeniero
Jacobacci

Gastre

Telsen

Puerto
Lobos

Ancud

Golfo
Nuevo

El Maitén

2440

Puerto
Madryn

Chiloe

Castro

Esquel

Gangan

Trelew

Rawson

Cabo Quilán

Chaitén

2260

Tecka

Chubut

Las Plumas

Chubut

Boca del Guafo

Golfo de Corcovado

2400

Florentino
Ameghino
Reservoir

José de
San Martín

Paso de los Indios

Gran
Laguna
Salada

Camarones

45°S

Puerto
Cisnes

Magdalena

2960

Facundo

Lago
Musters

Lago
Colhué
Huapi

Chico

Malaspina

Archipiélago
de los Chonos

Puerto
Aisén

Coihaique

Río Mayo

Sarmiento

Comodoro
Rivadavia

Golfo de
San Jorge

Lago
Buenos Aires

Caleta
Olivia

Península de
Taitao

San Valentín
4058

Chile
Chico

Perito
Moreno

Las Heras

Cabo Tres Puntas

Lago Gen.
Carrera

Pico
Truncado

Jaramillo

Golfo de
Penas

3440

Cochrane

3700
San Lorenzo

Bajo Caracoles

Deseado

Puerto
Deseado

Campana

Wellington

Lago
o'Higgins

Lago
Cardiel

Gobernador
Gregores

El Salado

3375

Lago
Viedma

Tres Lagos

Puerto
San Julián

50°S

Murallón
3800

Lago
Argentino

Chico

La
Julia

Piedrabuena

Puerto Santa
Cruz

2380

El Calafate
2150

Santa Cruz

Hanover

Lago del
Toro

Yacimiento

Esperanza

Bahía
Grande

Nelson Strait

1750

Puerto
Natales

Río
Turbio
1285

Gallegos

Río Gallegos

Laguna
Blanca

Punta Delgada

Magellan St.

Desolación

Punta Arenas

Brunswick
Peninsula

Magellan Straits

Porvenir

Cerro
Sombrero

Tierra del
Fuego

Grande

Río Grande

Cabo San Diego

Santa
Inés

Pen Sarmiento

Lago Fagnano

Ushuaia

Los Estad

Hoste

55°S

Cape Horn

80°W 75°W 70°W 65°W

This map shows 1/60 of the earth's surface. Area scale : 1 □ inch on the map ≃15,000 □ miles on the ground 1 □ cm on the map ≃ 6000 □ km on the ground

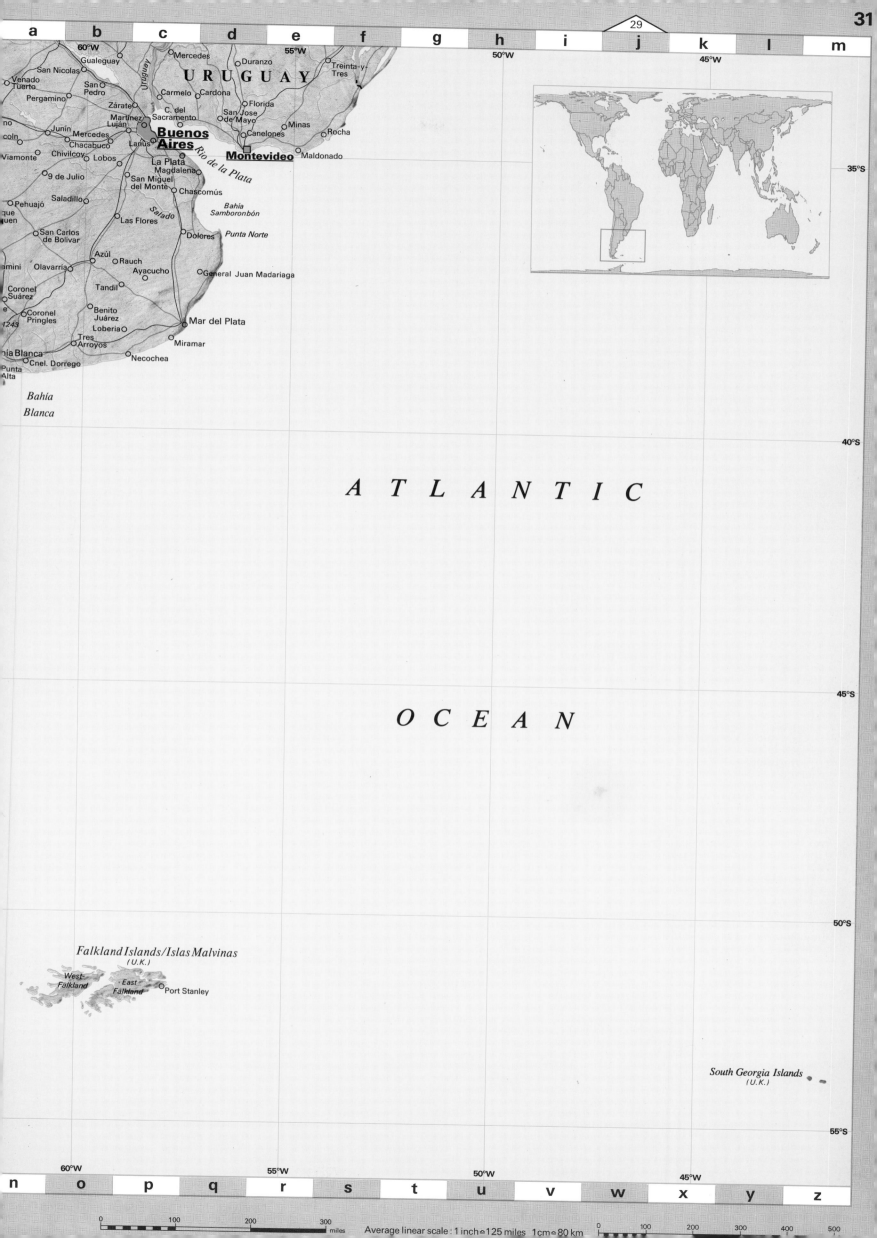

GREENLAND
(Denmark)
Scoresbysund
Scoresby Sund

70°N

20°W

15°W

10°W

5°W

0°

Denmark Strait

Cape Horn

Arctic Circle

Ísafjördur

Fontur

Hünaflöi

Akureyri

Breidifjördur

I C E L A N D

•1765

65°N

Akranes

•1400

Vatnajökull

Djúpivogur

Faxaflói

•Reykjavik

2119 •

Keflavik

Reykjanes

Faëroes
(Denmark)

Shetland
Islands

Lerwick

60°N

A T L A N T I C

Orkney
Islands

Cape
Wrath

Pentland Firth

Thurso

Lewis

Minch

Hebrides

Moray Firth

Inverness

Elgin

90

Skye

Loch
Ness

Highlands

•1309

Aberdeen

S C O T L A N D

Fort William O •1344

Mull

Perth

Dundee

Stirling

Edinburgh

Islay

Glasgow

Berwick
upon
Tweed

GREAT BRITAIN

N O R

55°N

Ayr

Newcastle
upon Tyne

S E

Londonderry

North Channel

AND

NORTHERN
IRELAND

Belfast

Carlisle

Sunderland

O C E A N

Donegal
Bay

Lough Neagh

NORTHERN IRELAND

Middlesbrough

Portadown

Sligo

Isle of
Man

Douglas

Leeds

York

Blackpool

Kingston upon Hull

Westport

Irish

Sea

Liverpool

Manchester

Sheffield

IRISH

Athlone

Irish
Sea

Galway

Shannon

Dublin

Holyhead

Stoke-on-
Trent

886

Anglesey

1085

Nottingham

Roscrea

Derby

Norwich

Limerick

Arklow

Birmingham

Leicester

920

Wexford

WALES

Coventry

Cambridge

REPUBLIC

Aberystwyth

Killarney

Waterford

St. George's Channel

Ipswich

Cork

Fishguard

Oxford

Luton

Swansea

Thames

Southend-
on-Sea

Cape Clear

Cardiff

Bristol

Reading

London

Dover

Oste

Bristol Channel

Southampton

Strait of

Calais

Bournemouth

Brighton

Lil

Exeter

Isle of
Wight

Valencie

Plymouth

Land's End

Penzance

English Channel

Abbeville

50°N

Cherbourg

Amiens

Guernsey

Le Havre

St

Channel Islands
(U.K.)

Jersey

Caen

Rouen

Golfe de St. Malo

Évreux

Seine

Paris

Granville

Brest

St. Brieuc

Alençon

Chartres

Rennes

F R A N

Le Mans

Orléa

Lorient

Angers

Loire

20°W

15°W

10°W

St. Nazaire

Nantes

Tours

5°W

0°

92

10°E · 15°E · 20°E · 25°E · 30°E

Söröya · Nordkapp · Kap Kiberg
Hammerfest · Alta · Lakselv · Tana · Kirkenes · 70°N · Pečenga
Tromsö · Skibotn · 1139 · 623 · Inarijärvi · Ivalo · Lotta · Paduhskoye More
Senja · Andöya · 1590 · Muonio · Kolari · Kemijärvi · 636 · 263
Lofoten · Vesterålen · Langöya · Narvik · Kebnekaise · Kiruna · 807 · SOVIET · Kalevala
Vest Fjord · Bognes · 2117 · Gällivare · Torne · 396 · Kemi · Kuusamo
Bodö · 1906 · 2090 Sarek · Lule · Oulu · UNION · 65°N
Svartisen 1599 · Lönsdal · Hornavan · 697 · 211 · Reboly
NORWEGIAN SEA · Mo-i-Rana · 1915 · 1609 · Arjeplog · Skellefte · Raahe · Oulu järvi · Kajaani · 355 · Pielinen
Mösjöen · Uddjaur · Storuman · Skellefteå · 239 · Joensuu
Kvigtind 1703 · Storman · Umeå · Kokkola · FINLAND · 279 · Sortavala
Vikna · Storuman · Ångerman · Jakobstad · Kuopio
Kristiansund · Grong 1390 · 530 · Vaasa · 125 · Kyyjärvi · Lake Ladoga
Molde · Steinkjer · Östersund · Kramfors · Örnsköldsvik · Parkano · Jyväskylä
Ålesund · Oppdal · 1796 · Storsjön · Näsijärvi · Saimaa · Imatra
Dombås 2469 · Trondheim · 1009 · Sundsvall · Pori · Tampere · Lappeenranta · Vyborg
Geldhöpiggen · Tynset · Sveg · Hudiksvall · Hämeenlinna · Lahti · 179 · 60°N
Sognefjord 2038 · Øvre Ardal · 2183 · Särna · Söderhamn · Lahti · Leningrad · Kolpino
Gudvangen · Lillehammer · 430 · Gävle · Åland Islands · Turku · Helsinki · Hangö · Narva · Chudovo
Eidfjord 1862 · Gol · Hamar · Siljan · Borlänge · Mariehamn · 62 · Espoo · Vantaa · Tallinn · Luga · Novgorod
Hardangerfjord 1660 · Hönefoss · Mjøsa · Kongsvinger · Uppsala · ESTONIA · Tartu · Ozero Pskovskoye
Grungedal · Drammen · Oslo · Västerås · Norrtälje · Hiiumaa · Pärnu · 145 · Pskov · Staraja Russa
Evje · Larvik · Oslofjord · Fredrikstad · Örebro · 279 · Södertälje · Stockholm · Saaremaa · Ostrov · Ozero Ilmen
Arendal · Uddevalla · Vänern · Lidköping Vättern · Linköping · Gulf of Riga · Valga · R.S.F.S.R.
Kristiansand · Cape Skagen · Västervik · Visby · Riga · 311 · Opochka · Velikije Luki
Skagerrak · Frederikshavn · Göteborg · Borås · 377 · Gotland · Ventspils · LATVIA · Dvina · Nevel'
Jönköping · Liepāja · Jekabpils · 259
Ålborg · Kattegat · Växjö · Kalmar Öland · Klaipeda · Šiauliai 228 · Daugav pils · Vitebsk
Holstebro · Randers · Halmstad · SOVIET UNION · Polotsk
Jylland 173 · Århus · Helsingör · Helsingborg · Kristianstad · Postavy · Orsha · Smolensk · 55°N
DENMARK · København · Karlskrona · Bornholm (Denmark) · Kaliningrad · Kaunas · Vilnius · Molodetschno · Borisov
Kolding · Odense · Malmö · Ystad · Neman · Sovetsk · R.S.F.S.R. · Chernyakhovsk · Lida · Minsk · Mogilev
Esbjerg · Fünen · Svendborg · Falster · Gdynia · Suwałki · Grodno · WHITE · Krichev
Flensburg · Lolland · Rügen · Gdansk · Olsztyn · Baranovichi · Dovsk
Kieler Bucht · Stralsund · Zatoka Pomorska · Słupsk · Gdansk · Łomza · Białystok · RUSSIA · Bobruysk · Klintsy
Deutsche Bucht · Lübecker Bucht · Greifswald · Koszalin · Tczew · Elblag · Slonim · 192 · Pripet
Frisian Islands · Wilhelmshaven · Kiel · 56 · Rostock · 176 · Szczecinek · Toruń · Pinsk · Marshes · Chernigov
Groningen · Emden · Lübeck · Wismar · Neubrandenburg · Szczecin · Stargard · 312 · Bydgoszcz · POLAND · Brest · Mozyr · Pripyat
Leeuwarden · Bremerhaven · Schwerin · Grudziadz · Warszawa · Slutsk · Gomel
Amsterdam · Hamburg · Bremen · GERMAN · Neuruppin · Gorzow-Wlkp. · Poznan · Kutno · Siedlce · Styr · Priyat · Nezhin
Enschede · Hannover · Wittenberge · Potsdam · Berlin · Włocławek · Warta · Łódź · Lublin · Kovel · Koresten · Kiyev Reservoir
Utrecht · Osnabrück · Magdeburg · Frankfurt · 162 · Leszno · Kalisz · 289 · Piotrków · 240 · Lutsk · Rovno · 252 · Kiyev
Arnhem · Münster · Dessau · Oder · DEMOCRATIC · Legnica · Radom · Zamość · Novograd-Volynskiy · Zhitomir
Eindhoven · Dortmund · Göttingen · Halle · Leipzig · Wrocław · Kielce · UKRAINE · Belaya Tserkov
Essen · Kassel 840 · Erfurt · Weimar · REPUBLIC · Dresden · Częstochowa · L'vov · Ternopol' · Khmel'nitskiy
Düsseldorf · Aachen · Bonn · FEDERAL · Gera · Marx-Stadt · 983 · Plauen · 1603 · Wałbrzych · Katowice · Przemyśl · 617 · Vinnitsa · Cherkassy
Liège · Koblenz · 689 · Bad Hersfeld · 774 · Karlovy Vary · Hradec Králové · Kraków · Rzeszow · Kamenets-Podol'skiy · Uman'
Wiesbaden · Frankfurt Main · 616 · Kolín · Mähr-Ostrava · Bielsko-Biala · Chernovtsy · Mogilev Podol'skiy
Luxembourg · Trier · Würzburg · Praha · Plzen · Pardubice · Olomouc · Zilina · CZECHOSLOVAKIA · Uzgorod · 383 · Pervomaysk
Nancy · Mannheim · Bamberg · České Budějovice · Jihlava · Brno · 1725 · Zakopane · Presov · 346 · Ivano-Frankovsk · Kolomyya · Dnestr
Metz · Saarbrücken · Nürnberg · Znojmo · 1592 · Gerlachovsky · Košice · Mukachevo · Belsty
Strasbourg · Karlsruhe · Regensburg · Donau · 1457 · Zvolen · 2043 · Miskolc · Chernovtsy · MOLDAVIA
REPUBLIC · Stuttgart · Passau · Linz · Wien · Moravia · Bratislava · Nyíregyháza · 2305 Pietrosu · Botoșani · Bel'tsy
Chaumont · Freiburg · 1366 · Augsburg · München · Salzburg · 2075 · Győr · Debrecen · Satu Mare · ROMANIA · Orgejev
Mulhouse · 1493 · Memmingen · Bodensee (Lake Constance) · 2963 Zugspitze · AUSTRIA · Dachstein 2996 · Leoben · Vác · Budapest · HUNGARY · Baia Mare · Prut · South Bug
Dijon · Besançon · Basel · Zürich · 10°E · Inn · 2743 · 15°E · 20°E · 25°E · 30°E
SWITZERLAND

50

35

0 100 200 300 miles · Average linear scale : 1 inch ≈ 125 miles   1 cm ≈ 80 km · 0 100 200 300 400 500 Km

a b c d e f g h i j k l m

32

GREAT BRITAIN
5°W
Southampton 0° Dover
Bournemouth Brighton Strait of Dover
Plymouth Exeter Isle of Wight
Land's End Penzance

Calais
Lille Gent Bruxelles Köln
50°N Abbeville Valenciennes **BELGIUM** Liège Aachen **Bonn** Bad Hersfeld Erfurt G.
Amiens St Quentin Charleroi **LUXEM-** Koblenz Karl-Marx Plauen
Cherbourg St Quentin Sedan **BOURG** Trier Wiesbaden Frankfurt 983
Le Havre Rouen Compiègne Thionville **Luxembourg** Saarbrücken Würzburg **GERMAN FEDERAL**
Guernsey Channel Islands (U.K.) Reims Metz Mannheim Bamberg
Caen Jersey Golfe de San Malo Évreux **Paris** Nancy Karlsruhe Nürnberg
St. Brieuc Alençon Chartres Troyes Strasbourg Stuttgart Donau Reg
Brest Rennes Le Mans Orléans Chaumont 1366 Freiburg Augsburg **REPUBLIC**
Lorient Angers Loire Tours Auxerre Mulhouse 1493 Bodensee München
St. Nazaire Nantes **F R A N C E** Dijon Basel (Lake Constance) Memmingen Zugspitze
Poitiers 288 Châteauroux Chalons-sur- Besançon Bern Zürich **LIECHTEN-** Landeck 2953 Inns
La Roche- Moulins Saône Luzern **SWITZERLAND** **Vaduz** STEIN 3772
sur-Yon Limoges Allier Mâcon Genève Lac 4158 Bernina Bolzano Dolomites 3344
A T L A N T I C La Rochelle Angoulême Clermont- St. Étienne Léman Monte Rosa 4052 **Milano** Brescia Lago di Vic
Saintes Ferrand 1886 Lyon Mont Blanc 4634 Aosta Como Bergamo Garda
O C E A N Bay of Brive Massif Grenoble 4807 Novara **Torino** Verona Padova
45°N Bordeaux Aurillac Central Valence Alpes Alessandria Piacenza Po Ferra
of Dordogne Le Puy Pelvoux Cuneo Genova Parma
Biscay Lot Côtevennes 4103 Digne Nice Imperia Golfo di Modena Bologna
Agen Garonne Rhône 3847 Genova **SA**
Adour Nîmes Avignon Aix-en- **MONACO** La Spezia **MARIN**
Gironde Landes Bayonne Toulouse Montpellier Provence Arles Toulon 2120 Firenze
Pau Tarbes Carcassonne Narbonne **Marseille** **LIGURIAN** Livorno Pisa D
Gijón Santander San 2604 Golfe du Lion **SEA** Siena
La Coruña Oviedo Cordillera Cantábrica Bilbao Sebastián Pamplona 3404 Perpignan Bastia 2710 Elba Grosseto
Cabo Santiago de 2583 Vitoria Jaca Pico de Corsica Ajaccio Civitavecchia Viterbo
Finisterre Compostela Ponferrada León Logroño Aneto 2923 **ANDORRA** Gerona (France)
Orense Burgos Costa Bonifacio **Ro**
Vigo Miño Soria 2142 Huesca Brava Str. of Bonifacio
Braga Zamora Valladolid Duero Zaragoza Lérida Sassari Olbia
Porto 1382 Salamanca Calatayud Ebro Tarragona **Barcelona** Nuoro Sardinia
Aveiro Douro Segovia Guadalajara Tortosa 1834 (Italy)
Guarda Ávila 2430 Teruel Castellón Oristano
Coimbra 2592 **Madrid** Islas Baleares Menorca Cágliari
40°N Leiria Talavera 2020 Alcudia Capo Teulada **TYRRH**
S P A I N de la Reina La Almarcha Palma Mallorca **S**
Tejo Toledo Tajo Valencia Ibiza
Cáceres Trujillo Ciudad Júcar Cabo de
Santarém Real Guadiana Albacete Gandia la Nao
Lisboa Mérida Puertollano Segura Alicante **M E D I T E**
Setúbal Badajoz Sierra Morena Murcia
Évora Córdoba Ubeda 2036 Lorca Cartagena
Beja Aracena Jaén Baza Aguilas
Sines Guadalquivir Écija Granada 3478 Almería
Odemira Mértola Algarve Huelva Sevilla Antequera Sierra Almería Bizerte Golfo de
Sagres Lagos Faro Golfo de Jerez de la Nevada Cap Bon Tunis Kélibia
Cabo Cádiz Frontera Málaga Motril Dellys **Tunis** Cap Bon
San Vicente Cádiz Costa del Sol **Alger** Bejaia Skikda Annaba Tabarka
Algeciras Gibraltar (U.K.) Ténès Tizi Constantine Beja Teboursouk
Str. of Ceuta (Sp.) Khemis Blida Ouzou Sétif 586 Zaghouan
Gibraltar Miliana **Médea** Souk Le Kef 1357 Sousse
Tanger Tétouan Cheliff Bordj Bou Ahras Ain Beida Kairouan Isole Pe
Asilah Chechaouen Melilla (Sp.) Mostaganem 1983 Arreridj Batna Khenchela El Djem Lamped
35°N Al Hoceima Mohammadia Relizane Tell Atlas Metlili Chaamba Tebessa Kasserine Mahdia
Ksar el Kebir Beni Saf Oran Sidi-bel- Tiaret Chellala 767 2326 Fériana Ras Kaboud
MOROCCO Aknoul Oujda Abbès Bou Saada Biskra Gafsa Sfax Îles
Oued Tlemcen **M o u n t a i n s** Djelfa Kerkenna
Marhoum P l a t e a u x Chott
Chott ech Ouled Melrhir Tozeur Gabès
Chergui Monts des Ouled Nail Djellal Chott Golfo de Gabès
Bougtob Aflou Messaad Ouled Djerid Kebili Île Djerba Zarzis
1977 Laghouat El Meghaier Diamaa El Oued Médenine
Méchéria H a u t s Brézina Tilrhemt Chebka Ghardaia Touggourt Ben
2236 Aflou Guerara du Mzab 238 Guerdane
Ain Sefra **A L G E R I A** El Goléa Ouargla Bordj Nalut 688
Safi Grand Erg Occidental 502 306 Hassi Messaoud Bourguiba
Essaouira Taouz El Goléa 145 Bir Zar
Amizmiz Rissani Bordj Bouarfa Sinawan
Jebel Igdet Toubkal Abadla Bir Zar L
3615 4165 Taouz 834 Grand Erg Oriental Al Az
5°W 0° 5°E 10°E

n o p q r s t u v w x y z

36

This map shows 1/60 of the earth's surface. Area scale: 1 □ inch on the map ≙ 15,000 □ miles on the ground 1 □ cm on the map ≙ 6000 □ km on the ground

33

POLAND

CZECHOSLOVAKIA

Wałbrzych · Wrocław · Czestochowa · Kielce · Zamość · Lutsk · Rovno · Korosten · Kiyev Reservoir · Nezhin · Sumy

Hradec Králové · Katowice · Krakow · Rzeszow · Przemyśl · L'vov · Novograd Volynskiy · Kiyev · Priluki · Akhtyrka

Kolin · Mähr-Ostrava · Bielsko-Biala · Zakopane · Stryy · Ternopol' · Zhitomir · Belaya Tserkov · Cherkassy · Kremenchugskoye Reservoir · Poltava · Khar'kov · Valki

SOVIET UNION

Olomouc · Žilina · Gerlachovsky · Prešov · Ivano Frankovsk · Khmel'nitskiy · Vinnitsa · Kremenchug · Pereshchepino

Jihlava · Brno · Znojmo · Zvolen · Košice · Užgorod · Mukachevo · Kamenets Podol'skiy · Uman' · Kirovograd · Dneprodzerzhinsk · Novomoskovsk

UKRAINE

Wien · Bratislava · Györ · Vác · Miskolc · Nyíregyháza · Satu Mare · Baia Mare · Suceava · Botoşani · Bel'tsy · Mogilev Podol'skiy · Pervomaysk · Krivoy Rog · Zaporozh'ye · Dnepropetrovsk

Linz · Budapest · Debrecen · MOLDAVIA · Orgejev · Nikopol

AUSTRIA · Leoben · Veszprém · Balaton Lake · Oradea · Dej · Iaşi · Kishinev · Tiraspol · Nikolayev · Kakhovskoye Reservoir

Graz · HUNGARY · Békéscsaba · Cluj Napoca · Tirgu Mureş · Bacău · Belgorod · Novaya Kakhovka · Melitopol

Maribor · Nagykanizsa · Szeged · Arad · Sibiu · Braşov · Galaţi · Odessa · Kherson

Klagenfurt · Pecs · Subotica · Timişoara · Deva · ROMANIA · Ploieşti · Tulcea · Bolgrad · Sea of Azov

Ljubljana · Osijek · Zrenjanin · Vršac · Negoiu · Dunărea Delta · Simferopol · Dzhankoy

Zagreb · Karlovac · YUGOSLAVIA · Novisad · Turnu-Severin · Piteşti · Craiova · Bucureşti · Constanţa · Crimea · Feodosiya

Dinara · Banja Luka · Mitrovica · Smederevo · Rosiori · Sevastopol · Jalda

Bihać · Beograd · Dunav · Ruse · Dunărea · BLACK SEA

Zadar · Tuzla · Titovo Užice · Vidin · Vraca · Pleven · Kolarovgrad · Varna

Šibenik · Sarajevo · Morava · Niš · Türnovo

Split · Jablanica · Leskovac · Pirot · Balkan · Sliven · Burgas

Brac · Hvar · Korčula · Pelješac · Planina · Ivangrad · Titograd · Pristina · Sofiya · BULGARIA · Stara Zagora

Dubrovnik · Shkodër · Prizren · Kumanovo · Musala · Plovdiv

ADRIATIC SEA · ALBANIA · Skopje · Titov Veles · Blagoevgrad · Rodopi · Kürdzali · Edirne · Luleburgaz

Pescara · Durrës · Bitola · Sérra · Komotini · Istanbul · Üsküdar · Bosporus · Karabük · Kastamonu · Samsun

Campobasso · Tiranë · Ohridsko ézero · Edessa · Kavála · Tekirdağ · Sea of Marmara · Adapazari · Geredé

Foggia · Benevento · Prispansko ézero · Thessaloniki · Thasos · Izmit · Bursa · Bilecik · Kizilirmak · Corum

Bari · Vlorë · Kozáni · Chalkidiki · Imbros · Canakkale · Bandirma · Balikesir · Eskişehir · Ankara · Kirikkale · Turhal

Brindisi · Korça · Thermaïkós Kólpos · Lemnos · Troy · Ayvalik · Anatolia · Yozgat

Taranto · Lecce · Pindhos · Kérkira · Jánina · Trikala · Lárisa · AEGEAN SEA · Kütahyá · Tuz Golu · Kayseri

Potenza · Vólos · Lesbos · Manisa · Afyon · Akşehir · Aksaray

TURKEY · Izmir · Alaşehir · Eğridir Gölü · Konya · Niğde

Coriglano · Northern Sporades · Lamia · Euböa · Chíos · Aydin · Denizli · Beyşehir Gölü · Eregli · Kozan

Cosenza · Lefkas · Delphi · SEA · Chalkis · Büyük Menderes · Muğla · Karaman · Adana

IONIAN SEA · Agrinion · Euböa · Sámos · Antalya · Taurus · Mersin · Iskenderun

Reggio · Kephallenia · Patras · Korinthiakós Kólpos · Athinai · Piraievs · Ándros · Tínos · Fethiye · Körfezi Adalia · Alanya · Silifke · Antakya

Messina · Etna · Riposto · Zante · Korinth · Kikládhes · Náxos · Southern Sporades · Finike · Anamur · Burun Anamur

Catania · Pyrgos · Tripolis · Kárpathos · Ródhos · Cape Andreas · Latakia

Siracusa · Kalamai · Mílos · Ródhos · CYPRUS · Famagusta

Valletta · Ákra Akrítas · Kría · Kánea · Iráklion · Sea of Crete · Cape Arnauti · Nicosia · Olympus · Larnaca · Tartus

Ákra Taínaron · Ákra Maléa · Kýthira · Tráblous

MEDITERRANEAN SEA · Paphos · Limassol

LEBANON · Beirut · Zahlé · Dimashq

LIBYA · Al Bayda · Darnah · Sour · Golan Heights · Dar'a · Haifa · Irbid

Al Marj · Al Jabal al Akhdar · Hadera · ISRAEL · Tel-Aviv-Yafo · Zarqa

Banghazi · Al Abyar · Tubruq · Nile Delta · Jerusalem · Amman · Dead Sea

Gulf of Sirte · Qaminis · Al Adam · Al Burdi · Rashīd (Rosette) · Baltīm · Dumyat · Port Said · Gaza · Beer Sheba · Al Karak

Buerát el Hsun · Sirte · Sīdi Barrāni · Mersa Matruh · Al Mansura · Suez Canal · Ar Arish · Al Qantara

Al Iskandariyah · Damanhūr · EGYPT

37 · 38

Average linear scale : 1 inch ≈ 125 miles · 1cm ≈ 80 km

0 100 200 300 miles · 0 100 200 300 400 Km

a b c d e f g h i j k l m

15°W 10°W 5°W 0°

PORTUGAL   SPAIN

Sines
Odemira   Ourique   Aljustrel   Aracena   Sevilla   Córdoba   Jaén   Huéscar   Lorca   Murcia
Mértola   2036   Baza   Guadix   Aguilas   Cartagena
Portimão   Tavira   Huelva   Marchena   Granada   3478   Sa. Nevada   Almería
Sagres   Lagos   Faro   Jerez de la   Frontera   1654   Antequera   Motril
Golfo   Ronda   Málaga
de Cádiz   Ubrique
Cádiz   Algeciras   Gibraltar (U.K.)   Mostaganem
Str. of Gibraltar   Ceuta (Sp.)   Oran
Tanger   Tetuan   Melilla (Sp.)   Relizane   Masc
Asilah   Chechaouen   Al Hoceima   Beni Saf   Mohammadia   Sidi-
El Arisch   Nador   Ghazaouet   bel-Abbes
Ksar el Kebir   Midar   Tlemcen   Marhoum
Mehdia   Ouezzane   Ouerrha   Aknoul   Taourirt   El Aricha   Boug
Sidi   Kacem   Fès   Taza   Guercif   Oujda   Ras-al-Ma   Hauts   Chot
Salé   Kenitra   Ain   Chei
Rabat   Meknès   3190   Debdou   Benimathar   El Baye   Méchéria
Casablanca   Khemisset   Sefrou   Outat-el-Hadj   Atla
(Dar-el-Beida)   Rommani   Azrou   Missour   Tendrara
Azemmour   Berrechid   Khouribga   Moyen   Atlas   Ain Sefra   2236
El Jadida   Oued   Zem   3741   Ksabi   Bou Arfa
Oualidia   Settat   Midelt   Talsinnt   Mengoub   Figuig
Sidi   Benguerir   Beni Mellal   Rich   2670   Beni Cunif
Safi   Bennour   Demnate   Goulmina   Ksar es Souk   Kenadsa   Colomb   Bechar   Abadla   Taghit   834
Tensift   Chichaoua   Marrakech   4071   Ighil   Tinerhir   Erfoud   Rissani   Abadla
Essaouira   Amizmiz   Haut   Atlas   Agdz   Tazzarine   Taouz   Igli   Beni Abbès   Grand Erg
Jebel Igdet   Toubkal   Tazenakht   Zagora   Kerzaz
3615   4165   Taroudannt   Ksabi   Charouîne
Agadir   Anti Atlas   Tinrhir   Tabelbala   Gourara
Ihezgane   2359   Tata   Tagounite   Tinfouchy   890   Kahal Tabelbala   Sbaa
Tiznit   Bani   Tabelbala   Adrar
Sidi Ifni   Djebel   Hamada du Dra   Bou Akba   ALGE   Tamentit
1250   Foum   El Mansour   Titaf
Bou Izakarene   El Aassane   Sali
Tantan   Dj. Ouarkziz   Ouahila   Reggane
El Eglab   Iguidi   Mcherrah   Bordj Flye
Tindouf   437   680   Sainte Marie   Chenachane

ISLAS
CANARIAS   (Spain)
Tenerife   Lanzarote
Pico   Santa   Arrecife
de Teide   Cruz   Puerto del Rosario
3718   Guia   Las   Fuerteventura
Gomera   Palmas   C. Yubi
1949   Tarfaya
Hagunia
Daora
Laayoune
WESTERN   SAHARA   Al Farcia
C. Bojador   Smara
Bojador   Lemsid   Tifariti
Amasin   Ain
ben Tili
701   Bir
Guelta   Oum Greine   Chech
Zemmour   Yetti   Chegga
Zemmour   Rhallamane   Aioun Abd
Bir el Khzaim   el Malek   Erg
Dakhla   370   Kreb en Naga   305
Aargub   Karet   315   Tanezrouft
Rio de Oro   Imlili   Zedness   El Mreiti   A El Ahmar   Taoudenit
Bir   500   Hamada Safia
Enzarah   Aguelt el Melah   Agueraktem   Hamada el Hericha   El Maia
Cap   Zouerate   322   273
Barbas   Fderik   Hammami   296   361
Agailas   Er Mreyer
Bir   Makteir   330   El Djouf   El Khenachich   321
Gandus   647   Ouarane   Douaouir   450
Tichla   Zug   Choûm   Guelb er
Nouâdhibou   Richet   Jafene   284   Bordj-Mo
Guera   Ouadane   MAURITANIA
Cape   Ksar
Nouâdhibou   Azefal   Torchane   Chinguetti
Atar   Oujeft   MALI
I. Tidra   Akchar   Mabrouk   Timétrine
C. Timiris   Akjoujt   Adafer   Azaouad   750
Nouamrhar   Faye   501   Agueloc
88   Méraia
Tamassoumit   Tidjikja   Dabar Tichitt   In Alay   Oudeîka
23   Tichitt   Agamor
Tagant   Akreijit   Dahar   Bamba   Niger   Bourem
Nouakchott   554   Oualata
Trarza   Moudjeria   334   318   Aouker   Oudeîka
Boutilimit   Boûmdeïd   Tamchaket
Aleg   Mal

n o p q r s t u v w x y z

20°N

25°N

30°N

ATLANTIC
OCEAN

Madeira (Portugal)
Funchal   Is. Desertas

MOROCCO

This map shows 1/60 of the earth's surface   Area scale : 1 ☐ inch on the map ≈ 15,000 ☐ miles on the ground   1 ☐ cm on the map ≈ 6000 ☐ km on the ground

5°E 10°E 15°E 20°E

ITALY

I. Egadi Marsala Corleone Etna 3340 Bova Marina
Sciacca Agrigento Caltanissetta Adrano Riposto
Licata Gela Enna Catania
Sicilian Channel Ragusa Syrakus Noto
Pantelleria (It.) Pachino

Alger Dellys Skikda Annaba Biserte Golfo de Tunis Cap Bon
Boufarik Tizi Ouzou Bejaia Djidjelli Mateur Tabarka Tunis Kélibia
Blida Constantine Guelma Beja Hammam Lif
Medea Setif Souk-Ahras Le Kef Teboursouk Zaghouan
Ksar el Boukhari Bordj-Bou-Arreridj Batna Aïn Beida 1357 Sousse
Metlili Chaamba Bou Saada Khenchela Tebessa Kairouan Mahdia
767 Biskra 2326 Kasserine El Djem
Djelfa Ouled Djellal Redeyef Gafsa Fériana Sfax
Messaad Tolga Metlaoui Ras Kaboudia Îles Kerkenna
Tilrhemt El Meghaier Tozeur Nefta Gabès
Berriane Guerara Dzioua Djamaa El Oued Chott Djerid Kebili Île Djerba Zarzis
Ghardaia Touggourt Temacine Médenine Ben Guerdane
Ain Oussera Ouargla Hassi Messaoud Bordj Bourguiba Remada Zuwarah

MEDITERRANEAN SEA

Golfo de Gabès Linosa Gozo Valletta
Isole Pelagie (Sicilia) Lampedusa **MALTA**

35°N

Tarabulus Janzur Tajura Khoms Zliten Misurata
Al Aziziyah Tarhuna Banghazi Qaminis
Jadu Nalut Gharian Zintan Beni Walid Mizda
Bir Zar Sinawan Buerát el Hsun Sirte Gulf of Sirte
Ghadames Darj Tripolitania Bu Ndjem Ash Shwayrif Ajdabiya
Hamada el Homra Al Qariyat Al Aqaylah
Waddan Hun Suknah Maradah
Hamada du Tinhert Hamadat Tingharat Awaynat Wanin Zella Tlisen
Ohanet Brak Idri Umm el Abid El Fugha Harudj el Asued
Bordj Omar Driss In Amenas Semnu Sabha
Tiguentourine Edjeleh **LIBYA** Tmed Bu Haschlscha
Ubari Jarma Zuwaylah Terbu Timsah
Fezzan Murzuq Wau el Kebir
Ghat El Barcat Qatrun Wau en Namus
Djanet Tajarhi
Anai Ramlat Rabyana Tropic of Cancer
Plateau du Mangueni Tumu Pic Toussidé 3265 Jabal Nuqay
Madama Auzu Bardai 3376 Aozi
Plateau du Djado Tibesti Yebbi Bou
Ténéré du Tafassasset Djado Dao Timni Zouar Tarso Ahon Sherda Emi Koussi

CHAD

NIGER

30°N 25°N 20°N

Average linear scale: 1 inch ≈ 125 miles 1cm ≈ 80 km

a b c d 35 e f g h i j k l m

20°E 25°E 30°E 35°E

GREECE

Kythira Ákra Maléa Ródhos 1215 30°E Finike Gulf of Antalya Anamur Silifke Antakya 1795 Alep
Sea of Crete 2540 Burun Anamur TURKEY Idlib Mas

Ródhos Kárpathos CYPRUS Cape Andreas Latakia Hama 1385

35°N Káros Cape Arnauti Nicosia Olympus 1951 Larnaca Famagusta Tartus Homs S

Paphos Limassol Trâblous Tall Kalakh Nabk 2659
Baalbek 308 Zahlé

MEDITERRANEAN Beirut LEBANON Dimashq
Sour Qunaitra Syr
Golan Heights

SEA Haifa Dara a 1735

Hadera Irbid Mafraq
1247 Zarqa
Tel-Aviv-Yafo ISRAEL Amman

Nile Delta Rashid (Rosette) Baltim Dumyat Gaza Jerusalem Al
Banghazi Al Mekhily Tubruq Al Burdi Sîdi Barrâni Mersa Matruh Damanhûr Al Mansura Port Said Beer Sheba Dead Sea Al Karak
Qaminis Al Adam Sallûm Al Iskandariyah Tanta Zagazig Suez Canal Ar Arish JORDAN Bayir
169 Fuka Al Hammam Ismâilîya 850 1641 Ma'an Al Isaw
Ajdabiyah Marmarica Al Alamein Zagazig Great Bitter Lake Quseima 1615 Petra 1615
Cyrenaica Fort Qarain Qattara Depression Shubra al Kheima Al Qahirah Nakhl Wadi al Arish Elat Aqaba Al Mudauwara
30 Wadi al Hamim Qara Giza Suez Sûdr Sinai Aqaba
30°N Al Jaghbub 113 123 Pyramids Helwân Ain Sukhna 1626 Nuweiba Al Bir
Jaghbub Oasis Memphis Al Faiyûm Peninsula Dahab 2580 Al Bad Tabuk
Awjilah Siwa Beni Suef Katherina 2637 Ofira Ash Sharmah
Jalu Siwa Oasis Nile Ras Ghârib Duba 1990
Jalu Oasis Baharîya Oasis Beni Mazâr Gemsa Ras Muhammad
Bawîti Al Minyâ Hurghada
L I B Y A Dairût Port Safaga
Farafra Farafra Oasis Asyût Abu Tig Wadi Qena Al Wajh
E G Y P T Akhmin Arabian Desert
Sohâg Qena Qusair Wadi al Qasr
Qasr Al Balyana Qus Karnak Marsa Alam
37 184 Tazirbû Dakhla Oasis Mût Al Khârga Thebes Luxor Ras Abu Madd
Zighan Isna Upper Nile
25°N Al Khârja Oasis Idfu Egypt Kom Ombo
Kufrah Oasis Bâris 1977 Berenice Ras Banas
Rabyanah Al Jawf 1st Cataract Aswân Wadi Garara Ya l
625 Gilf Kebir Lake Nasser Bir al Hasa
Tropic of Cancer Plateau Wadi Allaqi Ras Abu Dara
Abu Simbel Halaib
1893 Uweinat 2217 Ras Had
2nd Cataract Wadi Halfa Wadi Oko Dungunab Ras Abu
Nile 2218 Erba Muhar Qol
Kosha Nubian Desert 2260 Oda
20°N Delgo Port
CHAD Erdi Kerma Abu Hamed
Ounianga Kebir Dongola 3rd Cataract Umm Mirdi Amur Sinkat Sua
Fada 545 Karima 4th Cataract 5th Cataract Musmar Haiya
Archei S U D A N Al Khandaq Merowe Berber Derudeb
Mourdi Depression Debba Korti Atbara Adarama Baks3
Ennedi Baiyuda Atbara
Haouach Howar 738 Mitatib
al Milk White Nile Shendi E
Wadi Seidna 6th Cataract
20°E 517 Omdurman Al Khartum North
25°E 30°E 35°E

n o p 42 q r s t u v w x y z

a b c d e f g h i j k l m

54

IRAQ

IRAN

SAUDI ARABIA

KUWAIT

NEUTRAL ZONE

BAHRAIN

QATAR

UNITED ARAB EMIRATES

OMAN

YEMEN ARAB REPUBLIC

PEOPLE'S DEMOCRATIC REPUBLIC OF THE YEMEN

Al Hasakah
Sinjar
Tall 'Afar
Mosul
Arbil
Saqqez
Baneh
Qojur
Qazvin
Amol
Ghaem Shahr
Damghan
Mayamey
Takestan
Damavand Mts
Damavand
Suwar
Sharqat
Lesser Zab
Kirkuk
Bijar
Razan
Karaj
Zarand
Tehran
Semnan
Torud
Abu Zawr
Euphrates
Anah
Wadi ath Tharthar
Tigris
Tikrit
Tuz Khurmatu
Sulaimaniyah
Sanandaj
Hamadan
Saveh
Qom
Garmsar
Dasht-e-Kavir
Abu Kamal
Al Hadithah
Ravansar
Bakhtaran
Kangavar
Qareh Su
Malayer
Arak
Khor
Tabas
Mileh Tharthar
Jalaula
Diyala
Karand
Eslamabad-e-Gharb
Ilam
Borujerd
Azna
Mahallat
Kashan
Natanz
Anarak
Ar Ramadi
Ba'qubah
Baghdad
Mehran
Keshvar
Khorramabad
Daran
Meymeh
Ardestan
Nain
Aliabad
Dasht-e-Lut
Wadi al Ghadaf
Bahr al Milh
Karbala
Al Aziziyah
Dehloran
Dezful
Shahr-e-Kord
Najafabad
Isfahan
Ardakan
Yazd
Al Hillah
Al Kut
Shush
Qomsheh
Darband
Wadi Tibal
An Najaf
Ad Diwaniyah
Ar Rifa'i
Al Amarah
Ahwaz
Izadkhast
Abadeh
Abarqu
Mehriz
Bafq
Ravor
Al Jalamid
Wadi Ar'ar
As Samawah
An Nasiriyah
Hawr al Hammar
Al Qurnah
Ramhormoz
Ramshir
Behbahan
Dinar
Dehbid
Zarand
Ar'ar
Ash Shubaiyai
As Salman
Al Busaiyah
Basra
Umm Qasr
Bandar-e-Khomeini
Abadan
Hendijan
Nurabad
Saadatabad
Rafsanjan
Kerman
Baghin
Abu Qasr
Ad Duwaid
Sakakah
Rafha
Al Faw
Bubiyan
KUWAIT
Jahra
Kuwait
Bandar-e-Rig
Kazerun
Shiraz
Persepolis
Daryacheh-ye-Tashk
Hoseinabad
Sirjan
Jawf
Linah
Ansab
Ahmadi
Bushehr
Ras Halileh
Borazjan
Firuzabad
Daryacheh-ye-Bakhtegan
Laleh Zar Baft
An Nafud
Jubbah
Al Wafra
Mina Saud
Khormuj
Zeydan
Jahrom
Neiriz
Fasa
Aliabad
Dowlatabad
Ha'il
Al Maiyah
Bir Shari
Al Qaisumah
Safaniyah
Qaryat al 'Ulya
Abu Hadriyah
Kangan
Lar
Qotabad
Tabah
Samirah
Az Zilfi
Al Artawiyah
Sarar
Al Hasa
Al Jubayl
Ras Tannurah
Gavbandi
Bastak
Bandar-e-Margam
Bandar Abbas
Minab
Qeshm
Hulaifah
Uqlat al Suqur
Buraidah
Unaizah
Al Majm'ah
Ushairah
Ash Shumlul
Dhahran
Damman
Al Manamah
Ar Ruwais
BAHRAIN
Qeys
Bandar-e-Lengeh
Ash Sha'am
Str. of Hormuz
Musandam Pen.
OMAN
Khayber
Shaqra
Abqaiq
G. of Bahrain
QATAR
Ras al Khaimah
Dibba
Buwatah
Al Hanakiyah
Al Qurain
Khuff
Durma
Khurais
Al Udailiyah
Al Hufuf
Dukhan
Karana
Doha
Umm Sa'id
Sharjah
Dubai
Jebel Ali
Fujairah
Gulf of Oman
Shinas
Al Madinah
Ad Dawadimi
Riyadh
Sulaimaniyah
Harad
Salwa
Marawah
Abu al Abyad
Abu Dhabi
Al Khaznah
Al Ain
Al Khaburah
Sohar
Hunain
Afif
Muhairiqah
As Sila
Jabal adh Dhanna
Tarif
UNITED ARAB EMIRATES
Bu Hasa
Habshan
Ibri
Bahla
As Sidr
Mahd adh Dhahab
Halaban
Al Hillah
Sabkhat Matti
Taraq
An Nashash
Liwa Oasis
Al Jafurah
Umm al Samim
Wadi Aswad
Madrakah
As Suq
ARABIA
Layla
Ad Dahna
As Sawadah
Jabal Tuwayq
Zalim
Khulais
Makkah
At Ta'if
Ar Rauda
Wadi ad Dawasir
Ar Rub' al Khali
Al Uruq al Mutaridah
Arafat
Turabah
Wadi Bishah
Al Khamasin
As Sulaiyil
Al Lith
Bani Sar
Qal'at Bishah
Wadi Tathlith
Al Ulaya
Tathlith
Wadi bin Khawtar
Dhofar
Sharbithat
Ras Sharbithat
Al Qunfudhah
An Nimas
Asir
Khay
Abha
Khamis Mushait
Hima'
Sanaw
Wadi Shihan
Wadi Qitbit
Sahil al Jazir
Sauqira Bay
Ad Darb
Zahran
Thamarit
Jabal al Qara
Kuria Muria Islands
Najran
Sa'dah
Thamud
PEOPLE'S DEMOCRATIC REPUBLIC OF THE YEMEN
Salalah
Mirbat
Ras Mirbat
Farasan Is.
Jizan
Midi
YEMEN ARAB REPUBLIC
Al Hazm
Huth
Wadi al Jawf
Raisut
Jabal al Qamar
Wadi al Jiz
Al Ghaydah
Qamar Bay
ARABIAN SEA
Dahlak Islands
Hajjah
Haynan
Wadi Masilah
Sayun
Ras Fartak

Average linear scale : 1 inch ≈ 125 miles   1 cm ≈ 80 km

0 100 200 300 miles
0 100 200 300 400 500 Km

43
60

15°W
10°W
5°W

Moudjéria
Boûmdeïd
Tamchaket
In Alay
Oudeik

T r a r z a
A o u k e r
Bamba

Boutilimit
Oualata
Tombouctou

Mederdra
Aleg
Kiffa
Montagnes
de l'Affolé
·600
·318
Ayoûn el Atroûs
Néma
Lake
Faguibine
Goundam

Rosso
Bogué
Mâl
MAURITANIA
Néma
I r i g u i

Dagana
Senegal
Kaédi
Kankossa
Timbedgha
Amourj
Bassikounou
Niafounké
Hombori

St. Louis
Mbout
Kobenni
S a h
·1155

Louga
Matam
Hamoud
Nioro du Sahel
Nara
Lac Débo
e l

Linguère
Maghama
Balé
Nampala
Douentza

Fourdou
Sélibabi
Birou
Sokolo
Mopti
Bandiagara

15°N
Dakar
Thiès
Mbaké
F e r l o
Kidira
Diéma
M a c i n a
Djibo

Cape Verde
Diourbel
Kayes
Koniakari
M A L I
Ouahigouya

Mbour
Kaolack
Malème-Hodar
SENEGAL
Bamba
Didiéni
Niger
Djenné
B U R

Karang
Koumpentoum
Diamou
Bafoulabé
Ségou
Bani
San
Yako

Banjul
GAMBIA
Georgetown
Tambacounda
Toukoto
Kolokani
Bla
Nouna
FA

Sere Kunda
Gambia
Basse Santa Su
Dialakoto
Dialafara
Banamba
Koulikoro
Fana
Dédougou
Ouagad

Brikama
Bignona
Kolda
Niokolo Koba
Saraya
Satadougou
Kita
Bamako
Baguinéda
Mpessoba
Koutiala
Koundougou
Houndé

Casamance
Farim
Kédougou
Kati
Ouéléssébougou
Koundougou
Léo

Ziguinchor
GUINEA-BISSAU
Koundara
·1538
Bougouni
Sikasso
·820
·505
Bobo-Dioulasso
Tumu
Navrongo
Bolgatang

Mansôa
Bafatá
Gaoual
Siguiri
Garalo
Banfora
Lawra

Bissau
Corubal
Fouta Djalon
Tougué
Dinguiraye
Manankoro
Pogo
Gaoua
Wa
Yala

Bissagos Islands
Kogon
Labé
·1264
Pita
·1028
Kpouroussa
Samatiguila
Ouangolodougou
Baouna
Ga

Catió
Boké
Télémélé
Dabola
Kankan
Odienné
Ferkéssédougou
Korhogo
·430
Kong
Sawla
Bole

Fatala
Frie
Konkouré
Dalaba
·1015
Kissidougou
Boundiali
Kanawolo
Koutouba
Maluwe

Boffa
·1421
Kavendou
Mamou
·1094
Sanouyah
Bohodou
Morondo
Kani
Katiola
Bondoukou
Bamboi
Kintam

Kindia
Faranah
Kérouané
Bako
Koro
Séguéla
Goumeré
·700
Techiman
GHA

10°N
Conakry
Forécariah
Little Scarcies
Kabala
Kissidougou
Touba
Biankouma
Bouaké
Berekum
Sunyani

Kambia
Rokel
Loma Mts.
·948
Makeni
Koidu
Tibé
1504
Man
Kossou Reservoir
Yamoussoukro
Abengourou
Kuma
Konongo
Nkaw

Freetown
SIERRA LEONE
Bo
Pendembu
Guéckédou
Macenta
1656
Beyla
1257
IVORY COAST
Bouaflé
Agnibilekrou
Obuas
Ko

Sewa
Zorzor
Nzérékoré
1752
Sanniquellie
·1189
Daloa
Dimbokro
Akoupé
Tano
·554
Awaso
Dunkwa

Kenema
Loffa
Ganta
Danané
Duékoué
Toumodi
Agboville
Prestea

Sherbro Island
Pujehun
Mano River
St. Paul
Gbarnga
Guiglo
Grand-Lahou
Tarkwa

Bomi Hills
Bong
Tapeta
Toulépleu
Tchien
Tai
Soubré
Gagnoa
Lakota
Dabou
Abidjan
Grand-Bassam
Sekondi
Takorad

Monrovia
LIBERIA
Man
Buchanan
Cess
Juazohn
·396
Niénokoué
Sassandra
San Pédro
Grabo
Ivory Coast
Gold C

5°N
Grain Coast
Greenville
Cavally
Sassandra
Bendama
Comoé
Plibo
Harper
Tabou

A T L A N T I C
O C E

This map shows 1/60 of the earth's surface. Area scale : 1 ☐ inch on the map ≃ 15,000 ☐ miles on the ground   1 ☐ cm on the map ≃ 6000 ☐ km on the ground

a b c d e f g h i j k l m

NIGER

CHAD

BENIN

NIGERIA

TOGO

CAMEROON

CENTRAL AFRICAN REPUBLIC

EQUATORIAL GUINEA

SÃO TOMÉ AND PRINCIPE

GABON

CONGO

ZAÏRE

Gulf of Guinea

Slave Coast

Azaouak

Vallée de l'Azaouak

Kanem

Lake Chad

Bioko Island

Principe

São Tomé

Anou Mellene ·500
Ansongo
Ménaka
In Talak
Tillia
Tchin-Tabaradene
Tegguidda-n-Tessoum
·500
Agadez
Aouderas
Akrereb
Dibella
Kichi Kichi
Toro Doum
Abala
Tahoua
Illéla
Tilemsès
Aderbissinat
Tanout
Task
Idaye
Agadem
Ouyu Bezze Denga
Homodji
·280
Ngourti
Moul
·255
15°N
Salal
Torodi
Niamey
Tillabéri
Ouallam
Filingué
·302
Madaoua
Burni-Nkonni
Matankari
Dogondoutchi
Illela
·403
Tessaoua
Maradi
Zinder
Gouré
Goudoumaria
Mainé-Soroa
Nguigmi
Bosso
Rig-Rig
Nokou
Mao
Am Raya
Mondo
Moussoro
Ngouri
Massakori
Ngoura
Say
Dosso
Sokoto
Katsina
Dungas
Nguru
Gashua
Geidam
Mongouno
Baga
Massaguet
Djermaya
Karmé
550
Téra
Kantchari
Diapaga
·ourma
Kamba
Gaya
Koulou
Argungu
Birnin-Kebbi
Anka
Gusau
Faskari
Kano
Wudil
Hadejia
Potiskum
Damaturu
Dikwa
Maiduguri
Fort-Foureau
N'Djamena
·442
Massenya
Tanguiéta ·550
Natitingou
Bérroubouay
Bembéréké
Kandi
Yelwa
Zuru
Kontagora
Birnin Gwari
Kaduna
Zaria
Zalanga
Gongola
Gombe
Bara
Wuyo
Biu
Mubi
Mokolo
Maroua
Moutouroua
Ham
Bongor
Guélengdeng
Bousso
Boukombé
Wawa
Kainji Reservoir
Tegina
·1594 Goura
Bauchi
·1141
296
Djougou
Lama-Kara
Parakou
Yashikera
Kaiama
Minna
Kafanchan
·1625 Kagora ·1618
Pankshin
Jos
Zamko
Numan
Garoua
Pala
Kelo
Lai
Bassari
772
Sokodé
Blitta
Bassila
Kilibo
Igbetti
Agoaré
Ilorin
Jebba
Bida
Abuja
Akwanga
Wamba
Lafia
Ibi
Wukari
Jalingo
Poli
Guidjiba
Tchollité
Moundou
Koumra
Doba
·845
Savalou
Iseyin
Oyo
Ede
Oshogbo
Ilesha
Ado Ekiti
Okene
Kabba
Lokoja
Baro
Benue
Makurdi
Beli
Mbé
Touboro
Baïbokoum
Gore
Atakpamé
Nuatja
Abomey
Abeokuta
Iwo
Ife
Ikerre
Akure
Ondo
Owo
Oturkpo
Ayangba
Okene
Takum
Béka
Ngaoundéré
Bétaré-Oya
Bocaranga
Bossangoa
Kpalimé
Tsévié
Ilaro
Porto Novo
Lekki
Lagos
Ijebu Ode
Benin City
Ogoja
Nkambe
Banyo
Tibati
Meiganga
Garoua Boulaï
Bouar
Bozoum
Baboua
Bombale
Lomé
Ouidah Cotonou
Sapele
Onitsha
Enugu
Ikom
Mamfe
Bamenda ·2335
Foumban
Yoko
Goyoum
Bertoua
Carnot
Bossembélé
Warri
Afikpo
Cross
·1890
·3008
·2740
Bafoussam
Dschang
Bafang
Bafia
Ndjolé
Nanga Eboko
Batouri
Kenzou
Berbérati
Bania
Ughelli
Aba
Calabar
·2050
Nkongsamba
Yabassi
Edéa
Yaoundé
Abong Mbang
Yokadouma
Nola
Port Harcourt
Bonny
Brass
Mt. Cameroon 4100
Buea
Limbé
Douala
Malabo
·3090
Luba
·2662
Eséka
Nyong
Mbalmayo
Ebolowa
Sangmélima
Dja
Lokomo
Bayanga
Bomassa
Ebebiyin
Bitam
Ntam
Souanké
Moloundou
Ouesso
Ambam
Bata
Niefang
Oyem ·1200 Tembo
·937
Nkolabona
Mékambo
Sembé
Liouesso
Mbini
·1200
Evinayong
Mbini
Mitzic
Makokou
Pikounda
Cocobeach
Makokou
Libreville
Kougouleu
Lalara
Booué
Makoua
Mossaka
São Tomé ·2024
Ndjolé
Booué
Likouala ·500
Okondja
Ewo
Boundji
Okoyo
Pagalu (Equa.Guinea)
Port-Gentil
Lambaréné
Ogooué
·980
·875
Koulamoutou
Lastoursville
Okandja
Wandjo
Omboué
Mimongo
Moanda
Franc20ville
Mouila

37 44

n o p q r s t u v w x y z

0   100   200   300 miles
Average linear scale : 1 inch ≈ 125 miles   1 cm ≈ 80 km
0   100   200   300   400   500 Km

20°E 25°E 30°E

Toro Doum
Bodélé
Ennedi
Fada
Archei
Haouach
Ouagat
Karma
Maba
Kapka 1220
Thé
Umm Saggat
Sindi
Magrur
Wadi Howar
Wadi al Milk
Nile
Shendi
6th Cataract
Wadi Seidna
517
Omdurman
Al Khartum North
Al Khartum
Umm Inderaba

Koro Toro
15°N Salal
Sahel
Rime
Biltine
Abéché
al Ouaday
Haddad
Adré
al Junayna
Kebkabiya
El Fasher
Umm Keddada
Hamrat al Shaikh
Sodiri
Kordofan
Haraza 1127
Umm Saiyala
El Hasaheisa
El Gezira
Wad Medani

CHAD
Batha
Batha
Ati
Oum Hadjer
Mangalmé
Guedi 1506
Mongo
Zalingei 3071
Jebel Marra
Gurgei 2351
Kass
Menawashei
Dam Gamad
Wad Banda
Kirim 640
al Nahûd
AbuZabad
El Obeid
Bara
Er Rahad
Tendelti
Umm Ruwaba
al Dueim
Kosti
Rabak
Singa
Sennar

Bitkine
1613
Abou Deïa
Goz Beida
Azoum
Nyala
Ghubeish
al Udaiya
al Fûla
Dilling
Nuba Mountains 1325
Kadugli 842
Ed Damazin
Renk
Lake Roseires

Mélfi
Zakouma
Am Timan
Azoum
'Idd al Ghanam
Rahad al Berdi
al Da'ain
Babanusa
al Muglad
Talodi
Turum 1122
Kurmuk

SUDAN
Ibra
Sumaih
1093
Tungaru
Paloich

El guig
Chari
Salamat
Kendégué
Haraze Mangueigne
Ouandja
Oulou
Birao
Yata
Dango 790
Bahr al Arab
Sudan
Malakal
Bambeo 2185

10°N
Koumra
Sarh
Kéita ou Doka
Aouk
Tété
Tiroungoulou
Toussoro 1330
Bora
Raga
Aweil
Bahr al Ghazel
Sud
Tonga
Sobat
Nasir
Der
Gambe

Maro
Ouham
Bangoran
Ndélé
Massif des Bongos
850
Ouadda
1050
Ndji
Sopo
Pongo
Wau
Toni
Akobo

41
Kabo
Batangafo
Ouandago
Kaga Bandoro
Mbrès
Bemingui
Kotto
Haute Kotto
Busseri
Rumbek
White Nile
Maridi
Pibor Post

Bossangoa
Bouca
Dékoa
Bria
Yalinga
Bou ngo
CENTRAL AFRICAN
Mvolo
Bor
Kenamu Swamp

Sibut
Bambari
Kotto
Ouaka
Vovodo
Ouara
REPUBLIC
Tambura
Sue
Ibba
Angeleri 838
Mundri
Medi
Mongalla

5°N
Bogangolo
Damara
Bossembélé
Kouango
Alindao
Gambo
Chinko
Dembia
Rafaï
Zémio
Moomou
Obo
Li Yuba
Doruma
Yambio 1067
Maridi
1065
Garmabe
Juba
Ngangala
Kapoeta 1940

Bangui
Bimbo
Zongo
Gbadolite
Bosobolo
Mobaye
Mobayi-Mbongo
Yakoma
Uele
Bili
Api
Ango
Ese
Niangara
Dungu
Yei
Faradje
Aba
Lalyo
Torit
Kinyeti 3187
Lok

Mbaïki
Zinga
Boyabo
Libenge
Lua Dékere
Matundu
Monga
Bili
Api
Bambili
Baranga
Poko
Rungu
Watsa
Gombari
Arua 1310
Kajo-Kaji
Laropi
Nimule
Kaabong 2381

Lobaye
Enyélé
Businga
Gemena
Ebola
Abumonbazi
Angu
Titule
Dulia
Buta
Isiro
Medje
Nepoko
Wamba
Aru
Atiak
Kitgum
Loyoro

Kungu
Budjala
Mongala
Dua
Bodala
Likati
Tele
Ibembo
Zambeke
Kole
Medje
Wamba
Mahagi 2448
Gulu
Anaka
Lira
Kot
Mord

Dongou
Mobeka
Makanza
Lisala
Bumba
Izimbiri
Ituri
Bomili
Nia Nia
Mambasa
Komanda
Bunia
Fataki
Lake Mobutu
Masindi
Soroti

Impfondo
Giri
Zaïre (Congo)
Busu-Djanoa
Bongandanga
Basoko
Aruwimi
Banalia
Lindi
Bafwabalinga
Hoyo 1450
Ntoroko
Hoima
Nakasongola
Lake Kyoga
Mbale

ZAÏRE
Lopori
Basankusu
Yahuma
Yambuya
Bengamisa
Batama
Beni
Fort Portal
Kyanjojo
Kamuli
Kaliro
Iganga
Tororo

Lulonga
Waka
Lulonga
Lingomo
Yekana
Isangi
Yangambi
Kisangani
Madula
Boyoma Falls
Opiene
Butembo
Stanley 5109
Kasese
Mubende
Kayunga
Jinja

Mbandaka
Bolomba
Befale
Maringa
Samba
Djolu
Yatolema
Pene-Tungu
Maiko
Lubero
Lake Edward 2197
Masaka
Entebbe
Kampala

0°
Ruki
Ingende
Boende
Watsi
Wema
Yali
Befori
Ekoli
Ubundu
Opala
956
Kirundu
Lubutu
Mountains 2341
Lake Edward
Bushenyi
Mbarara
Sese Islands
Lake
Kisumu

Bikoro
Kalamba
Lomela
Watsi-Kengo
Tshuapa
Busanga
Ikela
Likoto
Lomani
Ishasha River
Kikagati
Lake Victoria
Tarime

Lake Tumba
Inongo
Kiri
Lake Mai-Ndombe
Momboyo
Monkoto
Yalifafu
Yolombo
Punia
Walikale
Masisi
Karisimbi 4507
Goma
Lake Kivu
Gisenyi
Ruhengeri
Kabale
Kyaka
Bukoba
Musoma
Ukerewe Island
Nansio
Banagi

Yandja
Bolia
Ntadembele
Mitumba
Lowa
Kabunga
Kavumu
Kigali
RWANDA
Kayonza
TANZANIA

CONGO
UGANDA

20°E 25°E 30°E

This map shows 1/60 of the earth's surface. Area scale : 1 □ inch on the map ≈ 15,000 □ miles on the ground 1 □ cm on the map ≈ 6000 □ km on the ground

a b c d e f g h i j k l m

39

40°E   45°E   50°E

Derudeb

Barka

2589

Mersa Teklay

Nakfa

Mitatib

Keren

·2617

Mitsiwa

Farasan Islands

Jizan

Red Sea

Sa'dah

YEMEN

Midi

Huth

al Hazm

8

sala

Showak

aref

Akordat

Asmara

2374

·2617

Dekemehare

Dahlak Islands

Hajjah

Az Zaydiyah

al Mahdad 3360

San'a 2242

Sirwa

ARAB

Adi Quala

Adi Keyih

Hodeida

Isbil ·3190

Dhamar

REPUBLIC

al Rawda

al Baida

al Shihr

15°N

Humera

Adi Arkay

Mesfinto

Metema

Aksum

Adwa

Asimba 3248

Adigrat

Bait al Faqih

Zabad

Manar ·3350

Ibb

Hays

Lawdar

Riyan ·2185

al Mukalla

Ta'izz

Ahwar

al Baida

PEOPLE'S DEMOCRATIC REPUBLIC OF THE YEMEN

Wadi al Jiz

Thamud

Al Ghaydah

Makrah

Qamar Bay

Ras Fartak

Sayhut

Mekele

Kwiha

Lake Assale

Ras 4620 Dashen

Maychew

Danakil

al Mukha

Turbah

Lahej

Musa Ali ·2063

Gonder 2223

Abune Yosef 4190

Kobbo

Ramlu 2130

Az Zuqar

Aseb

Turbah

850 Ghadir

Aden

Gulf of Aden

Abd al Kuri

Cape Guardafui

Bereda

Gorgora

Lake Tana

Addis Zemen

Debre Tabor

·435 Guna

Weldiya

Danakil

Randa 1783

Tadjourah

Hodda ·1400

El Gal

Bahir Dar

Tisisat Falls

Betehor

Tendaho

DJIBOUTI

Asayta

Arta

Djibouti

Bosaso ·2200

Beleya ·3131

Abay (Blue Nile)

Dangila

Bati

Dese

Kembolcha

Awash

Lake Abbe

Ali-Sabieh

Dikhil

Bure 4052

2960

Ethiopian

Mendebo

Karakore

Gewane

·1789

Berbera

Mait

al Mado ·1826

Las Koreh

Erigavo

Las Dave

Carcar Mountains

Ras Hafun

Debre Markos

Dejen

Fiche

Debre Birhan

Dire Dawa

Buramo

Arde ·1858

Wadi Giahel

ETHIOPIA

Highlands

Amara ·3145

3292

Sheno

Mieso

Harer

Babile

Jijiga

Hargeisa

Burao

Bur Anod ·1097

Gardo

Bender Beila

10°N

Gimbi

Nekempt

Arjo

Hagere Hiywot

2408

Adis Abeba

Awash

Asbe Tafari

Gugu 3060

Ahmar Mountains 1856

2064

El Dab

Kirit

Las Anod

Sinugif

Garoe

Eil

S O M A L I A

Bedele

Ghion

3719

Welkite

Debre Zeit

Nazret

Degeh Bur

Rabableh

Agaro

Jima

Lake Ziway

Asela

Kaka ·4190

Fik

Hamarro Hadad

Warder

Baduen

Ghelinsor

Berdale

El Hamurre

Maigudo 2386

Lake Abiyata

Lake Langano

Shashemene

2119 Awetu

Shebeli

Kebri Dehar

Galcaio

Mirsale

Bonga

Lake Shala

2743

Awasa

Goba

Megalo

Imi

Gode

Shilabo

Godinlave

Dusa Mareb

Shishinda an Teferi

Sodo

Dila

Wendo

Mendebo Mountains

Kibre Mengist

El Kere

Kelafo

Obbia

Omo

Lake Abaya

Lake Chamo

Negele

Hargele

Mustahil

Sinadogo

Maji

Arba Minch

1441

Filtu

Lema Shilindi

Ferfer

Jinka

Gidole

Dawa

Bokol Mayo

Yet

Belet Huen

El Bur

Maas

5°N

Key Afer

Konso

Dolo

Hoddur

Tigieglo

Bulo Burti

El Dere

Kelem

Yabelo

Chew Bahir Lake

Chelago

Ramu

Mandera

Lugh Ganana

Calie Corar 566

INDIAN

ng

Banya Fort

Mega

Moyale ·1280

Baidoba ·600

Mahaddei Uen

Adale

Lake Turkana

North Horr

Sololo

Buna

El Wak

El Uach

Bur Acaba

Uanle Uen

Giohar

OCEAN

war

Chalbi Desert

Dinsor

Afgoi

Nyiru 2752

Loiyangalani

Marsabit

Tarbaj

Bardera

Corioleo

Saco Uen

Mogadishu

Lokori

South Horr

Wajir

Juba

Dugiuma

Merca

Baragoi

Laisamis

·2375

KENYA

Kapedo

Maralal

Kisima

Archer's Post

Mado Gashi

Habaswein

Scebeli

Brava

Baringo Lodge

Isiolo

Meru

Garba Tula

Belesc Cogani

Afmadu

Gelib

Nyahururu 2360

Nanyuki

Kenya 5200

Saka

Liboi

Hagadera

Giamama

Araara

Nakuru

Gilgil

3994

Embu

Mwingi

Garissa

Tana

Kisimaio

Equator 0°

Kijabe

Thika

Kitui

Nairobi

Machakos

Narok

Magadi

Kajiado

Mutomo

Mokowe

Patta Island

Kolbio

Hola

45°E   50°E

n o p q r s t u v w x y z

45

100   200   300 miles

Average linear scale : 1 inch ≃ 125 miles   1 cm ≃ 80 km

0   100   200   300   400   500 Km

a   b   c   d   e   f   g   h   i   j   k   l   m

41   42

SÃO TOMÉ AND
PRINCIPE
São Tomé
Equator
0°

G A B O N

C O N G O

Z A Ï

A N G O L A

A T L A N T I C

O C E A N

CABINDA
(Angola)

N A M I B I A

BOTSWAN

Cocobeach
Mitzic
Mékambo
Lulonga   Waka   Yekana
Libreville   Kougouleu   Makokou   Pikunda   Bolomba   Befale   Lingomo
Lalara   980   Djolu
Gabon   10°E   Likouala   15°E   Samba   Maringa   Befori
Ndjolé   Booué   Kéllé   Makoua   Mbandaka   Yali
Ruki   Busira   Boende   Watsi   Wema   Ikela
Lambaréné   Okondja   Kouyou   500   Owando   Irebu   Ingende   Watsi Kengo   Lomela   Tshuapa   Yalifafu
Port-Gentil   Koulamoutou   Bonda   Ewo   Boundji   Mossaka   Kalamba   Bikoro
(Lastoursville)   Lake Tumba   Momboyo   Monkoto   Yolom
Ogooué   Mimongo   Moanda   Franceville   Okoyo   Bolia   Kiri   Lome
Lake Onangué   875   Gamboma   Yandja   Inongo   Lake
Omboué   820   Boumango   Bouanga   Mai-Ndombe
975   Mouila   Mayoko   Bambama   Nsah   Ntadembele
Ndendé   Mayumba   Ngo   Nioki   Kutu
Tchibanga   834   Inoni   Bandundu   Lukenie   Oshwe   Dekese   Lodja
Mossendjo   Congo/Zaïre   Masia-Mbio   Bagata   Kasai
Kibangou   Mapati   Brazzaville   Cuango   Fatunda   Kapia   Ilebo   Bena Dibele   Sankuru
Sounda   Madingou   Kinkala   Kenge   Kwilu   Bulungu   Bena-Tshadi
Loubomo   Boko   Kinshasa   Mayamba   Masi-   Mweka   Kakenge
Bas-Kouilou   Luozi   Madimba   Manimba   Kikwit   Idiofa   Mpata   Luebo   Demba   Dimbele
Pointe-Noire   5°S   Tshela   798   Inkisi-Kisantu   Banda   Kananga   Mbu
Zaïre   Seke Banza   Mbanza-Ngungu   Feshi   Gungu   Kilembe   Tshikapa   Kazumba   Kamiji
Lândana   Isangila Falls   Ngidinga   Kimvula   Popokabaka   Luiza   Gandaji   Mw
CABINDA   Lukula   Kimpese   Mwenge   Kania
Cabinda   Boma   Matadi   Kasongo-Lunda   Kahemba   Luachimo   Kapanga
Muanda   M'Pala   Maquela do   Warnba   Forte Carumbo   Lucapa
Soyo   M'Banza-Congo   Zombo   Verissimo
Damba   Quimbele   Cuango   1150   Sarmento
Tombôco   Sanza   Camaxilo
N'Zeto   Bembe   Pombo   Luremo   Caungula
Mussera   Uige   Negage   Camabatela   Camaxilo   Lucapa
Ambriz   Quitexe   Cuango   Saurimo   Sandoa   Tshimb
Nambuangongo   Quibaxe   Samba Caju   Xá-Muteba   Xinge   Mona-   Muriege   Dilolo
Caxito   Lucala   Kalandula   Cuango   Quimbundo
Luanda   Catete   N'Dalatando   Malange   Nova Gaia   Cacolo   Muconda   Luau   Ikele
Muxima   Dondo   Cuanza   Quitapa   Dala   Mald
Porto Amboim   Calulo   Quibala   Mussende   Cassai   Cazombo   Mw
Gabela   Andulo   Buçaco   Luena
Sumbe   Waco-Kungo   Camacupa   Luena   Moxico   Lucusse
Lobito   Alto Hama   Bailundo   Cuemba   Chicala   Lumbala   Luena
Benguela   Balombo   Kuito   Cassamba   Luzi   Zambezi
Catengue   Caala   Ganda   Cachingues   Luvuei   Zambesi   Kabo
Lucira   Chitembo   Lutembo
Caconda   Mumbué   Sessa   Lungué-Bungu   Lukulu
Negola   Lumbala N'Guimbo
Lucira   Cacula   Caconda   Menongue   Longa   Cuito Cuanavale   Chiume   Mongu
Gambos   Capelongo   Cuchi   Mavinga   Senar
Lubango   Cassinga   Cuvelai   Caiundo   Chibaranda
Chibia   Mulundo   1265   Cubango   1190   Rivungo   Luengué   1160   Luiana
Chianje   Quiteve   Rito   Cuito   Savate   Mucusso   Kongola   Capri
Roçadas   Cunene   Cuangar   Rundu   Shakamku   Strip
Oncócua   Naulila   N'Giva   Ondangwa   Shakawe
Ruacana   Oshakati   Savate   Numkaub   Sepopa
Cape Frio   Opuwa   Obombo   1096   Namutoni   Keibeb   20°E
1784   Purros   15°E   Etosha   Pan   10°E

5°S
10°S
15°S

2024   20°E

n   o   p   q   r   s   t   u   v   w   x   y   z

48

This map shows 1/60 of the earth's surface. Area scale : 1 □ inch on the map ≈ 15,000 □ miles on the ground   1 □ cm on the map ≈ 6000 □ km on the ground

43

a | b | c | d | e | f | g | h | i | j | k | l | m

30°E 35°E 40°E

sangani
Madula
Maiko
Lindi
Opienge
Beni 5109
Kyanjojo
Kayunga
Kaliro
Iganga
Tororo
Eldoret
Loruk
Archer's Post
Mado Gashi
Afmadu

Pene-Tungu
Butembo
Fort Portal
Mubende
Jinja
Kakamega
Baringo Lodge
Isiolo
Garba Tula
Hagadera
Belesc Cogani

Kampala
Entebbe
Kisumu
Kapsabet
Nyahururu
Meru
Saka
Liboi

Kirundu
Lubero
Kasese
Lake George 2197
UGANDA
Masaka
Sese Islands
Kericho
Kisii
2277
Nakuru
Gilgil
Nanyuki
Mt. Kenya 5200
Equator 0°
SOMALIA
Kisimaio

956
Lubutu
Lowa
Lubero
Kasindi
Bushenyi
Mbarara
Lake Victoria
Bukoba
Kilkoris
3100
Naivasha
Embu
Garissa

Lake Edward 2341
Ishasha River
Kikagati
Kyaka
Musoma
Tarime
Mara
Narok
2775
Kijabe
1662 Nairobi
Kitui
Machakos
Hola

Walikale
Masisi
Karisimbi 4507
Ruhengeri
Banagi
Nansio
Magadi
Lake Natron
Namanga
Kajiado
Mutomo
Mokowe
Patta Island

1040
Punia
Kabunga
Goma 3044
Gisenyi
KIGALI
Gitarama
Kayonza
Mwanza
Ukerewe Islands
Nyin Desert
2942
Oloitokitok
Meru 5895
4555
Kilimanjaro 5895
Moshi
Manyami

Kalima
Ulindi
Mwenga
Kavumu
Bukavu
RWANDA
Cibitoke
Kayanza
Nyakanazi
Geita
Ngudu
Oldeani 3188
Arusha
Makuyuni
Same
Malindi

Pangi 1047
Kasambule
Kitutu
2670
BURUNDI
Bujumbura
Kibondo
Shinyanga
Manonga
Nzega
Ndareda 3420
Babati
2124
Mbulu
Kwale
Kilifi

1019
Kingombe
Kipaka
Kalole
2073
Kibondo
Kahama
Ibologero
Katesh
Masai Steppe
Mkomazi
Lushoto
Mombasa

Samba
Kasongo
Kasulu
Kigoma
Uvinza
Tabora
Sikonge
Singida
2193
Kondoa Irangi
Korogwe
Handeni
Segera
Tanga
Pemba Island
5°S

Tshofa
Lubao
1052
Lukuga
Kalemie
Malagarasi
Igombe
Ugalla
Itigi
Manyoni
Kongwa
Gairo
Mvomero
INDIAN

Kabalo
Nyunzu
Niemba
2373
Lake Tanganyika
Mpanda
Rungwa
Kitunda
Kisigu
Dodoma
Mpwapwa
Msata
Zanzibar
Zanzibar Island

Katompi
Kaloko
Zaire
Luvua
Sange
Moba
Kapona
Namanyere
Sumbawanga
Lake Rukwa
2418
TANZANIA
Rungwa
Kilosa
2287
Morogoro
2646
Chalinze
Bagamoyo
Dar-es-Salaam

Pidi
Kikondja
Mulongo
Malemba Nkulu
2460
Marungu Mountains
Kasanga
Makongolosi
Chunya
Iringa
Mbuyuni
Mikumi
Kisarawe

1139
Lake Upemba
Mitwaba
Pweto
Sumbu
2418
Mbeya
Uyole 2961
Chimala
Sao Hill 2072
2576
Ifakara
Mahenge
Kibiti
Mafia Island
Kilindoni

Lake Mweru
Chiengi
Mpulungu
Mbala
Chambeshi
Nakonde
Itungi
Rungwa
Njombe
Luhombero
Mohoro
Nangurukuru
OCEAN
46

Kabondo Dianda
Mukana
Nchelenge
Mporokoso
Kasanga
Tunduma
Karonga
Livingstone Mountains
Lukumburu

Busanga
Bunkeya
Kasembe
Kawambwa
Kapatu
Kasama
Isoka
Mbesuma
Chilumba
Gumbiro
Nachingwea
Mingoyo
Lindi
Mtwara
10°S

Kambove
Luambo
Kasenga
Munungu
Luwingu
Chinsali
Luangwa
2606
Livingstonia
Songea
Tunduru
Nangomba
Masasi
Newala
Cape Delgado

Likasi
Minga
Mansa
Lake Bangweulu
1475
Chisoso
Chama
Rumphi
Lake Malawi
Chamba
Masuguru
Mueda
Diaca
Mocimboa da Praia

Lubumbashi
Kipushi
Mokambo
Kapalala
Mukuku
Mpika
Chilonga
Mpulu
Chikwa
Mzuzu
Nkhata Bay
Maniamba 1836
Litunde
Lugenda
Marrupa
Montepuez
Nantulo
Macomia

Solwezi
Chililabombwe
Mufulira
Chingola 1350
Kitwe
Ndola 1261
Serenje
Kanona
Chibembe
Lundazi
Jenda
Dwangwa
Nkhotakota
Lichinga
Malanga
Messalo
Nungo
Pemba

ZAMBIA
Luanshya
Chifwefwe
Luangwa
Kasungu
Maua
Namapa

Kapiri Mposhi
Chipata
Mchinji
MALAWI
Salima
Massangulo
Lurio
Nacaroa
Nacala

Kabwe
Petauke
Katete
Lilongwe
Dedza
Mandimba
Cuamba
Ribaue
Namialo
Lumbo
15°S

Lubungu
Landless Corner
Kachalola
Nyimba
2035
Mangochi
Balaka
Mutuali
Monapo
Mocambique

Mumbwa
Rufunsa
Fingoe
Chitunde
Bene
Zomba
Lake Chilwa
Gurue
2419
Nampula
Angoche

Lusaka 1279
Zumbo
Cabora Bassa Reservoir
Songo
560
Blantyre
Limbe 3000
2133
Alto Molocue
Nam.
Liupo

Namwala
Mazabuka
Zambezi
Kafue
Chiuta
Mulanje
2054
MOZAMBIQUE
Mucuba
Moma

Kariba Reservoir
1204
Kariba
Mkumbura
Tete
2054
Nsanje
Mocuba
Pebane

Kalomo
Choma
Karoi
Mount Darwin
Nyamapanda
Changara
Tambara
Sena
Namacurra
Quelimane

Livingstone
Victoria Falls
Zambezi
Binga
Gokwe
Kadoma
Bindura
Mutoko
Guro
Caia
Mopeia

Hwange
Gwai River
ZIMBABWE
HARARE 1472
Chegutu
Inyanga 596
1868
Catandica
Inhaminga
Chinde

Dete
Banket
Rusape
Gorongosa 105
40°E

n | o | p | q | r | s | t | u | v | w | x | y | z

30°E 35°E

49

0 100 200 300 miles

0 100 200 300 400 500 Km

Average linear scale: 1 inch ≈ 125 miles 1cm ≈ 80 km

a b c d e f g h i j k l m

25°E 30°E 35°E 40°E

ZAÏRE

TANZANIA

ZAMBIA

MALAWI

MOZAMBIQUE

ZIMBABWE

BOTSWANA

REPUBLIC OF SOUTH AFRICA

SWAZI-LAND

Lake Tanganyika
Lake Rukwa
Lake Mweru
Lake Upemba
Lake Bangweulu
Lake Malawi
Marungu Mountains
Muchinga Mountains
Kariba Reservoir
Cabora-Bassa Reservoir
Makgadikgadi Pans
Mafia Island
Kilindoni
Bassas da India (France)
Europe Island (France)
Sofala Bay
Straits of
Drakensberg

Kaloko, Kaniama, Kabongo, Manono, Luvua, Sange, Moba, Mpanda, Kitunda, Kisigu, Kilosa, Morogoro, Dar-es-Salaam, Bagamoyo, Chalinze, Kisarawe
Mulongo, Kiambi, Kapona, Namanyere, Rungwa, Rungwa, Mbuyuni, Mikumi, Kibiti
Kabondo, 1060, Pidi, Kikondja, Malemba Nkulu, Mitwaba, Pweto, Sumbu, Kasanga, Sumbawanga, 2418, Kipembawe, Iringa, 2576, Ifakara, Mohoro
Kamina, 1139, Mukana, Chiengi, Mpulungu, Mbala, Makongolosi, Chunya, Chimala, 2072, Sao Hill, Mahenge, Luhombero, Nangurukuru
Kabondo Dianda, Nchelenge, Mporokoso, Nakonde, Tunduma, Uvole, 2959, Mbeya, Makambako
Busanga, Bunkeya, Kawambwa, Kasembe, Kapatu, Isoka, Mbesuma, Itungi, Karonga, Lukumburu, Gumbiro, Nachingwea, Mingoyo, Lindi, Mtwara
Kolwezi, Luambo, Likasi, Minga, Kasenga, Mununga, Luwingu, Kasama, Chinsali, 2606, Chilumba, Livingstonia, Songea, Nangomba, Newala, Masasi
Mwinilunga, Chisasa, Kipushi, Lubumbashi, Chembe, Mansa, Samfya, 1475, Rumphi, Mzuzu, Chamba, Ruvuma, Tunduru, Masuguru, Diaca, Mocimboa, Mueda
Solwezi, Mokambo, Kapalala, Mukuku, Chisoso, Chikwa, Mzimba, Nkhata Bay, Maniamba, 1836, Lichinga, Malanga, Nantulo, Macomia
Chililabombwe, Mufulira, Chingola, Kitwe, 1350, Ndola, 1261, Kanona, Chilonga, Mpika, Chibembe, Lundazi, Jenda, Dwangwa, Nkhotakota, Kasungu, Litunde, Marrupa, Nungo, Montepuez, Metoro, Pemba
Kabompo, Kasempa, Luanshya, Serenje, Chifwefwe, Kapiri Mposhi, Chipata, Mchinji, Salima, Massangulo, Maúa, Ribauè, Namapa, Nacaroa, Naca
Kaoma, Lubungu, Kabwe, Petauke, Katete, Lilongwe, Dedza, 2035, Mandimba, Cuamba, Mutuali, Namialo, Lumbo, Moça
Mumbwa, Landless Corner, Kachalola, Nyimba, Chitunde, Bene, Balaka, Gurué, Nampula, Monapo
Lusaka, 1279, Rufunsa, Fingoè, Songo, Chiúta, Zomba, Blantyre, Limbe, Molócuè, Liupo, Nametil, Angoche
Namwala, Mazabuka, Zumbo, 560, Tetè, Mulanje, 3000, Errego, 760, Moma
Choma, Kariba, Karoi, Mkumbura, Changara, Tambara, Nsanje, 2054, Mocuba, Mucubela, Pebane
Seshéke, Katima Mulilo, Kazungula, Livingstone, Victoria Falls, Binga, 1204, Mhangura, Mount Darwin, Nyamapanda, Guro, Vila de Sena, Namacurra, Quelimane, Mopeia, Inhaminga, Chinde
Kataba, 1108, Pandamatenga, Hwange, Dete, Gwai River, Mvurwi, Bindura, Mutoko, Catandica, 1862, Caia, Gorongosa, 105, Dondo, Beira
Kanyu, Nata, Bulawayo, 1343, Masvingo, Chipinge, Rupisi, Espungabera, Chimanimani, 2436, Nova Golegã
Tsoe, Mosetse, 1028, Plumtree, Antelope Mine, Gwanda, Rutenga, Chiredzi, Macane, Jofane, Inhassoro, Bazaruto
Xhumo, 974, Letlhakane, Francistown, Tlalamabale, Mazunga, Bubye, Tswiza, Chicualacuala, Massangena, 167, Mabote, Pambarra, Mapinhane, 500
Metsiamonong, Serule, 1000, Selebi-Phikwe, Tuli, Beitbridge, Pafuri, 438, Mapai, Chigubo, Funhalouro, Massinga
Kikao, Shoshong, Palapye, Pontdrift, Messina, Louis Trichardt, Shingwedzi, Limpopo, 132, Inhambane
Molepolole, Jwaneng, Mahalapye, Soje, Marken, Ellisras, Pietersburg, Tzaneen, 2128, Phalaborwa, Massingir, Panda
Gaborone, Mosomane, Letlhakeng, Mmabatho, Thabazimbi, Vaalwater, Potgietersrus, 1856, Satara, Guijá, 169, Quissico
Kanye, Lobatse, Zeerust, Rustenburg, Dwarsberg, 2085, Nylstroom, Warmbad, Groblersdal, Sabie, Lydenburg, Witrivier, Magude, Macia, Xai-Xai
Lichtenburg, Roodepoort, Pretoria, 1233, Witbank, Middelburg, Steelpoort, Komatipoort, 515, Nelspruit, Manjacaze
Delareyville, Potchefstroom, Johannesburg, 1753, Germiston, Benoni, Springs, Bethal, Carolina, Ermelo, Maputo, Namaacha, Bela Vista
Klerksdorp, Vereeniging, 1440, Standerton, Middelburg, Mbabane, Manzini, Catuane

Zaïre, Luena, Luapula, Chambeshi, Luangwa, Kafue, Zambezi, Kariba, Hunyani, Gwai, Shashi, Tuli, Mwenezi, Save, Limpopo, Molopo, Lugenda, Messalo, Lúrio, Ruvuma

n o p q r s t u v w x y z

This map shows 1/60 of the earth's surface. Area scale : 1 □ inch on the map ≈ 15,000 □ miles on the ground 1 □ cm on the map ≈ 6000 □ km on the ground

45°E   50°E   55°E   60°E

*Aldabra
Island*

10°S

I N D I A N   O C E A N

Moroni
COMOROS

pel   Antsiranana
Moheli des   Anjouan
Comores   Dzaoudzi
                        *Mayotte
                        (France)*

Ambilobe
Nosy-Bé
Hell-Ville   Iharaña

Tsaratanana   Sambava
2876
Mountains   Andapa

Antsohihy   Antalaha

15°S

Befandriana Av.   Ambohitralanana
1218.
a   Maroantsetra   Mahalevona

Mahajanga   Port-Bergé-
                        Vaovao
                        Mandritsara
Marovoay   Mampikony   Mananara

b   *1301.*

i   Miarinarivo   *Nosy
                        1325.   Boraha*

*Juan de
Nova*   Maevatanana
                        Andriamena
M A D A G A S C A R
                        .1545
                        Morafenobe   Vohidiala
                                                Toamasina
                        Ankazobe

Antsalova

Tsiroanomandidy   **Antananarivo**
                        1381
Manambolo   *2643.*
                        Mandoto
Tsimafana   Betafo   Mahanoro
                        Tsiribihina   Antsirabe
Morondava   *2140.*   Fandriana
        Mahabo   20°S
                        Ambositra   **Port Louis**
Mandabe   **MAURITIUS**
                        Mananjary
Mangoky   Fianarantsoa
                        Irondro   Saint-Denis
orombe   *3069.*
                        Ambalavao   *La Réunion
                        Manakara   (France)*
Ankazoabo   *2658.*
.1348   Ihosy   Ivohibe
anombo   Farafangana
Toliara   Andranovory   *Manara*
                        Betroka   Vangaindrano
                        1824   *Tropic of Capricorn*
Betioky

Ampanihy   *.1957*
        Antanimora
                        Taolañaro
Tsihombe   Ambovombe

25°S

0   100   200   300
miles   Average linear scale : 1 inch≏125 miles 1cm≏80 km   0   100   200   300   400   500
                                                                                Km

a b c d e f g h i j k l m

10°E   15°E   20°E

Moçâmedes   Chibia   Cassinga   Chiume   Mc
Tômbua   Chianje   Mulundo   Cuito Cuanavale
(Porto Alexandre)   Cuvelai   Caiundo   Rivungo   Ser
900   Tambor   Quiteve   *1265*   A N G O L A
Oncócua   Roçadas   Savate   *1190*   Rito   Luengué
Iona   N'Giva   *1160*   Chibaranda   Lui
Foz do Cunene   Cunene   Náulila   Cuangar   Xamavera   Mucusso
2195   Ruacana   Ondangwa   Rundu
Orupembe   Obombo   Oshakati   O v a m b o l a n d   Shakamku   Shakawe
Opuwa   *1096*   Sepopa   Okavango
Cape Frio   *1784*   Etosha   Namutoni   Keibeb   Numkaub   *950*   Oka
Purros   Pan   *1093*   Gumare   Okav
Kowares   Okaukuejo   Tsumeb   Tsumkwe   Mount Aha   D.
Kamanjab   Otavi   *2149*   Grootfontein   *1070*   Tsau
868   Terrace Bay   Goreis   Outjo
20°S   Torra Bay   Khorixas   Otjiwarongo   *1932*   Okakarara   Dekar
Kalkfeld   Ghanzi
Brandberg   N A M I B I A   Hochfeld   Kalkfontein   B O
2579   Omaruru   Takatshw
Uis Mine   *2350*   Steinhausen   Kule   K a l a h
Cape Kruis   Usakos   Okahandja   *1537* Buitepos
Henties Bay   Windhoek   Witvlei   Gobabis   *1000*
Swakopmund   Anschluss   *1654*   Ukwi   Kang
Walvis Bay   *160*   Dordabis
Tropic of Capricorn   Rehoboth   Leonardville   Tshane
2334   Derm
Abbabis   Aranos   Mpaathutlwa   Mako
A T L A N T I C   Kalkrand   Stampriet   Pan
Sesriem   Mariental   Twee   Nossob
Naribis   Zaris   Maltahöhe   Gochas   Rivier   Tshabong
25°S   Asab   Asanib   *1046*   Koës
Helmeringhausen   Twee Rivieren   *1000*   Molopo   Fry
Great Tiras   *1185*   Gemsbok
1867   Bethanie   Ku
Lüderitz   Aus   Keetmanshoop   Aroab   Sishe
Goageb   Narubis   Gr. Karasberge   *1000*   *1832*   Da
Pomona   *2202*   Upington   Postma
Witpütz   *1107*   Orange   Grie
O C E A N   Grünau   Karasburg   Ariamsvlei   *903*   Keimoes   R
1341   Augrabies   Kakamas   Groblershoop
Alexander Bay   Orange   Falls   Onseepkans   Pofadder
Vioolsdrif   Steinkopf   Namies   Kenhardt
Port Nolloth   Nababeep   Springbok   Marydale
30°S   Coppertor
Garies   Platbakkies   Van Wyksvlei   Vosburg
Brandvlei
Loeriesfontein   Carnarvon
Bitterfontein   Nieuwoudtville   Williston   Loxton
Calvinia   Sak
Vanrhynsdorp   Fraserburg   S O U
Clanwilliam   Sutherland   Komsberg   B
Slippers Bay   Citrusdal   *1721*   W
Vredenburg   *1040*   Prince Albert Road   Little Swartberge   Wil
Saldanha   Gr. Winterhoek   Laingsburg   *2325*   Oudtshoorn   Ha
Malmesbury   *2078*   Touws River   Ha
Cape Town   Wellington   Little Karoo
Strand   Worcester   Swellendam   George
Cape of   Caledon   Witsand   Stilbaai
Good Hope   Mosselbaa
35°S   Cape Agulhas   Agulhas

n o p q r s t u v w x y z

This map shows 1/60 of the earth's surface. Area scale : 1 □ inch on the map ≙ 15,000 □ miles on the ground 1 □ cm on the map ≙ 6000 □ km on the ground

25°E Mumbwa Rufunsa 30°E Fingoè Chiúta Zomba 35°E Gurué Nampula 40°E Moçambique

Lusaka 1279 Zambezi Zumbo Cabora Bassa - Reservoir Songo **MALAWI** Blantyre Limbe 3000. Mulanje Errego Molócuè Liupo .200 Nametil

1220. Namwala Lake Kafue Kafue Mkumbura Tete Zambezi 2054. Nsanje Mocuba Mucubela Moma

Kalomo Choma Kariba Reservoir Kariba Karoi Mhangura Mount Darwin Changara Tambara .760 Angoche

sheke Livingstone Zambezi Binga Mvurwi Nyamapanda Guro Vila de Sena Caia Quelimane Pebane

Kazungula Victoria Falls Hwange Banket .1204 Bindura **Harare** Catandica Gorongosa Namacurra

Kataba Pandamatenga Dete Gwai River .1472 Chegutu Kadoma Rusape Inyanga 2592 .1862 Inhaminga Chinde

ZIMBABWE Gokwe Kwe Kwe Chivhu Mutare Chimoio .105

Kenmaur Nkayi 1447 Dorowa Chimanimani Beira

1000 Gweru Chatsworth Nyanyadzi Dondo Sofala Bay

Basotho Tsholotsho Masvingo Chipinge Nova Golegã 20°S

Nata Bulawayo 1343 Zvishavane Rupisi Espungabera

Tsoe Plumtree .1028 Mosetse Chiredzi .502 Save

Tlalamabele Gwanda Mwenezi Macane Jofane Inhassoro

Letlhakane Antelope Mine Rutenga .500 Massangena .167 Bazaruto Bassas da India (France)

74. Francistown Mazunga Bubye Mabote Pambarra

Serule Selebi- Tuli Beitbridge Chicualacuala Machaila Mapinhane Europe Island (France)

Metsiamonong Serowe .1000 Palapye Pikwe Pontdrif Messina Pafuri .438 Mapai Chigubo

Kalamare Mahalapye Groblersbrug Louis Trichardt Shingwedzi Funhalouro Massinga

Soje Ellisras Marken Phalaborwa 132. Panda Inhambane

ikao Mosomane 2128. Pietersburg Tzaneen Massingir Guijá 169 Inharrime

etlhakane Molepolole Vaalwater Potgietersrus 1856 Satara Magude Manjacaze

Gaborone .2085 Thabazimbi Nylstroom Steelpoort Sabie Skukuza Macia Xai-Xai Quissico 25°S

Kanye Warmbad Lydenburg Witrivier Komatipoort 46

1479. Dwarsberg Groblersdal Sabie Nelspruit .515

Lobatse Zeerust **Pretoria** 1333 Middelburg Waterval Boven **Maputo**

Molopo Rustenburg Witbank Carolina **Mbabane** Namaacha

veng Mmabatho Roodepoort 1753 Benoni Springs Ermelo Manzini Bela Vista

Delareyville Lichtenburg **Johannesburg** Germiston Bethal **SWAZI** Catuane

burg Potchefstroom Vereeniging 1440 Standerton Piet Retief **LAND** Lavumisa

Klerksdorp Parys Vaal Reservoir Frankfort Volksrust Pongola Mkuze

Schweizer-Reneke Wolmaransstad Vaal Heilbron Utrecht 2277 .1532 Vryheid Lake St. Lucia

Bloemhof Reservoir Kroonstad Reitz Newcastle Ulundi Mtubatuba

Christiana Bloemhof Bethlehem Dundee

nton Welkom Harrismith Ladysmith INDIAN

Barkly West Winburg Ficksburg Mont aux Estcourt Eshowe Richards Bay

Kimberley Senekal Sources Tugela Greytown

Bultfontein Clocolan 3285 Himeville Pietermaritzburg

1426 Bloemfontein .3482 Durban

LIC Maseru

Luckhoff Fauresmith Wepener .3096 **LESOTHO** Ixopo 1000 30°S

Trompsburg Smithfield Mafeteng Umzinto

K. le Roux servoir Moyeni Kokstad Harding Port Shepstone

Colesberg Aliwal North Zastron Mount Fletcher Umtata Port Edward

Hanover Burgersdorp .2052 Lady Grey Maclear Port St. Johns

Steynsburg Barkly East Elliot .1677

FRICA Queenstown Idutywa Coffee Bay

Graaff-Reinet Cradock Stutterheim King William's Town

Somerset East Fort Beaufort .500 East London

Kirkwood Grahamstown

tlerville Bell

Uitenhage Port Alfred

dorp Port Elizabeth Jeffreys Bay

MOZAMBIQUE Mozambique Channel

INDIAN OCEAN

25°E 30°E 35°E 40°E

n o p q r s t u v w x y z

0 100 200 300 miles   Average linear scale : 1 inch≈125 miles   1cm≈80 km   0 100 200 300 400 500 Km

35°E · 40°E · 45°E · 50°E · 55°E · 60°E · 65°E

85°N

A R C

80°N

Aleksandry Zemlya · *Georga Zemlya* · Solsberi · Dzheksana · *Rudol'fa* · *Yeva-Liv*
Luidzhi · Karla-Aleksandra · La Rons'yer
Gukera · Mak-Klintoka · Gallya · Vil'cheka Zemlya

F r a n z   J o s e f   L a n d   Zem

Sal'm

Russkaya Gavan

Smidovich

75°N

N o v a y a   Z e m l y a

K A R A   S E A

Sedova 1115
Stolbovoy
Litke

B A R E N T S   S E A

• 260

Krasino

70°N

Cape

Proliv Karskiye Vorota

Pechora Sea

• 162 Vaigač

Amderma

Baie

Kolgujev 166

Ust'-Kara

Pay-Khoy

Chernaya

Yangarey

Murmansk

Dresvyanka

Khal'mer-Yu

Tundr

• 201

Mončegorsk
• 1191
Kirovsk

Cape Kanin Nos

Kanin Peninsula

• 242

Nar'yan Mar

Bol'shezemel'skaya

Vorkuta

397

Češa Bay

Velikovisochnoye

Kolva

Koreyver

Yeletski

Kandalakša

• 106

Northern Ural

Pay-yer • 1499

Mezen' Gulf

Volonga

Makarikha

Abez'

Arctic Circle

Stafonovo

Usa

Inta

Laby

Kandalakša Gulf

Mezen'

Nonburg

Trosh

White Sea

Azopol'ye

Ust'Tsil'ma

• 155

Kosyu

Fe

Belomorsk

Izhma

Pechora

Narodnaya 1894

Onega Bay

Dvina Bay

Pinega

Mezen'

Kadzherom

Saranpaul'

Onega

Severodvinsk
Archangelsk

• 463

Kedva

• 164 Voyvozh

Kyrta 1617

Patrasuy

Berezovo

Segeža

Pinega

Politovo

Shomvukva

Ukhta

Muligort

• 417

Medvežjegors

North Dvina

Vendenga

Vym'

Vey Vozh

Nyaksimvol

Sergi

Lake Onega

259

Pinega

• 324

Zheleznodorozhnyy

Troitsko-Pechorsk

Sovetsk

Petrozavodsk

Kargopol

Verkhnyaya Toyma

Mikun

S O V I E

Puzla • 1108

Khang

Irta

Loptyuga

Syktyvkar

Vyčegda

Porog

Suyevatpaul

Podporoze

Ustya

Kizema

Kotlas

Vizinga

Ust'Kulom

Kur'ya

Komsomol'

Konoša

Vel

239

Kur'ya 303

Pionerskiy

Tichvin

Vaga

Velikiy Ustyug

Kazhim

• 213

U v a l y

Kolva

• 1027

Polunochnoye

Cherdyn

Ivdel'

Totma

Noshul'

• 1493 Denezkin Kamen

Sukhona

Pyatigory

Kama

Cerepovec

• 292

Nizhniy Yenangsk

Northern

Kirs

Solikamsk

162 •

Krasnotur'insk

Vologda

Nikol'sk

Murashi

Kudymkar

Berezniki

Lobva

Sos'va

Rybinsker Reservoir

Vetluga

Karnskoje Reservoir

Gubakha

• 883

Verkhniy Tura

Bui

Kirov

Glazov

Krasnokamsk

• 321

Turinsk

Rybinsk

Novo-Vyatsk

Dobryanka

Nizhniy Tagil

Kostroma

Volga

Vetluzhskiy

Pizhma

Kez

Perm'

Artemovskiy

Vyšni Voloček

Jaroslavl

Kinešma

Uren

Yaransk

Nolinsk

Igra

Kungur

Talitsa

• 343

Kalyazin

Krasnyye-Baki

Votkinsk

Bogdanovich

Ostashkov

Ivanovo

• 115

Kil'mez

Izhevsk

Krasnoufimsk

Pervoural'sk

Sverdlovsk

Torzhok

Kalinin

Dubna

Klin

Dmitrov

Kovrov

Yoshkar Ola

Malmyzh
217 •

Sarapul

Degtyarsk

Sysert'

Kamensk-Ural'skiy

Shadrinsk

Nelidovo
Ržev

Starica

Zagorsk

Vladimir

Agryz

Nyazepetrovsk

Kasli

Volokolamsk

Noginsk

Dzerzhinsk

Gor'kiy

Volga

Arsk

Naberezhnyye Celny

Ula

Moskva

Mytišci

Orechovo Zujevo

Cheboksary

Kazan'

35°E

Odintsovo

Elektrostal

Murom

Yadrin

235

45°E

50°E Mamadysh

55°E

65°E

This map shows 1/60 of the earth's surface. Area scale : 1 □ inch on the map ≃ 15,000 □ miles on the ground 1 □ cm on the map ≃ 6000 □ km on the ground

70°E   75°E   80°E   85°E   90°E   95°E   100°E

I   C   O   C   E   A   N   85°N

Severnaya   Zemlya

Ushakova   Schmidta
                                                              Komsomolets   Cape Berga
                                                                                              80°N
Vize   Pioner   262 *Oktyabr'skoy Revolyutsii*
                                                                              800   *Shokal'skogo Str.*
West Siberian Sea   Cape Mednyy   *Bolshevik*

Mys Zelaniya   Nordenshel'da
                                                    Isačenko   Russkiy
                                                                Arch.   Cape Oskara
                                          Troynoy   Taimyr

                                      Arkticheskogo   Niz Taimyra
                                        Instituta   Mikhaylova   171•   *T a i m y r   P e n i n s u l a*   75°N
                                                                                                              512
                          Pyasina Bay   Pjasina   • 223   *Byrranga Mountains*
Belyy   Šokalsky   Vilkicky   Makarova   279   Tareya   Verkh. Taimyra   Ozero
Drovyanaya   Sibirjakov   Dikson   Pura   Taimyr
        • 47   Oleni   • 415 Zyryanka   Novay
Tambey   Taran   Gol'chikha   Agapa   Ust'-Avam   Dudypta Payturma Boganida   Kheta
                  Gyda Bay   Yuribey   Oshmarino   Kresty   Volochanka Kargo   Isayevskiy Ozero
Yamal   Ozero   *Gyda   Peninsula* Yakovlevka   Chernaya Dolgany   Kochikha   Boyarka   Labaz Pol'kyko
        Neyto   Gyda   70°N
Peninsula   Napalkovo   Karaul   Ust'-Port   Ozero   Ayan   1403 *Putorana*
    75•   Khokiley   Dudinka   Pjasina Ozero Lama 1612 *Mountains*   Maimeča
    66• Yaptiksale   • 160   Ust'-Port Yenisey Noril'sk   • 1274   2030 Kamen   Kotui
                                                              • 766 Ozero Keta   Changada
Yarongo 82• Ozero   Antipayuta   Taz Bay   65•   Potapovo Ambar   Ozero
    Yarroto   Yamburg   202   Khantayka   Khantayskoye   Anama   Chirinda
Shchuch'ye Novvy Port   Yepoko   Nakhodka   Igarka   Khantayskoye Kureyka   Kotuikan
Yada   Tazovskiy   Taz   Reservoir   814• Agata Ozero   Kočečum
    Nyda   Nyamboyeto   Russkaya   Karasino   Vivi   • 619
Gornyy Kazymsk Shuga   Sidorovoko   Yermakovo Ust'-Kureyka   Severnaja   Tura Nidym
                  Yanov Stan   Turukhan Farkovo Severnaja   Tembenchi
    112• Pangody   Urengoy   Taz   Kostino Turukhansk   Tutonchany   Tembenchi   65°N
Kazymskaya Staryy Nadym Kazym   Krasnosel'kup   22• Bugarikta *Tunguskoye* Vivi
        Numto   Chasel'ka   698• Niznaja Tunguska Tutonchany Chiskovo   Uchami Tura
    • 168   Vyngapur 42• Tolka   Noginskiy   *Mountains* 552 Uchami Vivi
        Noyabr'sk Tolka Kikiakki   Nizhneimbatskoye   Bakhta   970•   Taimurá
Kedrovyy Pokacheva Khalesavoy Ratta Matyl'ka Verkhneimbatskoye Kuzmov'ka Poligus Baykit
U N I O N Yermakovo Kolik'yegan Sabun Yeloguy Kellog Bakhta Podkamennaya Tunguska Čunja
Pim • 77 Korliki Yeloguy Sumarokovo Podkamennaya Tunguska Korda Mutoray
Surgut Ust'Kolik'yegan 55• Osinovo Velmo1-oye Vayvida
Khanty-Mansiysk Nizhnevartovsk Vach Lar'yak Sym Yartsevo Ust'Kamo
Strezhevoy Vanzhil'kynak Sym Teya Kamo
Aleksandrovskoye Nazina Polkan 951 Taimba
Kintus Negotka Kadzhi Novoyerudinskiy 60°N
Demyanskoye Ust'Tym Tym Lugovatka Nazimovo 695• Yarkino Cadobec
Cherpiya Katyl'ga Vasjugan Kargasok Ust'Ozernoye Bryanka Panovo
Gerasmikova Onegva Yar Staritsa Alipxa Ket Ust'Pit Kamenka Bedopa
Tobol'sk Belyy Yar Vorozheyka Yeniseysk Angara Boguchany Kova
Bystryy Mogochin Kolpashevo Lesosibirsk Strelka Rodina Chuna Karamysheva 636•
S . S . R .) Baturino Komsomol'sk 211• Altat Galanino Oktyabr'sk
Tevriz 142• L'vovka Tegul'det Meletsk Birilyussy Predivinsk Asansk Shelayevo
Tara Bakchar Asino Shivera Aban Vydrino
Golyshmanovo Panovo 122• Biaza Moryakovskiy Achinsk Pamyat 698• Nevanka
Ishim 124• Bol'sherech'ye Pikhtovka 166• Zaton 258 Bogotol Kan Kansk Chunskiyo Bratsk
Tyukalinsk Chumakovo Yurga Tomsk Mariinsk Nazarovo 818• Krasnoyarsk Borodino Taysht
Nazyvayevsk Pokrovka Anzhero-Sudzhensk Uyar

70°E   75°E   80°E   85°E   90°E   95°E   100°E

0   100   200   300 miles   Average linear scale : 1 inch ≈ 125 miles   1cm ≈ 80 km   0   100   200   300   400   500 Km

105°E 110°E 115°E 120°E 125°E 130°E

Laptev Sea

Byrranga Mountains

75°N

Vezdekhodnaya

Ozero Taimyr *Bol. Balakhnya*

Korennoye Nordvik *Begichev* Cape Nordvik Khorgo

Novoryonye Novyy Kozhevnikovo *Suolama* *Uele* Dunay Turkannakh Sagastyr Antipinskiy

Novay Sagyr *Khatanga* Lukunskiy Bychez *Popigay* Popigay Uryung-Khaya Stannakh-Khocho Ary ·52 Trofimovsk

Khatanga *Fomich* Popigay Saskylakh Ust'-Olenëk 211. Taymylyr Tit-Ary Orto-Ayan

Star. Kayakhnyy Popigay ·268 Amakinskiy ·128 Ot-Siyen *Pur* Sklad ·921 Chekurovka Tiksi Buorkh

·536 Bor-Yuryakh 405. Khasalakh Kyusyur Tas-Tumu

Kotuykan Dzhelinde Kuoyka Govorovo ·982

70°N

Central

Tukalan Kirbey Mongolo Ulgumun Siktyakh Sakhandzha ·1291

Yessey *Kotui* Ylas-Yuryakh *Dzhara* Kirbey *Ukukit* Olenëk Sukhana Molodo *Lena* Kel' Sutu

Murukta *Moyero* *Arga-Sala* Kyuekh-Bulung *Siligir* *Olenëk* *Muna* Menkere Dzhardzhan Dzhelon

Siberian *Olenëk* *Motorchuna* Kystatyam *Menkere* Sencha ·2389

Vilyuy Mountains S O V I E T Zhigansk *Verkhoyanskiy* Tirekh

Ekonda Eyakit-Tërdë Khoronnokh Kharalakh

Uplands Udachnyy Onkuchakh Eyik Bakhynay Endybal Toy-Tire

65°N Aykhal *Tyung* Borolgustakh Tungus-Khaya

Kochechum ·823 *Markha* Andyngda Amysakh Bagadzha Mastakh *Linde* Dalgoye

Nizhnaya Tunguska Yeyka *Markoka* Engerdyakh Ulgumdzha Kyrgyday Vilyuy *Lena*

Kananda Malykay *Tyukyan* Vilyuysk Khampa Batamay

Amo Ust'-Ilimpeya Yukta Ankacho Chernyshevskiy Kysyl-Yllyk Nyurba Verkhnevilyuysk Ebe Kobya

501· Chuyengo *Ilimpeya* Simenga *Viljujskoje Reservoir* Novyy Khordogoy Sheya Khochot Ilbenge Tyugene

Tunor Bugorkan Mirnyy Almaznyy Suntar Olëng-Sala Tongulakh Kiriyestyakh Kangalassay

R O S S I Y S K A Yakutsk

Ayan Yerbogachen *Niznaya Tunguska* Dzhunkun Tas-Yuryakh Tenke Kerekyano Tyu

Čunja Strelka-Čunja Chamcha Ergedzhey Atakh-Yuryakh Yet-Kyuyel' *Sinyaya* Kytyl-Zhura Pokrovsk Ne

Sosna Khomokashevo Yerema Lensk Nyuya *Lena* Sangyyakhtakh Kachikattsy

Vanavara Kulinda Dulga-Kyuyel' Khamra Olekminsk Uritskoye Taloye Khorc

60°N *Tetere* Ust'-Chayka *Nyuya Khabalakh* *Bol. Patom* Patom Cherendey Tegyulte-Tërde

Chemdal'sk Tolon Vitim Andreyevskiy Berezovskaya Kudu-Kyuyel' Tokko *Tuolba* Verkhnyaya Amga

Panovo *Kamanga* Ayan Ika *Nepa* Chuya *Patomskoye Plateau* Polovinka *Chara* Khopporuo *Amga* Ugoyan

Kata Bur Kureyskaya Vorontsovka Chara Torgo *Olekma* Dikimdya Tommot

Angara Volokon Cherkashina Kropotkin ·1771 Usmun Aldan Ust'-Timpton

Ust'llimsk Ichera *Lena* Vitimskiy Severomuysk *Tokko* Yenyuka ·1612

Vorob'yeva Kirensk Bodaybo Berezovka *Aldan* Suon-Tit *Timpton* Chy

Garmenka Romanova Ul'Kan Gorno-Chuyskiy *Mama* Sinyuga Karalon Oron Chara Khani Bol. Khatymy *Gynym*

Ilimsk Ust'-Kut *Kirenga* Yermaki *Chaya* *Severo Baykal'skoye Nagor'ye* Ust'-Muya Udokan Taluma Neryungri Berkakit *Gonam* Go

Bratsk Vidim Riga Injaptuk 2573 Ueyan Tonnel'nyy 2467· Ust'Nyukzha 1870.

Suvorka Orlinga Kazachinskoye *Vitim* Bambuyka Sredniy Kalar *Kalar* Nagornyy Sutam Chapa

Bratskoye Reservoir Yukhta Nizhneangarsk *Plateau* Baunt Kadali Vetekhtina Lopcha Larba *Stanovoy* *Moun*

55°N ·763 Atalanka Žigalovo Sugdža Baykal'skoje ·1592 Tynda Ugagli Zeyski

Ust'-Kada *Lena* *Baykal'skiy Mountains* Oron Kalakan *Olëkma* Gulya Belen'kaya Zeya

Angara Balagansk 2069. Mogojto Bagdarin Ust'-Karenga Koltovkinda Tupik Bam Solov'yevsk Ogoron

Zima Zalari Bol. Onguren Sosnovka ·2573 Jeleninskij *Vitim* Zel'onoje Ozero Amazar Urusha Skovorodino Zeya

Čeremchovo 774· Manzurka Bugunda Chulugli 1911 Mogoča Luoguhe Dzhalinda Magdagachi

Usolje Sibirskoje *Ozero Baykal* Barguzin Romanovka *Nercha* Bukaćaća ·557 Petropavlovka

Angarsk Maksimicha 2049 Isinga Telemba Mošëgda *Silka* 1249. Gulian Ershiyizhan Ushumun

Selichov Ust'-Ordynskij Chaim 1322· *Uda* Cernyšev Ust'-Karsk Yimuhe Walagan Oktyabrskiy

Irkutsk Tataurovo Chörinsk Versino-Darasunski Sretensk Qiqian Ershiyizhan Novorossiyka

3265· Kamensk Ulan-Ude Chita *Silka* Ingoda Baley Mangui Linhai Shimanovsk

Kyren Listv'anka Darasun Nerchinskiy Zavod Kurleja By

Sl'ud'anka Tanchoj *Yablonovyy Mountains* Chilok Karymskoye *Ingoda* *Ergun* C H I N A Mordaga Jinhe Svobodnyy Novokiy

Gušinoozersk 2304 Petrovsk-Zabajkal'skij Ulety Olov'annaja Klin Qiqian Shisanzhan ·827 Belogorsk

Džida *Selenga* Tanga Il'a *Gol* Priargunsk Ergun Yuoqi Kalagi Oroqen Zizhiq Tulihe

Zakamensk *Džida* Damarovka 1248· Huma *Amur* Zeya

105°E *Chilok* 110°E 115°E 120°E 125°E 130°E

n o p q 57 r s t u v w 58 x y z

This map shows 1/60 of the earth's surface. Area scale : 1 □ inch on the map ≈ 15,000 □ miles on the ground 1 □ cm on the map ≈ 6000 □ km on the ground

Novosibirskiye Ostrova

Bennetta

75°N

Bel'kovskiy Kotel'nyy

Kotel'nyy
320.

Bol'shoye *Novaya Sibir'*
Zimov'ye

East Siberian Sea

Stolbovoy Ambardakh

Mal. Lyakhovskiy

Fedorovskiy

Kigilyakh *Bol. Lyakhovskiy*

Chay-Povarnaya 420.

Laptev Strait

Cape Kharstan
Buorkhaya

Uyёdey Star.Dom Chikhacheva

Kuogastakh Balagannakh Kokuora Kiseleva Tabor

Yana Kazach'ye Khroma Kolesovo

Kular Ust'-Kuyga Tumat Boru Ukta *Indigirka* Chokurdakh Ulovo 70°N

Tenkeli Byyangnyr Alekseyevo

Oyun-Yurege Uyandi .1221 914. Kondakovo Khara-Tala *Ozero*
Nerpich'ye

Bytantay Saydy Oyun- Deputatskiy Ozero *Kolymskaya* Ilimniir Kyrbana Balagannakh Mys Cherskiy
Kyuyel' *Ozhogino*

Bagata Tirekhtyakh Chibagalakh Ozhogino *Nizmennost* Khongsey Srednekolymsk Konzaboy Gorelova

Batagay Orto-Kyuyel' Uyandina Druzhina Shestakova Urdakh Malaya Oysurdakh Zhirkova *Chernyy* Volochsk
Mys

Tokuma Suordakh Bertes Pastakh Chernyy

U N I O N 1919. Tuostakh Khobolchan Tyugyuren Mayor-Krest Sededema Berezovka

1726. Ust'- Tuostakh Etykan Arga *Arctic Circle*

Kusagan- Charky 1926. Khastakh Khonu Erozionnyy Zatish'ye
Olokh .721

Nel'gese Astakh Cheulik *Mama* Kycham- Yugo-Tala *Bulun* Shcherbakovo
Udanna Kyuyel' Zyryanka

Khara- *Chibagalakh* 2703. Rassokha 65°N
Tas Tyubelyakh 3147.

Adycha Alyaskitovyy Oroyek Korkodon Korkodon

.1627 Ust'-Nera Abkit Munugudzhak

Suglan Marshal'skiy Nera Tirgelir Artyk .2558 Omolon

Tompo .2341 Khongo Razdolnoye .1550

Mountains Kysyl- Oymyakon Khuzdzhakh im Chapyeva .2038 *Kolyma*

Khara-Aldan Suluo Dal'stroy Arkagala .1347 Seymchan Omsukchan Galimyy

Dyalinnya Tomtor Sordongnokh .1830

Khandyga Byuchennyakh Adygalakh Burkhala Gizhiga

.1714 .2933 Debin Orotukan

Sayylyk Gvardeyets Khatyngnakh Pik Aborigen Strelka Nayakhan

A S. F. S. R. Kennya *Kolyma* .2586 Viliga-
Myakit Kushka

El'dikan Okhotskiy- im Gastello Vetrennyy Atka Tumany

Zolotoy Perevoz Burgakhchan Ust'Omchug Kandychan *Cape*
Taygonos

Allakh-Yun' Ancha Ugulan

Chertovo- Kencha .1585 Palatka *Gulf of*
Ulovo Ynykchanskiy *Inya* Malkachan *Shelekhova*

Ayaya Yudoma- 2350. Star. Kuntuk Talon Arman *Yama* Lesnaya
Krestovskaya Kheydzhan Nyurchan Sredniy

Ust'-Mil' Yugorenok Bulun Shilkan Balagannoye Magadan Yamsk Palana

Ust'-Maya Sordongnokh *Maya* Urak Motykleyka .1549 *Cape*
Tolstoy

Ulukuut Amka Okhotsk Inya *Cape* Sivuch 60°N
Alevina

Aim Kurun Uryak Ul'ya Ust'-Tigil'

Ingili Kaval'kan Khanyangda Tigil

Omnya Alachakh Utkholok .2531

Chiguj'bach Nel'kan Enkan *Sea of* Ust'-Belogolovoye

Chasovnya- Khakhar Kemkara *Okhotsk* Kekuk
Uchurskaya *Topko*
.1906 Ust'-Sopochnoye Klyuchi

Batomga Esso Atlasovo .4750

Maymakan Ayan *Icha* .3621 *Kamchatka*

Nemuy Oblukovino Tvayan *Ichinskaya*
Sopka Mil'kovo 55°N

Maya .1500 Chumikan *Shantar* Kirovskiy Kronok

Udskoye Burandzha *Cape* Pushchino
Yelizavety *Kamchatka*

Shevli Nyvrovo Pymta Zhupanovskiy
.602

Baladek Litke Malka Nalchevo

Ekimchan Tugur Usal'gin Okha *Sredinnyy* Paratunka
.2295 *Ozero* Bol. Oktyabr'skiy
Orel' Vlas'evo .1870 Petropavlovsk-

Guga Nikolayevsk- *Mountains* Kamchatskiy
Yashkino na-Amure

Sofiysk Gaktsynka Tyr Paromay Bol'sheretsk

Duki *Ozero* .1462 Mariinskoye Boatasyn *Paramušir*
Chukehagirskoye *Sakhalin*

Ust' Niman Sofiysk Nysh
Bolodzhak Kondon De Kastruskoye

Urgal 2010. Boktor Aleksandrovsko- .1609 145°E 150°E 155°E 160°E
Gornyy *Amur* Novoilinovka Sakhalinskiy Tymovskoye

Mogdy Komsomol'sk- Siziman
na-Amure

0 100 200 300 miles

Average linear scale : 1 inch≃125 miles 1cm≃80 km

0 100 200 300 400 500 Km

a b c d e f g h i j k l m

50

35°E 40°E 45°E 50°E

Ostashkov
Torzhok
Nelidovo
Rzhev Staritsa
Volokolamsk Klin
Vyaz'ma
.320
Gagarin
Smolensk
Dne'or
Roslavl
Shostka
Klintsy
Priluki
Lubny
Znamenka
Kremenchug
Kremenchugskoye
Reservoir

Jaroslavl'
Kalinin
Dubna
Dmitrov
Zagorsk
Balashikha
Noginsk
Mytišči
Moskva
Odintsovo
Mozhaysk
Obninsk
Podolsk
Serpuchovo
Kaluga
Chekalio
Sukhinichi
Belev Plavsk
Bryansk
Karchev Navlya
Orel
Zmiyevka
Yelets
Lipetsk
Livny
Fatzeh
Kursk
Gorshechnoye
Oboyan
Staryy Oskol
Belgorod
Akhtyrka
Poltava
Valki
Khar'kov
UKRAINA
Izyum
Pereshchepino
Novomoskovsk
Kramatorsk
Pavlogard
Dnepropetrovsk
Gorlovka
Dneprodzerzhinsk
Kirovograd
Krivoy Rog
Zaporozh'ye
Chaplino
Makeyevka
Donetsk
Nikopol
Kakhovskoye
Reservoir
Kherson
Melitopol
Novaya
Kakhova
Berdyansk
Dzhankoy
Kerch'
Kavkaz
Crimea
Simferopol'
.1259
Feodosiya
Sevastopol'
Jalda
Karkinitskiy
Zaliv
18

Ivanovo
Kovroy
Kineshma
Dzerzhinsky
Gor'kiy
Vladimir
Muром
Volga
.235
Arzamas
ROSSIYSKAY
Nazarovka
Zubova-
Polyana
Saransk
Temnikov
Inza
Baryšh
Ul'yanovsk
S.F.S.S.R.
Alatyr
Shatsk
Morshansk
Michurinsk
Kamenka
Tambov
Kirsanov
Rtishchevo
Mordovo
Tugolukovo
Vyzakova
Penza
Vol'sk
Kuznetsk
Syzran
Chapayevsk
Kuybyshev
Maryevka
Balakovo
Buzuluk
Bol'shaya
Glushitsa
Andreyevka
Volga Heights
Voronezh
Borisoglebsk
Rogachevka
Kantemirovka
Veshenskaya
Log
Volga
Primorsk
Elton
.67
Kalininsk
Balashov
Saratov
Engel's
.122
Pushkino
Atkarsk
Rudnya
Jrvupinsk
Mikhaylovka
Millerovo
Voroshilovgrad
Stakhanov
Kamensk-
Shakhtinskiy
Yenakiyevo
Morozovsk
Kalach-
na-Donu
Volgograd
Krasnoslobodsk
Kamyshin
Nikolayevsk
Kaysatskoye
Furmanovo
Mergenevo
SOV
Antonovo
Masteksay
Novo
Uzensk
Inderborskiy
Kulagino
Chapayevo
Ozero
Aralsor
.12
Caspian Depression
Kapustin-Yar
Solodniki
Chernyy
Yar
Mikhaylova
Kharabalio
Volga
Krasnyy-Yar
Astrakhan
Zelenga
Mumra
Gur'yev
Zhagaly
Canyushikino
Sarychik
Iskine
.27
Makat

S Y R T

Krasnyye-Baki
Uren
Yaransu
Yoshkar Ola
Cheboksary
Kazan'
Tetyushi
Kuybyshevskoje
Reservoir
Severnoye
Bugul'ma
Krotovka
Buguruslan
Sorochinsk
Ob'šči
Ural
Ilek
Ural'sk
Dergachi

Yoshkar Ola
Kilmez
Malmyzh
Izevsk
.217
Agryz
Votkinsk
Naberezhnyje
Celny
Al'met'yevsk
Oktja
Aksakovo
Sha

.115
Volga
Yadrin
Sergach
Kanash

Shakhty
Novoshakhtinsk
Volgodonsk
Tsimlyanskoye
Reservoir
Kotel'nikovo
Dubovskoye
Taganrog
Zhandov
Batajsk
Rostov
Novocherkassk
Sal'sk
Yeysk
Primorsko-
Akhtarsk
Tikhoretsk
Sosyko
Kropotkin
Kugulta
Ozero
Manych
Gudilo
Elista
Yashkul'
Divnoye
Utta
Ulan-Khol
Velichayevskoye
Kochubey
Kuban'
Krasnodar
Armavir
Stavropol'
Kura
Novorossiysk
Maykop
Tuapse
.2867
Čerkessk
Kislovodsk
Pjatigorsk
Prochladnyj
Kiz'lar
.25
Elbrus
5631
Nal'čik
Groznyi
Terek
.3238
Soči
Caucasus
Suchumi
Ordžonikidze
Kazbegi
.5047
.4151
Machačkala
Poti
Kutaisi
Chasuri
GRUZIYA
S.S.R.
Tbilisi
Rustavi
Derbent
Batumi
Kura
Marneuli
Hopa
.3438
Ardahan
Kazach
Mingecaurskoje
Reservoir
.2205
Kuba
Trabzon
Leninakan
.1357
Kirovakan
Kirovabad
Jevlach
Achsu
Samsun
Kars
Askale
Kagizman
Yerevan
ARMENIYA S.S.R.
Agdam
Sumgait
Baku
Žioj
Erzurum
Aras
Ozero
Sevan
AZERBAYDZHAN
S.S.R.
Saljany
Araks
Erzincan
Ağri
5156
Aranrt
Nachičevan
Ožalilabad
Astara
Patnos
Maku
Ahar
Van-
Gölü
Van
Khovy
Marand
Tabriz
1362
.4811
Ardebil
Hakkâri
.4168
Oroumieh
Maragheh
Mianeh
.3050
Rasht
Bandar Anzeli
Ramsar
Daryachen-
ye-Oroumieh
Amol
Sočfit

Machačkala

CASPIAN SEA

Zaliv-
Kara-
Bogaz-
Gol
Kara-Bogaz
Bekdaš
Karshi
Omch
Krasnovodsk
Čeleken
Ogurčinskij

Fort-Sevčenko
.44
Say-
Kulaly
P
Shetpe
Ševčenko
.132
Kyzyk
Fetisova
Kultay
U

MEDITERRANEAN
SEA
Cape
Andreas
Ince
Burun
Sinop
Kastamonu
Karabük
.2565
Gerede
Kizilirmak
Çorum
Ankara
Kirrikkale
Yozgat
Sivas
.2062
Fatsa
Giresun
Gümüshane
.3065
Kara Dağ
Divriği
Erzincan
Yozgat
Tokat
Turhal
Kayseri
.3916
Keban
Lake
Elaziğ
Gürün
Malatya
.2500
Ar Dağ
.3031
Kara Dağ
.2345
Anatolia
TURKEY
Bingöl
.4424
Murat Nehri
Tatvan
Siverek
Diyarbakir
Kurtalan
Pontine
Mountains
Tuz
Golu
Aksaray
Nigde
.3488
Ereğli
Karaman
Kozan
Ceyhan
Gaziantep
Urfa
Kiziltepe
Nusaybin
Tall
'Afar
Sinjar
.1463
Mosul
Arbil
Saqqez
Qojur
Baneh
Bijar
Razan
Qazvin
Karaj
Takestan
Damavand
.5671
Tehrān
Zanjan
Elburz
Mountains

Taurus
Adana
Mersin
Iskenderun
.1795
Antakya
Silifke
Anamur
Cape Anamur
CYPRUS
Aleppo
SYRIA
Latakia
Idlib
Maskana
Raqqah
Euphrates
Suwar
Al Hasakah
.Zab
Tigris
Leser Zab
Sharqat
Kirkuk
Sulaimaniyah
IRAQ
35°E
40°E
45°E
50°E

35

45°N

50°N

55°N

40°N

BLACK
SEA

Sea of
Azov

Ponti ne Mountains

n o p q r s t u v w x y z

39

This map shows 1/60 of the earth's surface. Area scale : 1 □ inch on the map ≈ 15,000 □ miles on the ground 1 □ cm on the map ≈ 6000 □ km on the ground

a b c d e f g h i j k l m

Kungur · Pervoural'sk · **Sverdlovsk** · Talitsa · Tevriz · Irtyš · Tara · .142

Krasnoufimsk · 60°E · Bogdanovich · Yalutorovsk · .122 · Panovo · Tara · Biaza

Ufa · Degtyarsk · Kamensk-Ural'skiy · 65°E · Golyshmanovo · Ishim · Tyukalinsk · Bol'sherech'ye

Nyazepetrovsk · Syšert' · Shadrinsk · Tobol · 70°E · Nazyyayevsk · .124

Asha · Min'yar · Suleya · Zlatoust · Kasli · Kurgan · Makushino · Petukhovo · Isil'kul · Lyubinskiy · **Omsk** · 55°N · Pokrovka · Tatarsk · Barabinsk

Ufa · Chernikovsk · Ust' Kata · **Chelyabinsk** · Shumikha · Kurtamysh · Presnovka · Petrovka · Krasnoarmeyesk · Ozero Ul'kenkaroy · Cherlak · Chistoozernoye · Ozero Chany · Kupino

Krasnosol'skiy · Beloretsk · Chudinovo · Ust'-Uyskoye · Troitsk · Plast · Presnogor'kovka · Dem'yanovka · Mar'yevka · Volodarskoye · Kokchetav .887 · Stepnyak · Aksu · Kzyltu · Shuga · Kachiry · Zhelezinka · Karasuk

Sterlitamak · Kaga · Verkhneural'sk · Magnitogorsk · Varna · Kartaly · Kustanay · Stavropolka · Uritskiy · Peski · Ruzayevka · Aydabul' · Makinsk · Bestobe · Ozero Seletyceniz · Pavlodar · Jamyšev

Kumertau · Baymak · .447 · Bredy · Dznetygara · Tobol · Tobol' · Kushmurun · Yesil · Dzhaksy · Atbasar · Zhaltyr · Zholymbet · Yermentau · Tortkuduk · Yermak · Maykain · Ozero Azhbulat

Troitskoye · Saraktash · Krasnoyarskiy · Akkarga · Dzhambul · Naurzum · Ishim · Zhaltyr · Novoishimskiy · Sabyndy · Nura · Novodolinka · Ekibastuz · Karashoky · Ajryk

Mednogorsk · Orsk · Terensay · Dombarovskiy · Tolybaya · Derzhavinsk · .391 · Arkalyk · Ozero Tengiz · Kurgal'dzhino · Tselinograd · Aktau · .621 · Ul'yanovskoye

Martuk · Aktubinsk · Khrom-Tau · Karabutak · Turgay · Shenber · Temirtau · Saran · Karaganda · Korobovskiy · Kiikkaškan

E T U N I O N · Akkabak · Saga · Zahksykan · Ozero .633 · Sonaly · Abay · **K a z a k h** · Karagayly · Myylybulak · Kajnar · 50°N

Alga · Temir · Emba · Irgiz · Turgay Valley · Ulu Taun · Ulutau · Atasu · Kyzyl-Dzhar · Dzhezkazgan · Dar'inskiy · Uspenskiy · Nuru · **U p l a n d s** · Agadyr

.316 · Karaulkeldy · Shakhty · Kyzyluy · Nikol'skiy · Baykonyr · Ayshirak · Kiik · Zhamshi

K A Z A · Chelkar · Togyz · **Z A K** · **H** · Brali · Baykonur · **S** · **A** · Mointy · Balkhash · Sajak

Chushakyl' · .343 · Akespe · Aral'sk · Beleutty · Ozero 59. Arys · **Betpak-Dala Steppe** · Karazhingil · Ozero Balkhash · Tomar · Karabas

Sokyrbulak · Kulanoy · Kokaral · Bugun · Kazalinsk · Leninsk · Bet-Pak-Dala · Kashkanteniz · Mynaral · Karoy · .603

Barsa-Kel'mes · **Aral Sea** · Vozrozhdeniya · Zhanay · Dzhusaly · Čи · Kamkaly · Algatart · Kuyygan · Burylbaytal · Uštobe · 56

Urt · Satlyk · Muinak · Kazakdarya · .146 · Erimbet · Kyzyl-Orda · Chilli · Aksumbe · Furmanovka · Čи · .1506 · Kapčagajskoje Reservoir · Taldy-Kurgan · 45°N

tau · Urga · Karaozek · Uzynkair · Syrdarja · Yany-Kurgan · .2176 · Uyuk · Khantau · Aktogaj · Saryozek

Ozero Sudocje · Chimbay · Kungrad · .473 · Mynbulak · Uchkuduk · Kentau · Turkestan · Kara Tau · Tatty · Kaskelen · Kapčagaj · Čilik

Sarykamyškoje Ozero · Bol'ševik · Kun'a-Urgenč · Chodzeili · Tašauz · .335 · **K y z y l K u m** · Arys' · Džambul · Lugovoi .3817 · Frunze · Kara-Balta · Čemolgan · **Alma Ata** 482 · **Ala Tau**

Taškent · Cimkent · .592 · Cirčik · .4503 Toktogul Res. · Toktogul · Čajek · **KIRGIZIYA** · Ananjevo · Ozero Przeval'sk · Issyk-Kul · Bubačga

UZBEKISTAN · Urgenč · Turtkul' · Zarafshan · Cardara · Taš-Kumyr · Naryn · Taragaj · Naryn · **S.S.R.** · Karasaj · Ottuk

TURKMENIYA · Lebap · **S.S.R.** · Cardara · Cardarinskoje Reservoir · Jahgiyul' · Namangan · **Tian Shan** · Kok-Jangak · Ozero Catyrk'ol · Čatyrtaš · .4929 · Pik Dankowa 5982 · Toxkan He

S.S.R. · Darvaza · Gorel'de · Amudarja · Gizhduvan · .2165 · Navoi · Angren · Andižan · Ozero Catyrk'ol · Sari Bulak · Akaj

K a r a K u m · Jerbent · Bucharа · Kagan · Kattakurgan · Gulistan · Kokand · Margilan · Oš · Gul'ča · .4641

Kizyl-Arvat · Kabakly · .224 · Alat · Mubarek · Džizak · Leninabad · Kajrakkumskoje Reservoir · Fergana · Gul'ča · Sugun · 40°N

Bachardok · Čardžou · Šachrisabz · Ura J'ube · Bekabad · .5509 · Darаut-Kurgan · Irkeštam · Sanchakou

andžik · Kizyl-Arvat · Karši · Ajni · **Ala Tau** · Lenina 7134 · Ozero Karakul · Opal · Kashi

Arčman · Bachardok · Tezejet · Repetek · Novabad · Pik Kommunism 7495 · Bulunkol · Shache

auk · Aščhabad · Mary · Bajram Ali · Nička · Keriči · Denau · Dušanbe · .2227 · Kurgan-T'ube · Viščary · **P a m i r** · Arkbajtal · Murgab · Kungur 7719 · **C H I N A**

eh · Bojnurd · Artyk · Tedžen · Iolotan · .293 · Termez · Dust · Chorog · Mamazair · .6083 · Yecheng

vamey · Quchan · Dušak · Karakumskiy Canal · Andkhoy · Aqcha · Khulm · Kunduz · Faidabad · Zebak · Qala Panja · Hašalbag · Muji

Dasht · **N** · Sarakhs · Takhta Bazar · Sar-i-Pul · Maimana · Aibak · Baghlan · Taliqan · **H i n d u K u s h** · Tirich Mir 7690 · Mastuj · Yasin · Rakaposhi 7788 · Mazar He · Misgar 6525 · Mazar

Neishabur · .3476 · Bala Murghab · Qaisar · Balkhab · Doabi · Doshi · Mikhe Zarin · **A F G H A N I S T A N** · Chitrāl 5715 · **P A K I S T A N** · **Karakoram Range** · .7228 · Ponda

Mashhad · Sabzevar · .3415 · **Khurasan** · **T A D Z H I K I S T A N S.S.R.** · Novabad · Džirgatal · Darvaza · Chlias · .7261 · Gilgit · Drosh · Indus · 75°E

n o p q r s t u v w x y z

60°E · 65°E · 70°E · 60

0 100 200 300 miles

Average linear scale : 1 inch ≏ 125 miles · 1cm ≏ 80 km

0 100 200 300 400 500 Km

a b c d e f g h i j k l m

55

Onegva Yar · Vasyuganye · 80°E Staritsa · Kolpashevo · Ket · 85°E Belyy Yar · Mogochin · Baturino · 90°E Yeniseysk · Vorozheyka · Lesosibirsk · Strelka · 95°E Rodina · Čuna · Boguč · Oktyab

·142 · L'vovka · Parabel · Bakchar · parbig · Komsomol'sk · Čulym · Meletsk · ·211 · Altat · Birilyussy · Predivinsk · Asansk · Shelayevo

Tara · Biaza · Chumakovo · Pikhtovka · Moryakovskiy Zaton · ·258 · Mariinsk · Bogotol · Achinsk · Nazarovo · Shivera · ·898 · Aban · Kan · Kansk

Pokrovka · Barabinsk · Chulym · Ob' · Tomsk · Yurga · Anzhero-Sudzhensk · Kemerovo · Uzhur · ·818 · Pamyat · Krasnojarsk · Uyar · Borodino · Zam

55°N · Chistoozernoye · Ozero Chany · Kupino · Novosibirsk · Ordynskoye · Cherepanovo · T'agun · Tsentral'nyy · Čulym · Krasnojarskoye Reservoir · Mina · Niž

Ozero Azhbulat · Karasuk · Kamen-na-Obi · Suzun · Krasnobrodskij · Kisel'ovsk · Sira · Bujedžul · Sum · Gut

Kachiry · Khabary · Pavlovsk · Tal'menka · Prokopjevsk · Novokuzneck · Sorsk · Černogorsk · Minusinsk · Burgon · Pik Grandioznyj 2922 · Pokr

Pavlodar · Kulunda · Blagovščenka · Barnaul · Troickoje · Mundybaš · Taštagol · Abakan · Sušenskoje · Sajanogorsk · Kazyr · Udg Alygdžer

Yermak · Jamyševo · Kulundinskaya · Rodino · Len'ki · ·286 · Bijsk · ·621 · Bija · Biričul · Taštyp · Idzim · ·2456 · Bujba · Sevi · Toora-Chem · ·2682 · Bol Yenisey

Ajryk · Molgary · Dolon · Pospelicha · Alej · Altai · Čaryšskoje · Gorn'ak · Ozero Teleckoje · Cel'us · 2930 · Cadan · 2972 · Orog Nuur · Uvs Nuur · Kyzyl · Saryg-Sop · Uš-Bel'dir · 2668 · Kyzyl-Chem

Semipalatinsk · Bel'agaš · Semonaicha · Tuekta · 2820 · Inja · Kuraj · Čodro · 3487 · Ak-Dovurak · Tannu Mountains · Turgen · Sagonar · Balgazya · ·2584 · Samagaltaj · Naryn

50°N · Kiikkaskan · Kajnar · Čarsk · Serebr'ansk · Georgiievka · ·1608 · Katun' · 2776 · 4506 · Argut · Koš-Agač · 4029 · Kyzyl-Chaja · Malčin · Baruun Turuun · Bajan-Uul · Ojgon Nuur

KAZAKHSTAN · Bestamak · Ajaguz · Kökpekty · Bol'šenarymskoje · 2645 · Ozero Markakol · Korti Linchang · Čagaan Gol · Ulgij · Čagaan Nuur · Chirgis Nuur · 2928 · Telmen Nuur · PEO

Madenijet · ·1305 · Karaaul · Žarma · Kurčum · Burán · Ertix He · Burqin · Altay · Altaj · Erdene Buren · Kobdo · Char Us Nuur · 2896 · Jaruu · Han

S.S.R. · Sajak · Aktogaj · Tarbagataj · Belaja Škola · Zajsan · Ertix He · Beitun · 3743 · Tolbo Nuur · Döröö Nuur · Aldar · Uliastaj · ·3905

Taskesken · Urdžar · 2992 · Muz Tau · 3816 · Ulungur Hu · Beitun · Fuyun · Manchan · 4362 · Chajrchan · Dzereg · Mönch · Bujan

Im Frunze · Ozero Sasykkol · Tacheng · Utubulak · Jili Hu · Sarbulak · Ovoot · 3578 · Čagaan-Qlom · Delger

Lepsy · 756 · Žarsuat · Ozero Balchaš · Matataj · ·603 · 2923 · Toli · Karamay · Ulungur · Urho · Hh · Bulgan · Tamč · Tamč · Altaj · Beger

Sarkand · 1442 · Ebinur Hu · Tachakou · Manas Hu · Junggar Pendi · 3479 · Türgen · Bugat · Altaj

45°N · Uštobe · Taldy-Kurgan · Wenquan · Bole · Jinhe · Sayram Hu · Gov'Chonin · ·3802 · Dzachuj · O

Aktogaj · Saryözek · Panfilov · Borohoro Shan · Yining · Nilka · Usu · Shihezi · Jiangjumiao · Santanghu · Altaj · Ondč

Kapčagaj · Kapchagayskoye Reservoir · Čilik · Qapqal · Manas · Changji · Ganhezi · Qitai · Barkol Hu · Nom

Čemolgan · Alma Ata · ·4876 · Ili He · Cundža · Tekes · Xinyuan · Narat · Ürümqi · Bogda Feng · ·5445 · 3951 · Qijiaojing · Barkol Kazak · Yiwu · G

Kaškelen · 3638 · Zhaosu · Tekes · Tien Shan · Houxia · Baiyanghe · Qiquanhu · Liaodun · 4925 · Karlik Shan · Mergol

Rubačje · Ananjevo · Narynkol · Kegen · Keyi · 5500 · Bulguntay · Ewirgol · Shanshan · Liushuquan · Hami · Mingshui · Gongpoquan

Öttuk · Ozero Issyk-Kul · Prževal'sk · 4553 · Yengisar · Qarqi · Yanqi Huizu Zizhixian · Turpan · 154 · Yandun · Xingxingxia

KIRGIZIYA S.S.R. · Pik Pobedy · Kuqa · Dalaoba · Korla · Bosten Hu · 1524 · Weiya · Daquan · 2584 · Jiangjuntai

Naryn Taragay · Karasaj · Yakrik · Xinhe · Yuli · 1762 · Hongluyuan · Jiangquanzi

Čatyrtaš · Pik Dankowa · 5982 · Torkan · Aksu · Karayulgun · Tarim · Beis · Shan · Zhangjiaquan · Anxi · Qiaowan

4929 · Sari Bulak · Akqi · Awat · Aral · Tarim Liuchang · 1238 · Kongi · Shule · Kumkuduk · Dunhuang

40°N · Sanchakou · Bachu Liuchang · Yarkant · Tarim · Yengisu · Lop Nur · 1099 · Shazaoyuan · Dongbatu · Jiayu

Sugun · Yopurga · Tarim Basin · ·1082 · 1066 · Ikanbujmal · Luobuzhuang · Dongluk · C · Aksay · Dang · Changma

Markit · Takla Makan Desert · Miran · Ruoqiang · Qilian Shan · 5547 · Choush

East Turkestan · 1570 · Tongguzbasti · Koxlax · Aktaz · Waxxari · Qargan · Altun Shan · Xorkol · 5798 · Obo Liang · Lenghu · Huahaizi · 5827

Hasalbag · Yecheng · Muji · 1082 · Qiemo · Niubiziliang · 2774 · Youshashan · Qaidam Basin · Iqe · Har Hu

Zangguy · Zawa · Hotan · Qira · Minfeng · Hadilik · Andirlangar · 6140 · Tura · Gas Hu · Mangnai · Shaliangzi · Da Qaidam · 5030

Karakax · Tekiliktag · 5466 · Yutian · Bostan · 6748 · Aqqikkol Hu · Ayakkum Hu · 5810 · Nur Turu · Suli Hu 3099 · Dabsan Hu · Xitieshan · Qarhan

Mazar · Yarkant · ·7228 · 80°E · Pulu · Karasay · Aktag · 85°E · Muztag · 7723 · 7720 · Boluntay · De Juh · 90°E · Golmud · Nomhon · Nan Hulsan Hu · 5026 · 95°E · Xia

Kangxiwar

This map shows 1/60 of the earth's surface. Area scale: 1 □ inch on the map ≈ 15,000 □ miles on the ground, 1 □ cm on the map ≈ 6000 □ km on the ground

a b c d e f g h i j k l m

U N I O N

Kova
Karamysheva
636
Vorob'yeva
Garmenka
Bratsk
kiyo
Ilir
Oka
Zima
Čeremchovo
Usolje Sibirskoje
Angarsk
Mondy 3266
Kyren
be Chanch
Chövsgöl
Nuur
chatgal

Ust 'Ilimsk
Romanova
Suvorka
Vidim
Bratskoye
Reservoir
Atalanka
Balagansk
763
Ust'-Kada
Žigalovo
Zalari
774
Usolje Sibirskoje
Selichov
Irkutsk
Listv'anka
Sl'ud'anka
Tanchoj
Zakamensk
Tešig
Egin Gol

Volokon
Kirensk
Ul'kan
Riga
Orlinga
Yukhta
Kazachinskoye
Yermaki
Kirenga
Injaptuk
2579
Tonnel'nyj
Uoyan
Nizhneangarsk
Baykal'skoje
2089
Bol.Onguren
Barguzin
Manzurka
Maksimicha
Ust'-Ordynskij
Chaim
2049
Tataurovo
Kamensk
Ulan-Ude
Gusinoozersk
Džida
K'achta
Süchbaatar
Urluk

Lena
Uoyan
Kirensk
Gorno-Chuyskiy
Chuya
Severo
Baykal'skoye
Nagor'ye
Chara
Mama
Vitimskiy
Bodaybo
Sinyuga
Berezovka
Ozero
Nichatka
Tokko
Orokami
Yenyuka
Taluma
Ust'
Nyukzha

S F S R

Vitim
Plateau
Baunt
2573
Oron
Mogojto
Jeleninskij
Ust'-Džilinda
Romanovka
Isinga
Telemba
1322
Uda
Chorinsk
Selenga
Chilok
Petrovsk-
Zabajkal'skij
Jamarovka
Chilok
Menza
2523

Bukačača
Veršino-
Darasunskij
Cernyševsk
Ust'-Karsk
1249
Yimuhe
Gulian
Luoguhe
Qiqian
Mangui
Kurleja
Argun
Mordaga
Jinhe
Kalagi
Tulihe
Yuanlin
1395

55°N

Chita
Chilok
Darasun
Tanga
Ulety
Il'a
Narasun
1248

Yablonovy Mountains
Karymskoje
Ingoda
Balev
Šilka
Olov'annaja
Onon Gol
Borzya
Priargunsk

Šilka
Nerchinsky
Zavoid
Klin
Solovjevsk
Borshchovochny Mts.
Argun Zuoqi
Argun Youqi

50°N

E'S   R E P U B L I C

Tarialan
2263
Möron
Chutag
Bulgan
Chišig-Öndör
Bat Cengel
Cecerleg
Chašaat
tuut
ntains
ndal
Orog Nuur 3690
Bajanleg
Chovd
Mandal-Ovoo
Bulgan
2631
Bajan-
Dalaj
Ovoot Chural
Qen
Soga
Nur
Ejin Qi
roi

Erdenet
Darchan
Charaa
Orchontuul
Mandal
Batšireet
Ulaanbaatar 1309
Lün
1843
Tariat
Bajan
Bajan
Baraat
Delgerchaan
Arvaj Cheer
Erdenedalaj
Mandalgov'
3535
1962
Tuul Gol
Sümber
Dalandžargalan
Sajnšand
Cogt-Ovoo
1521
Manlaj
Dalandzadgad
1791
Chan Bogd
Nomgon
Sulan
Cheer
1865
Suj

Cencher
Mandal
Öndör Chaan
1706
Cherlen Gol
Bajan
Ovoo
1260
Tüvšinširee
Bajšint
Etap
Bajanmönch
Erdene
Xilin Qagan Obo
1150
Chövsgöl
Bayan Obo

Orchontuul
Norovtin
1595
Bajan-Uul
Gurvan
Ozagal
Chavirga
Ar Dzargala
Baruun-Urt
Qahan Qulut
1750
Xar Hudak
Érenhot
Orgon Tal
Qagan
Nuur
Yanga Sum
Ondor Sum
Baixingt
Xar Moron

M O N G O L I A

M O N G O L I A

Bulgar
Cojbalsan
Öndör
Tamsagbulag
Erdene
Cagaan
Bulag Sum
Dong Ujimqin Qi
Xi Ujimqin Qi
Jirin Gol
Holt Sum
Xilin Hot
2029
Linxi
Bairin Zouqi
Hexigten Qi
Ongniud Qi
Zhenglan Qi
Zhenghuang Qi
Chifeng
1081

Manzhouli
Hailar
Huluun
Nuur
Qagan
Hailar
Xin Barag Youqi
Xin Barag Zouqi
Buyr
Nuur
Handgai
1712
Yirshi
Xikou
Shumougou
1394
Nungnain Sun
1950
Da Hinggan Ling
1474
Goukou
Dashizhai
Horqin
Youyi
Qianqi
Tuquan
45°N
510
Jarud Qi
Bairin Youqi
Kailu He
Tongliao
Baixingt
Naiman Qi
Chen Barag Qi
Qagan
Yakeshi
Yolin Mod

I N N E R   M O N G O L I A

I N N E R   M O N G O L I A

Taibus Qi
Shangdu
Zhengxiang Qi
Weichang
Luan
1941
Jianping
Longhua
866
Fuxin
Yi Xian
Jinzhou
Chengde
Jinxi
Yingkou
Kuancheng
Xi
Harqin
Gai Xian
Liaodong
Wan
40°N
Wudao

C H I N A

Hanggin
Houqi
Wuyuan
Ulansuhai
Nur
2187
Guyang
Shiguaigou
Hohhot
2174
Jining
Shangyi
Zhangjiakou
Xuanhua
Huai'an
Great Wall
Miyun
1677
Qinhuangdao
Beijing
Tangshan
Fu Xian

Bayan Mod
Urad
Qianqi
Linhe
Dengkou
Baotou
Xar Burd
Huang
Togtoh
Dai
Hai
Datong
Huairen
Yu Xian
Laiyuan
Lulong
Badain Jaran
1766
Jartai
Wuda
2149
Shizuishan
Dongsheng
Juntuliang
Pianguan
Shuo Xian
Ba Xian
Cangzhou
Yanshan
Tianjin
Luda
Suhait
Yabrai
Yanchang
Otog Qi
Shenmu
Xin Xian
3058
Baoding
Bo Hai
Maiodao
Islands

N o r d o s

A l a s h a n   D e s e r t

Yinchuan
Nangsin Sum
Wuzhong
Dingbian
Yulin
2831
Ding Xian
2393
Penglai
Dongle
Shandan
Dongzhen
Alxa Zuoqi
Zichang
Yan'an
Suide
Linqing
Dezhou
Laizhou
Wan
Yantai
Minne
Jinchang
Zhongwei
Tianshui
Wuqi
Yanchang
2069
Xingtai
Zibo
Weifang
220
3616
Dongle
Great
Wall
4079
Huang
Huan Jiang
Huo Xian
Handan
950
Jinan
Laiyang
Wuwei
Manyuan
Yondeng
Tongxin
Guyuan
Taiyuan
Taigu
Fengfeng
Jiao Xian
Gangca
Häiyan
Datong
Jingyuan
Taiyuan
Yucion
Yangquan
Anyang
Tai'an
1619
Qingdao
4832
Minhé
2244
Xining
Shijiazhuang
Changzhi
120°E
Gonghe
Nangdol
Lanzhou
1608
Shan
Yunhe (Grand Canal)
Huang (Yellow River)
Boxing
Shantung

105°E   110°E   115°E   120°E

n o p q r s t u v w x y z

Average linear scale : 1 inch ≈ 125 miles   1cm ≈ 80 km

0   100   200   300 miles

0   100   200   300   400   500 Km

a b c d e f g h i j k l m

52

120°E 125°E 130°E 135°E

Ingoda Baley

Nerchinskiy Zavod Mordaga Jinhe Linhai Huma Shimanovsk Svobodnyy Novokiyevskiy Uval Ust'Niman Urgal Chegdomyn Mogdy Bolodzhak Kondor Duki

Klin Argun Zuoqi Kalaqi 827 Shisanzhan Belogorsk Zeya 2010 Komsomo-na-Am.

SOVIET UNION Borzya Priargunsk Argun Youqi Tulihe Oroqen Zizhiqi 1212 Dayangshu Huolongmen Heihe Blagoveshchensk Zavitinsk Bureya ROSSIYSKAYA Chekunda Ust'Tyrma Tyrma Bolon

Yuanlin Xiao'ergou 1395 188 Raychikhinsk Bureya Arkhara Talandzha 1381 SOVIET UN

50°N Chen Barag Qi Hailar Yakeshi 1474 Goukou Morin Dawa Nenjiang Longzhen 701 Sunwu Xunke Izvestkovyy Birobidzhan Khabarovs

Manzhouli Qagan Hailar Da Hinggan Ling Arun Qi Nehe Bei'an Wuyiling Jiayin Kukan Litovka Kruglikovo

Hulun Nur Handgai 1712 Yirshi Zalantun Fuyu Yi'an Baiquan Suiling 1150 Yichun Luobei Fuyuan Khor

Xin Barag Youqi Xin Barag Zuoqi Buyr-Nur Longjiang Nen Jiang Qiqihar Xiao Hinggan Ling Nancha Hegang Fujin Tongjiang Kotikova

PEOPLE'S REPUBLIC OF MONGOLIA Tamsagbulag Jalaid Qi Dorbod Qing'an Suihua Jiamusi Shuangyashan 831 Bikin

Gobi Xikou Dashizhai Daqing Laoxi Anda Fangzheng Qitaihe Dongfanghong 1014 Luchegorsk Svetlovodna

Bulag Sum Nungnain Sum Horqin Youyi Qianqi 1394 Tailai Baicheng 190 Manchuria Harbin Shuangcheng Shangzhi Dier Songhua Jiang 1060 Jixi Hulin Lesozavodsk Dal'nerechensk

Dong Ujimqin Qi Qagan Qulut Shumugou Tao'an Zhaoyuan Lalin He 1322 Linkou Xiachengzi Ozero Khanka Kirovskiy Yasnaya Velikaya

45°N Mongolia 1950 Tuquan Qian Gorlos Dehui Dier Songhua Jiang Yushu Mudanjiang Ning'an Dongjingcheng Suifenhe Spassk Dal'niy Rudnaya

Xi Ujimqin Qi Jarud Qi 510 Tongyu Xinkai He Horqin Zuoyi Zhongqi 1397 Jiaohe Emu Wangqing Hunchun Arsen'yev Kavalerovo

CHINA Holt Sum Yolin Mod Kailu He Changchun Jilin 2404 Dunhua Yanji 1498 Ussuriysk 1855 Vangou

Jirin Gol Bairin Zuoqi Linxi Tongliao Xar Moron Shuangliao Siping Liaoyuan Huinan Huadian Hunchun Hoeryong Artem Margaritovo

Xilin Hot 2029 Bairin Youqi Qi Baixingt Dongliao He Kaiyuan Huanan Jingyu Liuhe Paektu-san 2744 Najin Vladivostok Nakhodka

Zhenglan Qi Hexigten Qi Ongniud Qi Naiman Qi Xinmin Fushun Qingyuan Tonghua Hunjiang Changbai Shan Tumen Ch'ongjin Chuuronjang

Chifeng 866 Fuxin Xi He Shenyang Benxi Huanren 1823 Hyesanjin Kapsan

Weichang 1081 Jianping Yi Xian Liaoyang Kuandian Yalu 2522 Kimchaek SEA OF

Luan He 1941 Longhua Jinzhou Anshan 940 NORTH Hüich'on Pukch'ong

Fengning Jinxi Yingkou 1132 Dandong Sinuiju Hamhung

Chengde Harqin Kuancheng Liaodong Wan Gai Xian Fu Xian KOREA Anju JAPAN

Miyun 1677 Great Wall Wudao Korea Bay Pyongyang Wonsan

57 40°N Beijing Lulong Qinhuangdao Lüda Chinnamp'o Hwangju Ich'on Sokch'o

Tangshan Yongding He Miaodao-Qundao Haeju Kaesong Ch'unch'on 1708 Kangnüng

Tianjin Ba Xian Penglai Yantai Ongjin Inch'on Seoul Wonju Tonghae

Bo Hai Laizhou Wan Chengshan Jiao 220 Ch'ungju

Cangzhou Yanshan Huang He Boxing Ch'ongju Andong

Ziya He Dezhou Laiyang SOUTH Taejon Oki Kanazawa

Grand Canal Zibo Weifang Chengshan Jiao Chonju Taegu Fukui

Jinan Tai'an 950 Jiao Xian Yellow Kunsan 1260 Ulsan Matsue 1214

35°N Yanzhou Jining Junan Qingdao Sea KOREA 1915 Masan Tottori

Zaozhuang Liangcheng Kwangju Chinju Pusan Masuda 1339 Fukuyama Kyoto

Xuzhou Lianyungang Mokp'o Yosu Korea Strait Yamaguchi Okayama Nishinomiya Himeji Kobe Osaka

Huaibei 1366 Binhai Cheju Tsushima (Japan) Shimonoseki Hiroshima Takamatsu Sakai Wakayama

Su Xian Hongze Hu Huaiyin Cheju-do (S. Korea) Sasebo Kita-Kyushu Ube Sea Tokushima 1915 Tanabe

Bengbu Gaoyou Hu Hongze East China Fukuoka Inland Shikoku Kochi

Huainan Yangzhou Taizhou Nantong Sea Nagasaki Kumamoto Oita Bungo-suido Nakamura

Hefei Chu Xian Nanjing Changzhou Yatsushiro 1700 Miyazaki

Lujiang Wuhu Wuxi Suzhou 1791

Tongling Xuancheng Tai Hu Shanghai Kagoshima Kyushu Osumi-Kaikyo Tanega

1860 1187 Jiaxing Zhoushan Qundao Yaku

Anqing 120°E Hangzhou 1841 125°E 130°E 135°E

n o p q r s t u v w x y z

63

This map shows 1/60 of the earth's surface. Area scale : 1 □ inch on the map ≙ 15,000 □ miles on the ground 1 □ cm on the map ≙ 6000 □ km on the ground

a b c d e f g h i j k l m

53

140°E 145°E 150°E 155°E

Sofiysk Mariinskoye
De Kastruskoye Nysh
Novoilinovka Aleksandrovsk- *1609*
...koye Sakhalinskiy Tymovskoye
1628 Siziman
Koto *Sakhalin*
U.S.S.R.
1324 Poronaysk
Gavan
Makarov
Adzhima
...vetlaya Samarga Kholmsk Yuzhno-Sakhalinsk
...imovka Korsakov

SEA OF

OKHOTSK

Kamchatka

Paramušir

50°N

Onekotan

K
u
r
i
l

I
s
l
a
n
d
s

Simušir

La Pérouse Strait
Wakkanai *Urup*
45°N
1129 *Iturup*

Kunašir
Asahikawa Kitami
2290
Asahi-dake
Otaru *Hokkaidō* Nemuro
□ **Sapporo**
2052 Obihiro Kushiro
Muroran
Uchiura-
wan Erimo
Hakodate
Ōma
Tsugaru-Kaikyō
Aomori

PACIFIC

40°N
1625
Akita Marioka
1914
Sakata
Kesen
Ishinomaki
Yamagata
Sendai
Niigata
2105 Fukushima
Kashiwazaki Kōriyama
1917
Iwaki

OCEAN

...onshū
...agano Utsunomiya
Maebashi Mito
...sumoto **JAPAN**
...lachioji
...e-san **Tōkyō** Chōshi
Kawasaki Chiba
...76 □ **Yokohama**
Yokosuka
Shizuoka 35°N
...atsu

140°E 145°E 150°E 155°E

n o p q r s t u v w x y z

0 100 200 300 miles
Average linear scale : 1 inch ≃ 125 miles 1 cm ≃ 80 km
0 100 200 300 400 500 Km

a b c d e f g h i j k l m

60°E 65°E 70°E

SOVIET UNION

Quchan
Mayamey Sabzevar
Neishabur
Sarakhs
Mashhad
·3347
3416.

Takhta Bazar
Andkhoy Aqcha Mazar-i Sharif Khulm Kunduz Faidzabad Qala Panja
Sheberghan Sari-i-Pul Baghlan Taliqan Zebak
Maimana Aibak Doshi ·736
Bala Murghab Doab-i Mikne Mustuj
Qaisar Zarin Charikar Tirich Mir
Kuska Daulat Yar Kuh-e-Baba Bamian ·5715
Quala-i Nau Chaghcharan ·3704 Qarah Tarai Behsud Kota-i Ashro Asadabad Drosh
Torbat-e-Heidariye Tayebad Kabul Sorabi Besham Qila
Kashmar Torbat-e-Jam ·3592 ·3850 Khurd ·1799 Jalalabad Khyber Pass Kabul Mardan Muze
Bardeskan Ghorian Herat Hari Rud Sangan ·3925 Gardez Peshawar Abbotabad
35°N Farsi ·4182 Qaisar Ghazni Matun Rawalpindi Islamab

Dasht-e-Kavir
Bidokht ·2578 AFGHANISTAN Gujarkha
Ferdows Shindand Farah Rud Kabul Bannu Kalabagh
Tabas Qaen Khash Rud Uruzgan Zarghunshar Razmak Lakki Mianwali
Deihuk Yazdan Farahrod ·2560 Shahjui Dera Ismail Khan ·3374 Sargodha
Khusf Birjand Farah Dilaram Nauzad Qalat-i Chilzai Port Sandeman Jhang Maghiana Faisalaba
Aliabad Sarbisheh ·2561 Lasho Joayin Girishk Kandahar Toba & Kakar Ranges ·3092 Leiah
·2992 Naiband ·2729 Lashkargah Arghandab Tarnak ·3276 Qila Saifullah Jhang
Bafq Darband Nehbandan ·2488 Zabol Registan ·1314 Ghaman Kand Muslimbagh Kingri Multan
·2438 716. Zaranj ·2641 Zargun Loralai Dera Ghazi Khan
Zarand Ravor Safar ·1371 ·3578 Quetta Chenab
IRAN Mirabad Helmand Rudbar ·1746 Mach Sutlej
Rafsanjan ·3143 Nosratabad Ribat ·2208 Kahan Uch Bahawalpur
Kerman Namakzar-e Shadad ·1643 ·2462 Chagai Hills Chagai Nushki Sibi ·1262 Dera Bugti
30°N Baghin Siraj Zahedan ·2333 Sultan ·2101 Kalat Rajanpur Pugal
Hoseinabad ·2062 Ras Koh PAKISTAN Rahimyar-Khan
Sirjan Laleh Zar Tahrud Mirjaveh Dalbandin ·3003 Kharan Surab Shikarpur Tanot
Baft 4374 Darzin Dehak Taftan Nok Kundi Rasin Besima Khuzdar Jacobabad Sri Mohangarh
Aliabad Bam ·3941 Khash Kharan Larkana Shahgarh Bap
Hajiabad Sabzevaran ·2548 ·3503 Bazman Qila Ladgasht Khairpur Jaisalmer Pokaran
Dowlatabad Kahnuj Baluchistan Patandar Wad Moro Myajlar Phalsund
Qotbabad ·3379 Hamun-e Jaz Murian Saravan ·2283 Jebri Sehwan Sanghar Balotra
1564 Bampur Iranshahr Awaran Bela Mirpur Khas Barmer
Bandar Abbas Jaghin Bampur Kuhak Panjgur Central Makran Range Kirthar Range Gurha
Qeshm Minab ·1950 Sarbaz Kikki Turbat Hoshab ·1464 Kotri Hyderabad Gurha
Qeshm Remeshk Nikshahr Dasht Hab Aravalli Ra
39 Straits of Hormuz ·2110 ·2100 Pishin Bahu Kalat Pasni Ormara Hab Chauki Badin Sirohi 1722
Al Sha'am Ras Musandam Jask Chabahar Ras Nuh Thatta Jati Virawah Tharad Guru Sikhar
·2061 Ras Kuh Lab Jiwani Karachi Rann of Kachchh Palanpur
Ras al Khaimah Dibba Indus Delta Radhanpur
Sharjah Fujairah Gulf of Oman Lakhpat Mahesana
Dubai OMAN Tropic of Cancer Rampur Bhuj New Kandla Ahmedabad
25°N Shinas As Suwaiq Badin Mandvi Gulf of Kachchh Jamnagar Morvi Dhandhuka
Sohar Muscat ARABIAN Dwarka Rajkot Khambhat
Al Ain As Sib Sumail Quraiyat Kathiawar Bharuch
Al Khaburah Nazwa Izki Sur Porbandar Bhavnagar Sura
Ibri 5018 Sur Ras al Hadd SEA Junagadh Na
Al Hajar ash Sharqi Adam Al Kamil Veraval Gulf of Khambhat
Wadi Aswad Al Ashkhirah Diu Valsad Daman
Umm as Samim OMAN Ramlat al Wahiba Jawha

Masirah

20°N Duqm

Thane

Ras Madrakah Bombay

Sahil al Jazir

Sharbithat Ras Sharbithat Janjira

Kuria Muria Islands Ko Rese

Chiplun

Ratnagiri

This map shows 1/60 of the earth's surface. Area scale : 1 □ inch on the map ≈ 15,000 □ miles on the ground 1 □ cm on the map ≈ 6000 □ km on the ground

Moyu 80°E Qira Minfeng Karasay Bostan *Altun Shan* Aqqikkol Hu Boluntay

Mazar Karakax He Yutian Kerlya 85°E *Aktag* 6748 Muztag 7723 7720

Yarkant He 1728 Kangxiwar Pixa Tekiliktag Pulu Keriya He 6250 Hoh Xil Shan Qumar Heyan

K2 8611 Dahongliutan 6282 Yingkax He *K u n l u n   S h a n* Xijir Ulan Hu 35°N Luanhaizi 4974

Ronda 7821 Kizyl Jilga Tielongtan 6920 Margai Caka Moron Us/He Tongtianheyan

Skardu Saser 7672 *Siach* Como 6800 Dogai Coring 7500

JAMMU AND KASHMIR Leh Pangong Tso Wujang *C H I N A*

Anantnag Zangla Chushul 6406 6392 *T i b e t* Banvalot 6549 Tanggula Shan Wenquan 6104

Kishtwar *Chenab* Zaskar 6400 *Transhimalaya* Parding Amdo Nyainrong

Jammu 4413 Chamba Jaggang 7315 Rabang Lugu Kangro Lhazhong Do'gyaling Dongqiao Baingoin Nagqu

Dharmsala Danknar Shiquanhe Gê'gyai Qagcaka Yanhuqu Nyima Urru Co Siling Co Damxung Nu Jiang

Amritsar Hoshiarpur Kulu Garyarsa Xungba Gêrzê Zhaxi Co Ombu Namco

Jalandhar Simla 2202 Kalpa Moincer Yagra 7216 Ngangla Ringco Coqên Tangra Yumco Zhari Namco Tomra Xainza 7088

Ludhiana 6315 Nilang Zanda La'nga Co Barga Mapam Yumco Lunggar Kangmar Gyaring Co Nam Co Damxung

Chandigarh Kamet 7756 Nanda Devi 7316 Burang 7728 Samsang Kangmar Paryang 7088

Dehra Dun Pauri Karnaprayag Almora 7040 Simikot Zhongba Saga Raka Zangbo Yarlung Zangbo Jiang Nyêmo Lhasa (Brahmaputra) Maizhokunggar 30°N

Ambala Patiala Saharanpur Dandeldhura 7043 Mustang Maquan Ngamring Lhazê Zigazê Gonggar Nêdong

Meerut Moradabad Dailekh Bheri Annapurna 8091 Gyirong Tingri 6482 Dinggyê Yamzho Yumco Comai Lhünzê

Delhi Hapur Rampur Pilibhit Nepalganj Dhaulagiri 8176 Makalu Xixabangma Feng 8012 Everest Kangto 7060

New Delhi Ghaziabad Bareilly Butwal Pokhara *N E P A L* Namlam 6749 Kangchenjunga 8586 7554 Cona

Rewari Budaun Shahjahanpur 1337 Kathmandu Bhaktapur Bhojpur Darjiling Thimphu Tongsa Dzong Dirang

Sikar Aligarh Etah Sitapur Balrampur Rapti Sun Kosi *B H U T A N* 4736 Tarka La Tashigang

Alwar Hodal Farrukhabad Kannauj Lucknow Faizabad Gorakhpur Bettiah Birganj Sirha Shiliguri Jalpaiguri Tezpur 62

Mathura Etawah Balrampur Motihari Biratnagar Koch Bihar Brahmaputra Nowgong

Bharatpur Agra Gangapur Gwalior Orai Kanpur Sultanpur Azamgarh Muzaffarpur Darbhanga Purnia Rangpur Tura 1412 Guwahati

Jaipur Chambal Jhansi Fatehpur Ghaghara Patna Raniganj Dinajpur Dhuburi Goalpara Shillong 1961

Tonk Banas Betwa Banda Allahabad Ghazipur Ganges Arrah Bihar Munger Ghugri Bhagalpur Bogra Jamalpur Sylhet Karimganj 25°N

Kota Shivpuri 521 Sind Chhatarpur Panna Varanasi Mirzapur Sasaram Gaya Kodarma Ingraj Bazar Mymensingh Maulvi Bazar

Baran Guna Lalitpur Maihar Rewa Son Garwa Hazaribagh Dhanbad Dumka Pabna Dhaka Agartala Aizawl

Ghandi Sagar Rajgarh Sagar Damoh Govind Ballash Pant Sagar 1026 Sonhat Ambikapur Ranchi Purulia Barddhaman Navadwip BANGLADESH Comilla

Narsinghgarh Shajapur Bhopal Jabalpur Shahdol Jashpurnagar Bankura Faridpur Jessore Chandpur

Ujjain *I N D I A* Narsimhapur Narmada Mandla Bilaspur Sundargarh Rourkela Jamshedpur Chaibasa Calcutta Khulna Barisal Barkal

Indore *Range* Hoshangabad 1350 Seoni Balaghat Raipur Hirakud Reservoir Baripada 1165 Kharagpur Hugli Barkal

Mhow Harda Chhindwara Betul Katgi Sarangarh Deogarh Baleshwar Bhadrakh Cox's Bâzâr BURMA

Khargon Khandwa Burhanpur 1178 Mandla Balaghat Mahanadi Sambalpur Talcher *Ganges Delta* Kyauktaw

Jalgaon Nagpur Bhandara Raj Nandgaon Balangir Bhadrakh Cuttack Palmyras Point Sittwe

Akola Amravati Wardha Garhchiroli Bhawanipatna Phulabani Bhubaneshwar 20°N

Buldana Yavatmal Chandrapur Kanker Bhanjanager Puri

Parbhani Adilabad Sirpur Makri 1501 Berhampur Chhatrapur *B a y   o f*

Ahmadnagar Jalna Nanded Jagtial *Penganga* Sironcha 1240 Jagdalpur Jaypur Parvatipuram

Beed *Deccan* Nizamabad Karimnagar Warangal Chintalnar Venkatapuram 1680 Srikakulam *B e n g a l*

Barsi Latur Manjira Bhadrathalam Khammam Vizianagaram Vishakhapatnam

Solapur Bidar Sangareddi Hyderabad Godavari Tuni *Eastern Ghats*

Gulbarga Mahbubnagar Nalgonda Eluru Kakinada Rajahmundry

Bijapur 75°E 80°E Gunter Vijayawada Krishna 85°E 90°E

0 100 200 300 miles Average linear scale : 1 inch ≈ 125 miles 1cm ≈ 80 km 0 100 200 300 400 500 Km

95°E   Da Qaidam   100°E   105°E

Mangnai   Shaliangzi   •5030   Delingha   Tianjun   Gangca   Menyuan   Wuwei   Dingbian

Gang   Suli Hu   Holt Taria   Wuqi   Zi

Nur Turu   •3099   Dabsan Hu   Xitieshan   Ulan   4711   Qinghai Hu   Haiyan   Datong   Yongdeng   •4070   Zhongwei   Tianshui   Tongxin

Boluntay   De Juh   Qarhan   Nan Hulsan Hu   Nomhon   Dulan   Dashuiqiao   Xining   2244   Jingyuan   Guyuan   Qingyang

•5972   Golmud   Nangdoi   Minhe   150E   Lanzhou   Luoch

Qumar Heyan   Naij Tal   5026   Xiangride   Daheba   •4832   Gonghe   Linxia   Dingxi   2143   Pingliang   Tongchu

Luanhaizi   4974   Ngoring   Guinan   Tongren   Lintao   Longxi   Qian Xian   Sanyuan

35°N   Tongtianheyan   Cowargarzê   Huashixia   Madoi   Maqên Gangri   •6282   Min Xian   Tianshui   Wei He   Baoji   Xianyang   Xi'an

Q i n g   Z a n g   Zhidoi   Qumarlêb   Cyaring Hu   Chalaxung   Darlag   4063   Maqên   Xingsagoinba   Huang He   Zhugqu   Liuba   Lüeyang   Ningsha

Wenquan   •6104   Bagan   5876   Chindu   4396   Sangruma   Hongyuan   3002   Qingchuan   Guangyuan   •1950   Wanyuan   Hanzhong   Xixiang

G a o y u a n   Zadoi   Yushu   Sêrxu   Jigzhi   Baima   Aba   •4820   Q i n l i n g   Sh

Amdo   Nyainrong   Domba   5189   Nangqên   Dainkog   Dêgê   4820   Garzê   Barkam   H   Jiuding Shan   4984   Mianyang   Nanbu   Daxian   Fe

Nagqu   Nu Jiang   Baqên   Dengqên   Riwoqê   Jomda   Jinchuan   Dawu   Guan Xian   S i c h u a n   Santai   Nanchong   Wanxian   Chan

Biru   Banbar   4750   Qamdo   C H I N A   Chengdu   Jianyang   Suining   Dazhu   Lich

Damxung   Lhari   •6692   Lhorong   Zhag'yab   Danba   Qionglai   Hechuan   P e n d i   E

30°N   Maizhokunggar   Gongbo'gyamda   Bomi   Baxoi   Markam   Yidin   Batang   Litang   Kangding   Ya'an   Meishan   Zigong   Neijiang   Chongquing   •1682

Nyingchi   Zogang   Minya Konka   3099   Yongchuan   Ba Xian   Qiar

Nyainqentanglha Shan   Namjagbarwa Feng   •7756   Zayü   •4353   Dêqên   Xiangcheng   5445   Wutongqiao   Qianwei   Qijiang   2251   Youyang   •2942

Yarlung Zambo Jiang   Mainling   Nang Xian   H e n g d u a n   S h a n   6740   Dêrong   5040   Min Jiang   Yibin   Luzhou   Julian   Tongzi   Tongren

Nêdong   Gongshan   Zhongdian   Xide   Meigu   Xuyang   Jinsha   Zunyi   Xinhuang   D a l o u   S h a n

Comai   Lhünze   Takpa Shiri   6685   Pangin   Saikhoa Ghat   Man Kabat   4578   Dechang   Zhaotong   Weining   Bijie   Xifeng   Shibing   Keili   Jir

BHUTAN   Cona   Kangto   7060   Zirò   Tinsukia   Putao   Yulongxue Shan   •5586   Lijiang   Huize   Xuanwei   Zhenning   Dushan   Rongj

Tashigang   Dirâng   Dibrũgarh   Mazunzut   Huaping   Huili   Dongchuan   •2159   Anshun   Duyun

61   Tezpur   Itanagar   Tagap Ga   Sumprabum   Jianchuan   Jinsha Jiang   Dukou   Guiyang   Rong

Guwahati   Nowgong   Jorhât   Brahmaputra   Makaw   Bijiang   Yongren   Pan Xian   Wangmo   Hechi

INDIA   P a i k a i   M t s   •3824   2569   Gaojian   •4122   Xiaguan   •1560   Qiansuo   Qujing   Xingyi   Anlong   •1424   Yishan

Shillong   Kohima   Lonkin   Lawa   Yipinglang   Tianlin   Bose   •1760   Pingguo

•1961   Lumding   Myitkyina   Baoshan   Chuxiong   •1893   Kunming   Mile   Guangnan   Yu Jiang

25°N   Sylhet   Silchar   Hopin   Tengchong   Fengqing   Anning   Dian Chi   Nanpang Jiang   Funing

Maulvi Bazâr   Karimganj   Imphâl   Bhamo   Luxi   Jingdong   Tonghai   Shiping   Tianlin

998   Tamu   Mansi   Naba   1672   Wandingzhen   Lincang   Zhenyuan   Yuanjiang   Jianshui   Kaiyuan   Wenshan   Hongshui He   Hechi

Agartala   Aizawl   Kawlin   Shuangjiang   Gejiu   •1740   Wenshan   •1760

Comilla   Tonzang   Kennedy   2704   Kalemyo   2168   Lashio   Salween   Pu'er   Simao   Lancang   Jiangcheng   3076   Lüchun   Jinping   Ha Giang   Nanning   Lingshan

BANGLA-   Barkal   A r a k a n   Gangaw   Mogok   Kyaukme   Mông Yai   Fan si Pan   •3143   Cao Bang   Ningming   Qinzh

Chittagong   DESH   Monywa   Shwebo   Tonking   Tuyen Quang   •1193   Pingxiang   Lang Son   •1507

Cox's Bâzâr   Victoria   3053   Kanbetlet   Mandalay   •2320   Daluo   Phongsali   Lai Chau   Tuan Giao   VIETNAM   Ha Coi   Beihai

Pakkoku   Myingyan   Mông Küng   •1842   Muang Khoa   Hanoi   Bac Ninh

Kyauktaw   Chauk   1518   Meiktla   Loi-lem   Ta-Kaw   Jinghong   Jiangcheng   Vien Pou Kha   Hoa Binh   Haiphong

Sittwe   M o u n t a i n s   BURMA   Taunggyi   1907   Xam Nua   Nam Dinh

20°N   Magwe   Langhko   Mông Ton   L A O S   Mekong   Thanh Hoa   Gulf of Tongking

Kyaukpyu   Pyinmana   Chiang Rai   Louangphrabang   Quynh Luu   Don

Toungoo   1854   Phayao   Sayaboury   Xieng   Khouang   •2820   Vinh

INDIAN OCEAN   Sandoway   Prome   Doi Inthanon   2590   Chang Mai   Nan   Vang Vieng   Pak Sane   Ha Tinh

Myanaung   Pyu   1056   Salween   Irrawaddy   Phrae   Lampang   Vientiane   Nong Khai   Nape   2286   Kham Keut   Rao Go

Gwa   Henzada   Phu Soai Deo   2102   T H A I L A N D   Thakhek   Dong Hoi

Pegu   Milang   2316   Wang Saphung   Udon Thani   Sakhon Nakhon

Thingangyun   Insein   Rangoon   Kyaikto   Thaton   Phitsanulok   Se

95°E   100°E   105°E

This map shows 1/60 of the earth's surface. Area scale : 1 ☐ inch on the map ≏15,000 ☐ miles on the ground 1 ☐ cm on the map ≏6000 ☐ km on the ground

a b c d e f g h i j k l m

Taiyuan
Yuci
Taigu
Yangquan
•2069
115°E
Dezhou
120°E
Penglai
Yantai
Chengshan Jiao
125°E
Ongjin
Inch'ŏn
Kangnŭng
Wǒnju
Sǒul

Xingtai
Linqing
Zibo
Boxing
•220
Laiyang
Ch'ŏngju
Andong

Huo Xian
Fengfeng
Handan
Jinan
950
Weifang
Jiao Xian
Qingdao
SOUTH
Taejǒn
•1918
Taegu

Changzhi
•1619
Anyang
Heze
Tai'an
Liangcheng
Qingdao
KOREA
Chŏnju
Masan

Houma
•2322
Hebi
Xinxiang
Yanzhou
Junan
Kwangju
35°N
Chinju
Yosu

eng
Jiaozuo
Zhengzhou
Kaifeng
Jining
Lianyungang
Mokp'o
Cheju

Sanmenxia
•1440
Qi Xian
Shangqiu
Xuzhou
Binhai
Cheju-do

Luoyang
Xuchang
Zhecheng
Bo Xian
Huaibei
•366
Huaiyin
Hongze

Pingdingshan
Nanzhao
Luohe
Zhoukouzhen
Su Xian
Hongze Ho
Gaoyu Hu

Shangnan
G r e a t
Fuyang
Bengbu
Yangzhou
EAST CHINA

Zhenping
Nanyang
Tanghe
Xincai
Huainan
Chu Xian
Nanjing
Changzhou
Wuxi
SEA

•612
•1140
Xinyang
Huangchuan
Hefei
Tai Hu
Suzhou
Shanghai

Xiangfan
Sui Xian
Luoshan
Huai He
Lujiang
Wuhu
Xuancheng
Jiaxing

Nanzhang
N
Yunmeng
Macheng
Chang Jiang
Tongling
•1187
Hangzhou

Yidu
Plain
Wuhan
•1860
Anqing
Shaoxing
Ningbo
Guoju
Zhoushan Islands
30°N

Shashi
Mianyang
Huangshi
Tongshan
•1841
Tunxi
Shaoxing

Li Xian
Jiujiang
Xingzi
Jingdezhen
Xin'anjiang
Jinhua
Linhai

Changde
Dongting He
Yueyang
1596
Xiushui
Poyang Hu
Shangrao
Quzhou
Lishui
Wenzhou

Yiyang
Nanchang
Gao'an
Cuixi
Pucheng
Yunhe

Changsha
Xinyu
Fuzhou
2158
Zhenghe

Xiangtan
Zhuzhou
Pingxiang
Gongxi
Nanfeng
Shaowu
Fuding

Liahuan
1290
Ji'an
Gan Jiang
Ningdu
•1199
Nanping
Ningde

Shaoyang
Hengyang
Leiyang
1871
Sanming
1494
Minqing
Fuzhou

Xiang Jiang
Ganzhou
Ruijin
Yong'an
Minqing

Quanzhou
Chen Xian
Longyan
Putian

Ningyuan
Nanxiong
Chilung
Taoyüan
Taipeh

Lian Xian
•1902
Shaoguan
Ilan
25°N
Hsinchu

ngle
Yingde
Zhangzhou
3884
Xueweng
Miyako

Qiuling
•1560
Mei Xian
Xiamen
Taiwan Strait
Taichung
Changhua
Hualien
Iriomote

Huaiji
•1282
Longchuan
Zhangpu
Chiai
3997

ngnan
Wuzhou
Jieyang
Chao'an
Tainan
TAIWAN
Tropic of Cancer

Xi Jiang
Guangzhou
Shantou
Chaoyang

Luoding
Foshan
Huizhou
Lufeng
Kaohsiung
Pingtung

1704
Jiangmen
Shunde
Fangshan

Zhuhai
Kowloon
Victoria
Hengchun

Yangjiang
Macao *(Port.)*
HONG KONG
(U.K.)

Maoming
PACIFIC

njiang
Bashi Channel

Luzon
Strait
Batan Islands
20°N

OCEAN

Hainan
nning

Babuyan Islands

Cape Bajeador
Cape Engaño
Aparri

Laoag
Tuguegarao

Vigan
Bangued
Luzon
Ilagan
PHILIPPINES

Pulog
2934

n o p q r s t u v w x y z

115°E
120°E
125°E

67

Yellow Sea

Ryūkyū Islands
(Japan)
Okinawa
Naha

Han Shui

Huang He
Yun He
Grand Canal

Wuyi Shan
Min Jiang

Dong Jiang

Cordillera Central
Sierra Madre

100 200 300
Average linear scale : 1 inch≈125 miles 1cm≈80 km
100 200 300 400 500

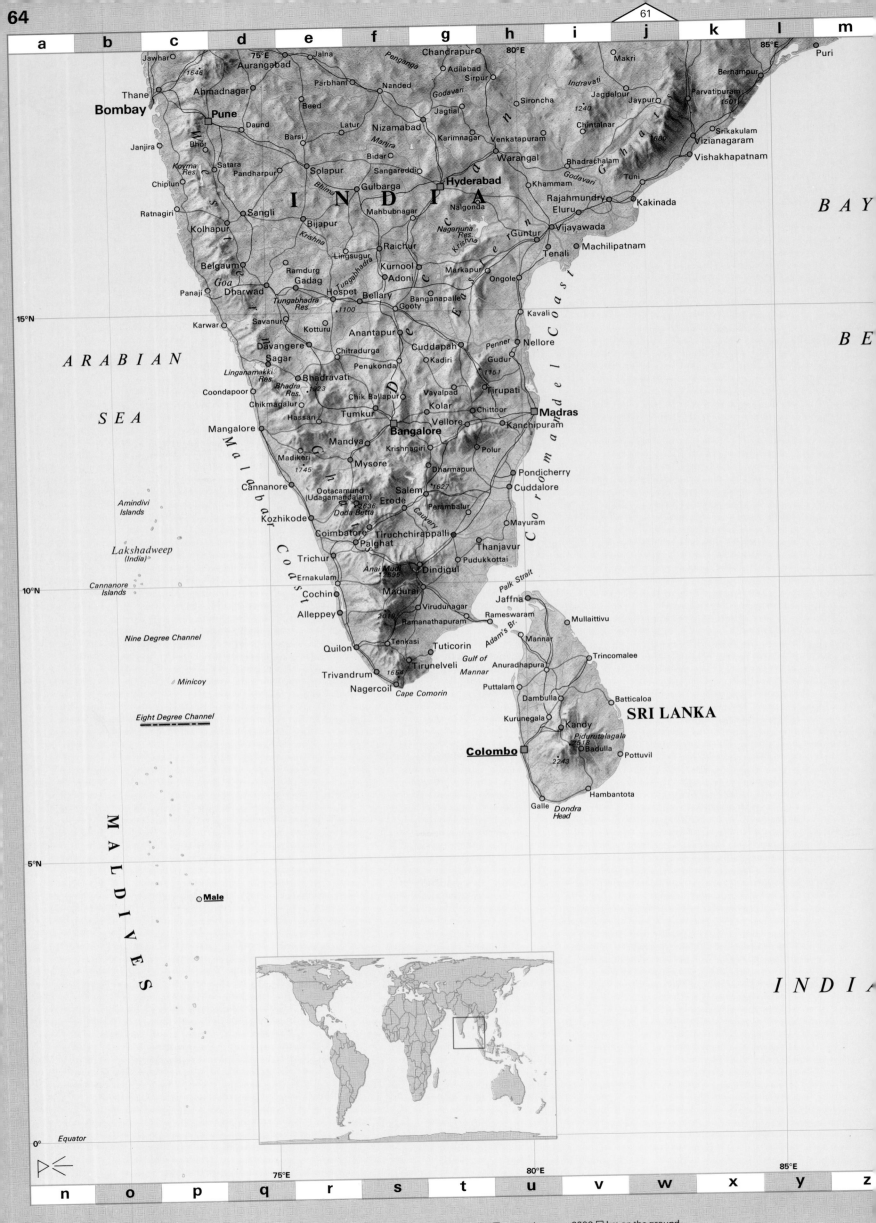

a   b   c   d   e   f   g   h   i   j   k   l   m

Jawhar   75°E   Jalna   Chandrapur   80°E   Makri   85°E   Puri

1646   Aurangabad   Adilabad   Indravati   Berhampur

Thane   Ahmadnagar   Parbhani   Nanded   Sirpur   Jagdalpur   Jaypur   Parvatipuram

Bombay   **Pune**   Daund   Beed   Godavari   Sironcha   1240   Chintalnar   1501

Janjira   Bhor   Barsi   Latur   Nizamabad   Jagtial   Karimnagar   Venkatapuram   1680   Srikakulam

Koyna   Satara   Pandharpur   Solapur   Bidar   Sangareddi   Manjira   Warangal   Bhadrachalam   Vizianagaram

Chiplun   Res.   Bhima   Gulbarga   **Hyderabad**   Khammam   Godavari   Tuni   Vishakhapatnam

Ratnagiri   Sangli   Kolhapur   **I N D I A**   Nalgonda   Rajahmundry   Kakinada   **B A Y**

Bijapur   Mahbubnagar   Nagarjuna   Eluru

Belgaum   Krishna   Lingsugur   Raichur   Res.   Guntur   Vijayawada   Machilipatnam   **B E**

Goa   Ramdurg   Gadag   Kurnool   Markapur   Tenali

Panaji   Dharwad   Hospet   Adoni   Ongole   Krishna

Tungabhadra   Bellary   Banganapalle   Kavali

Res.   .1100   Gooty   Coast

15°N   Karwar   Savanur   Anantapur   Nellore

Kotturu   Penner   Gudur

A R A B I A N   Davangere   Chitradurga   Cuddapah   1151

Sagar   Penukonda   Kadiri   Tirupati

Linganamakki   Bhadravati   1923   Vayalpad   Coromandel

S E A   Res.   Bhadra   Chik Ballapur   Kolar   Chittoor   **Madras**

Coondapoor   Res.   Chikmagalur   Tumkur   Vellore   Kanchipuram

Hassan   **Bangalore**

Mangalore   Madikeri   Mandya   Krishnagiri   Polur

1745   Mysore   Dharmapuri   Pondicherry

Cannanore   Ootacamund   Salem   1627   Cuddalore

Malabar   (Udagamandalam)   2636   Erode   Parambalur

Kozhikode   Doda Betta   Cauvery   Mayuram

Coimbatore   Tiruchchirappalli   Thanjavur

Trichur   Palghat   Pudukkottai

Coast   Anai Mudi   Dindigul

Ernakulam   2695

10°N   Cochin   Madurai   Palk Strait   Jaffna   Mullaittivu

Alleppey   Virudunagar   Rameswaram   Trincomalee

Nine Degree Channel   2019   Ramanathapuram   Adam's Br.   Mannar

Quilon   Tenkasi   Tuticorin   Gulf of   Anuradhapura

Tirunelveli   Mannar   Puttalam

Trivandrum   1654   Dambulla   Batticaloa

Nagercoil   Cape Comorin   Kurunegala   **SRI LANKA**

Minicoy   Kandy   Pidurutalagala

Colombo   2518   Badulla

Eight Degree Channel   2243   Pottuvil

Hambantota

Galle   Dondra Head

Amindivi Islands

Lakshadweep (India)

Cannanore Islands

M A L D I V E S

Male

5°N

I N D I A

0°   Equator

75°E   80°E   85°E

n   o   p   q   r   s   t   u   v   w   x   y   z

This map shows 1/60 of the earth's surface. Area scale : 1 ☐ inch on the map ≈ 15,000 ☐ miles on the ground   1 ☐ cm on the map ≈ 6000 ☐ km on the ground

90°E

Ramree

Cheduba

Pyinmana
Loikaw
Muang Chiang Rai *1854*
Luang Prabang
Ban Ban

Thayetmyo
Toungoo
Phayao
Sayaboury
Vang Vieng *2820*
Xieng Khouang
Pak Sane

Prome
Pyu
Nan
L A O S *Bia*

Myanaung
Inthanon 2590
Chiang Mai
Lampang
Phrae
Vientiane
Wang Saphung
Nong Khai
Kham Keut
Thakhek

Henzada
Salween 1056
Sittang
Mae Sot
Tak
Phitsanulok
Chum Phae
Udon Thani
Sakhon Nakhon

Pegu
Kyaikto
Thaton
Soai Dao 2102
Khon Kaen
Phetchabun
Kalasin

Insein
Thingangyun
Rangoon
Kanbe
Miang 2316
Nakhon Sawan
Chaiyaphum
Maha Sarakham
Roi Et
Yasothon

Basseein
Moulmein
T H A I L A N D
Nakhon Ratchasima
Si Sa Ket
Ubon Ratchathani

Gulf of Martaban
Ye
Sing Buri
Lop Buri
Buri Ram
Surin
15°N

Pyapon
Mouths of the Irrawaddy
Preparis
Suphan Buri
Kanchanaburi
Nakhon Pathom
Khiaw 1282
Prachin Buri *849*
Samrong

Tavoy
Ban Pong
Bangkok (Krung Thep)
Chon Buri
Angkor

Cocos Islands (Birma)
North Andaman
Phetchaburi
Siracha
1633
Battambang
KAMPUCHEA
Tonle Sap

Andaman Islands (India)
Middle Andaman
Klaeng
Rayong
Chantaburi
Pursat
Kompong Chhnang *1813*

South Andaman
Kadan
Mergui
Hua Hin
Laem Ngop Chang
Hat Lek

Mergui Archipelago
1251 Prachuap Khiri Khan
Kut
Phnom Penh

Little Andaman
Letsok-Aw
Lanbi
758
Gulf of Thailand
Kompong Som

Chumphon
Phu Quoc

Ten Degree Channel
Ranong
St. Matthew's
Isthmus of Kra
Ko Phangan Ko Samui
10°N

Car Nicobar
Sea
Takua Pa
Surat Thani
Ban Na San
Cape Mau

Nicobar Islands (India)
Thap Put
Khao Luang 1835
Nakhon Si Thammarat

Katchall
Karbi
Malay

Little Nicobar
Phuket
Trang
Phatthalung Thale Luang

Great Nicobar
Songkhla
Hat Yai
Pattani
Sai Buri

Terutao
Satun
Yala
Narathiwat

Langkawi
Alor Setar
Sungai Ko-lok
Kota Baharu

Sungai Petani
Pangkal Kalong

Banda Aceh
Sigli
Lhokseumawe
Pinang (George Town)
Butterworth
2171 Chamah
Kuala Terengganu
5°N

Bireuen
Idi
Taiping
Sungai Siput Utara
Dungun

Calang
2855 Geureudong
Lhoksukon
Peureulak
Ipoh **M A L A Y A**

Langsa
Kampar *2131*
Kuala Lipis *Tapis 1512*

Meulaboh
Pangkalanbrandan
Raub
Kuantan

Leuser 3404
Tanjungpura
Medan
Kutacane
Tebingtinggi
Kuala Kubu Baharu
Bentong
MALAYSIA

Tapaktuan
Kabanjahe
Petaling Jaya
Kuala Lumpur (PENINSULAR)

OCEAN
Pematangsiantar
Kelang
Seremban
Segamat
Tioman

Simeulue
Singkilbaru
Lake Toba
Malakka
Muar *Blumut 1010*
Keluang

Nias
Tuangku
2300 Sihabuhabu
Tarutung
Rantauprapat
Rupat
Kulai
Johor Baharu

Sibolga
Dumai
Duri
SINGAPORE

Tanahbala
Padangsidempuan
Balaipungut
Riau Islands

Hutanopan
Pakanbaru

Pini
Panyabungan
Ophir 2912
Lubuksikaping
Lingga Islands

Bukittinggi
Payakumbuh
Rengat
Singkep
0°

Padangpanjang

90°E
95°E
100°E

Average linear scale: 1 inch ≈ 125 miles 1cm ≈ 80 km

Gulf of Tongking

Hainan

1854
100°E
1056
Inthanon 2590

BURMA

Toungoo
Prome
Myanaung
Pyu
Henzada
Pegu
Insein Thingangyun
Kanbe
Rangoon
Pyapon
Gulf of Martaban
Thaton
Moulmein
Kyaikto

Sittang
Salween

Chiang Mai
Lampang
Phrae
Nan
Phayao
Sayaboury
Vang Vieng 2820
Bia
Xieng Khouang
Pak Sane
Kham Keut Nape 2286
Rao Go
Quynh Luu
Vinh
Dongfang
Yaxian
1879

Ha Tinh
Dong Hoi

Vientiane

Nong Khai
Wang Saphung
Udon Thani
Phitsanulok
Miang 2316
Soai Dao 2104
Tak
Mae Sot

THAILAND

L A O S

V I E T N A M

Khon Kaen
Chum Phae
Phetchabun
Kalasin
Sakhon Nakhon
Savannakhet
Thakhek
Sepone
Hue 2500 Atouat
Da Nang

15°N

Nakhon Sawan
Chaiyaphum
Maha Sarakham
Roi Et
Khemarat
Yasothon
Ubon Ratchathani
B.Thateng 2009
Pakse
Phiafay
Attopeu

Nakhon Ratchasima
Lop Buri
Sing Buri
Buri Ram
Surin
Si Sa Ket
Warin Chamrap
Det Udom
Khong 1570 An Tuc
Kontum
Pleiku

Suphan Buri
Kanchanaburi
Nakhon Pathom
Khiaw 1282
Prachin Buri 849
Samrong
Stung Treng
Qui Nhon

Tavoy

Ban Pong
Thon Buri
Bangkok (Krung Thep)
Sisophon
Angkor
Battambang
Tonle Sap
KAMPUCHEA
Ban Me Thuot
Mdrak

Phetchaburi
Chon Buri
Siracha
Klaeng 1633
Chantaburi
Rayong
Pursat
Kompong Chhnang
Kratie
Kompong Cham
1544
Nha Trang
1813
Da Lat
Cam Ranh

Mergui Archipelago
Kadan
Mergui
Hua Hin
Laem Ngop
Chang
Kut
Hat Lek
Phnom Penh
Bao Loc
1532
Di Linh

Andaman

Letsok-Aw
1251
Khiri Khan Prachuap
Lanbi 758
Phu Chong
Bien Hoa
Saigon (Ho Chi Minh)

Kompong Som
Chau Phu
My Tho
Vung Tau

Chumphon
Long Xuyen
Rach Gia
Can-Tho

10°N
St Matthew's
Ranong
Isthmus of Kra
Phu Quoc
Khanh Hung
Mekong Delta

Sea
Phangan
Samui
Takua Pa
Surat Thani
Ban Na San
Nakhon Si Thammarat
Nam Can
Cape Mau
Spratly Islands

65

Thap Put
Luang 1835
Karbi
Phuket

Malay

Phatthalung
Thale Luang
Trang
Hat Yai
Songkhla
Pattani
Sai Buri
Yala
Narathiwat
Kota Baharu
S o u t h

Terutao
Satun
Langkawi
Alor Setar
Sungai Ko-lok
Pangkal Kalong

Banda Aceh
Sigli
Lhokseumawe
Idi
Sungai Petani
Pinang (George Town)
Butterworth
Pinang
Kuala Terengganu

Bireuen
Geureudong 2855
Peureulak
Perak
Chamah 2171
Kelantan
Natuna Utara

5°N
Calang
Langsa
Taiping
Sungai Siput Utara
Ipoh
Dungun
Natuna

Meulaboh
Pangkalanbrandan
Tanjungpura
Kampar
2131
Kuala Lipis
Raub
Kuala Kubu Baharu
Tapis 1512
Kuantan
Natuna Selatan Islands

Strait of
Leuser 3404
Medan
Tebingtinggi
MALAYA
Bentong
Natuna Islands (Indonesia)

S u m a t r a
Kutacane
Kabanjahe
Pematangsiantar
Tanjungbalai
Kuala Lumpur
MALAYSIA (PENINSULAR)
Petaling Jaya
Kelang
Seremban
Malakka
Muar
Keluango
Segamat
Tioman
Anambas Islands (Indonesia)
Binatang
Sarike

Tapaktuan
Lake Toba
Sihabuhabu 2300
Rantauprapat
Blumut 1010
Johor
Datuk Bay
Tanjung Datu
Kuching

Simeulue
Singkilbaru
Tarutung
Dumai
Rupat
Kulai
Malakka
Johor Baharu
Sambas
Pamangkat
Singkawang
Lupar

Nias
Sibolga
Padangsidempuan
Panyabungan
Duri
Balaipungut
SINGAPORE
Riau Islands
Tambelan Islands
Pinang
Ngabang
Sanggau

INDIAN
Hutanopan
Pakanbaru
Lingga Islands

0° Equator
Pini
2912
Lubuksikaping
Kampar
Singkep
Pontianak
Kapuas
Bengkolan Bay

OCEAN
Tanahbala
Bukittinggi
Payakumbuh
Padangpanjang
Rengat
Indragiri
Berhala Strait
Cape Jabung
Maya
Nanga Sokan

Siberut
Padang
Solok
100°E
105°E
110°E

This map shows 1/60 of the earth's surface. Area scale:

95°E   100°E   105°E   110°E

S O U T H

THAILAND

Phatthalung
Thale Luang
Trang
Songkhla
Hat Yai
Pattani
Sai Buri
Satun
Yala
Narathiwat
Terutao
Sungai Ko-lok
Kota Baharu
Langkawi
Alor Setar
Pangkal Kalong
Sungai Petani
Butterworth
Kuala Terengganu
Pinang (George Town)
Pinang

S E A

Banda Aceh
Sigli
Lhokseumawe
Lhoksukon
5°N
Bireuen
Idi
2855 Geureudong
Peureulak
Taiping
Sungai Siput Utara
Dungun
Natuna Utava
Calang
Langsa
Ipoh
Kuala Lipis
Pangkalanbrandan
2171 Chamah
Natuna (Bunguran)
Meulaboh
Kampar
2131
Raub
Tapis 1512
Leuser 3404
Tanjungpura
Kuala Kubu Baharu
Kuantan
Natuna Islands (Indonesia)
Medan
Tebingtinggi
Bentong
South Natuna
Kutacane
MALAYA
Tapaktuan
Kabanjahe
Pematangsiantar
Kuala Lumpur
Kelang
Petaling Jaya
MALAYSIA (PENINSULAR)
Anambas Islands (Indonesia)
Simeulue
Tanjungbalai
Seremban
Tioman
Lake Toba
Sihabuhabu 2300
Rantauprapat
Malakka
Segamat
Tanjung Datu
Singkilbaru
Tarutung
Dumai
Rupat
Muar
Keluang 1010 Blumut
Johor
Datuk Bay
Sibolga
Barumun
Duri
Kulai
Johor Baharu
Sambas
Kuc
Nias
Padangsidempuan
Panyabungan
Balaipungut
SINGAPORE
Pamangkat
Singkawang
Hutanopan
Pakanbaru
Riau Islands
Tambelan Islands
Pinang
Ngabang
Lubuksikaping
Kampar
Pini
Ophir 2912
Payakumbuh
Rengat
Lingga Islands
Pontianak
Sa
Tanahbala
Bukittingi
Padangpanjang
Indragiri
Singkep
Bengolan Bay
Equator   0°
Solok
Berhala Strait
Maya
Siberut
Padang
Muarabungo
Hari
Jambi
Cape Jabung
Karimata Strait
Karimata
Ketapang
Sipora
Kerinci 3805
Sarolangun
Muntok
Pangkalpinang
Nang
65
Sungaipenuh
Barisan Mountains
Bangka
Pagai Utara
Palembang
Tanjungpandan
Gaspar Strait
Belitung
Pagai Selatau
Lubuklinggau
Sungaigerung
Perabumulih
Bengkulu
Lahat
Dempo 3159
I   N   D
Bintuhan
Kotabumi
Pesagi 2231
5°S
Tanjungkarang
Telukbetung (Bandarlampung)
Enggano
Merak
Jakarta
Krakatau
Sunda Strait
J
Cape Cangkuang
Bogor
Cirebon
Pekalongan
Sukabumi
Bandung
Tegal
Sema
Tasik Malaya
Purwokerto
Slamet 3418
I   N   D   I   A   N
Cilacap
Magelang
Yogy

O C E A N

Christmas Island (Australia)

10°S

95°E   100°E   105°E   110°E

This map shows 1/60 of the earth's surface.   Area scale : 1 □ inch on the map ≈ 15,000 □ miles on the ground   1 □ cm on the map ≈ 6000 □ km on the ground

67

I N A

Malayan Sea

Balabac Strait
Banggi
Jambongan

Sulu Sea

Cagayan
Sulu

Pagadian

PHILIPPINES

Zamboanga   Moro Gulf   Cotabato

Tagum

Davao
Apo
2954

Davao
Gulf

Mindanao

Kota
Kinabalu

Kinabalu
4101

Labuk
Bay

Sandakan

Basilan

Basilan

Digos

Koronadal

SABAH

Beaufort

Panqutaran Group

Jolo

General Santos

Brunei Bay

Lahad Datu

Tawitawi

Sarangani

Bandar Seri Begawan

Darvel Bay

Tawitawi
Group

Sulu Archipelago

5°N

Kuala Belait

Miri

BRUNEI

Baram

Tawau

Mulu
2371

Sebuku
Bay

Sulawesi Sea

Kawio

Talaud
Islands

**MALAYSIA
(EASTERN)**

Sesayap

Tarakan

Morotai

SARAWAK

Bintulu

2550

Kayan

Sangihe

Sangihe Islands

Tobelo

Akelamo

Rajang

Guguang
2467

Tanjungredeb

Klabat
2022

Manado

Jailolo

Saolat
1508

Liangpran
2240

Manyapa
2000

Rapak

Dondo Bay

Buol   Paleleh

2217

Tondano

Kuandang

Kotamobagu

Ternate

Halmahera

Weda

a l i m a n t a n

Mahakam

Ogoamas
291

Moutong

Tilamuta

Gorontalo

*Molucca
Sea*

Weda Bay

Pinoh

(B o r n e o)

Mapaga

Dongkalang

*Gulf
of
Tomini*

Tongian Islands

0°

*Raya
2278*

Muarabadak

Samarinda

Donggala

Palu

Malik

Teku

2400

Labuha

Batjan

Obi

*M
o
l
u
c
c
a
s*

Pasangkayu

Poso

Uebonti

Batui

anbuun   Sampit

Tumbangsamba

Buntok

Balikpapan

Lumu

*Sulawesi
(Celébes)*

Wotu

Peleng

Gulf of Tolo

Banggai Islands

Taliabu

Mangole

Sula Islands M

*Ceram
Sea*

Palangkaraya

Tanjung

Sarempaka
1380

Gandadiwata
3074 Masamba

Palopo

Buru

Namlea

Ceram

Kandangan

Muaus Mountains

Besar
1892

Rantekombola
3455

*Gulf
of
Bone*

Mekongga
2799

Strait of Manipa

Banjarmasin

Kotabaru

Majene

Kendari

Ambon

Batakan

Laut

Parepare

Kolaka

Kolono

N

E

S

I

A

*Cape
Selatan*

Watampone

Raha

Muna

Butung

a   S e a

Jatisiri

Ujung Pandang

Sinjai

Kabaena

Baubau

5°S

Bawean

Masalembo

2871

Salajar

Kabaena

*Tukangbesi
Islands*

B a n d a   S e a

Madura

Kangean

Tanahjampea
Kalao

*Barat Daya
Islands*

ngkalan

Surabaya

Madura Strait

Bali Sea

F l o r e s   S e a

S u n d a   I s l a n d s

Wetar

*Semeru
3676*

Probolinggo

Banyuwangi

L e s s e r

Alor

Dili

alang   Jember

2276 *Bali*

Lombok

Sumbawa
Besar

Raba

Ruteng

2400

Maumere *Solor Islands*

Atambua

2960

Denpasar

Mataram

Sumbawa

Mataram

Flores

Ende

Timor

Sumba

Waikabubak

Waingapu

Sawu Sea

Kupang

Besikama

10°S

Sawu

Roti

T i m o r   S e a

72

115°E   120°E   125°E

0   100   200   300 miles
Average linear scale : 1 inch ≃ 125 miles   1 cm ≃ 80 km
0   100   200   300   400   500 Km

130°E   135°E   140°E

Yap Islands

Faraulep Atoll

Ngulu Atoll   Sorol Atoll

F e d e r a t e

Palau   Babel Thuap   Woleai Atoll
Islands   Koror   Ifalik Atoll
                                                                 Eauripik Atoll
Palau
(U.S.A. Trust Territory)

C a r o l i n e

5°N   Sonsorol

Pulo Anna   P A C I

Merir

Tobi

Helen Reef
                                                              O C E

Morotai   Mapia Islands

Akelamo   Ayu Islands
Halmahera

Waigeo
0°
Dampier Strait   Kwoko   Manokwari   Biak
Sorong   3000   Peg Ariak
                                      2939
Cenderawasih   Yapen
Misool   Sarmi
   990   Steenkool   Gulf of
                                    Cenderawasih   Jayapura   Vanimo
C   Babo   Van Rees Mountains   Aitape
e   Ceram   Bula   I R I A N   Lumi   Dreikikir Wewak
r   3019   Tobo   Fakfak   Bomberai   Mamberamo
a   Ambon   Kaimana   Ma o Ike A   Wamena   Sepik
m   INDONES I A   JAYA Mountains   New
                    Jaya   5039   Mandala   Ramu
                    Kokonau   4702   Telefomin
5°S   G u i n e a   Kopiago Wabag
Kai   Moun
Banda Sea   Islands   Tanahmerah   Strickland Mendi Hage
                    Aru   2895   Kubor
                  Islands   4359
Damar   Mappi   Digul   Lake
Tanimbar   Murray   N E W
Islands   Babar   Kolepom   Fly   Kikori
Sermata   Selaru   (Dolak)
                                      Cape Vals   Merauke   Gul
A R A F U R A   S E A   Pa

                                                              Daru
                                          Torres Strait
10°S
                                          Badu   Moa
130°E   135°E   Prince of Wales   Cape York
                                          Island

n   o   p   q   r   s   t   u   v   w   x   y   z

This map shows 1/60 of the earth's surface. Area scale : 1 ☐ inch on the map ≈15,000 ☐ miles on the ground 1 ☐ cm on the map ≈6000 ☐ km on the ground

a   b   c   d   e   f   g   h   i   j   k   l   m

150°E   155°E   160°E

Namonuito
Atoll
Murillo Atoll
t Fayu   *Fayu*
Pikelot   *Hall Islands*
Minto
Atoll
S   t   a   t   e   s   o   f   M   i   c   r   o   n   e   s   i   a
Lamotrek
Atoll   (U.S.A. Trust Territory)   *Truk Islands*
Elato
Atoll   *Satawal*   *Oroluk*
Atoll
Losap   *Ponape*   *Mokil Atoll*
Atoll
Senjavin Group
Pingelap Atoll
s   l   a   n   d   s   *Namolok*
Ngatik
Atoll
Satawan *Mortlock*   *Kosrae*
Atoll   *Islands*
5°N

I   C

Kapingamarangi
Atoll
N

Equator   0°

Admiralty
Islands
Kavieng
B   i   s   m   a   r   c   k   A   r   c   h   i   p   e   l   a   g   o
New
Ireland
B   i   s   m   a   r   c   k   S   e   a
Rabaul
P   A   P   U   A   *Sinewit*
2438
5°S
dang
Balbi
2743
Walinga   *New Britain*   *Bougainville*   *Kieta*
Bangeta   *Kandrian*   (Papua New Guinea)
4107   *Choiseul*   S O L O M O N
Lae   *Fauro*   I S L A N D S
G   U   I   N   E   A   *Alu*
Mono   *Santa Isabel*
Morobe   *Vella*   *Nukiki*
ema   *Lavella* *New Georgia*
Popondetta   *Trobriand or*   S   *Vanunu*   *Malaita*
Victoria   *Kiriwina Island* o l   *New Georgia*
4073   m o   *Islands*
Woodlark   o n
Port   *Sogeri*   D'Entrecasteaux   S   **Honiara**
Moresby   *Islands*   e a   *Popomanaseu*
Kwikila   *Guadalcanal*   *2331*
10°S
Alotau   *San Cristóbal*

150°E   155°E   160°E

0   100   200   300   Average linear scale : 1 inch ≏ 125 miles   1cm ≏ 80 km   0   100   200   300   400   500
miles   Km

110°E   115°E   120°E   125°E

Java *Bali* Denpasar *Lombok* Mataram *Sumbawa Besar* Raba Ruteng Maumere *Solor* *Alor* Dili
·3726 ·1400 ·2460 Ende *Flores* ·2960 Atambua
Sumbawa Waingapu ·2427 Besikama *Timor*

I N D O N E S I A *Sawu*

Waikabubak *Sawu Sea*

Sumba ·1175 Kupang

Sawu *Roti*

· Cartier

10°S

Cape Bougainville *Lo*

Bonaparte Archipelago *Ka*

I N D I A N *Theda*

Kuri Bay *Kimbe*

15°S *Mount Hann* ·776 *Pla*

Collier Bay Panter Downs *Ka*

Cape Lévêque Beverley Springs *Gib River*

O C E A N Lombardina Oobagooma Mount House *Tableta*

Beagle Bay ·927 *Mt. Broome* ·836 Mount Ord

Coulomb Point *Dampier Land* Derby Kimberley Downs Glenroy

King Leopold Ranges

Broome Roebuck Plains Camballin

Fitzroy Fitzroy Crossing

Myroodah *Mount Huxley* ·522 *Marga*

Dampier Downs Nerrima *River*

Lagrange ·247 Christmas Creek *Bohe*

Frazier Downs *Down*

Anna Plains

Eighty Mile Beach

20°S *Great Sandy Desert* *Mount* ·4 *Elliott*

Wallal Downs

Port Hedland Goldsworthy

Barrow Island Dampier Roebourne Shay Gap

Whim Creek Kangan Yarrie

Cooya Pooya *Yule* Marble Bar Warrawagine

Bamboo Creek

Percival Lakes

North West Cape Onslow Yarraloola **W E S T E R N**

Exmouth Pannawonica Millstream Mount Florance Nullagine

Mount Minnie Wittenoom *Lake Dora* *Lake Auld*

Learmonth *Hamersley* *Tabletop* ·427

Yanrey Tom Price *Fortescue* *Lake Blanche*

Mount Tom Price ·1073 Talawana **A U S**

Uaroo Wyloo *Range* ·1251

Winning *Mount Palgrave* ·704 Ashburton Downs Paraburdoo *Mount Meharry* ·1053 *Mount Newman*

Tropic of Capricorn Ullawarra *Lake Disappointment*

Lyndon *Ashburton* Newman *Gibson Desert*

Minnie Creek Turee Creek Bulloo Downs

Cape Cuvier *Lake McLeod* *Lyons* Augustus Mount Vernon

Mount Augustus ·1105 *Waldburg Range* Kumarina **A U S T R A L I**

25°S Carnarvon Three Rivers

Gascoyne Junction Dairy Creek *Gascoyne* Milgun *Mount Essendon* ·906 *Carnarvon Range* Glenayle

Cape Inscription *Shark Bay* Mount Seabrook Peak Hill Neds Creek ·738 Granite Peak

·552 *Lake Nabberu*

Denham Byro Carnegie

Useless Loop ·732 *Mount Hale* Karalundi *Lake Carnegie* Warburton

Tamala Mileura Wiluna Yelma *Ta*

Hamelin Pool Curbur Meekatharra Wonganoo

Kalli

Wannoo ·530 Big Bell Cue Tuckanarra Gidgee

Yallalong Murgoo Sandstone Booylgoo Springs

Kalbarri Billabalon ·594 *Gre*

110°E   115°E   120°E   125°E

This map shows 1/60 of the earth's surface. Area scale : 1 ☐ inch on the map ≈ 15,000 ☐ miles on the ground 1 ☐ cm on the map ≈ 6000 ☐ km on the ground

a b c d e f g h i j k l m

70

130°E | 135°E | 140°E | 145°E

eti Islands

PAPUA NEW GUINEA

Gulf of Papua

A R A F U R A   S E A

Daru

Torres Strait

Coral

10°S

Badu   Moa

Sea

Prince of Wales Island

Cape York

Bamaga

183.

Cape Van Diemen

Cape Croker

Wessel Islands

Murgenella

Andoom

Weipa

Iron Range

555.

Lockhart River

Wenlock

Bathurst Island

Melville Island

Van Diemen Gulf

Maningrida

Milingimbi

Galiwinku

Nhulunbuy

Yirrkala   *Cape Arnhem*

Aurukun

Beagle Gulf

Belyuen   Darwin

Noonamah

Oenpelli

Mount Howship

385.

Mudginbarry

Camburinga

Great Dividing

Coen

506.

Cape

Princess Charlotte Bay

Darwin River

Batchelor

Adelaide River

El Sherana

366.

Camburinga

Arnhem Land

Umbakumba

Groote Eylandt

York

640.

Anson Bay

Burrundie

Pine Creek

Angurugu

Rose River

Strathmay

.213

Breeza Plains

Cape Flattery

Joseph Bonaparte Gulf

Port Keats

Daly River

Tipperary

.213

Bamyili

Katherine

Roper Bar

Ngukurr

Roper

Limmen Bight

Edward River

Mitchell River

Peninsula

Cooktown

Laura

15°S

Ninbing

Wyndham

Willeroo

Elsey

Mataranka

Larrimah

Nathan River

Bing Bong

Sir Edward Pellew Group

366.

Strathleven

Dunbar

Rossville

1375.

Daintree

Victoria

Timber Creek

Delamere

.227

Nutwood Downs

Borroloola

Inkerman

Galbraith

Mossman

Gamboola

Lake Argyle

Victoria River Downs

Daly Waters

Hidden Valley

O.T. Downs

McArthur

103.

Robinson River

Mornington

.152

Wellesley Islands

Bentinck

Delta Downs

Vanrook

Walsh

Mareeba

Cairns

Chillagoe

Almaden

Atherton

1611.

Turkey Creek

Top Springs

Mallapunyah

Calvert Hills

Wollogorang

Westmoreland

Karumba

Maggieville

Miranda Downs

Abingdon Downs

Earl Freres

Innisfail

Silkwood

Ord River

Inverway

Wave Hill

Newcastle Waters

.251

Elliott

Lake Woods

Creswell Downs

Benmara

Corinda

Doomadgee

Burketown

Floraville

Normanton

Blackbull

Croydon

Gilbert River

Georgetown

Einasleigh

Forsayth

742.

Conjuboy

Tully

Ingham

Silkwood

Barkly Tableland

.288

Hooker Creek

Renner Springs

Brunette Downs

.347

291.

Lawn Hill

Gregory Downs

Augustus Downs

Donors Hill

Iffley

Esmeralda

Claraville

.194

Robinhood

Savannah Downs

Greenvale

Lyndhurst

Sturt Creek

Gordon Downs

NORTHERN

Tanami

Alexandria

Alroy Downs

Frewena

Riversleigh

.200

Herbert Vale

Kamileroi

Thorntonia

Canobie

Maryvale

Tennant Creek

436.

240.

Wonarah

Camooweal

Gunpowder

Kajabbi

Millungera

Mount Sturgeon

732.

Lolworth

Mount Stewart

1067.

20°S

Nicholson

T E R R I T O R Y

Desert

.464

Mount Davidson

Wauchope

Kurundi

Avon Downs

Yelvertoft

Mount Isa

Cloncurry

Dalgonally

Boonderoo

Flinders

Pentland

Torrens Creek

Lake White

Hatches Creek

Elkedra

Warrabri

Austral Downs

Lake Nash

Annitowa

Mary Kathleen

Duchess

McKinlay

Julia Creek

Maxwelton

Richmond

Hughenden

Lake Buchanan

Willowra

Barrow Creek

Argadargada

.339

Kynuna

Whitewood

Aberfoyle

Lake Mackay

.808

Yuendumu

Tea Tree

Utopia

Oratippra

Woodgreen

Urandangi

Carandotta

380.

Dajarra

Chatsworth

Corfield

Winton

Lerida

Corinda

Lake Galilee

Eastmere

QUEENSLAND

Aileron

1067.

Mount Wedge

Harts Range

Indiana

Lucy Creek

Marqua

Linda Downs

Roxborough Downs

Toolebuc

Middleton

Chorregon

Morella

Muttaburra

Aramac

Lake Macdonald

Mount Liebig

1524.

Haast Bluff

Hamilton Downs

.1167

Glenormiston

Boulia

392.

Diamantina

Longreach

Barcaldine

R A L I A

Lake Neale

.901

Mount Cockburn

1138.

Glen Helen

Alice Springs

Ringwood

Santa Teresa

Areyonga

Deep Well

.236

Marion Downs

Vergemont

Arrilalah

Isisford

Yalleroi

Blackall

Simpson

Coorabulka

Breadalbane

Bedourie

Diamantina Lakes

Davenport Downs

Connemara

Stonehenge

Emmet

.594

Petermann Range

Docker River

Henbury

Angas Downs

Finke

Engoordina

Glengyle

Lake Machattie

Monkira

Palparra

Jundah

Yaraka

25°S

Curtin Springs

867.

Ayers Rock

Erldunda

Finke

New Crown

Desert

304.

Galway Downs

Retreat

Listowel Downs

Mount Davies

1058.

Kulgera

Mulga Park

Amata

Tieyon

Abminga

Birdsville

Durrie

Betoota

Tonbar

Windorah

Lynwood

Adavale

.329

Musgrave Ranges

1439.

Ernabella

De Rose Hill

Pedirka

Alton Downs

Pandie Pandie

Cadelga

Lake Yamma Yamma

.300

Thylungra

Quilpie

316.

Cheepie

Westgate

Charleville

S O U T H   A U S T R A L I A

917.

Everard Park

Fregon

Granite Downs

Welbourn Hill

Alberga

Oodnadatta

Goyder Lagoon

Clifton Hills

Cordillo Downs

120.

Eromanga

Toompine

Wyandra

Coongola

oria Desert

Mount Dutton

Cowarie

Lake Eyre

Warburton

Innamincka

Cooper Creek

Tobermory

Nockatunga

Thargomindah

130°E | 135°E | 140°E | 145°E

n o p q r s t u v w x y z

77

0   100   200   300 miles

Average linear scale : 1 inch ≈ 125 miles   1cm ≈ 80 km

0   100   200   300   400   500 Km

74

145°E   150°E   155°E   160°E

Honiara
Guadalcanal
▲2331

**SOLOMON
ISLAND**

Owen
1925
Mount
Suckling
3676
**Port
Moresby**
Kwikila
Baniara
*D'Entrecasteaux
Islands*
3129
Robinson
River
Normanby
10°S
M
Alotau
Louisiade Archipelago
PAPUA NEW GUINEA

e
S O L O M O N

l

S E A

*Renne
Isla*

Cape
York

183

Iron
Range
Lockhart
River
Wenlock

Cape

Coen
506
*Princess
Charlotte*
York
640
Breeza
Plains
Cape
Flattery
15°S
Peninsula
366
Cooktown
Laura
Strathleven
Rossville
1375
Daintree
Mitchell
Gamboola
Mossman
Walsh
Mareeba
Cairns
Chillagoe
Atherton
*Bartle
Frere*
1611
Innisfail
Almaden
Silkwood
Abingdon
Downs
Tully
Gilbert
River
Mount
Surprise
Georgetown
73
Forsayth
742
Einasleigh
Ingham
Esmeralda
Greenvale
Robinhood
Lyndhurst
Willis Islands
C O R A L

Gregory
Townsville
Ayr
Mount Elliot
1234
Bowen
S E A
20°S
Mount
Sturgeon
732
Lolworth
*Mount
Stewart*
1076
Charters
Towers
Proserpine
*Îles
Chesterfield*
(France)
Richmond
Torrens
Creek
Pentland
Collinsville
*Mount
Dairymple*
1259
Hughenden
Suttor
Finch
Hatton
Mackay
Whitewood
*Lake
Buchanan*
Mount
Coolon
Sarina
Aberfoyle
Mount
Douglas
Nebo
Tangorin
*Lake
Galilee*
Carmila
Winton
Chorregon
Eastmere
Blair
Athol
Peak
Downs
St. Lawrence
Muttaburra
Clermont
Marlborough
Morella
Aramac
Capella
Fitzroy
Yeppoon
Cato
Longreach
Barcaldine
Alpha
Emerald
Rockhampton
Thomson
Arrilalah
Bogantungan
Quaringa
Mount Morgan
P
Q U E E N S L A N D
Gladstone
Isisford
Barcoo
Yalleroi
Springsure
Wowan
Stonehenge
Blackall
594
Rolleston
Baralaba
Biloela
Yaraka
Emmet
Tambo
Consuelo Peak
1219
806
Theodore
Monto
Miriam Vale
25°S
Retreat
Listowel
Downs
Bundaberg
*Hervey
Bay*
Childers
Windorah
Carnarvon Ra
Taroom
Mundubbera
*Fraser
Island*
A U S T R A L I A
Lynwood
Augathella
Injune
Gayndah
Maryborough
Adavale
329
Wandoan
Murgon
Gympie
Thylungra
Charleville
Morven
Mitchell
Kingaroy
Nambour
Maroochydore
Eromanga
Westgate
Miles
Yarraman
*Moreton
Island*
Quilpie
376
Roma
Chinchilla
410
Cheepie
Dalby
Caboolture
Tobermory
Wyandra
Albany
Downs
Surat
Toowoomba
Esk
Brisbane
Thargomindah
Coongoola
Glenmorgan
Moonie
Gatton
Ipswich
Gold Coast
Bulloo
Downs
Cunnamulla
Bollon
Westmar
Clifton
Warwick
Murwillumbah
Eulo
St. George
Nindigully
Inglewood
Stanthorpe
Dirranbandi
Talwood
Goondiwindi
Casino
Lismore
Hebel
Thallon
145°E
150°E
155°E
160°E

This map shows 1/60 of the earth's surface.   Area scale : 1 □ inch on the map ≙ 15,000 □ miles on the ground   1 □ cm on the map ≙ 6000 □ km on the ground

165°E   170°E   175°E   180°

Kirakira
San Cristobal

Santa Cruz
Island

n

e

Banks
Islands

s

*Espíritu
Santo*   *1879*

i

*New
Hebrides*

Malekula

a

15°S

VANUATU

Efate

o **Vila**

*Vanua
Levu*
Lambasa
o *1032*

FIJI   *Koro
Sea*

o
Tavua
Nandi o *Mount Victoria
Viti Levu   *1324*
Singatoka o   **Suva**

Erromango

20°S

1626

New
Caledonia
(France)   Houailu
o
Bourail
o

*Loyalty
Islands*
(France)

Nouméa
o

Tropic of Capricorn

C   I   F   I   C

25°S

C   E   A   N

0   100   200   300
miles

Average linear scale : 1 inch ≃ 125 miles   1 cm ≃ 80 km

0   100   200   300   400   500
Km

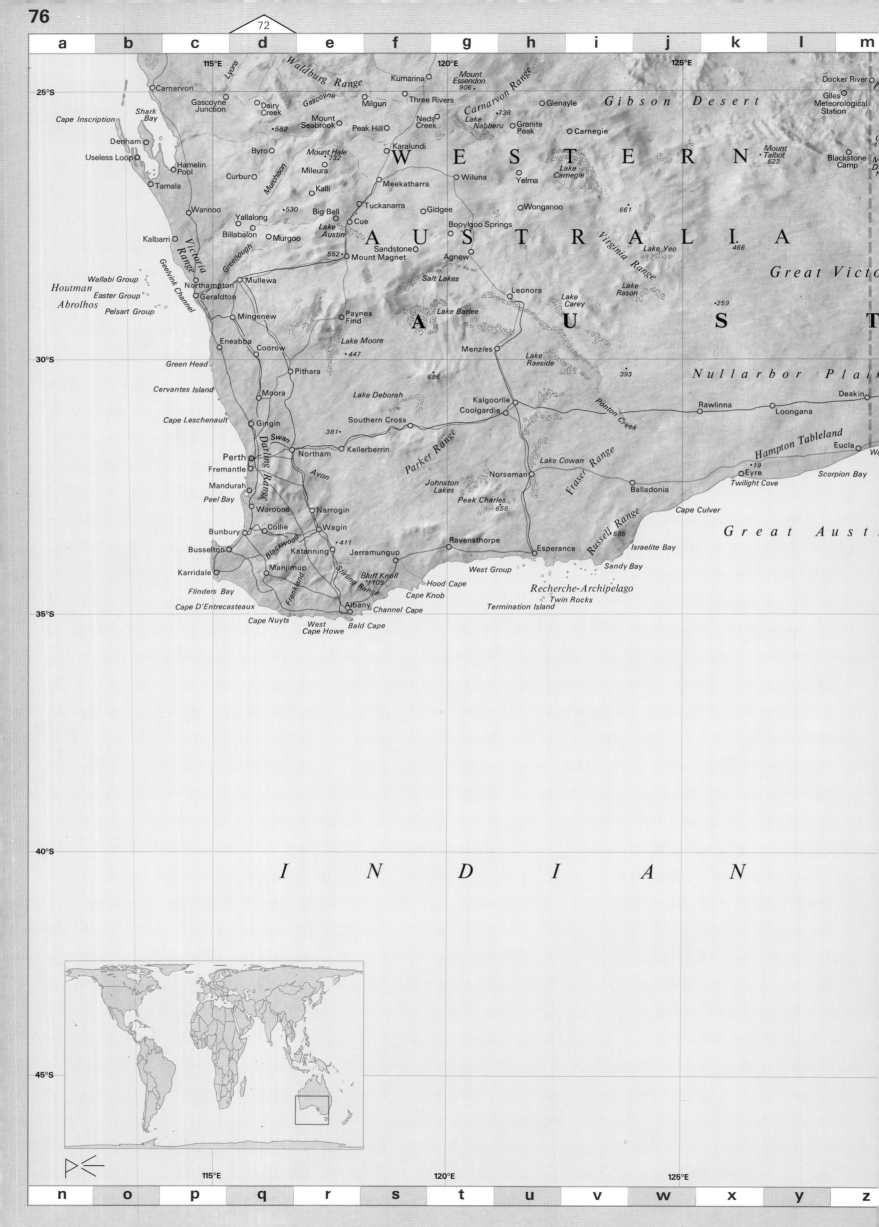

Cape Inscription

Carnarvon

Gascoyne
Junction

Dairy
Creek

Gascoyne

Milgun

Kumarina

Three Rivers

*Mount
Essendon
906*

Carnarvon Range

Glenayle

Gibson Desert

Docker River

Giles
Meteorological
Station

*Shark
Bay*

582

Mount
Seabrook

Peak Hill

Neds
Creek

*Lake
Nabberu*

738

Granite
Peak

Carnegie

Denham

Byro

*Mount Hale
732*

Mileura

Karalundi

Wiluna

Yelma

*Lake
Carnegie*

W　E　S　T　E　R　N

Blackstone
Camp

*Mount
Talbot
623*

Useless Loop

Hamelin
Pool

Curbur

Kalli

Meekatharra

Gidgee

Wonganoo

661

Tamala

Wannoo

Yallalong

530

Big Bell

Tuckanarra

Gidgee

A　U　S　T　R　A　L　I　A

Kalbarri

Billabalon

Murgoo

*Lake
Austin*

Cue

Booylgoo Springs

Virginia Range

Lake Yeo

466

Sandstone

552

Mount Magnet

Agnew

*Lake
Carey*

Great Victo

*Victoria
Range*

Northampton

Mullewa

Greenough

Salt Lakes

Leonora

*Lake
Rason*

S

T

Houtman

Wallabi Group

Geraldton

Mingenew

Paynes
Find

Lake Barlee

A　U　S

259

Great Victo

Easter Group

Abrolhos

Pelsart Group

Geelvink Channel

Eneabba

Coorow

Lake Moore

447

Menzies

*Lake
Raeside*

393

Nullarbor Plai

Green Head

30°S

Pithara

686

Cervantes Island

Moora

Lake Deborah

Kalgoorlie

Coolgardie

Ponton Creek

Rawlinna

Loongana

Deakin

Cape Leschenault

Gingin

Southern Cross

381

Hampton Tableland

Eucla

Swan

Northam

Kellerberrin

Parker Range

Darling Range

Avon

Norseman

Lake Cowan

Fraser Range

Balladonia

19

Eyre

Twilight Cove

Scorpion Bay

Perth

Fremantle

Mandurah

Johnston
Lakes

*Peak Charles
658*

Cape Culver

Peel Bay

Waroona

Narrogin

*Russell Range
585*

Great Aust

Bunbury

Collie

Wagin

Ravensthorpe

Esperance

Israelite Bay

Busselton

Blackwood

Katanning

411

Jerramungup

West Group

Sandy Bay

Karridale

Manjimup

Stirling Range

*Bluff Knoll
1109*

Hood Cape

Recherche-Archipelago

Twin Rocks

Flinders Bay

Frankland

Cape Knob

Termination Island

Cape D'Entrecasteaux

Albany

Channel Cape

Cape Nuyts

*West
Cape Howe*

Bald Cape

I　N　D　I　A　N

25°S

115°E

120°E

125°E

35°S

40°S

45°S

115°E

120°E

125°E

This map shows 1/60 of the earth's surface. Area scale: 1 ☐ inch on the map ≈ 15,000 ☐ miles on the ground. 1 ☐ cm on the map ≈ 6000 ☐ km on the ground

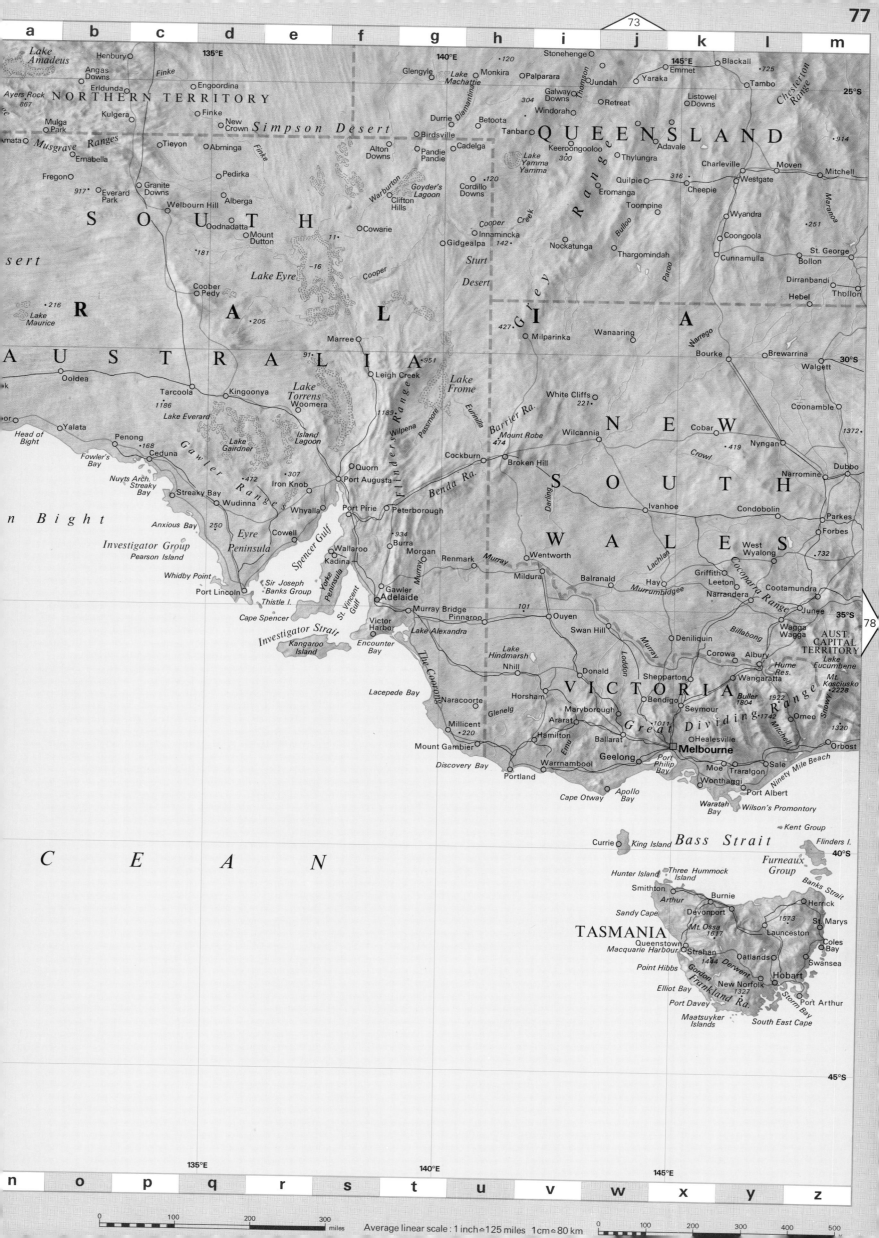

75

165°E   170°E   175°E   180°E

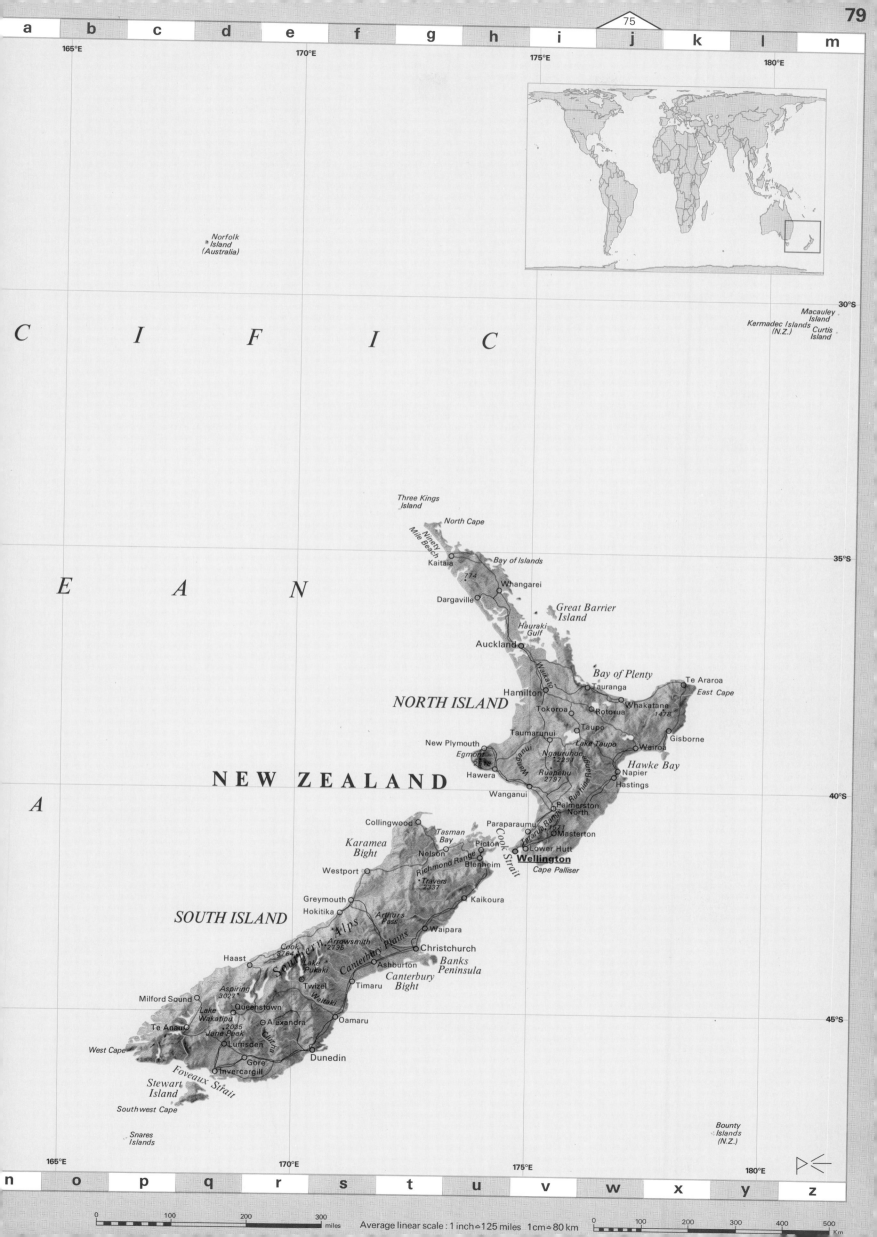

30°S

C   I   **F**   I   **C**

Norfolk
*Island
(Australia)*

Macauley
Island
Kermadec Islands   Curtis
(N.Z.)   Island

E   **A**   **N**

*Three Kings
Island*

35°S

North Cape

Ninety
Mile Beach
Kaitaia   *Bay of Islands*
774   Whangarei
Dargaville   *Great Barrier
Island*
*Hauraki
Gulf*
Auckland

Waikato   *Bay of Plenty*   Te Araroa
Hamilton   Tauranga   *East Cape*
NORTH ISLAND   Tokoroa   Rotorua Whakatane
Taupo   1478
Taumarunui   Gisborne
New Plymouth   *Lake Taupo*   Wairoa
Egmont   Ngauruhoe
518   2291   *Hawke Bay*
Hawera   Ruapehu   Napier
2797
NEW ZEALAND   Hastings
Wanganui
40°S

A

Wellington

Palmerston
North
Collingwood   Paraparaumu   Tararua Range
*Tasman   1571   Masterton
Bay*   Picton   Lower Hutt
*Karamea   Nelson   **Wellington**
Bight*   Richmond Range   Blenheim *Cape Palliser*
Westport
*Travers
2337*
Greymouth   Kaikoura
Hokitika
Arthur's
SOUTH ISLAND   Pass
Southern Alps   Waipara
Cook   Arrowsmith   Christchurch
3764   2795   *Canterbury Plains*
Haast   Lake   Ashburton   *Banks
Pukaki   Peninsula*
Aspiring   *Canterbury
3027   Twizel   Timaru   Bight*
Milford Sound   Waitaki
Lake
Wakatipu   Queenstown
Te Anau   Jane Peak   Oamaru
2035   Alexandra
45°S
West Cape   Lumsden
Clutha
Gore
Invercargill   Dunedin
Foveaux Strait

*Stewart
Island*

Southwest Cape

Bounty
Islands
(N.Z.)

*Snares
Islands*

165°E   170°E   175°E   180°E

0   100   200   300 miles   Average linear scale : 1 inch≏125 miles 1cm≏80 km   0   100   200   300   400   500 Km

60°S

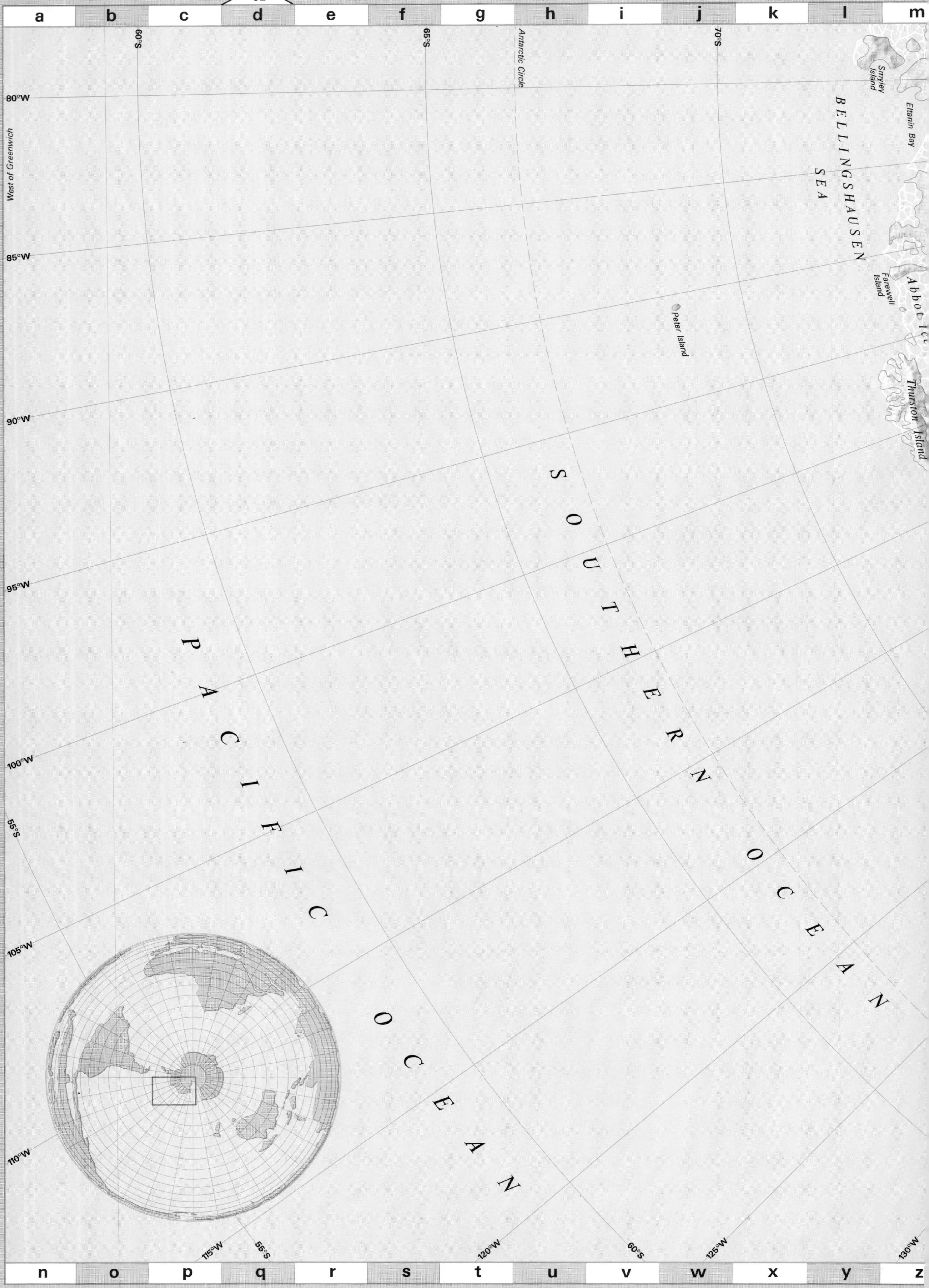

65°S

70°S

80°W

85°W

90°W

95°W

100°W

105°W

110°W

115°W

West of Greenwich

Antarctic Circle

Antarctic Circle

Smyley Island

Eltanin Bay

B E L L I N G S H A U S E N

S E A

Abbot Ice

Thurston Island

Farewell Island

Peter Island

S O U T H E R N   O C E A N

P A C I F I C

O C E A N

120°W

55°S

60°S

125°W

130°W

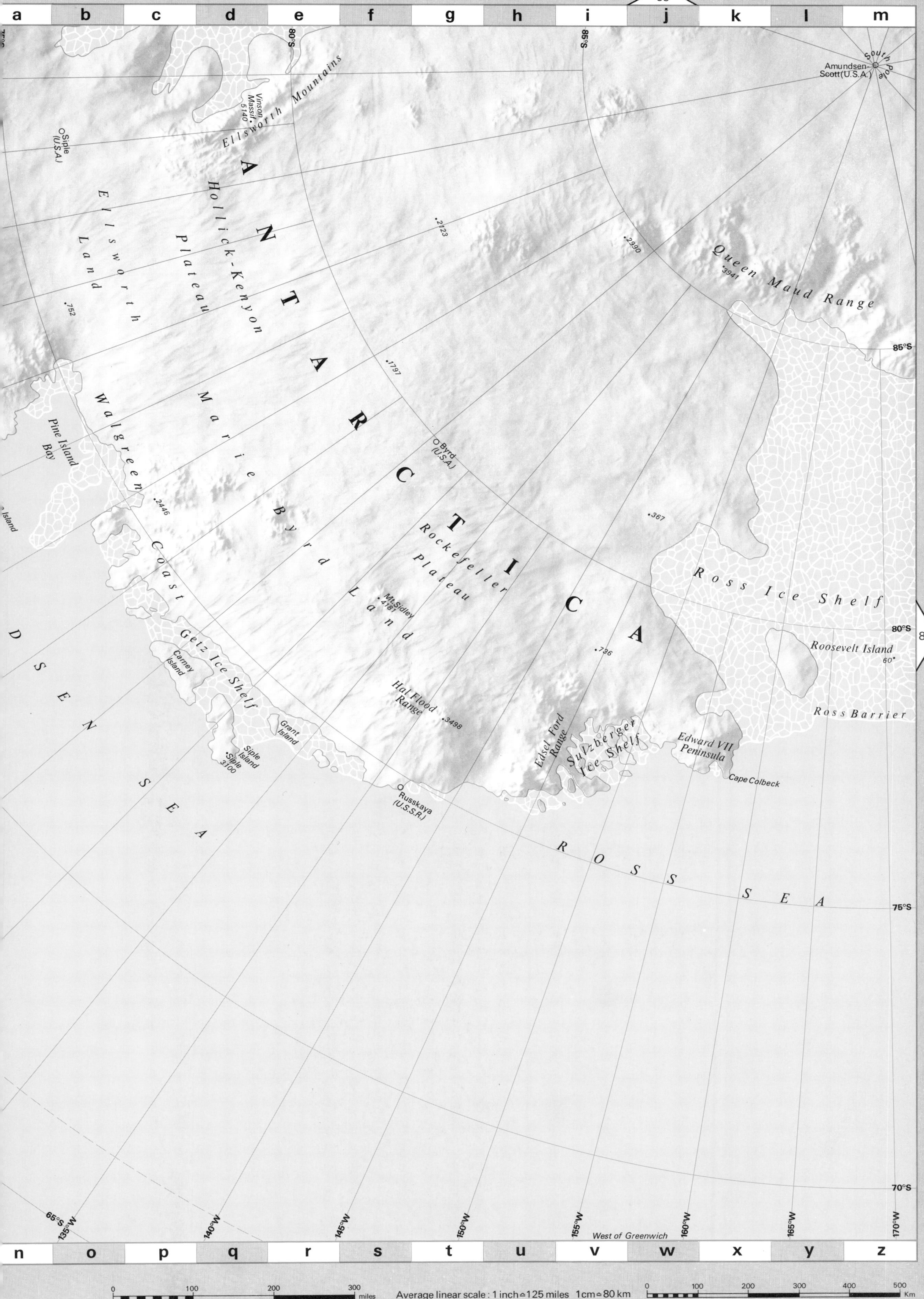

83

South Pole

Amundsen-Scott (U.S.A.)

○ Siple
(U.S.A.)

*Vinson Massif.
5140*

Ellsworth Mountains

A

Queen Maud Range
.3941

·2123

·2390

85°S

80°S

85°S

N

Ellsworth Land

Hollick-Kenyon Plateau

·752

·1797

T

·367

A

R

○ Byrd
(U.S.A.)

Marie

Walgreen Coast

Pine Island
Bay

·2446

C

Rockefeller Plateau

Byrd Land

T

Ross Ice Shelf

85°S

·736

80°S

86

Island

Getz Ice Shelf

Carney
Island

I

Mt. Sidley
·4181

Hal Flood Range
·3498

C

Roosevelt Island
60·

A

Ross Barrier

D

Grant
Island

Siple
Island
·Siple
3100

Edsel Ford
Range

*Sulzberger
Ice Shelf*

Edward VII
Peninsula

Cape Colbeck

S

○ Russkaya
(U.S.S.R.)

R

O

E

S

N

S

S

E

A

S

75°S

E

A

70°S

65°S
W·65·
140°W

145°W

150°W

155°W

West of Greenwich

160°W

165°W

170°W

0   100   200   300 miles   Average linear scale : 1 inch ≙ 125 miles 1 cm ≙ 80 km   0   100   200   300   400   500 Km

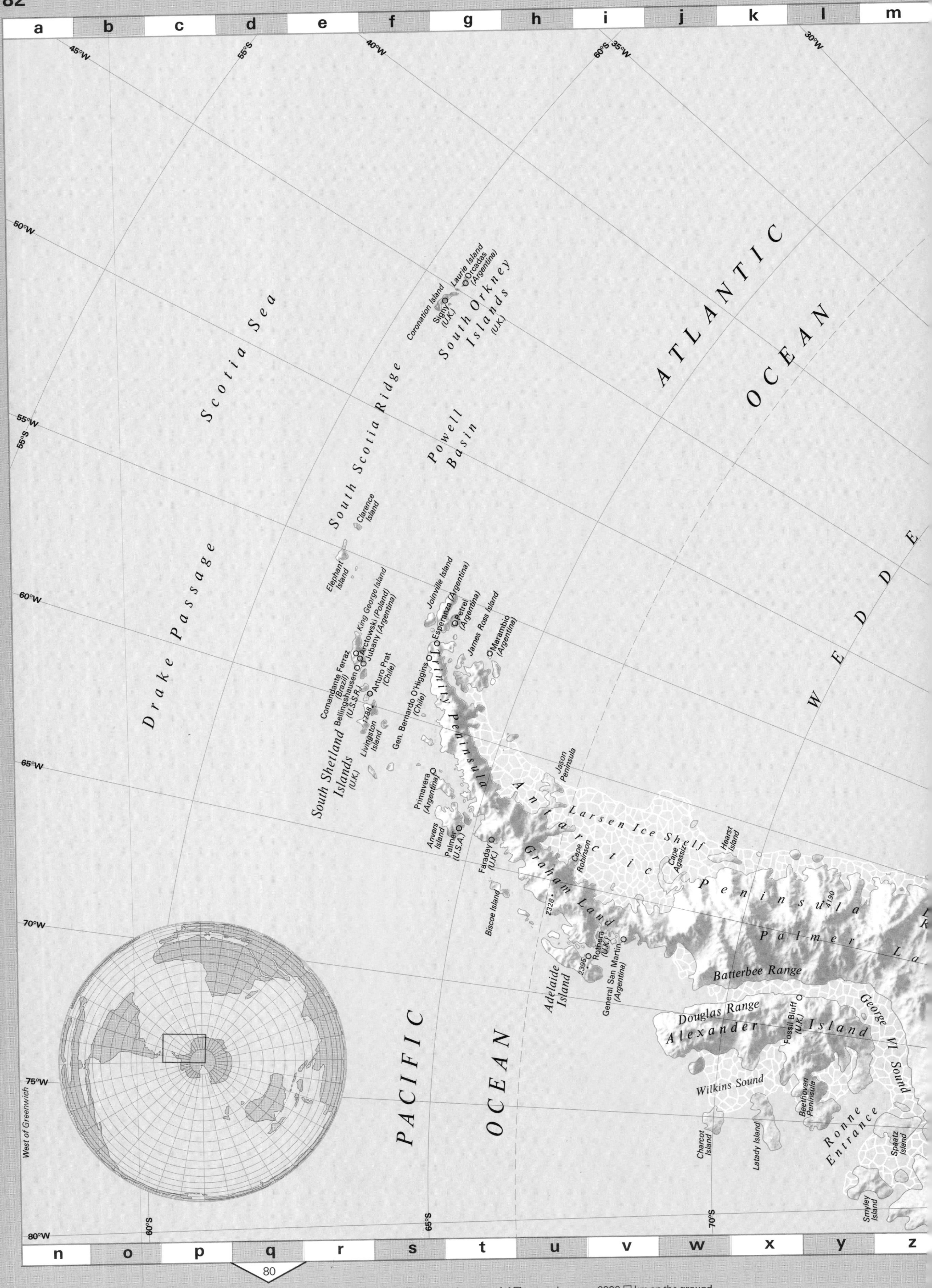

a b c d e f g h i j k l m

45°W

50°W

55°W

55°S

60°W

65°W

70°W

75°W

80°W

30°W

35°W

40°W

40°S

50°S

55°S

60°S

65°S

70°S

60°W

PACIFIC

OCEAN

ATLANTIC

OCEAN

Scotia Sea

Drake Passage

South Scotia Ridge

Powell Basin

W E D D E

South Orkney
Islands
(U.K.)

Coronation Island

Laurie Island

Signy
(U.K.)

Orcadas
(Argentina)

Clarence
Island

Elephant
Island

King George Island

Comandante Ferraz
(Brazil)

Bellingshausen
(U.S.S.R.)

Arctowski (Poland)

Jubany (Argentina)

Arturo Prat
(Chile)

Livingston
Island

1798

Gen. Bernardo O'Higgins
(Chile)

Joinville Island

Esperanza (Argentina)

Petrel
(Argentina)

James Ross Island

Marambio
(Argentina)

Trinity Peninsula

Jason
Peninsula

Larsen Ice Shelf

Hearst
Island

Cape
Robinson

Cape
Agassiz

Primavera
(Argentina)

Anvers
Island

Palmer
(U.S.A.)

Faraday
(U.K.)

Graham Land

Antarctic

Peninsula

Palmer La

4190

2328

Biscoe Island

Rothera
(U.K.)

2396

General San Martin
(Argentina)

Batterbee Range

Adelaide
Island

Douglas Range

George VI Sound

Alexander Island

Fossil Bluff
(U.K.)

Wilkins Sound

Beethoven
Peninsula

Charcot
Island

Latady Island

Ronne
Entrance

Spaatz
Island

Smyley
Island

South Shetland
Islands
(U.K.)

West of Greenwich

n o p q r s t u v w x y z

80

This map shows 1/60 of the earth's surface. Area scale : 1 □ inch on the map ≃ 15,000 □ miles on the ground 1 □ cm on the map ≃ 6000 □ km on the ground

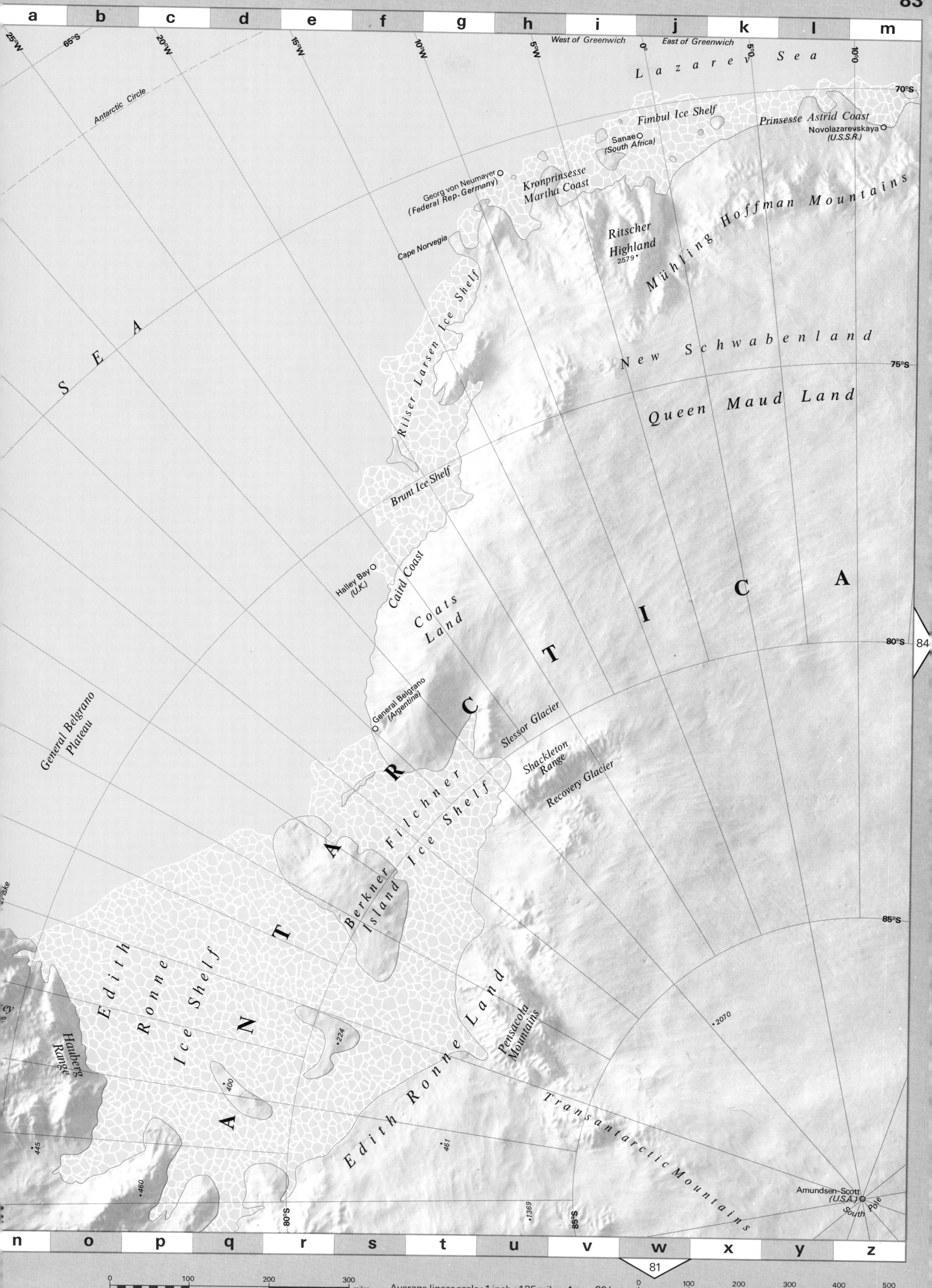

a b c d e f g h i j k l m

L a z a r e v   S e a

25°W 65°S 20°W 15°W 10°W 5°W West of Greenwich East of Greenwich 5°0 10°0 70°S

Antarctic Circle

Fimbul Ice Shelf
Prinsesse Astrid Coast
Sanae○ (South Africa)
Novolazarevskaya○ (U.S.S.R.)

Georg von Neumayer○ (Federal Rep. Germany)
Kronprinsesse Martha Coast

Mühling Hoffman Mountains

Ritscher Highland 2579

Cape Norvegia

New Schwabenland 75°S

Riiser Larsen Ice Shelf

Queen Maud Land

S E A

Brunt Ice Shelf

Caird Coast

Halley Bay ○ (U.K.)

Coats Land

A N T A R C T I C A

80°S 84

General Belgrano Plateau

General Belgrano ○ (Argentina)

Slessor Glacier

Shackleton Range

Recovery Glacier

Filchner

Berkner Island Ice Shelf

85°S

Edith Ronne Ice Shelf

Hauberg Range

Pensacola Mountains

•224

Edith Ronne Land

•2070

Transantarctic Mountains

•400

85°S

•445

•461

•460

•1369

Amundsen-Scott (U.S.A.)
South Pole

80°S

n o p q r s t u v w x y z

81

0 100 200 300 miles   Average linear scale : 1 inch≈125 miles 1cm≈80 km   0 100 200 300 400 500 Km

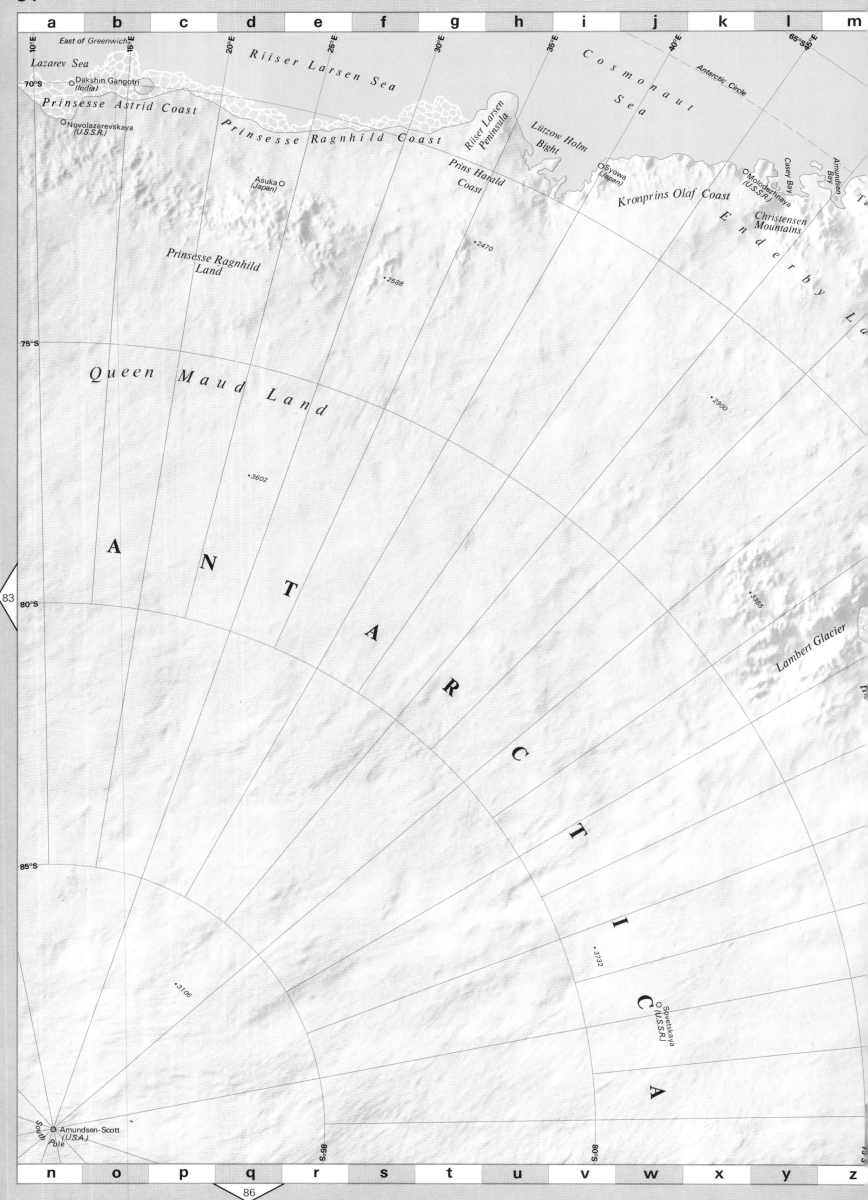

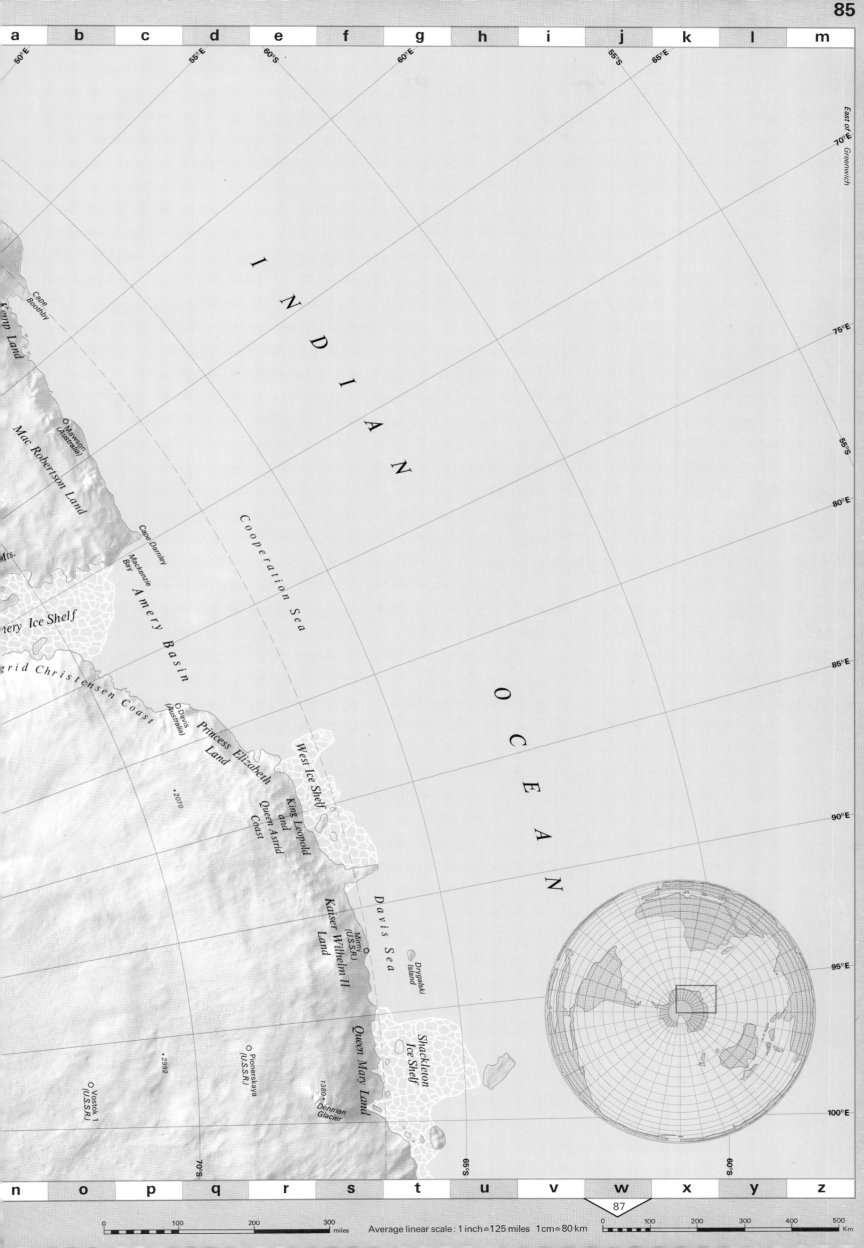

50°E   55°E   60°S   60°E   55°S   65°S

East of Greenwich

70°E

75°E

I N D I A N

Cape Boothby

Kemp Land

Mac Robertson Land

O Mawson (Australia)

55°E

80°E

C o o p e r a t i o n   S e a

Cape Darnley

Mackenzie Bay

A m e r y   B a s i n

Mts.

Amery Ice Shelf

rid Christensen Coast

85°E

O C E A N

Princess Elizabeth Land

O Davis (Australia)

West Ice Shelf

King Leopold and Queen Astrid Coast

•2070

90°E

D a v i s   S e a

Kaiser Wilhelm II Land

O Mirny (U.S.S.R.)

Drygalski Island

95°E

•2992

O Pionerskaya (U.S.S.R.)

Queen Mary Land

Shackleton Ice Shelf

Denman Glacier

1380•

O Vostok 1 (U.S.S.R.)

100°E

70°S   65°S   60°S

0   100   200   300 miles

Average linear scale : 1 inch ≙ 125 miles   1cm ≙ 80 km

0   100   200   300   400   500 Km

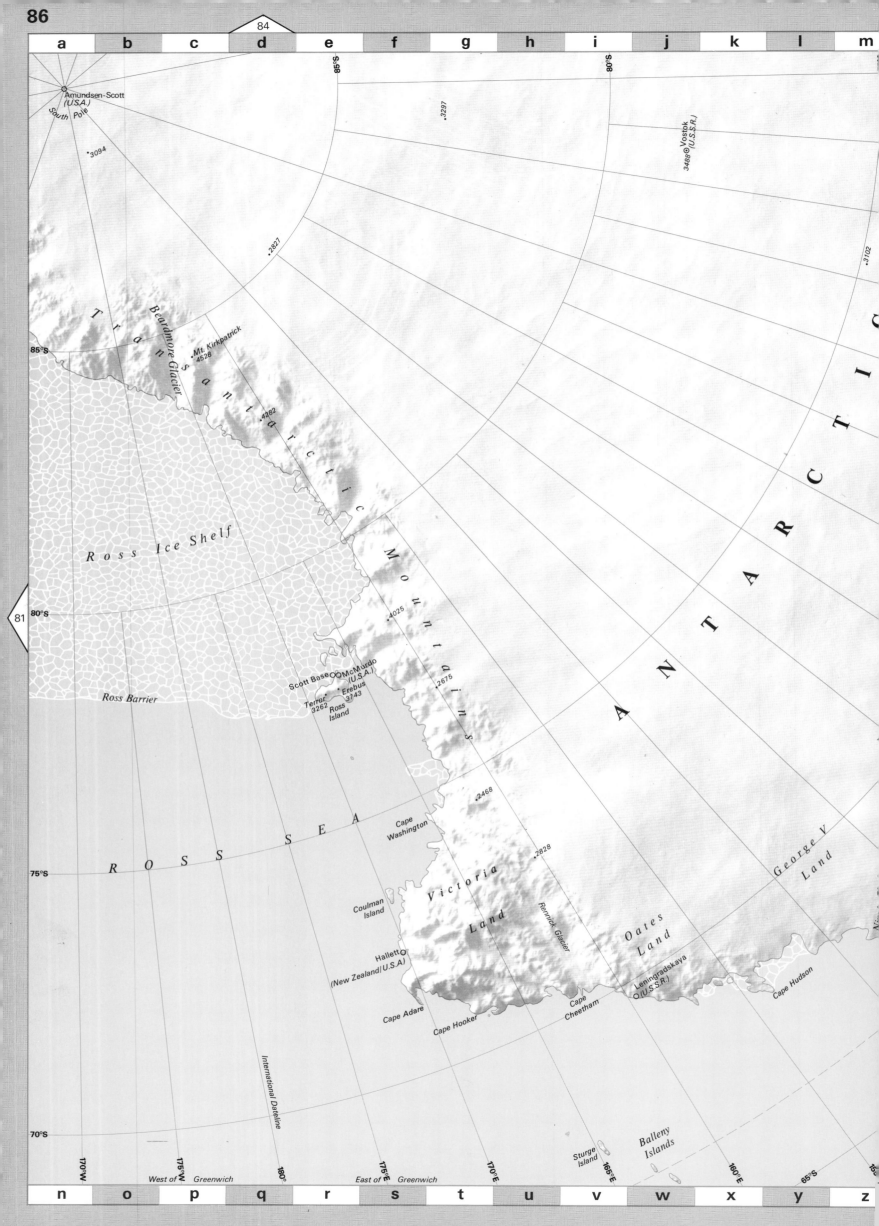

Amundsen-Scott
(U.S.A.)
South Pole

·3094

·3297

Vostok
3488 ⊙ (U.S.S.R.)

·3102

·2827

T r a n s a n t a r c t i c

Beardmore Glacier

·Mt. Kirkpatrick
4528

85°S

·4282

A N T A R C T I C

Ross Ice Shelf

M o u n t a i n s

·4025

80°S

81

·2675

Scott Base ○○McMurdo
(U.S.A.)
Terror · · Erebus
3262   Ross   3743
Island

Ross Barrier

·2468

R O S S   S E A

Cape
Washington

75°S

George V
Land

·2828

V i c t o r i a

Coulman
Island

L a n d

Rennick Glacier

O a t e s
L a n d

Cape Hudson

Hallett ○
(New Zealand/U.S.A.)

Leningradskaya
○ (U.S.S.R.)

Cape Adare

Cape Hooker

Cape
Cheetham

International Dateline

70°S

Sturge
Island

Balleny
Islands

170°W

West of Greenwich

175°W

180°

175°E   East of Greenwich

170°E

165°E

160°E

65°S

| n | o | p | q | r | s | t | u | v | w | x | y | z |

This map shows 1/60 of the earth's surface.   Area scale : 1 ☐ inch on the map ≏ 15,000 ☐ miles on the ground   1 ☐ cm on the map ≏ 6000 ☐ km on the ground

85

100°E

East of Greenwich

105°E

Antarctic Circle

Knox Coast

110°E

Casey O
(Australia)

Cape Poinsett

Budd Coast

115°E

Sabrina Coast

.2868

Banzare Coast

Wilkes Land

Voyeykov
Ice Shelf

120°E

S O U T H E R N   O C E A N

.400

Porpoise Bay

Terre Adélie

55°S

125°E

Dumont-d'Urville
Of (France)

Dumont d'Urville Sea

Cape
Gray

.South Magnetic Pole
(1987)

130°E

150°E

145°E
80°S

140°E

55°S

135°E

0   100   200   300   miles

Average linear scale : 1 inch ≃ 125 miles 1cm ≃ 80 km

0   100   200   300   400   500   Km

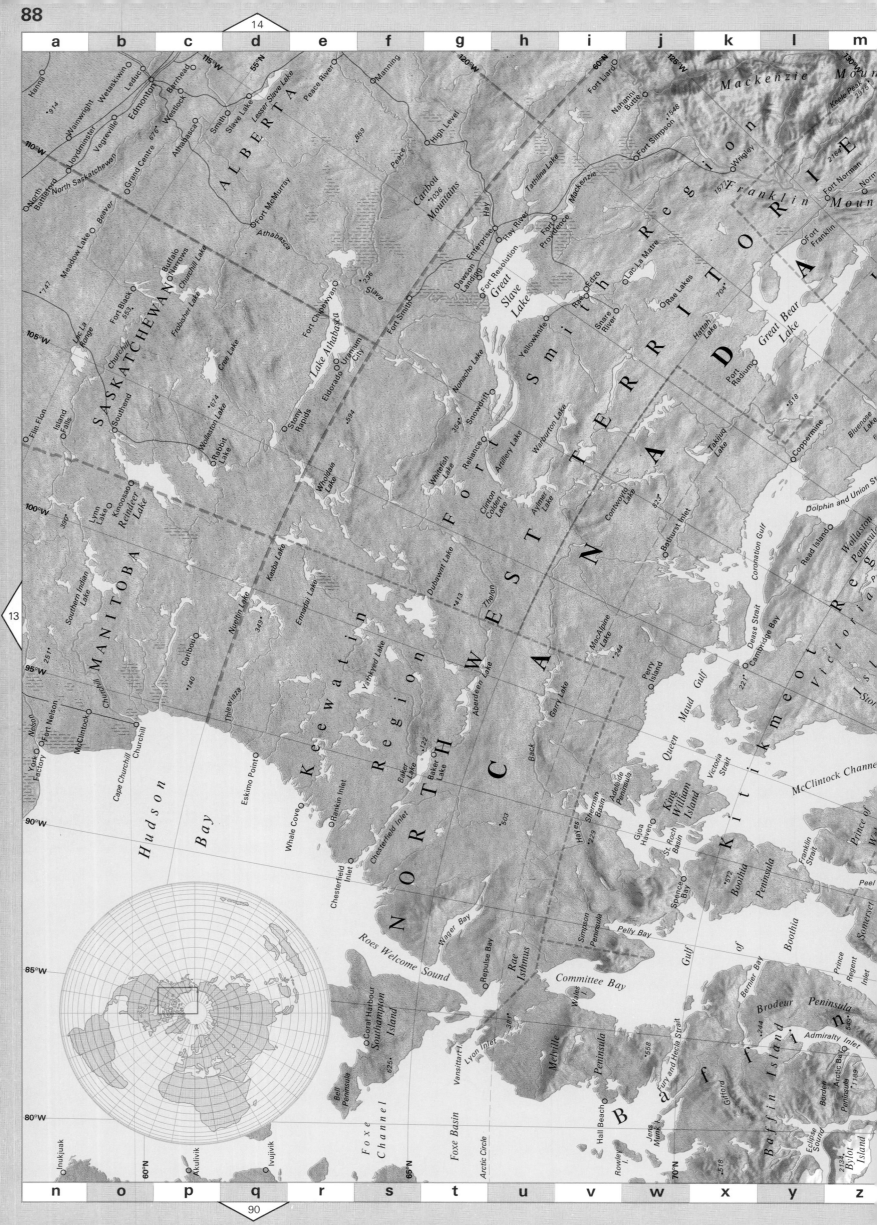

Mackenzie Moun
Keele Peak 2375
Franklin Moun
Fort Norman
Norm
Nahanni Butte 1548
Fort Liard
Fort Simpson
Wrigley 2161
Fort Franklin
115°W 55°N
Hama
914
Wainwright Wetaskiwin Leduc
Lloydminster Vegreville Edmonton Barrhead Westlock Smith Slave Lake Lesser Slave Lake Peace River Manning
110°W Meadow Lake Beaver Grand Centre 676 Athabasca High Level Hay High Level
North Battleford North Saskatchewan Fort McMurray 859 Peace 1036 Caribou Mountains Hay River Fort Providence Fort Resolution Fort Rae Edzo Lac La Martre Rae Lakes Port Radium
Fort Black 503 Churchill Lake Athabasca 236 Slave Fort Smith Great Slave Lake Dawson Landing Enterprise Hay River Yellowknife Stare River 823 Takijuq Lake 518 Great Bear Lake Coppermine
ALBERTA
SASKATCHEWAN
105°W Lac La Ronge Churchill Frobisher Lake Fort Chipewyan Lake Athabasca Eldorado Uranium City 594 Stony Rapids Nonacho Lake 354 Snowdrift Reliance Clinton Colden Lake Artillery Lake Aylmer Lake Warburton Lake Contwoyto Lake Bathurst Inlet Bluenose Dolphin and Union St
Flin Flon Island Falls Southend 674 Wollaston Lake Rabbit Lake Cree Lake Whitefish Lake Fort Smith Region Northwest Canada Territories Read Island Wollaston Peninsula
100°W Lynn Lake Kinoosao Reindeer Lake 390 Wholdaia Lake Kasba Lake Dubawnt Lake 613 Thelon MacAlpine Lake 244 Coronation Gulf Cambridge Bay Dease Strait Victoria
MANITOBA Southern Indian Lake Caribou 140 Nueltin Lake 349 Ennadai Lake Yathkyed Lake Aberdeen Lake Garry Lake Back Perry Island 221 Queen Maud Gulf Adelaide Peninsula King William Island McClintock Channel Prince of
95°W 251 Churchill Thlewiaza Kewatin Region 122 Baker Lake Baker Lake Victoria Strait Gjoa Haven Franklin Strait Peel
13 Nelson Fort Nelson McClintock Churchill Cape Churchill Eskimo Point Whale Cove Rankin Inlet 503 Chesterfield Inlet 229 Sherman Basin St. Roch Basin Spence Bay 572 Boothia Peninsula Boothia
York Factory Hudson Bay Chesterfield Inlet Hayes Simpson Peninsula Pelly Bay Gulf of Boothia
90°W Wager Bay Repulse Bay Rae Isthmus Committee Bay Bernier Bay Prince Regent Somerset
Roes Welcome Sound Coral Harbour Southampton Island 625 Bell Peninsula Vansittart I. Lyon Inlet 381 Melville Peninsula 558 Fury and Hecla Strait 244 Brodeur Peninsula Admiralty Inlet Arctic Bay 169
85°W Inukjuak Akulivik Ivujivik Foxe Channel Foxe Basin Arctic Circle Hall Beach Jens Munk Rowley I. Wales I. Baffin Island Eclipse Sound Bylot Island 2131
80°W BAFFIN 518
60°N 65°N 70°N

This map shows 1/60 of the earth's surface. Area scale : 1 ☐ inch on the map ≈ 15,000 ☐ miles on the ground 1 ☐ cm on the map ≈ 6000 ☐ km on the ground

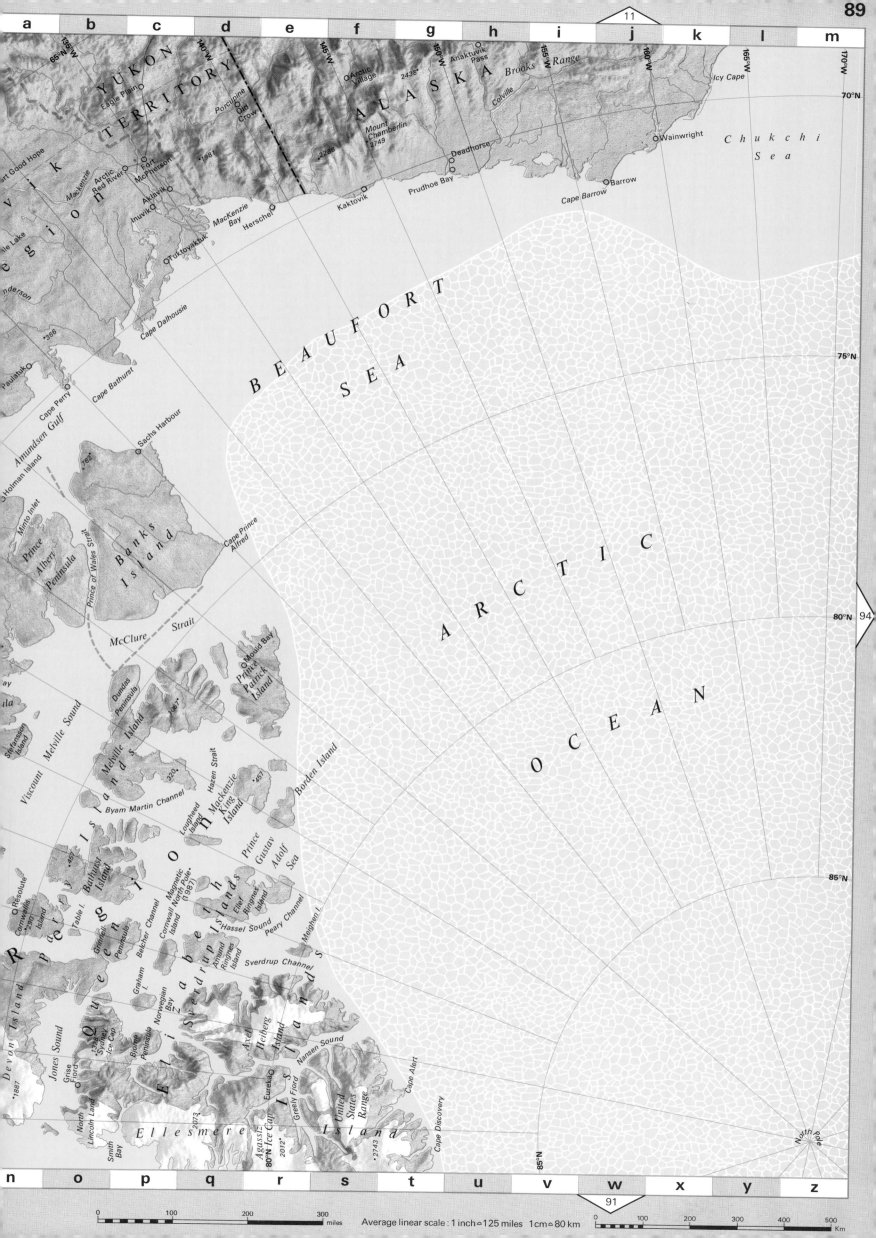

YUKON
TERRITORY

ALASKA

Eagle Plains
Porcupine
Old Crow

Arctic Village

2438

Mount Chamberlin
2749

Anaktuvik Pass

Brooks   Range

Colville

Icy Cape

Chukchi
Sea

70°N

Fort Good Hope

Mackenzie

Arctic Red River

Fort McPherson

Inuvik

Aklavik

·1981

·2286

Deadhorse

Wainwright

Kaktovik

Prudhoe Bay

Cape Barrow

Barrow

MacKenzie Bay

Herschel

Nile Lake

·366

Anderson

Tuktoyaktuk

Cape Dalhousie

BEAUFORT   SEA

Paulatuk

Cape Perry

Cape Bathurst

75°N

Amundsen Gulf

Holman Island

Minto Inlet

762·

Sachs Harbour

Prince Albert Peninsula

Banks Island

Cape Prince Alfred

ARCTIC

80°N 94

Prince of Wales Strait

McClure   Strait

Stefansson Island

Mould Bay

Prince Patrick Island

OCEAN

Dundas Peninsula

Viscount   Melville Sound

Melville Island

·1067

Hazen Strait

320·

·457

Byam Martin Channel

Lougheed Island

MacKenzie King Island

Borden Island

P a r r y   I s l a n d s

Prince Gustav Adolf Sea

85°N

·457

Bathurst Island

Resolute

Cornwallis Island

·2007

Table I.

Belcher Channel

Magnetic North Pole (1987)

Cornwall Island

Ellef Ringnes Island

Amund Ringnes Island

Eglinton

Hassel Sound

Peary Channel

Meighen I.

Q u e e n   E l i z a b e t h   I s l a n d s

Grinnell Peninsula

Graham I.

Norwegian Bay

Sverdrup Channel

Devon Island

Jones Sound

·1887

Grise Fiord

·1394

Sydkap Ice Cap

Bjorne Peninsula

Axel Heiberg Island

Nansen Sound

Cape Alert

Cape Discovery

North Pole

Lincoln Land

Smith Bay

Eureka

Greely Fiord

Agassiz Ice Cap

80°N

2012·

·2073

United States Range

Ellesmere   Island

·2743

85°N

0   100   200   300 miles

Average linear scale : 1 inch ≃ 125 miles   1cm ≃ 80 km

0   100   200   300   400   500 Km

a   b   c   d   e   f   g   h   i   j   k   l   m

80°W

60°N
Hudson
Bay

Oloukjouak

Opouvungnituk

Q U E B E C

U n g a v a   P e n i n s u l a

Akulivik

Ivujivik

•540

Mansel
Island

Salluit

Nottingham
Island

Salisbury
Island
•305

Nabukjuak

Foxe
Channel

Foxe
Peninsula

•411

Cape
Dorset

Prince
Charles
Island

Foxe
Basin

T E R R I T O R I E S

C A N A D A

Arctic Circle

65°W

75°W

Opurtung
•99

Kangiqsujuaq

R   Hudson   Strait

U   n   g   a   v   a

Big
Island

Lake
Harbour

Meta   Incognita
Peninsula

Iqaluit
(Frobisher Bay)

Frobisher
Bay

Hall
•1148

P e n i n s u l a

Kigisa

Koukdjuak
Netilling
Lake

Amadjuak
Lake

B   a   f   f   i   n

Jens Munk
Island

Rowley
Island

Foley
Island

Barnes
Ice Cap
•1750

Rowley

578•

I s l a n d

70°N

N O R T H W E S T

B a f f i n

Bylot
Island •2134

Eclipse
Sound

Pond Inlet

Buchan Gulf

Clyde

•1554

B   a   y

70°W

aux Feuilles

Koksoak

L   a   b   r   a   d   o   r

Okuujjuaq

Cape Hopes
Advance

Akpatok
Island

Ungava
Bay

Port
Burwell
Cape
Chidley

•661

Resolution
Island

Harper
Island

B   a   f   f   i   n   R   e   g   i   o   n

Cumberland   Sound

Kigisa

Nunatak
Pangnirtung

Penny
Ice Cap
2591•

Cumberland
Peninsula

•2143

Hoare
Bay

Home
Bay

Henry Kater
Pen.

Kivitoo

Broughton Island

Exeter
Sound

Cape Dyer

D   a   v   i   s

65°W

•390

Kangiqsualujjuaq

•604

N E W F O U N D L A N D

Fraser

•1076

ONutak

ORamah

ONain

L   a   b   r   a   d   o   r   S   e   a

Holsteinsborg

Godhavn

Disko

Disko Bugt

Svartenh

Karrais Fi.
•130

Uummannaq
•2197

Nugssuaq

G   r

60°W

A   T   L   A   N   T   I   C

Sukkertoppen

Søndre Strømfjord

•1610

Søndre Strømfjord

•2140

Godthåb

•13

•1790

S   t   r   a   i   t

G

55°N

O   C   E   A   N

Frederikshåb

Ivittuut

Julianehåb

Nanortalik

•1643

Kong Frederik VI Kyst

Kong   Frederik   VI   Kyst

Narssalik

•2140

Kong Cl

Kong C

Mt. Fore
3360•

Kronprins Frederik
•2056

Angmagssalik
Kap Dan

Dannebrog Øer

K. Løvenørn

Gyldenløves Fi.

K. Mosting

Bernstorffs Isfjord

Danells Fi.

Prins Christian Sd.

K. Farvel

45°W

50°W

55°W

40°W

55°N

35°W

60°N

30°W

50°W

n   o   o   p   q   r   s   t   u   v   w   x   y   z

This map shows 1/60 of the earth's surface. Area scale : 1 ☐ inch on the map ≏ 15,000 ☐ miles on the ground 1 ☐ cm on the map ≏ 6000 ☐ km on the ground

a   b   c   d   e   f   g   h   i   j   k   l   m

75°N
Devon Island
North Lincoln Land
1882
2073
80°W
Greely Fiord
E l l e s m e r e I s l a n d
Agassiz Ice Cap
United States Range
2143
Cape Discovery
85°N
Smith Bay
Smith Sound
Kane Basin
Washington Land
Kennedy Channel
Robeson Channel
Hall Land
Nyeboe Land
Alert O
L i n c o l n   S e a
A R C T I C   O C E A N
North Pole

Hayes Halvφ
Inglefield Land
1500
Prudhoe Land
O Thule (Qânâq)
Dundas O
Kap Atholl
796
Hval Sund
Kap York

Melville Bay
Cape Seddon
Steenstrups Gletscher
Holm Øer

K n u d   R a s m u s s e n s   L a n d

Nansen Land
1920
Peary Land
1910
Melville Land
Independence Fjord
Frederick E. Hyde Fjord
1010
Wandels Sea
85°N

f f i n

G r e e n l a n d
(Denmark)

Danmark Fjord
Kronprins Christian Land
769
Ingolf Fjord
Nordost Rundingen

W a n d e l s   S e a

Kong Frederick VIII Land
1100
Lambert Land
Norske Øer
Île de France
Skaerfjorden
80°N
92
Spitzbergen
1454
Prins Karls Forland
Isfjorden

Dronning Louise Land
Duc d'Orleans Land
Jøkel
Germania Land
550
Dove Bugt
Kap Bismarck
Store Koldewey

G r e e n l a n d   S e a

Kong Christian X Land
Kong Wilhelms Land
1932
Ardencaple Fjord
Shannon

Andrée Land
Hudson Land
1604
Clavering Øer
Wollaston Forland
Hold with Hope Pen.
1900
Kaiser Franz Josephs Fjord
Geographical Society Øer
Scoresby Land
Renland
1740
Kong Oscar's Fjord
Traill Øer
Milne Land
Jameson Land
Liverpool Land
Scoresby Sund
Scoresbysund O
Kap Brewster
Kap Dalton

N o r t h   S e a
75°N

and
Gunnbjørn Fjeld
Kangerlussuaq

D e n m a r k   S t r a i t

Jan Mayen
(Norway)

I C E L A N D
Isafjördur O
Cape Horn
Breida Fjördur
961
Húnaflói
66°N
20°W

70°N

n   o   p   q   r   s   t   u   v   w   x   y   z

0   100   200   300 miles
Average linear scale : 1 inch ≏ 125 miles   1cm ≏ 80 km
0   100   200   300   400   500 Km

North Pole

ARCTIC

OCEAN

85°N

80°N

Byrranga

76°N

80°N

Cape Berg^a

Cape Peschanyy

Komsomolets

Shokal'skogo Str.

Bol'shevik

Vilkitskogo Strait

Shmidta

Okhnaby'skor

Revoljutsii

Cape Medvy

Severnaya

Zemlya

Pioner

Russkiy

Nordenshel'da

Arch. Cape Oskara

Taimyr

Ushakova

West Siberian Sea

Taimyr Peninsula

Vize

Isačenko

Troynoy

Mikhaylova

Arktícheskogo Instituta

Yeva-Liv

Greem Bell

Rudol'fa

La Rohs'yor

Vil'cheka Zemlya

606

Gellya

Saf'm

Vilicky

Karla-Aleksandra

Dzheksana

Solsberi

Luidzhi

Gukera

Mak-Klintoka

Franz Josef Land

Sokal'sky

Aleksandry Zemlya

Georga Zemlya

370

Belyy

Kvitøya (White I.)

Mys Zelaniya

80°N

1052

Nordaustlandet

Russkaya Gavin

91

80°N

Hinlopenstr.

Spitzbergen

145⁴

West Spitzbergen

BARENTS

KARA SEA

Smidovich

Novaja

Barentsøya

Edgeøya

Isfjorden

Longyearbyen

Barentsburg

SEA

Sedova

115

Zemlja

933

Stolbovoy

Litke

Krasino

260

Proliv Karskiye Vorota

162

75°N

Pechora S

Bjørnøya (Bear I.) (Norway)

Kolgujev

166

Cape Kanin Nos

242

Malozemel'skaya Tundra

North Cape

Kap Kiberg

Kanin

Češa Bay

Volonga

Velikovisochnic

Søröy

Hammerfest

Tana

Sta fanovo

Lakselv

Kirkenes

Pečenga

Murmansk

Mezen' Gulf

Mezen'

NORWAY

Alta

1139

Tana

623

Lotta

Padunskoye More

397

Kola

Arctic Circle

Azopol'ya

NORWEGIAN SEA

Tromsø

Skibotn

Inarijärvi

Lapland

30°E

35°E

40°E

65°N

Senja

Ivalo

FINLAND

636

Mončegorsk

Kirovsk

10°E

15°E

20°E

25°E

n o p q r s t u v w x y z

This map shows 1/60 of the earth's surface. Area scale : 1 ☐ inch on the map ≃ 15,000 ☐ miles on the ground 1 ☐ cm on the map ≃ 6000 ☐ km on the ground

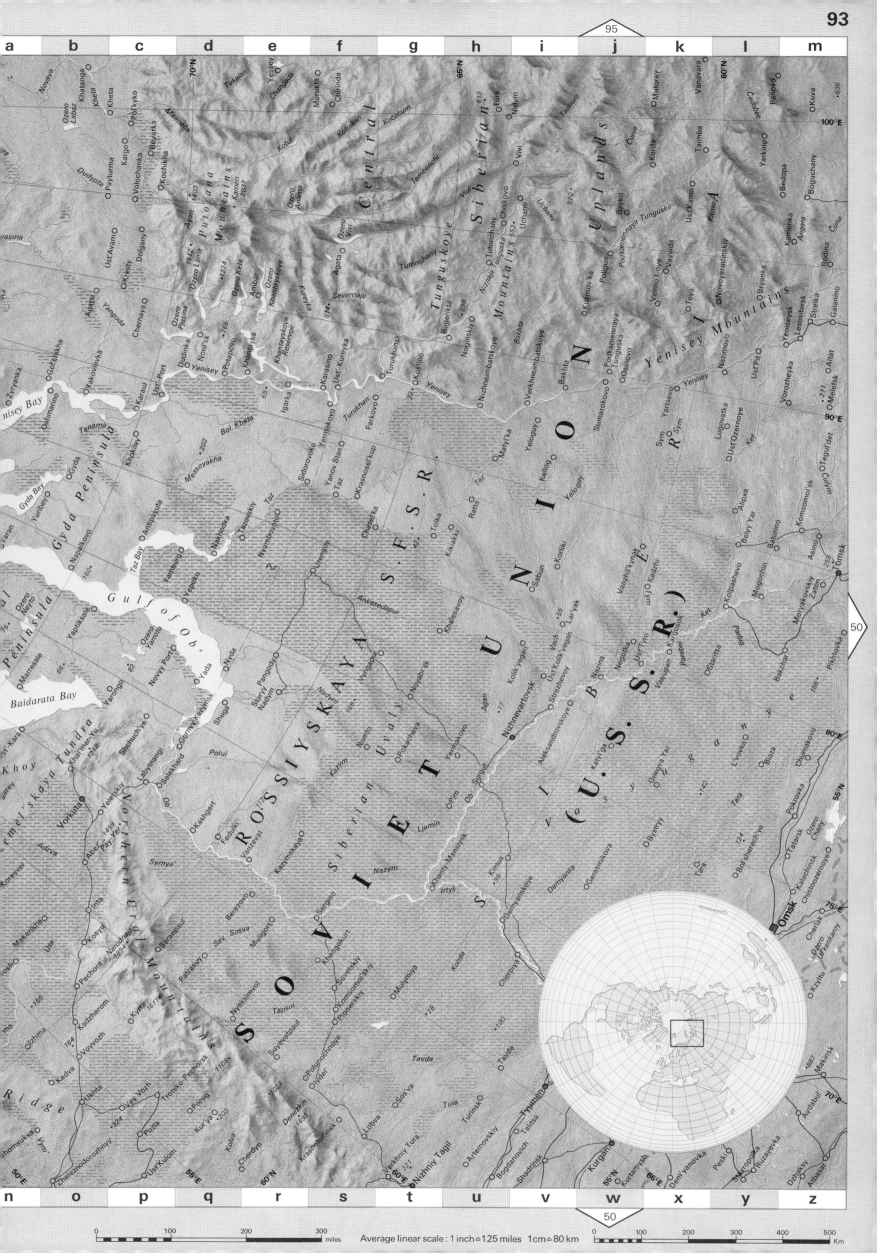

Average linear scale : 1 inch ≃ 125 miles   1cm ≃ 80 km

a b c d e f g h i j k l m

Chukchi Mys
Shmidta
Krasnoarmeyskiy
Sea Retkucha
Pevek
•1097
Wrangel Island

Ilirney
Southern Anyuskiy Mountains
•1641 Oscrovnoy
Mal. Anyuy
Cherskiy
Mal. Ambarchik
Baranikha Mys
Kolymskiy Mountains
Zatish'ye
Gorelova
Volochsk
Konzaboy
Chernyy
Mys
Oysurdakh
Ozero
Nerpich'ye
Chukochye
Balagannakh
Kyrbana
Khara-
Tala
Kolymskaya
Nizmennost
Ilimniir
Tenair
Kondakova
Ozhogino
•975
Ulovo
Byvangnyr
Indigirka
Chokurdakh
Ukta
Tabor
Kolesovo
Kiseleva
Khroma
Chikhacheva
Kokuora
Kharstan
Laptev Str.
Chay-Povarnaya
Star Dom
Kigilyakh
Bol'
Lyakhovsky
Fedorovskiy
Mal.
Lyakhovsky
Ambardakh
•320
Stolbovoy
Berkovskiy
Kotel'nyy
Antipinskiy
Bol'shoye
Zimov'ye
Novaya
Sibir'
Novosibirskiye Ostrava
Kotel'nyy

East Siberian
Sea
Bennetta

A R C T I C

O C E A N

North
Pole
Komsomolets
Cape
Berga
Mal. Taimyr'
Cape
Peschany
Oktyabr'skoy
Revolyutsii
Bolshevik
Vilkicki Str.
Cape
Oskara
•313
Byrranga Mountains
Vezdekhochnaya

Korkodon
Korkod
Bulun
R
Yugo
Sededem
Pastakh
Srednekolymsk
Khongseyo
Malaya
Urdakh
Shestako
Alekseyevo
Boru
Balagan
R
Berezovka
Zhirkova

Southern Anyuskiy
Mountains
Northern Anyuskiy Mountains
Bol Anyuy
•65°N

n o p q r s t u v w x y z

This map shows 1/60 of the earth's surface. Area scale : 1 □ inch on the map ≃ 15,000 □ miles on the ground 1 □ cm on the map ≃ 6000 □ km on the ground

PRINCIPAL SOURCES OF INFORMATION
REPRESENTED ON THE THEMATIC MAPS

Börsenverein des deutschen Buchhandels (ed.): Buch und Buchhandel in Zahlen. Frankfurt 1987.

British Geological Survey, Natural Environment Research Council: World Mineral Statistics 1979-1983. London 1985.

Dathe, Heinrich and Paul Schöps (eds.): Pelztieratlas. Jena 1986.

Deutsche Gesellschaft für Luft- und Raumfahrt: Astronautische Start-Verzeichnisse und Raumflugkörper-Statistiken 1957-1987.

Diercke Länderlexikon. Braunschweig 1983.

Durrell, Lee: State of the Ark. London 1986.

Encyclopedia Britannica. 15th ed. 32 vls. 1985.

Encyclopedia Britannica Book of the Year 1986. 1987. 1988.

Food and Agricultural Organization of the United Nations (FAO), Rome: FAO Production Yearbook 1985. 1986. FAO Food Balance Sheets 1975-1977. 1979-1981. FAO Yearbook of Fishery Statistics 1983. FAO Trade Yearbook 1986.

Fischer Weltalmanach 1986. 1987. 1988.

Haack. Atlas zur Zeitgeschichte. Gotha 1985.

Herre, Wolf and Manfred Röhrs: Haustiere-zoologisch gesehen. Stuttgart 1973.

The International Institute of Strategic Studies (ILSS): The Military Balance 1986-1987. London 1986.

International Labour Organization (ILO), Geneva: Yearbook of Labour Statistics 1978. 1979. 1980. 1981. 1982. 1983. 1984. 1985. 1986. 1987. Income Distribution and Economic Development. An Analytical Survey. Geneva 1984. Sixth African Regional Conference. Application of the Declaration of Principles and Programme of Action of the World Employment Conference. Geneva 1983.

International Road Transport Union: World Transport Data. Geneva 1985.

International Telecommunication Union: Table of International Telex Relations and Traffic. Geneva 1987.

Inter-Parliamentary Union (IPU): Women in Parliament 1988.

Participation of Women in Political Life and in Decision-Making Processes. Geneva 1988. Distribution of Seats Between Men and Women in National Assemblies. Geneva 1987.

Jain, Shail: Size Distribution of Income. Compilation of Data. World Bank Staff Working Paper No. 190. Nov. 1974. Washington 1975.

Kidron, Michael and Ronald Segal: The State of the World Atlas. London 1981. The New State of the World Atlas (revised ed.). London 1987.

Krüger, Hanfried, Werner Löser et al (eds.): Ökumene Lexicon. Frankfurt 1983.

Kurian, George Thomas: The New Book of World Rankings. New York 1984.

Länder der Erde. Berlin 1985.

Meyers Enzyklopädie der Erde (8 vls.). Mannheim 1982.

Moroney, John R.: Income Inequality. Trends and International Comparisons. Toronto 1979.

Myers, Norman (ed.): GAIA — Der Öko-Atlas unserer Erde. Frankfurt 1985.

Nohlen, Dieter and Franz Nuscheler (eds.): Handbuch der Dritten Welt. 8 vls. Hamburg 1981-1983.

Peters, Arno: Synchronoptische Weltgeschichte. 2 vls. München 1980.

Saeger, Joni and Ann Olson: Der Frauenatlas. Frankfurt 1986.

Serryn, Pierre: Le Monde d'aujourd'hui. Atlas économique, social, politique, stratégique. Paris 1981.

South: South Diary 1987. 1988. Statistisches Bundesamt, Wiesbaden: Statistik des Auslandes. Vierteljahreshefte zur Auslandsstatistik. 1985-1987. Statistik des Auslandes. Länderberichte.

Stockholm International Peace Research Institute (SIPRI): SIPRI Yearbook 1987. World Armaments and Disarmament. New York 1987.

Taylor, Charles Lewis and David A. Jodice: World Handbook of Political and Social Indicators. New Haven, London 1983.

Tietze, Wolf (ed.): Westermann Lexikon der Geographie. Braunschweig 1968.

UNESCO: Statistical Yearbook 1974. 1975. 1976. 1977. 1978. 1979. 1980. 1981. 1982. 1983. 1984. 1985. 1986. 1987.

UNICEF: The State of the World's Children 1987.

The United Nations (UN): UN Statistical Yearbook 1983/84. UN Demographic Yearbook 1972. 1979. 1984. 1985. 1986. National Accounts Statistics. Compendium of Income Distribution Statistics. New York 1985. UN Energy Statistics Yearbook 1984. UN Yearbook of International Trade Statistics 1982. 1983. 1984. 1986. Selected Indicators of the Situation of Women 1985. UN Industrial Statistics Yearbook 1983. 1984. World Conference of the United Nations Decade for Women: Equality, Development and Peace. Copenhagen 1980. Activities for the Advancement of Women: Equality, Development and Peace. Report of Jean Fernand-Laurent. 1983.

University of Stellenbosch, Department of Development Administration and the Institute for Cartographic Analysis: The Third World in Maps. 1985.

World Almanac & Book of Facts 1985. 1986. 1987.

The World Bank: The World Bank Atlas 1987. World Development Report 1980. 1981. 1982. 1983. 1984. 1985. 1986. 1987. World Labour Report 1984. World Tables 1984. World Atlas of the Child 1979. Social Indicators of Development 1987. World Economic and Social Indicators. Document of the World Bank. 1980.

World Energy Conference 1978: World Energy Resources 1985-2020. Renewable Energy Resources. The Full Reports to the Conservation Commissions of the World Energy Conference. 1978.

The World in Figures. Editorial information compiled by The Economist. London 1987.

World Health Organization (WHO), Geneva: World Health Statistics. Annual.

Völker der Erde. Bern 1982.

Voous, K.H.: Atlas of European Birds. New York 1960.

NATURE, MAN AND SOCIETY
IN 246 THEMATIC MAPS

Each map represents a single theme. As a result, it is possible to dispense with symbols and to allow the information to be expressed entirely in terms of colour. Dark colours stand for high values, light colours stand for low ones. This makes it easy to take in and remember the essential data shown on each map—an important feature, since up to 16 maps can be dedicated to a particular subject.

The maps should be considered in relation to each other. The interweaving and mutual interaction of all spheres of life, the intricacies of nature and culture, of economics, nations and society, mean that each of the 46 topics can be fully understood only when placed in the context of the other 45 double-page spreads.

These 246 thematic maps represent over 40,000 individual pieces of factual data. The main sources of this stupendous wealth of information are the published materials of the United Nations and other international bodies of comparable standing. Where such official figures are not available, estimates have been drawn up in consultation with the leading experts in the various fields concerned.

No interpretation or evaluation of information has been undertaken, in order not to detract from the aim of this Atlas—to enable the user to form an objective and unprejudiced personal picture of the world.

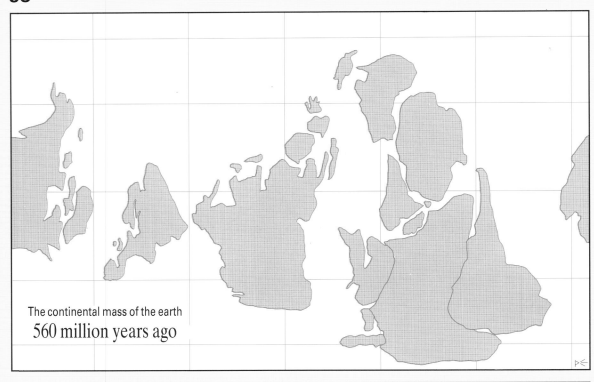

The continental mass of the earth
560 million years ago

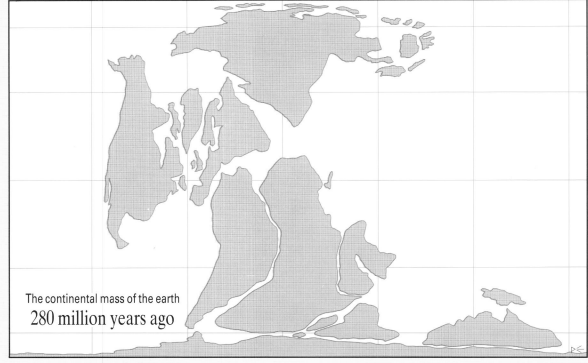

The continental mass of the earth
280 million years ago

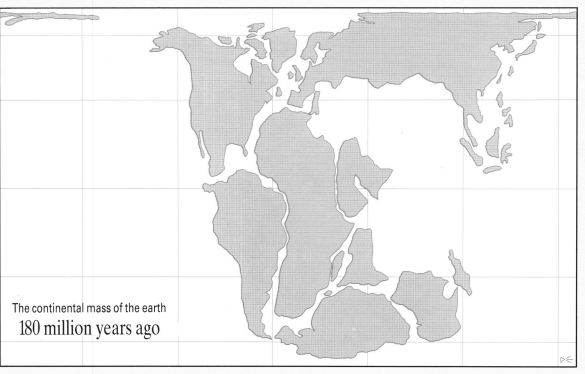

The continental mass of the earth
180 million years ago

The continental mass of the earth

TODAY

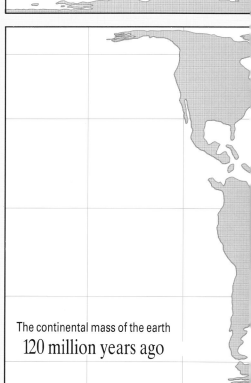

The continental mass of the earth
120 million years ago

THE CO

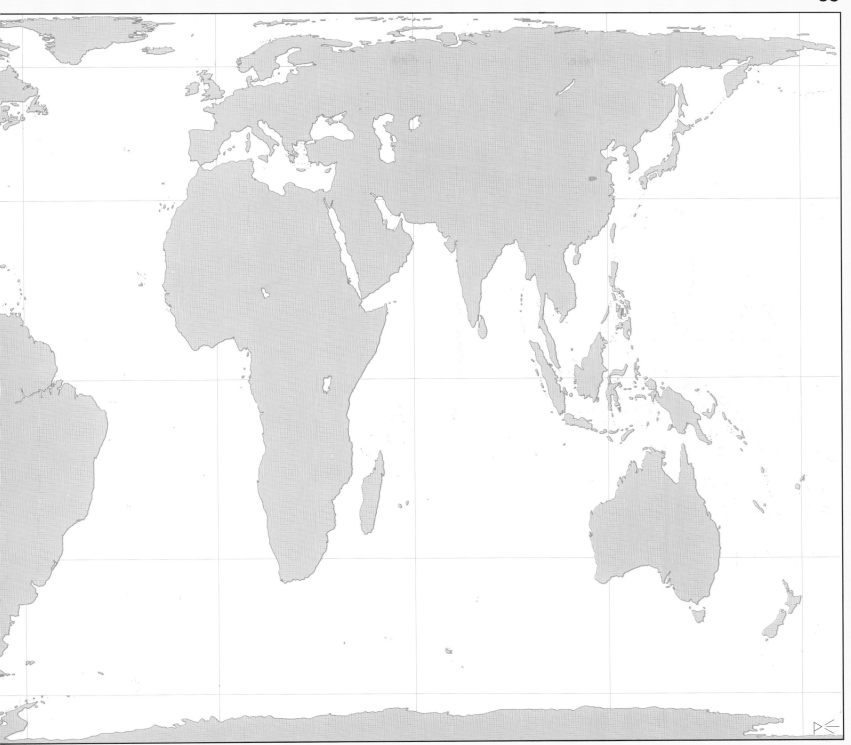

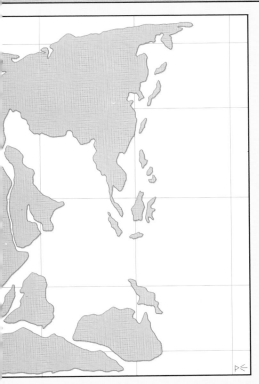

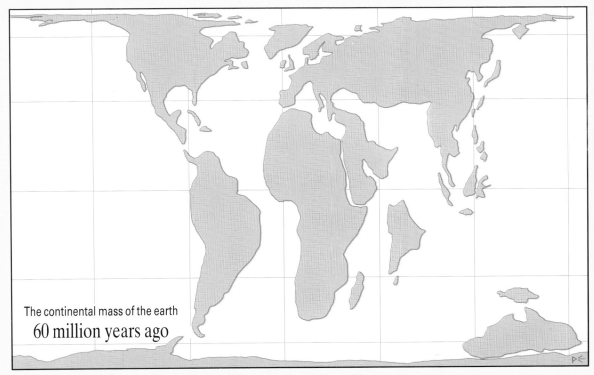

The continental mass of the earth
60 million years ago

TINENTS

MOUℕ

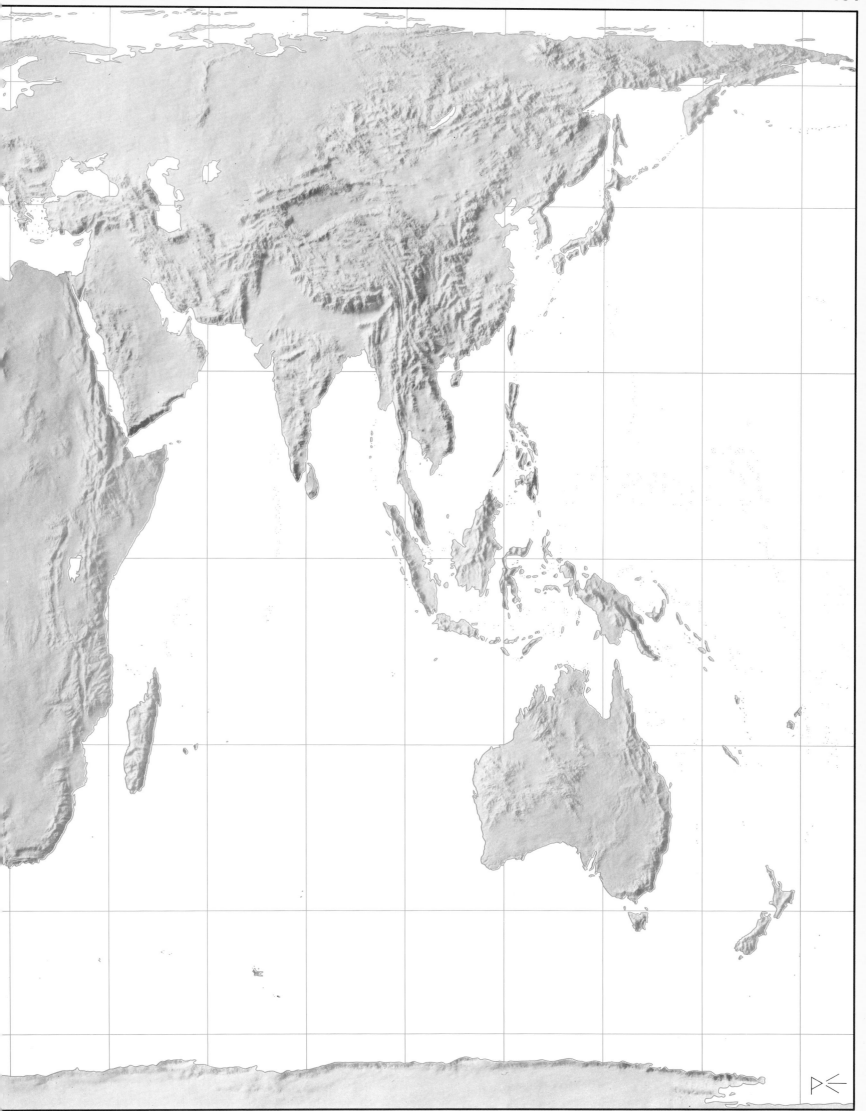

TAINS

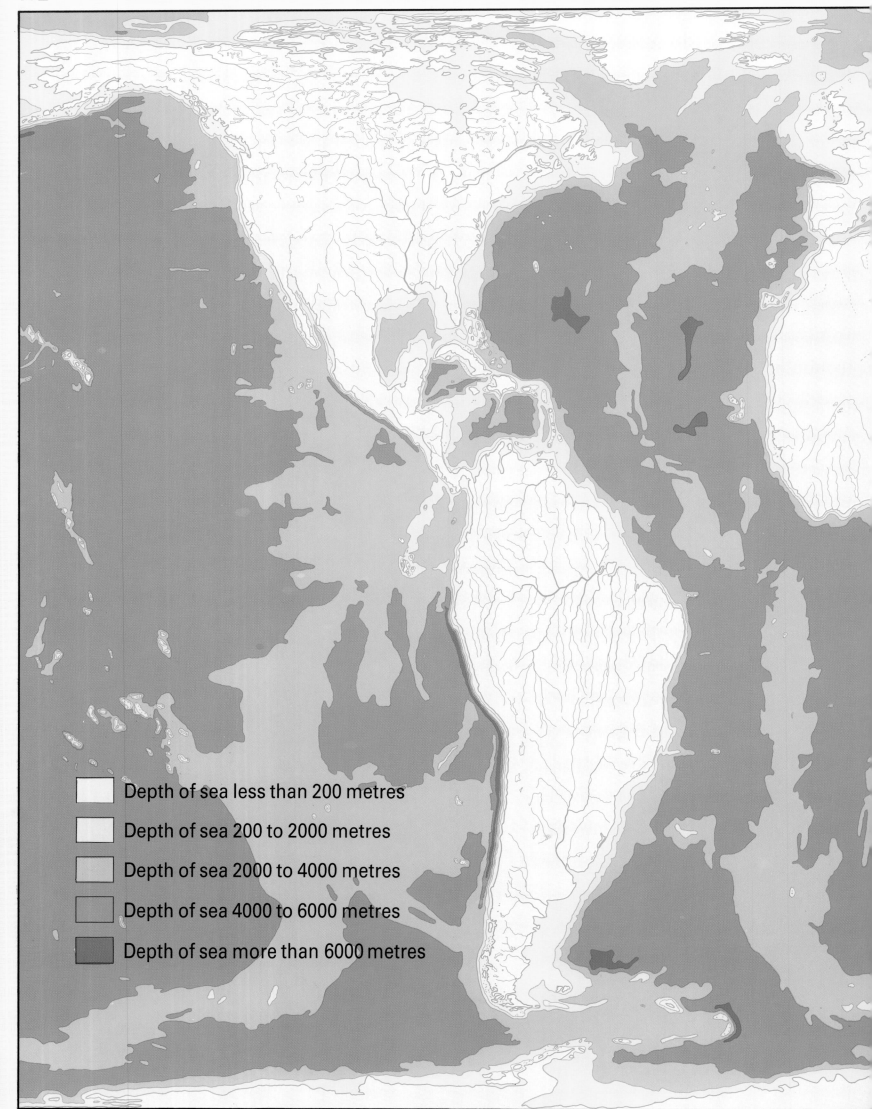

Depth of sea less than 200 metres

Depth of sea 200 to 2000 metres

Depth of sea 2000 to 4000 metres

Depth of sea 4000 to 6000 metres

Depth of sea more than 6000 metres

RIVERS A

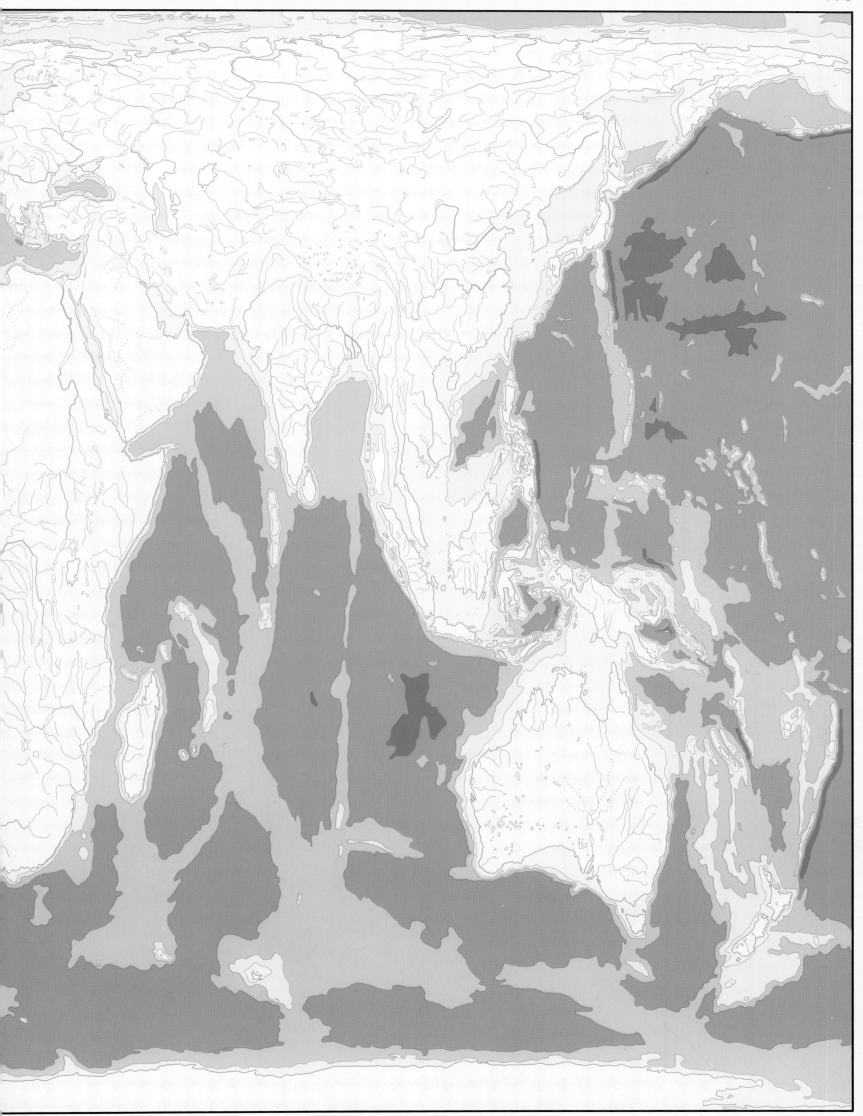

ND SEAS

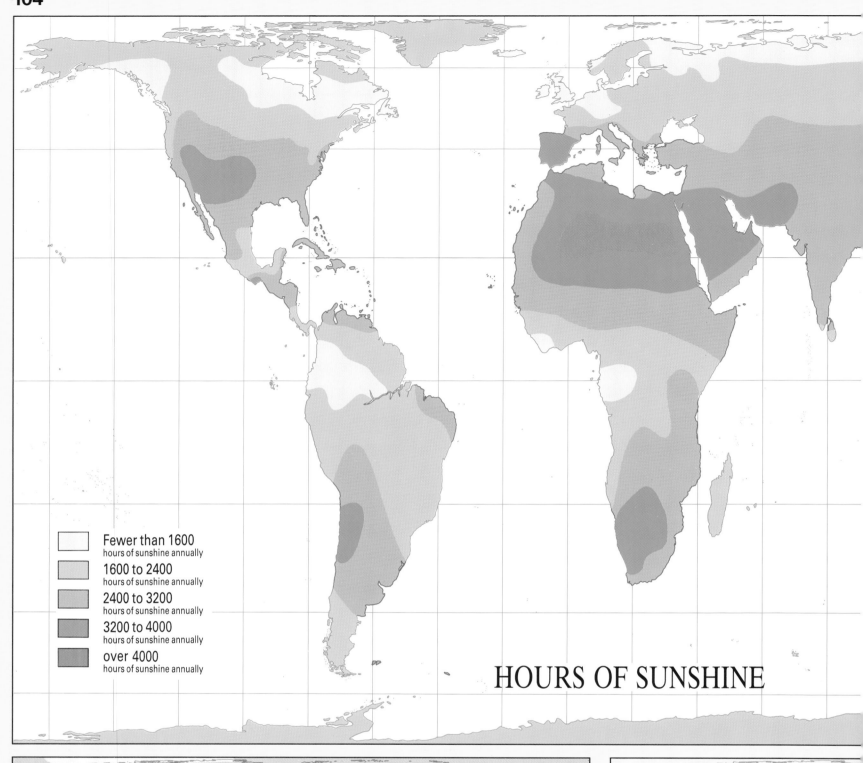

Fewer than 1600
hours of sunshine annually

1600 to 2400
hours of sunshine annually

2400 to 3200
hours of sunshine annually

3200 to 4000
hours of sunshine annually

over 4000
hours of sunshine annually

HOURS OF SUNSHINE

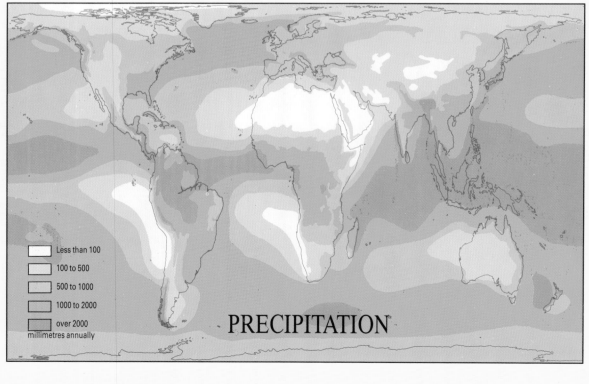

Less than 100

100 to 500

500 to 1000

1000 to 2000

over 2000
millimetres annually

PRECIPITATION

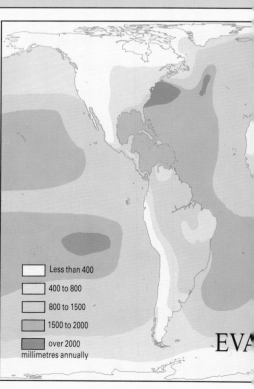

Less than 400

400 to 800

800 to 1500

1500 to 2000

over 2000
millimetres annually

EVA

SUN ANI

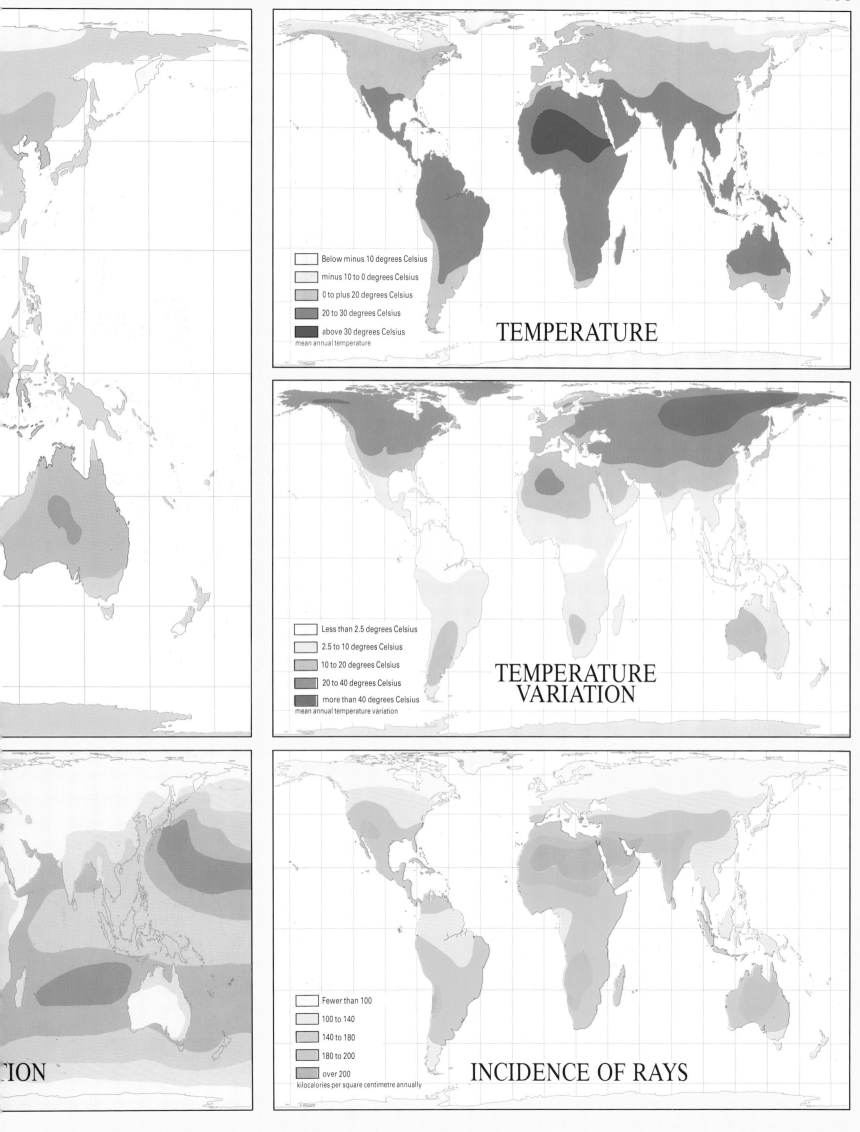

Below minus 10 degrees Celsius

minus 10 to 0 degrees Celsius

0 to plus 20 degrees Celsius

20 to 30 degrees Celsius

above 30 degrees Celsius

mean annual temperature

TEMPERATURE

Less than 2.5 degrees Celsius

2.5 to 10 degrees Celsius

10 to 20 degrees Celsius

20 to 40 degrees Celsius

more than 40 degrees Celsius

mean annual temperature variation

TEMPERATURE VARIATION

Fewer than 100

100 to 140

140 to 180

180 to 200

over 200

kilocalories per square centimetre annually

INCIDENCE OF RAYS

TION

CLIMATE

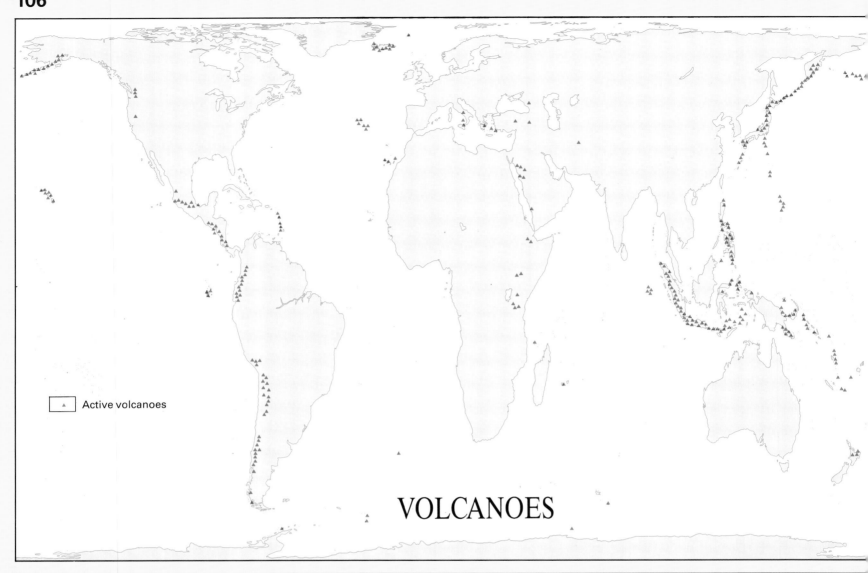

VOLCANOES

Active volcanoes

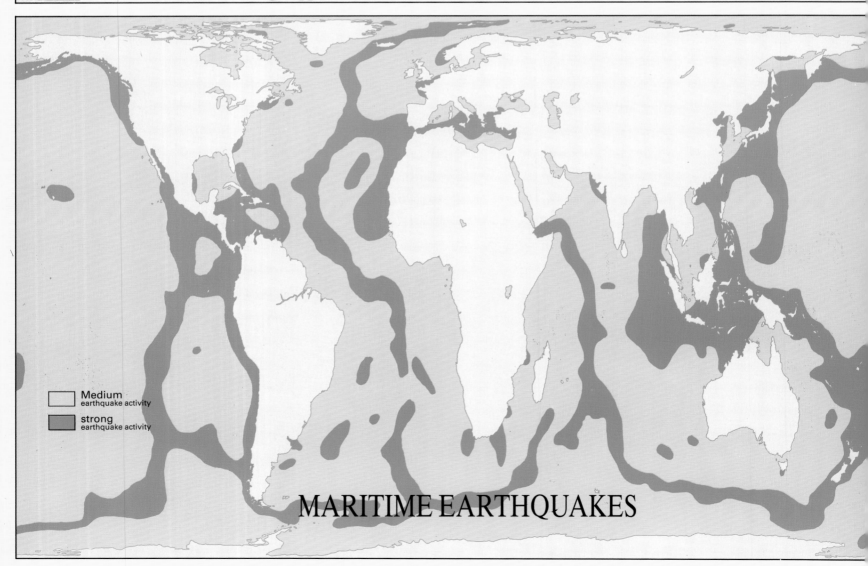

Medium
earthquake activity

strong
earthquake activity

MARITIME EARTHQUAKES

NATURAL

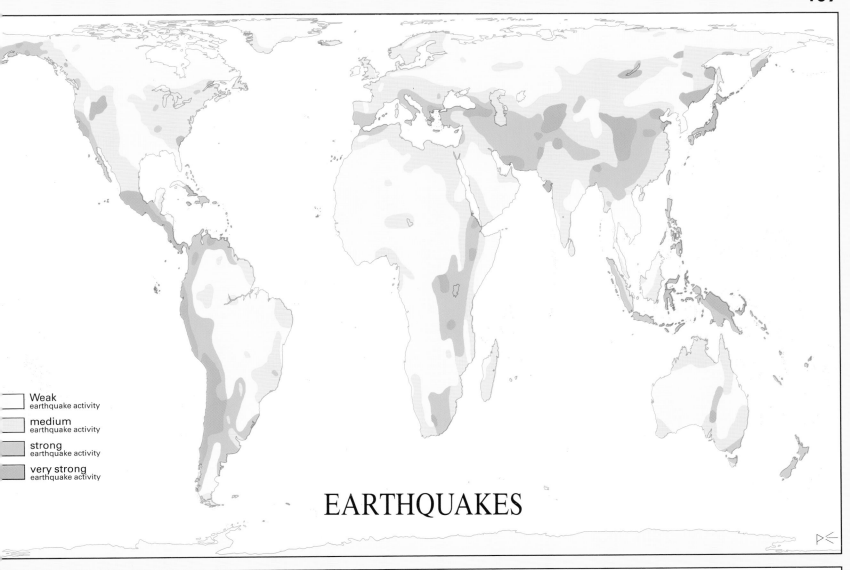

Weak
earthquake activity

medium
earthquake activity

strong
earthquake activity

very strong
earthquake activity

EARTHQUAKES

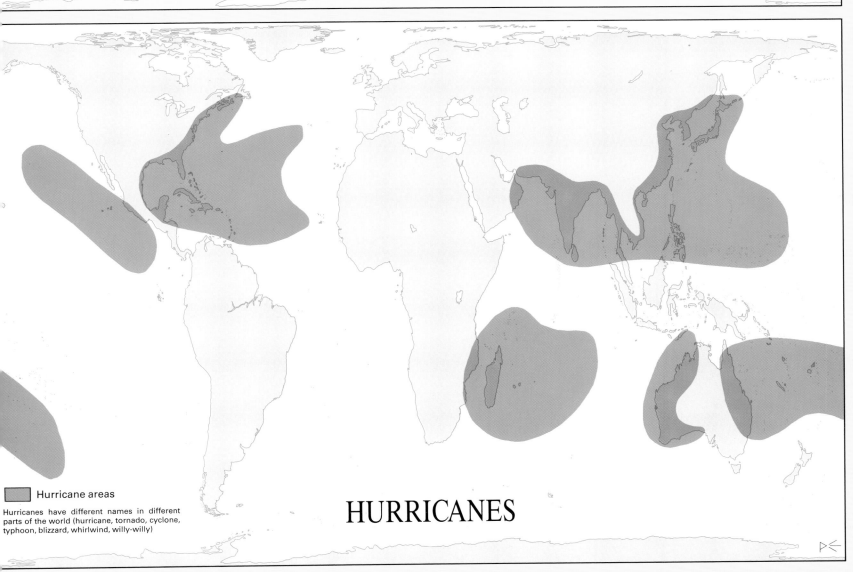

Hurricane areas

Hurricanes have different names in different
parts of the world (hurricane, tornado, cyclone,
typhoon, blizzard, whirlwind, willy-willy)

HURRICANES

DANGERS

108

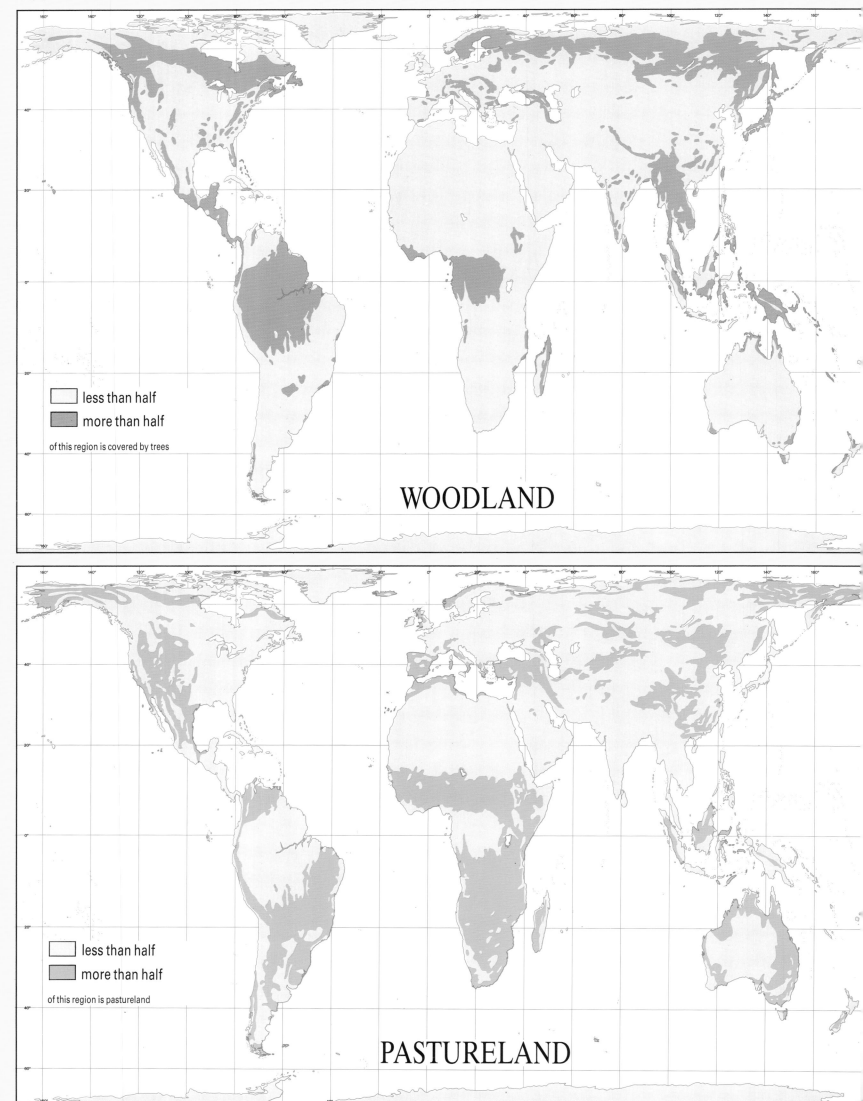

less than half

more than half

of this region is covered by trees

WOODLAND

less than half

more than half

of this region is pastureland

PASTURELAND

VEG

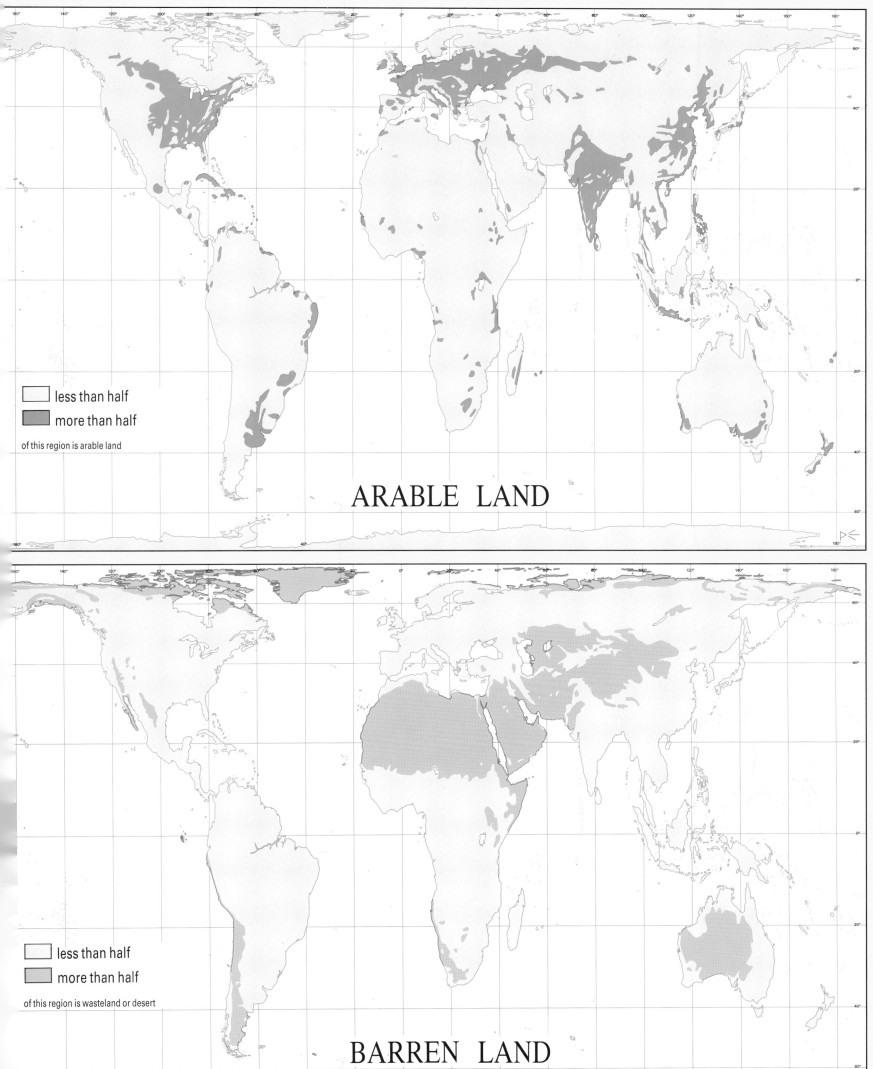

less than half

more than half

of this region is arable land

ARABLE LAND

less than half

more than half

of this region is wasteland or desert

BARREN LAND

TATION

20° 40° 60° 80° 100° 120° 140° 160° 180°

60°

FINLAND

S O V I E T   U N I O N

(U. S. S. R.)

PEOPLES' REPUBLIC
OF MONGOLIA

POLAND
CZECH
HUNGARY
ROMANIA
YUGOSLAVIA
BULGARIA
ALB.

40°

GREECE
TURKEY
NORTH KOREA

C H I N A

JAPAN

CYPRUS
LEBANON
SYRIA
ISRAEL
JORDAN
IRAQ
IRAN
AFGHANISTAN
SOUTH KOREA

PAKISTAN
KUWAIT

SAUDI
BAHRAIN
QATAR
UNITED
ARAB
EMIRATES

NEPAL
BHUTAN

BYA

EGYPT

ARABIA

INDIA

BANGLADESH

BURMA

20°

OMAN

TAIWAN

HAD

SUDAN

YEMEN

P.D.R. YEMEN

DJIBOUTI

THAILAND

LAOS

VIETNAM

KAMPUCHEA

PHILIPPINES

CENTRAL
AFRICAN
REPUBLIC

ETHIOPIA

S O M A L I A

SRI LANKA

MALDIVES

BRUNEI

UGANDA

KENYA

M A L A Y S I A

0°

RWANDA
BURUNDI

SINGAPORE

KIRIBATI

ZAIRE

TANZANIA

SEYCHELLES

I N D O N E S I A

PAPUA
NEW GUINEA

SOLOMON
ISLANDS

COMOROS

GOLA

ZAMBIA

MALAWI

WESTERN SAMOA

ZIMBABWE

MADAGASCAR

VANUATU

FIJI

BIA

MOZAMBIQUE

MAURITIUS

20°

BOTSWANA

TONGA

SWAZILAND

AUSTRALIA

SOUTH

LESOTHO

AFRICA

NEW ZEALAND

40°

60°

c   t   i   c   a   180°

ES

Fewer than 1 inhabitant
per square kilometre

1 to 10 inhabitants
per square kilometre

10 to 100 inhabitants
per square kilometre

100 to 1000 inhabitants
per square kilometre

more than 1000 inhabitants
per square kilometre. The symbols mean
· 500,000 to 1 million inhabitants
● 1 million to 10 million inhabitants
◆ more than 10 million inhabitants

PEOPLE A

D CITIES

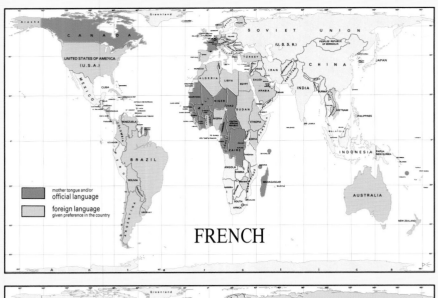

FRENCH

legend: mother tongue and/or official language; foreign language given preference in the country

SPANISH

legend: mother tongue and/or official language; foreign language given preference in the country

GERMAN

legend: mother tongue and/or official language; foreign language given preference in the country

RUSSIAN

legend: mother tongue and/or official language; foreign language given preference in the country

MALAY

legend: mother tongue and/or official language

PROPORTION OF THE WORLD'S POPULATION SP ONE OF THESE MAJOR LANGUAGES AS THE MO

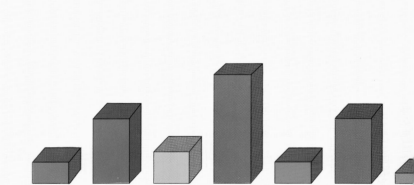

| French | Spanish | Portuguese | English | German | Russian | Ita |
| 2 % | 6 % | 3 % | 10 % | 2 % | 6 % | 1 |

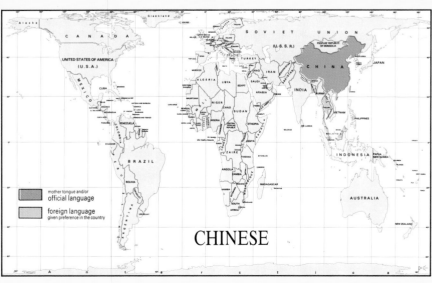

CHINESE

legend: mother tongue and/or official language; foreign language given preference in the country

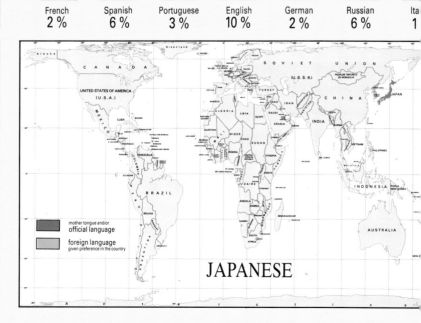

JAPANESE

legend: mother tongue and/or official language; foreign language given preference in the country

LAN

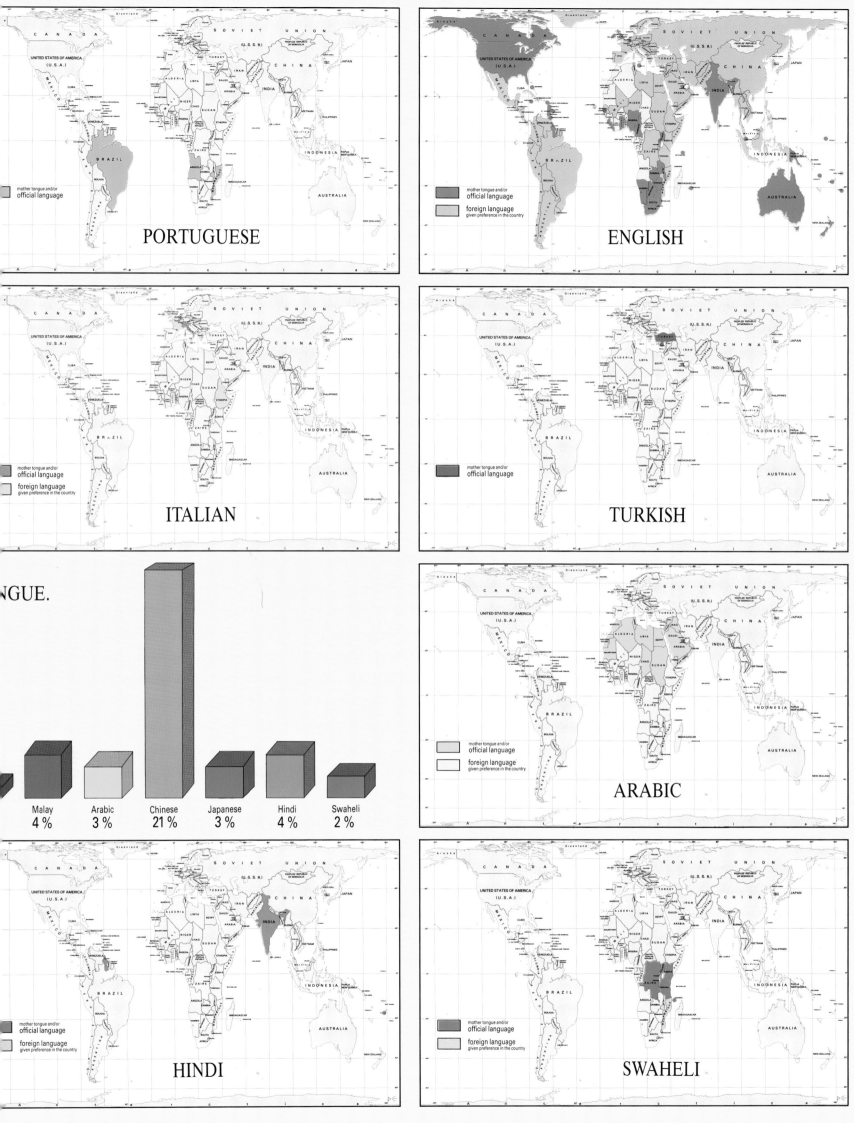

PORTUGUESE

ENGLISH

mother tongue and/or
official language

mother tongue and/or
official language

foreign language
given preference in the country

ITALIAN

TURKISH

mother tongue and/or
official language

foreign language
given preference in the country

mother tongue and/or
official language

NGUE.

| Malay 4 % | Arabic 3 % | Chinese 21 % | Japanese 3 % | Hindi 4 % | Swaheli 2 % |

ARABIC

mother tongue and/or
official language

foreign language
given preference in the country

HINDI

SWAHELI

mother tongue and/or
official language

foreign language
given preference in the country

mother tongue and/or
official language

foreign language
given preference in the country

UAGES

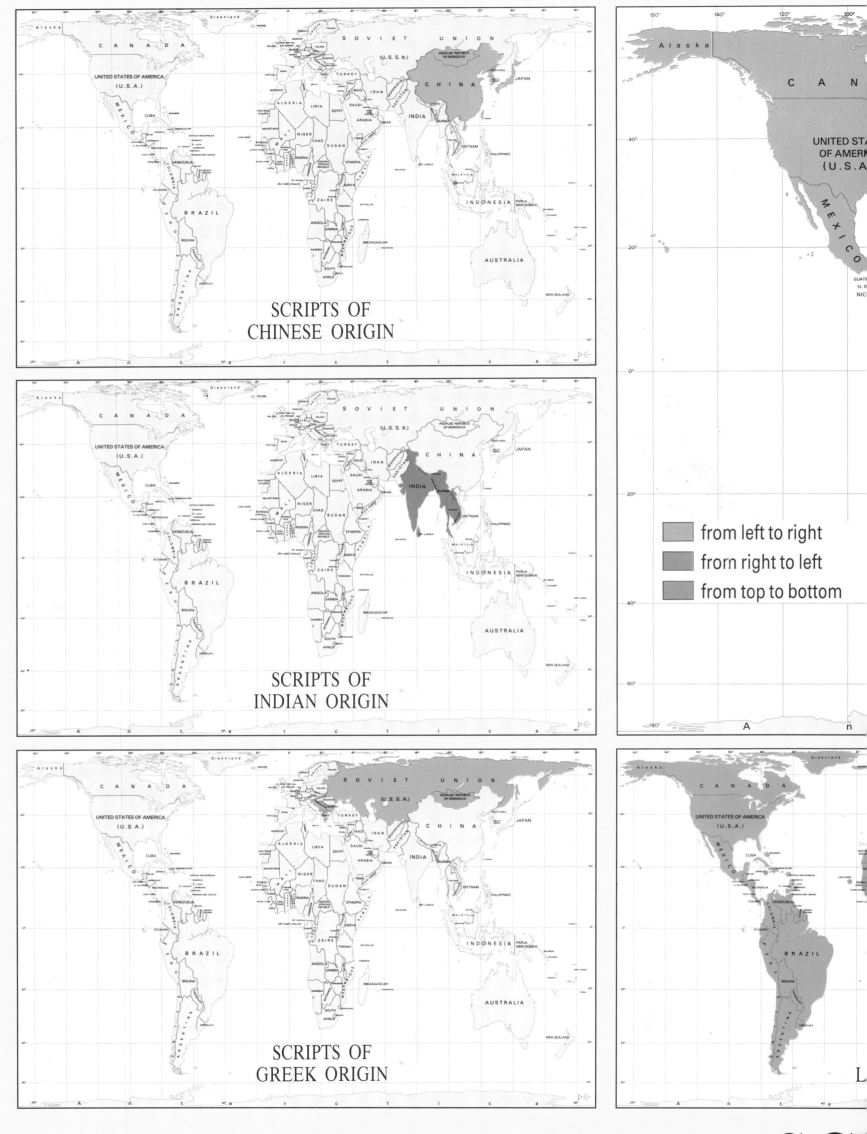

SCRIPTS OF
CHINESE ORIGIN

SCRIPTS OF
INDIAN ORIGIN

from left to right

frorn right to left

from top to bottom

SCRIPTS OF
GREEK ORIGIN

SC

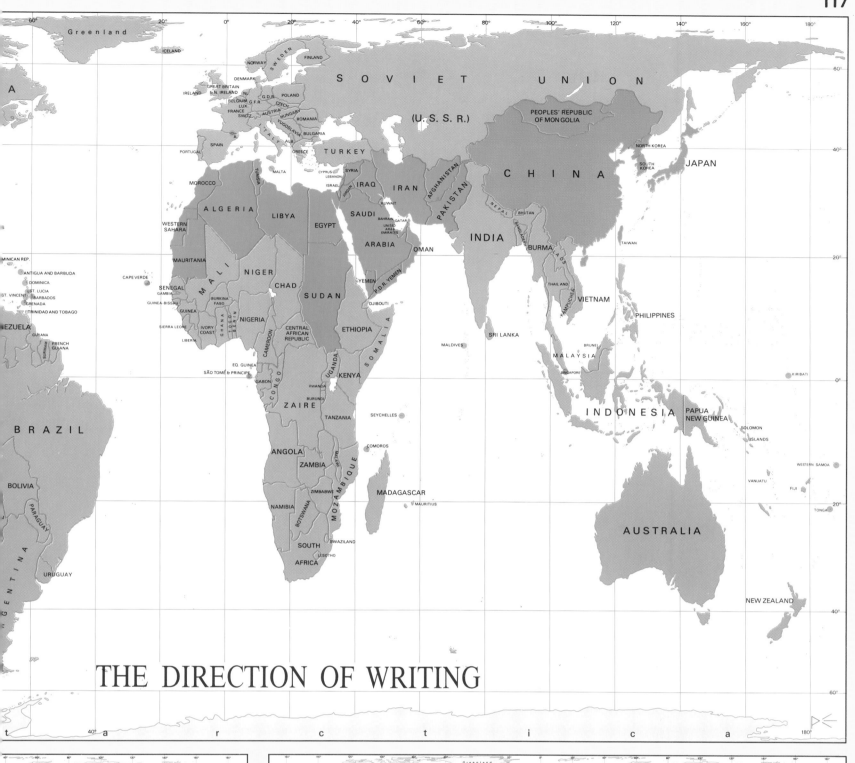

THE DIRECTION OF WRITING

OF
GIN

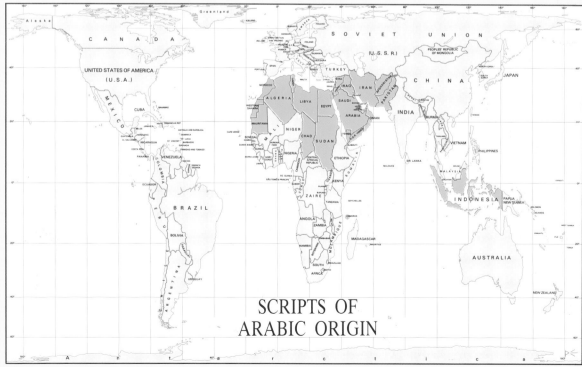

SCRIPTS OF ARABIC ORIGIN

PTS

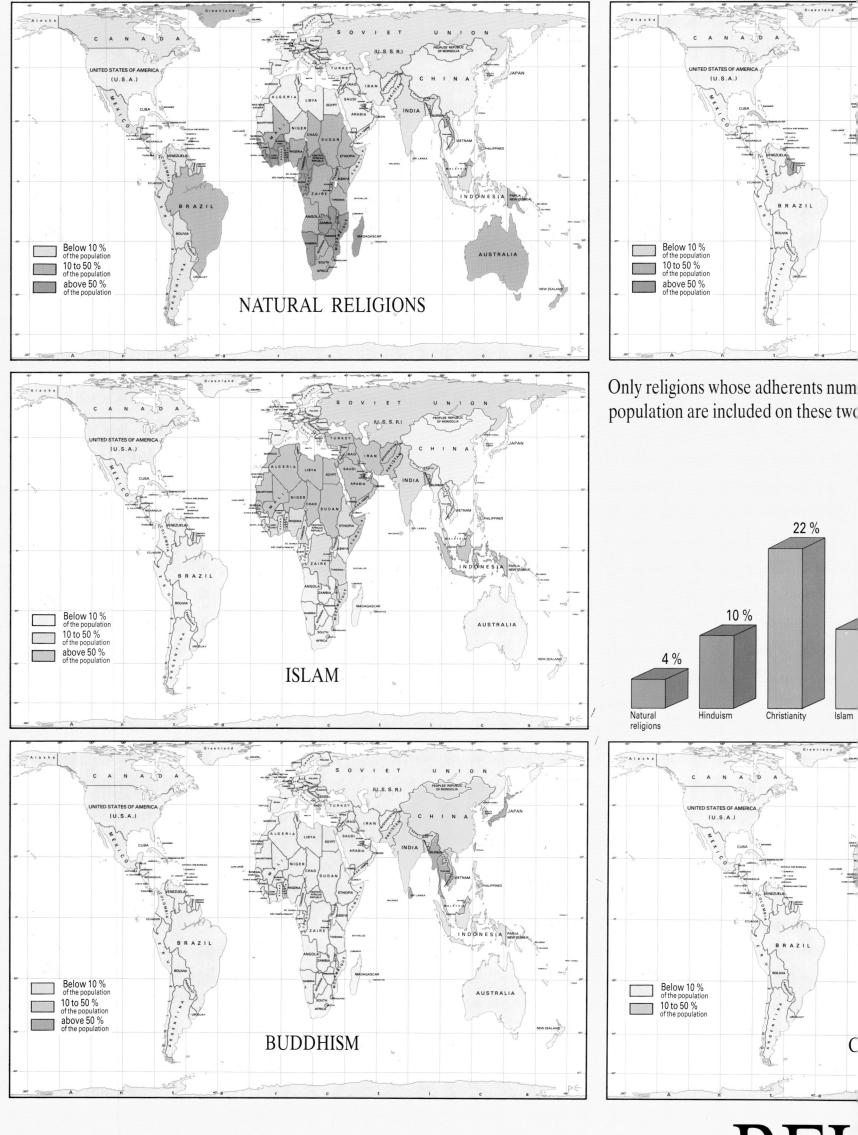

NATURAL RELIGIONS

Below 10 %
of the population
10 to 50 %
of the population
above 50 %
of the population

Below 10 %
of the population
10 to 50 %
of the population
above 50 %
of the population

ISLAM

Below 10 %
of the population
10 to 50 %
of the population
above 50 %
of the population

BUDDHISM

Below 10 %
of the population
10 to 50 %
of the population
above 50 %
of the population

Below 10 %
of the population
10 to 50 %
of the population

Only religions whose adherents num
population are included on these two

22 %

10 %

4 %

Natural
religions   Hinduism   Christianity   Islam

REL

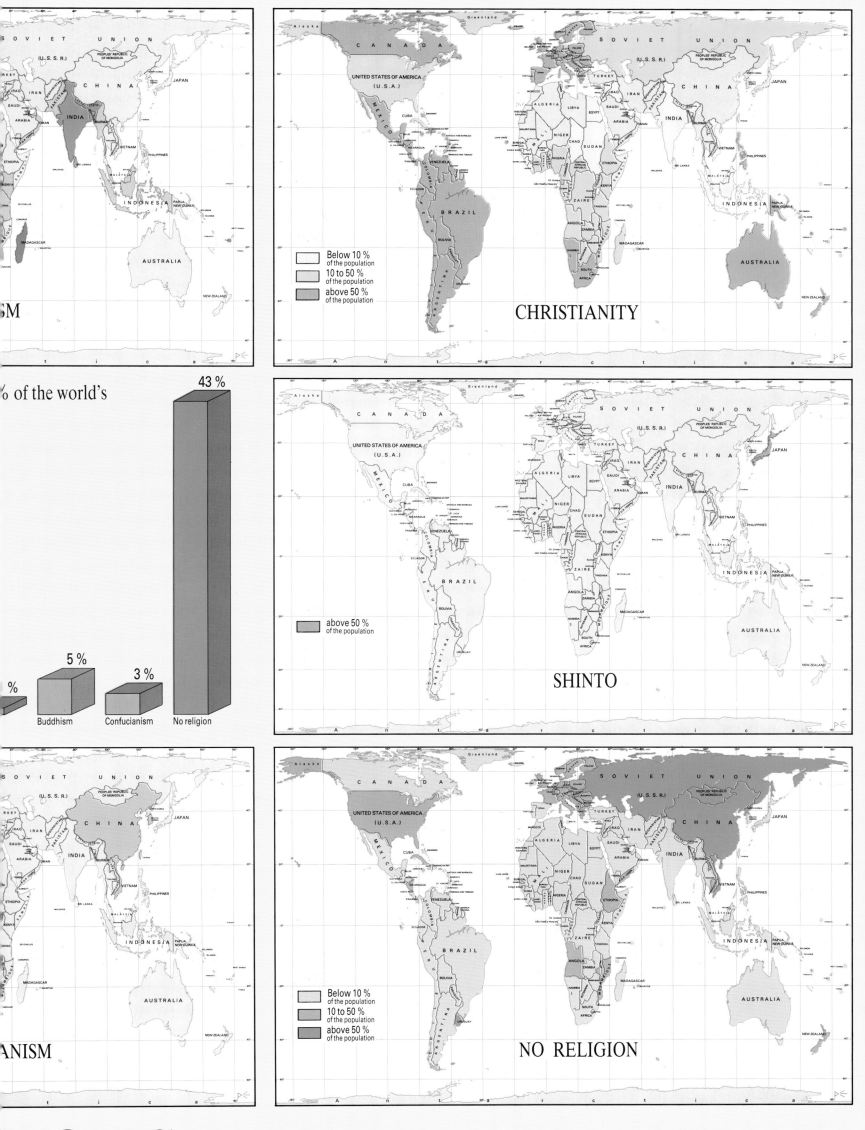

% of the world's

43 %

5 %

Buddhism

3 %

Confucianism

No religion

CHRISTIANITY

Below 10 %
of the population

10 to 50 %
of the population

above 50 %
of the population

SHINTO

above 50 %
of the population

NO RELIGION

Below 10 %
of the population

10 to 50 %
of the population

above 50 %
of the population

GIONS

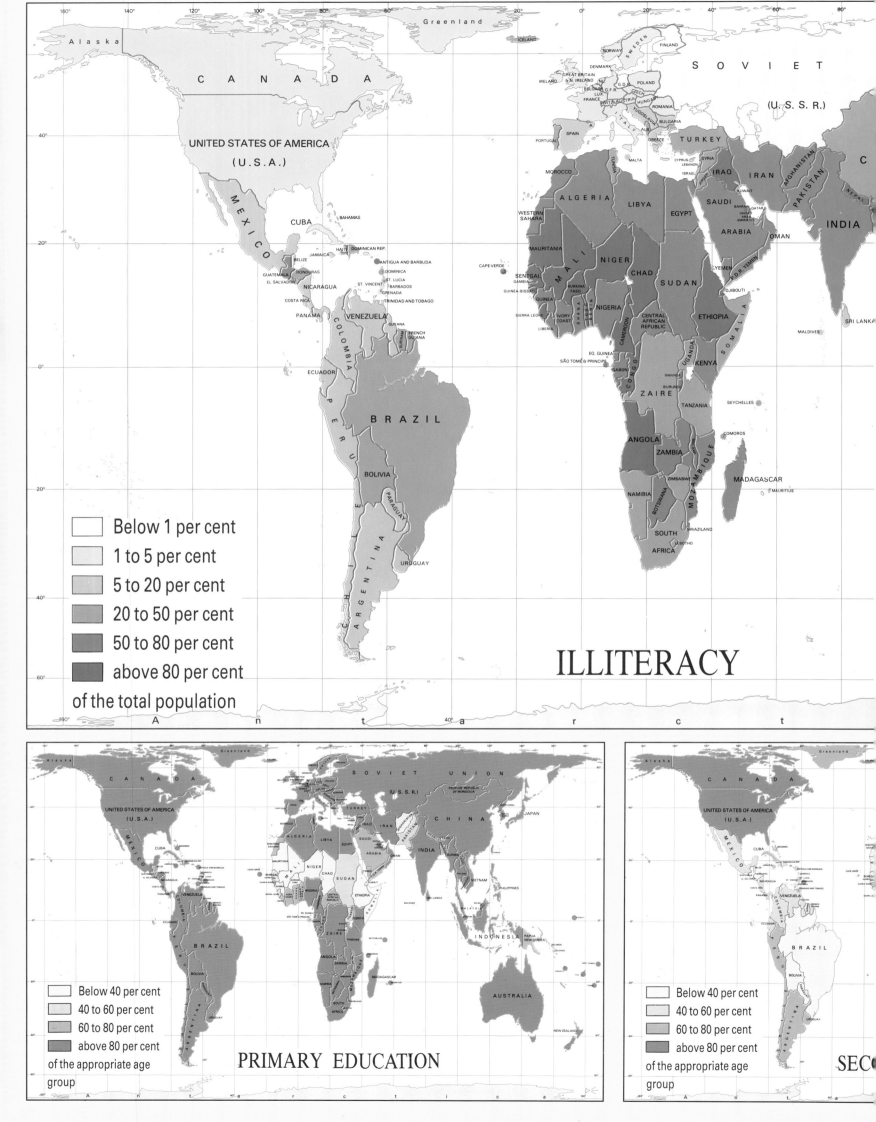

Greenland

Alaska

C A N A D A

UNITED STATES OF AMERICA
(U.S.A.)

ICELAND

NORWAY SWEDEN FINLAND

GREAT BRITAIN
IRELAND & N. IRELAND
DENMARK
BELGIUM G.D.R. POLAND
LUX.
FRANCE SWITZ. AUSTRIA HUNGARY ROMANIA
SPAIN ITALY YUGOSLAVIA BULGARIA
ALBANIA
GREECE

S O V I E T

(U.S.S.R.)

TURKEY

PORTUGAL

MOROCCO

WESTERN
SAHARA

ALGERIA

MAURITANIA

SENEGAL
GAMBIA
GUINEA-BISSAU
GUINEA
SIERRA LEONE
LIBERIA

MALTA CYPRUS LEBANON SYRIA
ISRAEL IRAQ IRAN
KUWAIT
JORDAN QATAR
SAUDI UNITED
ARAB
ARABIA EMIRATES
OMAN
YEMEN
P.D.R. YEMEN
DJIBOUTI

AFGHANISTAN
PAKISTAN
NEPAL

INDIA

LIBYA
EGYPT

MALI
NIGER
CHAD
SUDAN

BURKINA
FASO
IVORY NIGERIA
COAST
CAMEROON CENTRAL
AFRICAN
REPUBLIC

ETHIOPIA

SRI LANKA
MALDIVES

CAPE VERDE

MEXICO

CUBA
BAHAMAS
JAMAICA HAITI DOMINICAN REP.
BELIZE
GUATEMALA HONDURAS
EL SALVADOR
NICARAGUA
COSTA RICA
PANAMA

ANTIGUA AND BARBUDA
DOMINICA
ST. LUCIA
ST. VINCENT BARBADOS
GRENADA
TRINIDAD AND TOBAGO

VENEZUELA
GUYANA
SURINAM FRENCH
GUIANA

COLOMBIA

ECUADOR

EQ. GUINEA
SÃO TOMÉ & PRÍNCIPE
GABON CONGO

RWANDA
BURUNDI

ZAIRE

UGANDA KENYA

SOMALIA

TANZANIA

SEYCHELLES

P E R U

BRAZIL

BOLIVIA

PARAGUAY

C H I L E

A R G E N T I N A

URUGUAY

ANGOLA
ZAMBIA
ZIMBABWE
NAMIBIA
BOTSWANA
SOUTH
AFRICA
SWAZILAND
LESOTHO

MOZAMBIQUE

COMOROS

MADAGASCAR

MAURITIUS

☐	Below 1 per cent
▨	1 to 5 per cent
▨	5 to 20 per cent
▨	20 to 50 per cent
▨	50 to 80 per cent
▨	above 80 per cent

of the total population

ILLITERACY

A   n   t   a   r   c   t

C A N A D A

Greenland
Alaska

UNITED STATES OF AMERICA
(U.S.A.)

S O V I E T   U N I O N
(U.S.S.R.)

PEOPLES REPUBLIC
OF MONGOLIA

CHINA

JAPAN

TURKEY

IRAN
AFGHANISTAN
PAKISTAN

MEXICO

CUBA

WESTERN
SAHARA

ALGERIA
LIBYA
EGYPT

SAUDI
ARABIA

INDIA

OMAN

VIETNAM

CAPE VERDE

MALI
NIGER
CHAD
SUDAN

NIGERIA
CENTRAL
AFRICAN
REPUBLIC
ETHIOPIA

SRI LANKA
MALDIVES

MALAYSIA

PHILIPPINES

VENEZUELA

COLOMBIA

ECUADOR

ZAIRE

I N D O N E S I A
PAPUA
NEW GUINEA

BRAZIL

BOLIVIA

ANGOLA
ZAMBIA

A R G E N T I N A

URUGUAY

MADAGASCAR

SOUTH

AUSTRALIA

NEW ZEALAND

☐	Below 40 per cent
▨	40 to 60 per cent
▨	60 to 80 per cent
▨	above 80 per cent

of the appropriate age
group

PRIMARY EDUCATION

A   n   t   a   r   c   t   i   c   a

C A N A D A

Greenland
Alaska

UNITED STATES OF AMERICA
(U.S.A.)

MEXICO

CUBA

WESTERN
SAHARA

VENEZUELA

COLOMBIA

ANTIGUA AND BARBUDA
ST. VINCENT
NICARAGUA
PANAMA

CAPE VERDE

ECUADOR

P E R U

BRAZIL

BOLIVIA

A R G E N T I N A

URUGUAY

☐	Below 40 per cent
▨	40 to 60 per cent
▨	60 to 80 per cent
▨	above 80 per cent

of the appropriate age
group

SEC

EDU

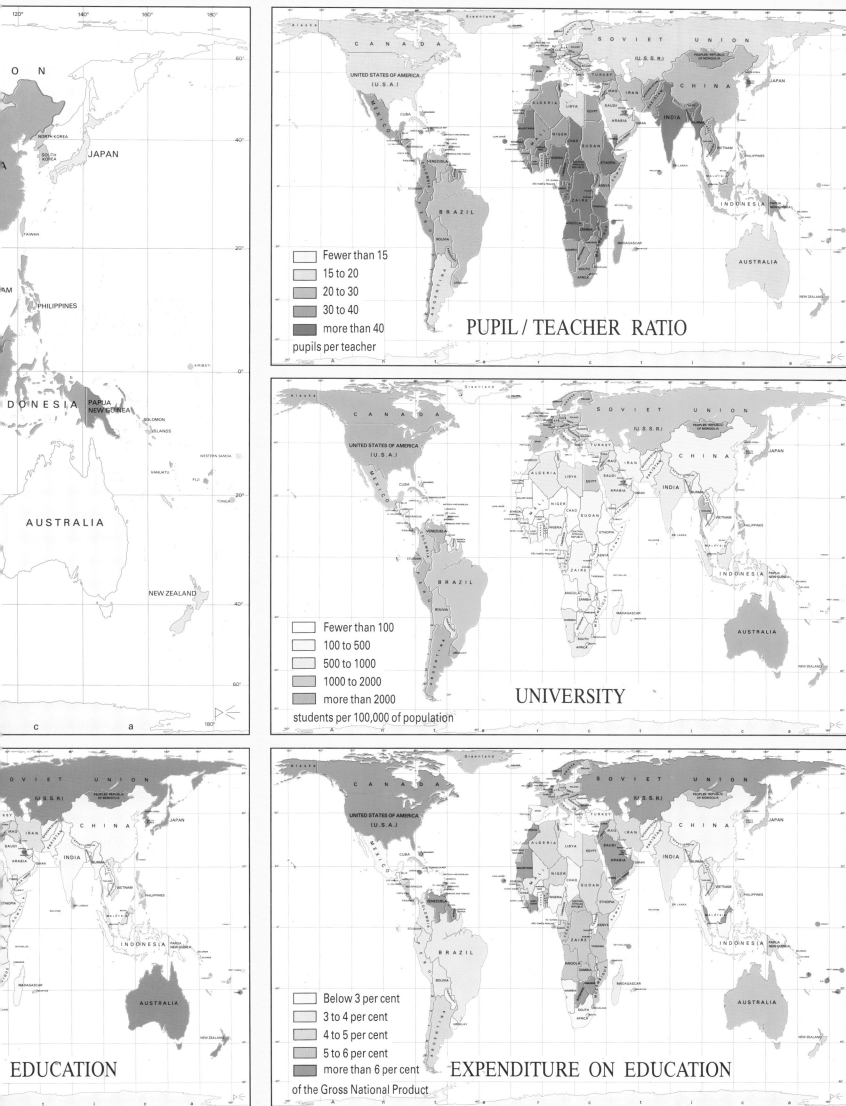

PUPIL / TEACHER RATIO

Fewer than 15
15 to 20
20 to 30
30 to 40
more than 40
pupils per teacher

UNIVERSITY

Fewer than 100
100 to 500
500 to 1000
1000 to 2000
more than 2000
students per 100,000 of population

EDUCATION

EXPENDITURE ON EDUCATION

Below 3 per cent
3 to 4 per cent
4 to 5 per cent
5 to 6 per cent
more than 6 per cent
of the Gross National Product

TION

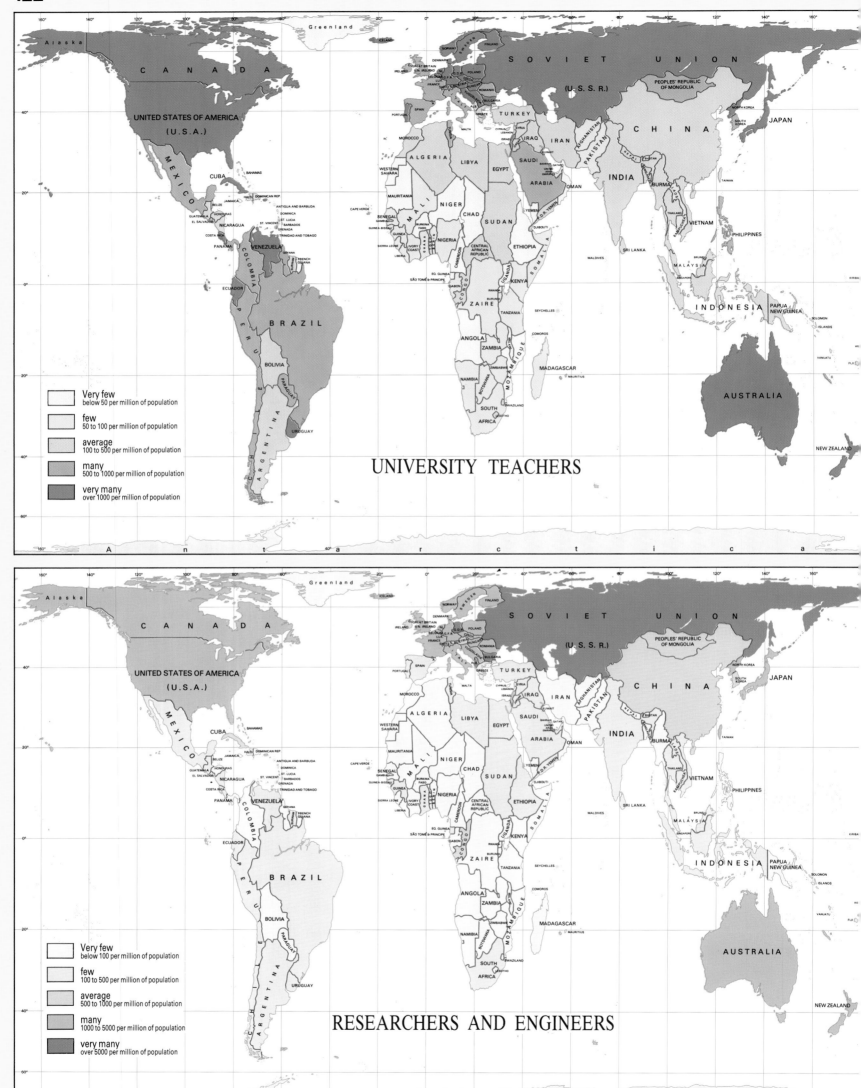

UNIVERSITY TEACHERS

Very few
below 50 per million of population

few
50 to 100 per million of population

average
100 to 500 per million of population

many
500 to 1000 per million of population

very many
over 1000 per million of population

RESEARCHERS AND ENGINEERS

Very few
below 100 per million of population

few
100 to 500 per million of population

average
500 to 1000 per million of population

many
1000 to 5000 per million of population

very many
over 5000 per million of population

THE S

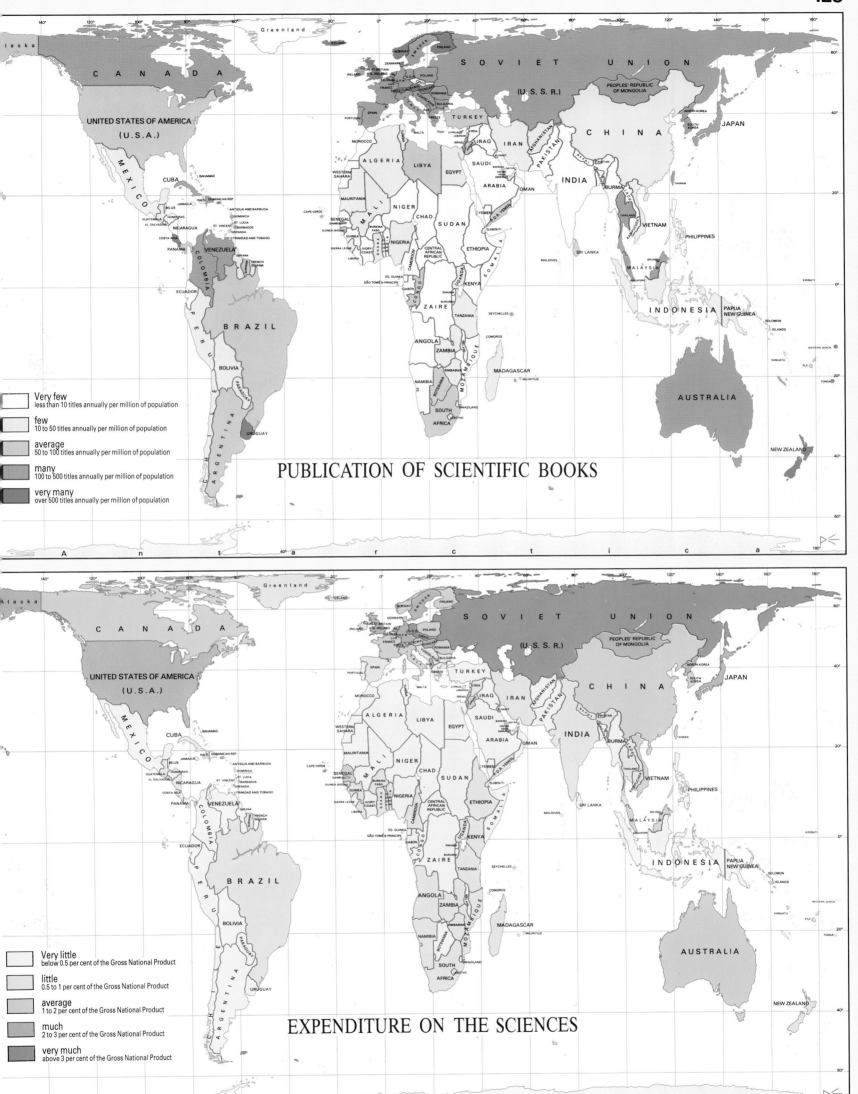

PUBLICATION OF SCIENTIFIC BOOKS

Very few
less than 10 titles annually per million of population

few
10 to 50 titles annually per million of population

average
50 to 100 titles annually per million of population

many
100 to 500 titles annually per million of population

very many
over 500 titles annually per million of population

EXPENDITURE ON THE SCIENCES

Very little
below 0.5 per cent of the Gross National Product

little
0.5 to 1 per cent of the Gross National Product

average
1 to 2 per cent of the Gross National Product

much
2 to 3 per cent of the Gross National Product

very much
above 3 per cent of the Gross National Product

ENCES

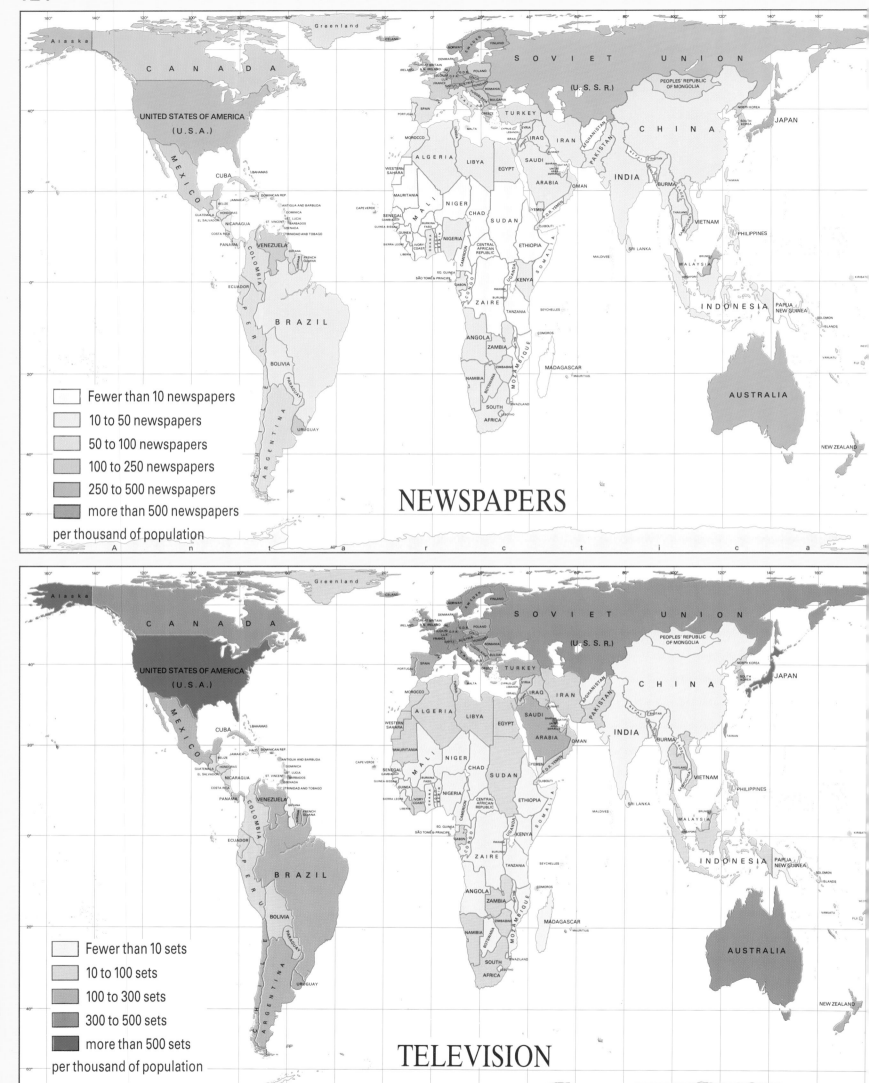

NEWSPAPERS

Fewer than 10 newspapers
10 to 50 newspapers
50 to 100 newspapers
100 to 250 newspapers
250 to 500 newspapers
more than 500 newspapers
per thousand of population

TELEVISION

Fewer than 10 sets
10 to 100 sets
100 to 300 sets
300 to 500 sets
more than 500 sets
per thousand of population

INFORM

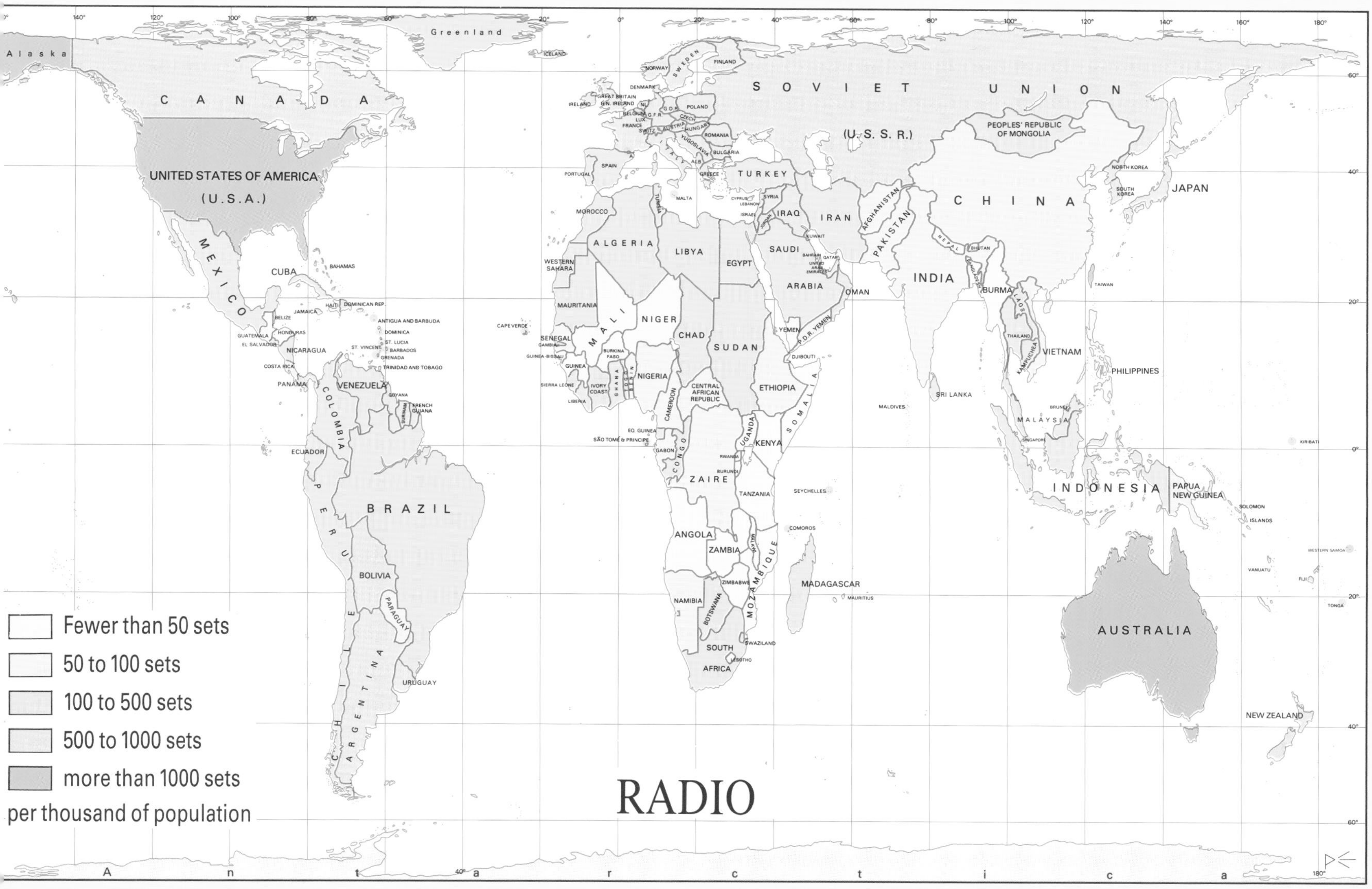
Fewer than 50 sets
50 to 100 sets
100 to 500 sets
500 to 1000 sets
more than 1000 sets
per thousand of population
RADIO

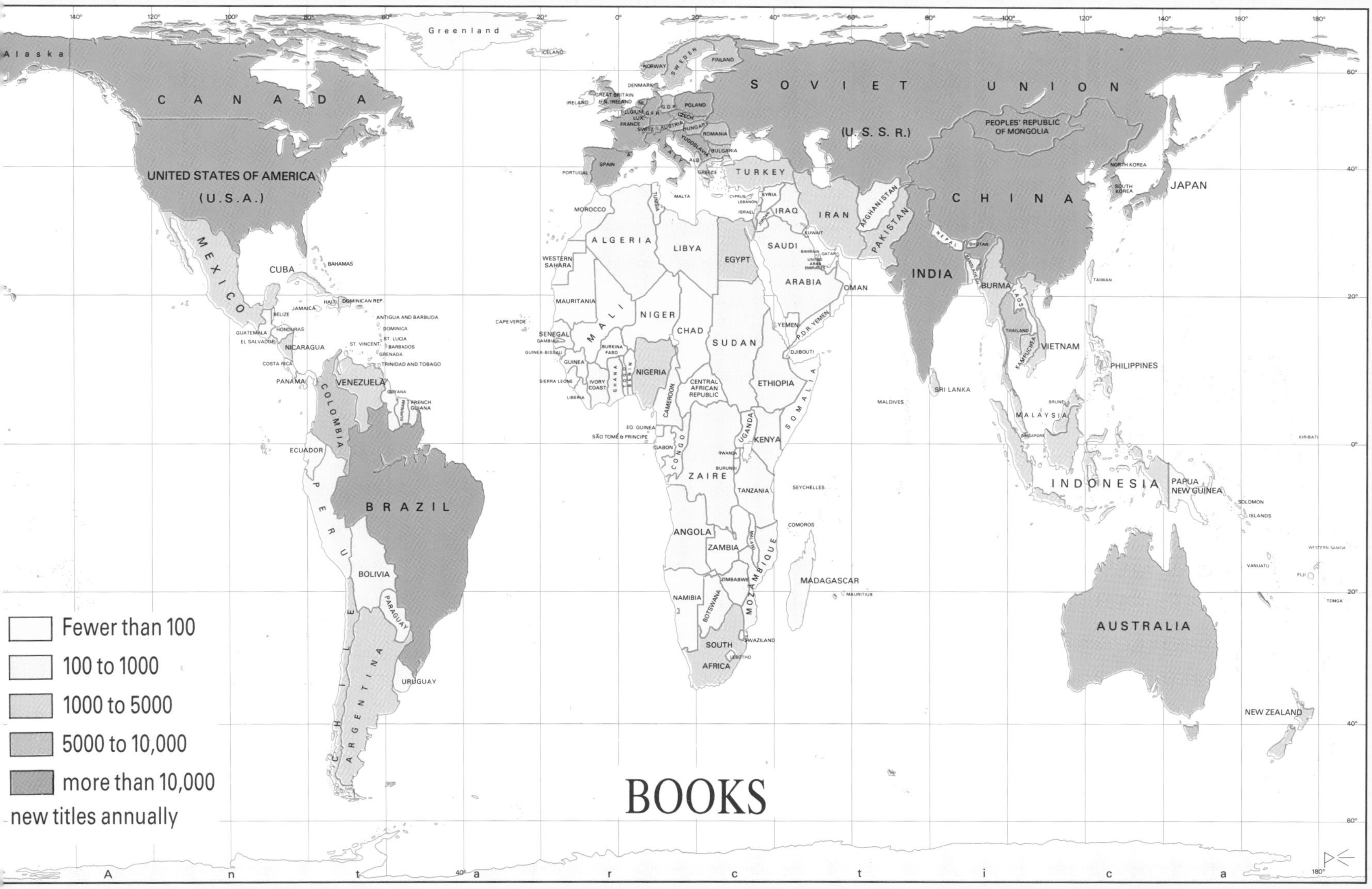
Fewer than 100
100 to 1000
1000 to 5000
5000 to 10,000
more than 10,000
new titles annually
BOOKS

TION

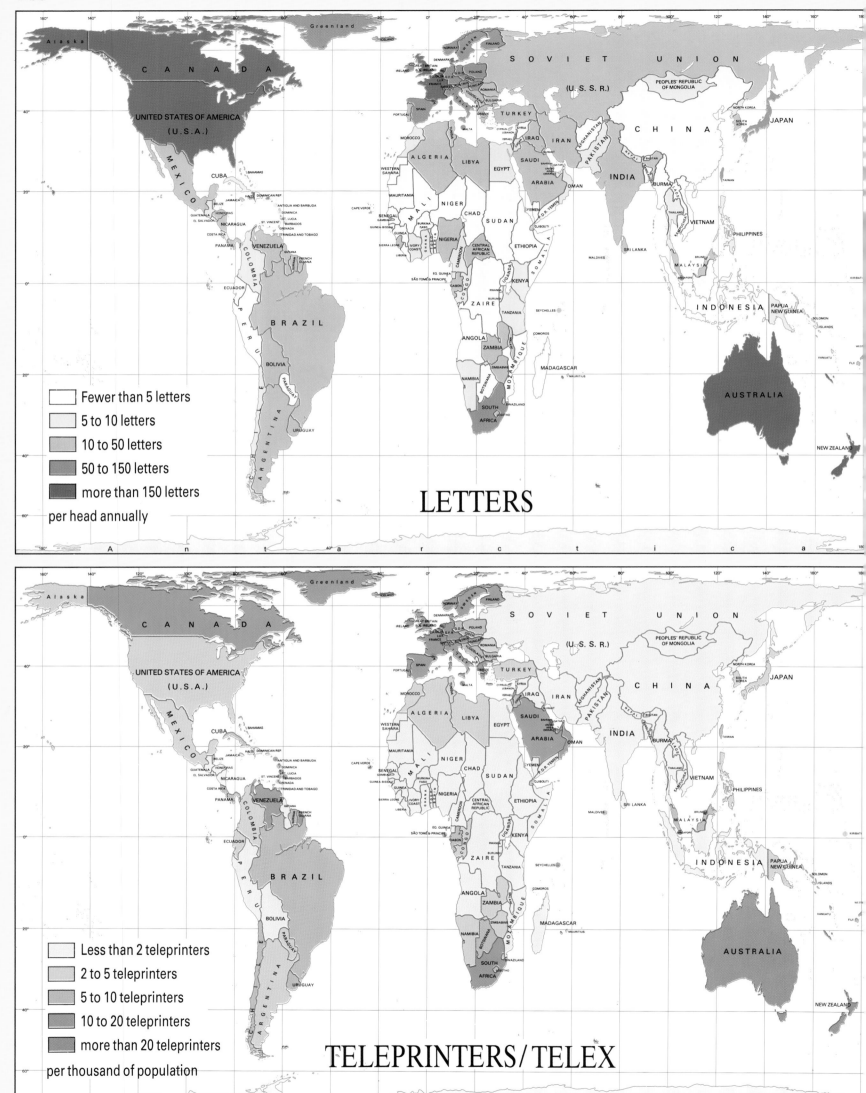

LETTERS

Fewer than 5 letters
5 to 10 letters
10 to 50 letters
50 to 150 letters
more than 150 letters
per head annually

TELEPRINTERS/TELEX

Less than 2 teleprinters
2 to 5 teleprinters
5 to 10 teleprinters
10 to 20 teleprinters
more than 20 teleprinters
per thousand of population

COMMU

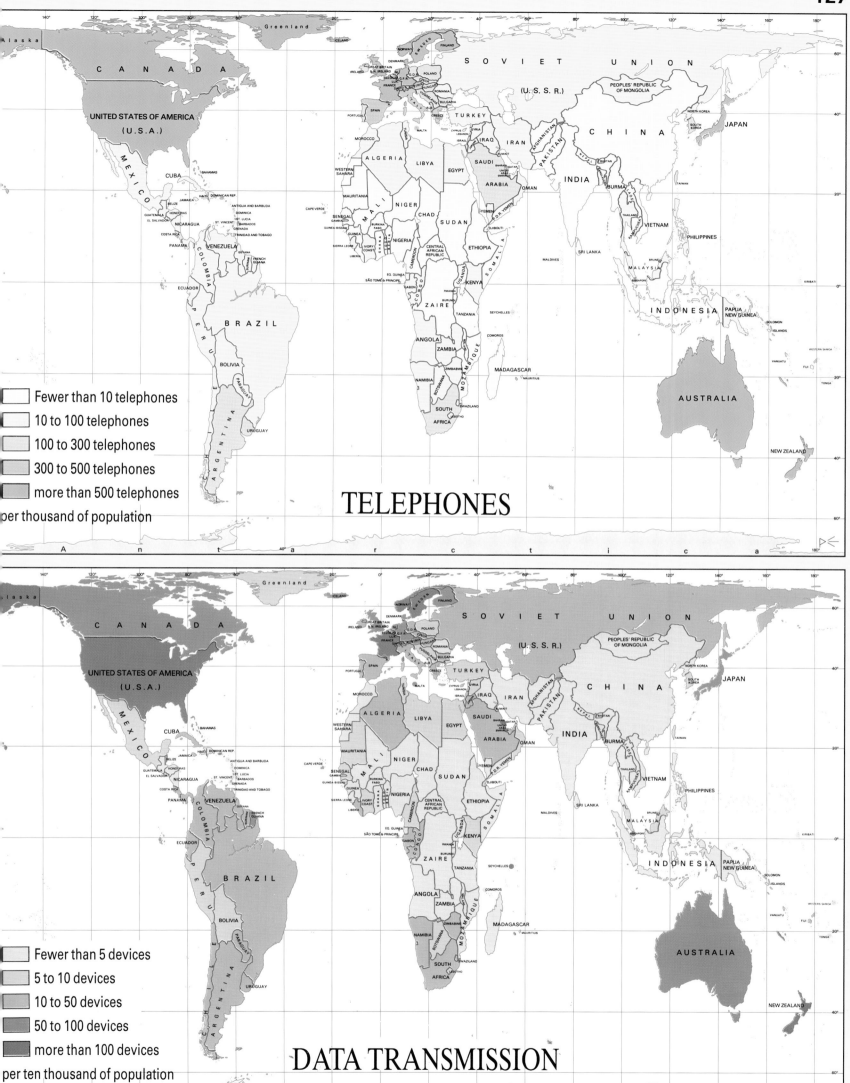

TELEPHONES

Fewer than 10 telephones
10 to 100 telephones
100 to 300 telephones
300 to 500 telephones
more than 500 telephones
per thousand of population

DATA TRANSMISSION

Fewer than 5 devices
5 to 10 devices
10 to 50 devices
50 to 100 devices
more than 100 devices
per ten thousand of population

CATIONS

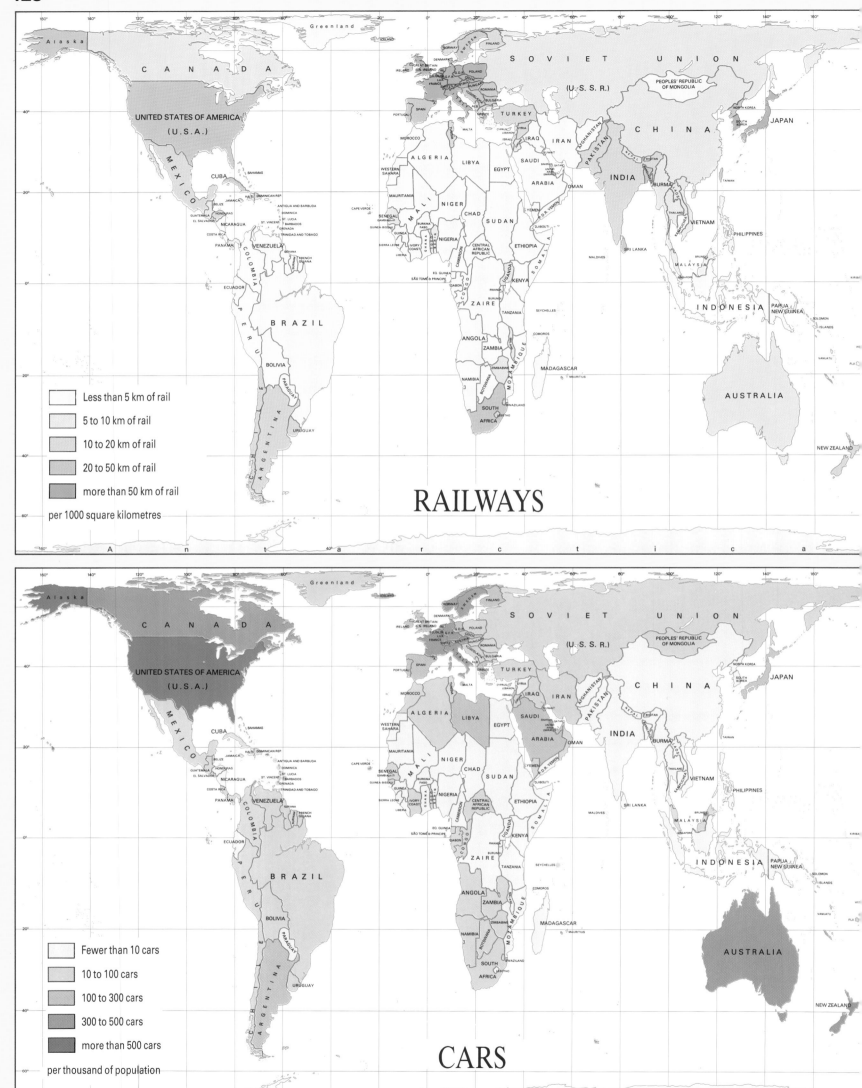

RAILWAYS

Less than 5 km of rail

5 to 10 km of rail

10 to 20 km of rail

20 to 50 km of rail

more than 50 km of rail

per 1000 square kilometres

CARS

Fewer than 10 cars

10 to 100 cars

100 to 300 cars

300 to 500 cars

more than 500 cars

per thousand of population

TRAFFIC

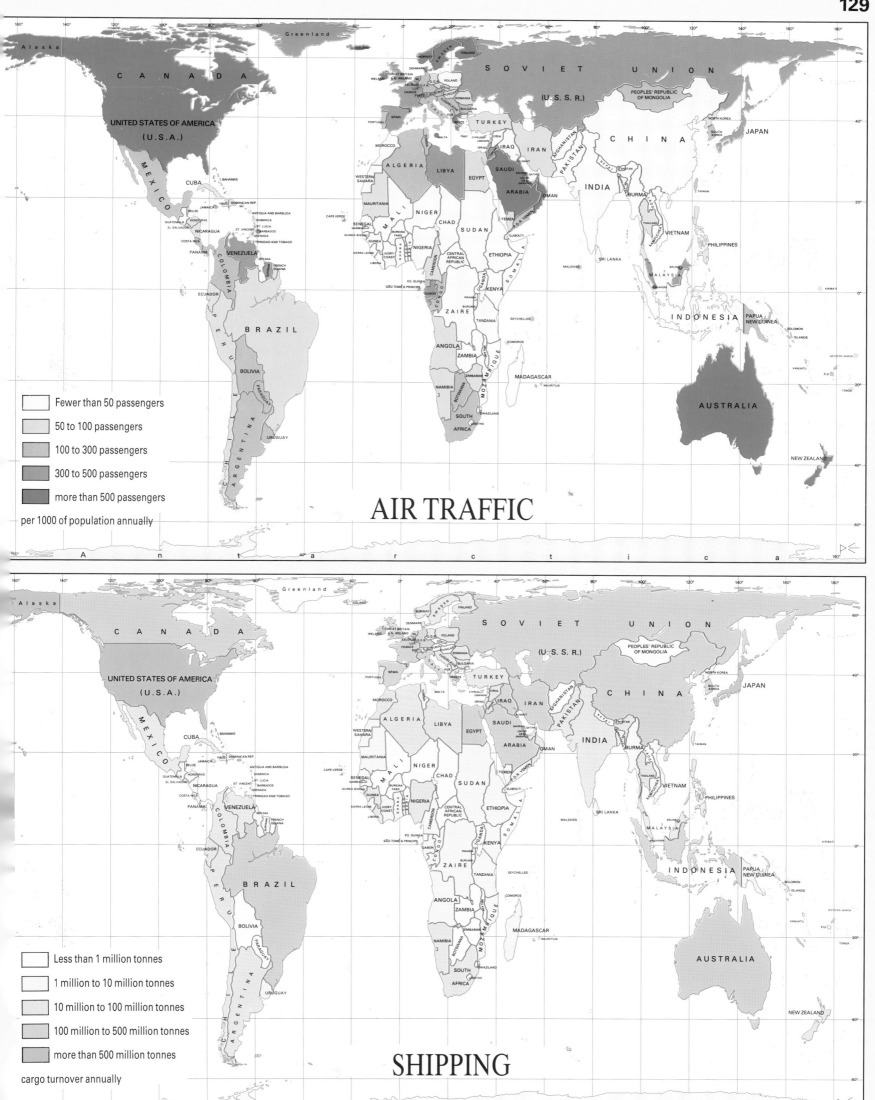

AIR TRAFFIC

Fewer than 50 passengers

50 to 100 passengers

100 to 300 passengers

300 to 500 passengers

more than 500 passengers

per 1000 of population annually

SHIPPING

Less than 1 million tonnes

1 million to 10 million tonnes

10 million to 100 million tonnes

100 million to 500 million tonnes

more than 500 million tonnes

cargo turnover annually

DENSITY

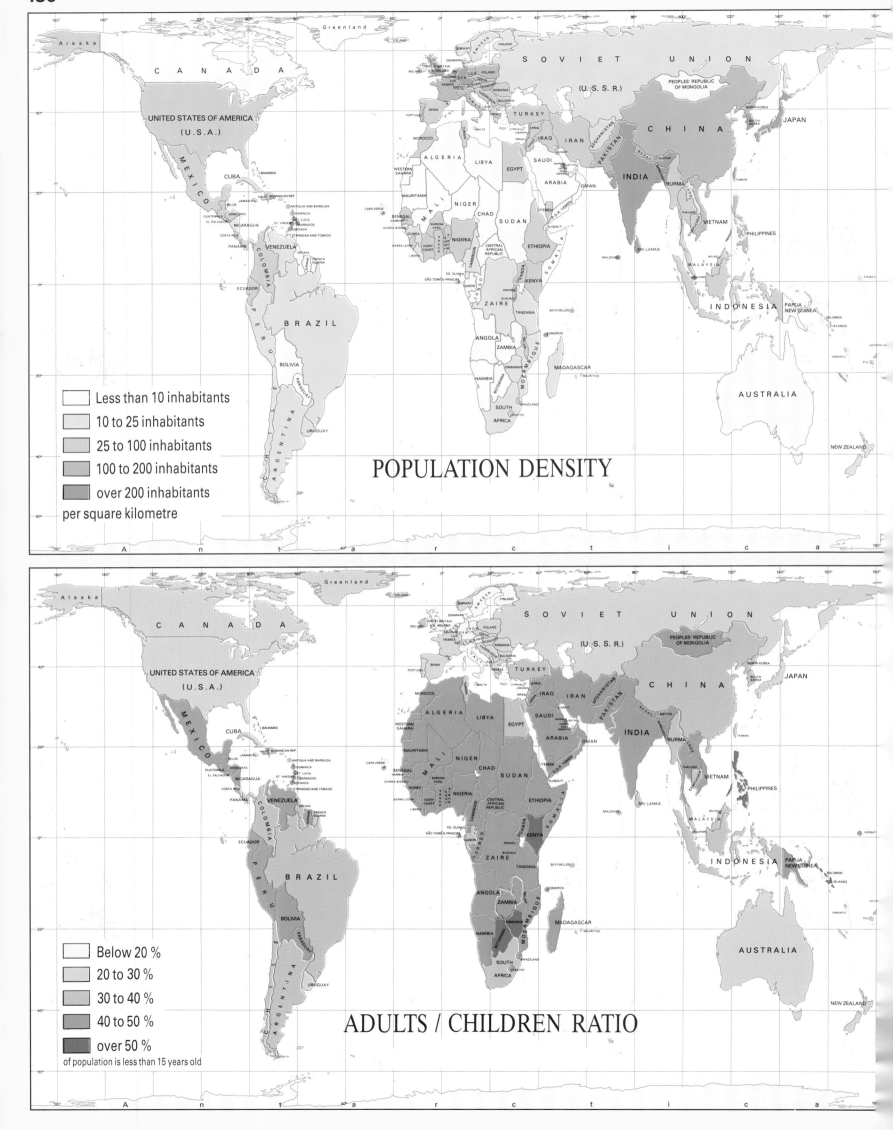

POPULATION DENSITY

Less than 10 inhabitants
10 to 25 inhabitants
25 to 100 inhabitants
100 to 200 inhabitants
over 200 inhabitants
per square kilometre

ADULTS / CHILDREN RATIO

Below 20 %
20 to 30 %
30 to 40 %
40 to 50 %
over 50 %
of population is less than 15 years old

POPULATIO

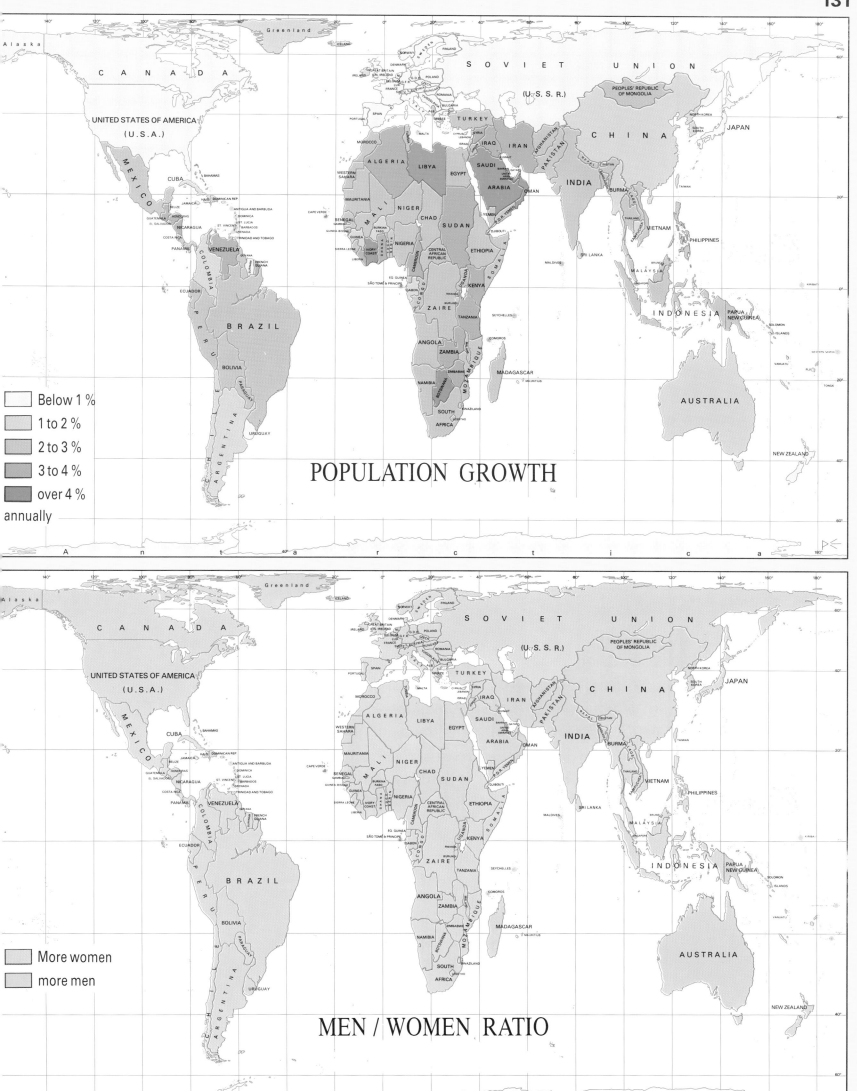

POPULATION GROWTH

Below 1 %
1 to 2 %
2 to 3 %
3 to 4 %
over 4 %
annually

MEN / WOMEN RATIO

More women
more men

STRUCTURE

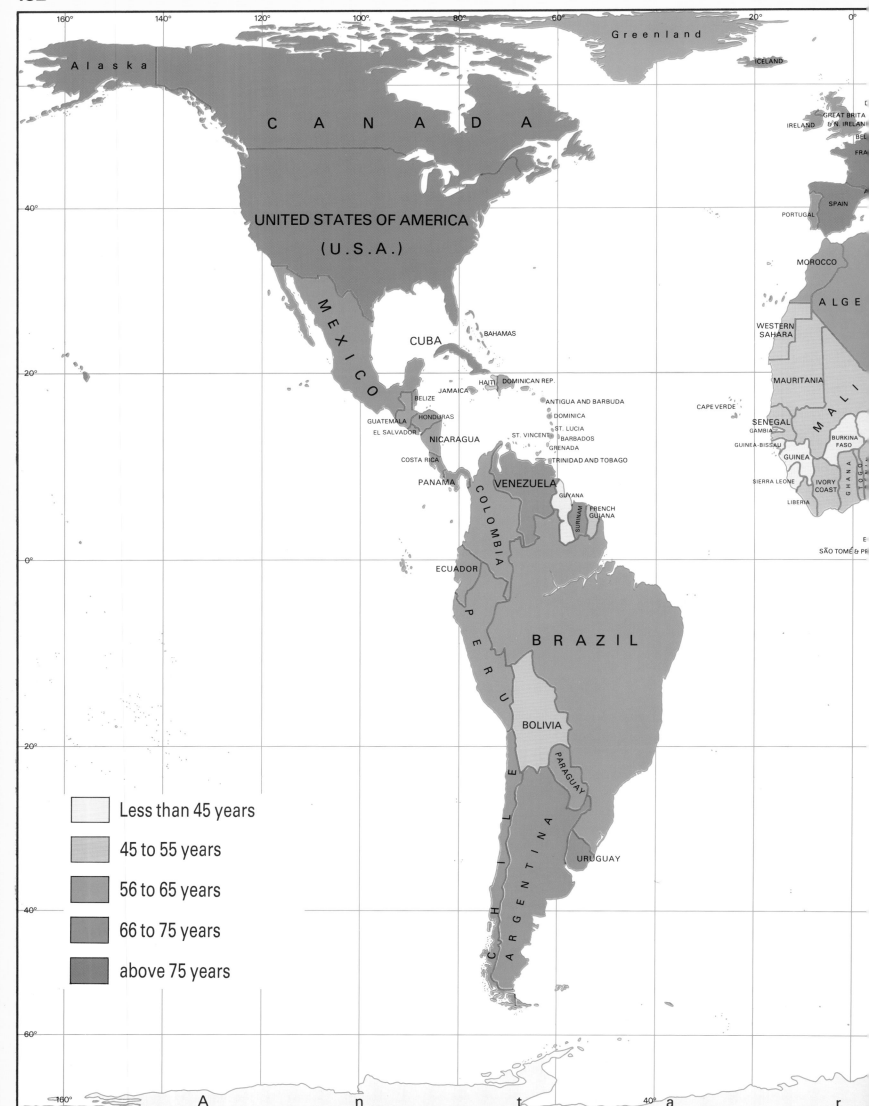

Less than 45 years

45 to 55 years

56 to 65 years

66 to 75 years

above 75 years

LIFE EX

CTANCY

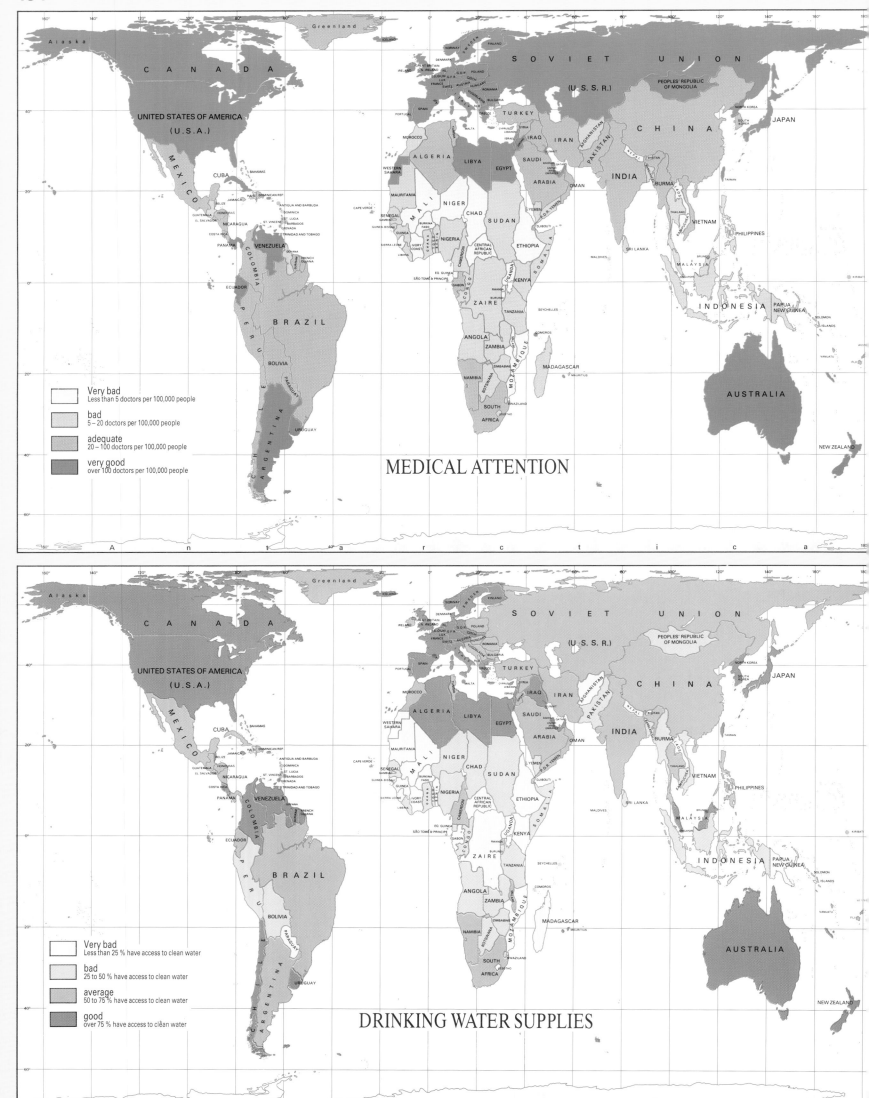

MEDICAL ATTENTION

Very bad
Less than 5 doctors per 100,000 people

bad
5 – 20 doctors per 100,000 people

adequate
20 – 100 doctors per 100,000 people

very good
over 100 doctors per 100,000 people

DRINKING WATER SUPPLIES

Very bad
Less than 25 % have access to clean water

bad
25 to 50 % have access to clean water

average
50 to 75 % have access to clean water

good
over 75 % have access to clean water

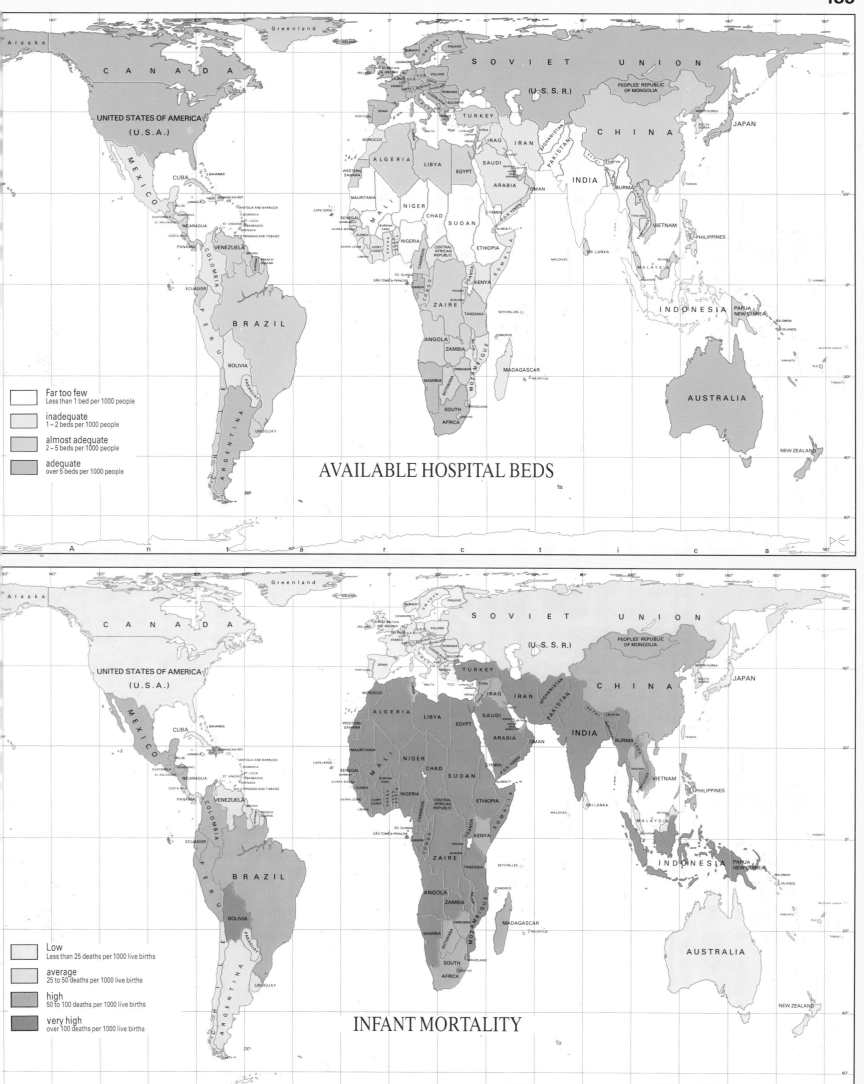

AVAILABLE HOSPITAL BEDS

Far too few
Less than 1 bed per 1000 people

inadequate
1 – 2 beds per 1000 people

almost adequate
2 – 5 beds per 1000 people

adequate
over 5 beds per 1000 people

INFANT MORTALITY

Low
Less than 25 deaths per 1000 live births

average
25 to 50 deaths per 1000 live births

high
50 to 100 deaths per 1000 live births

very high
over 100 deaths per 1000 live births

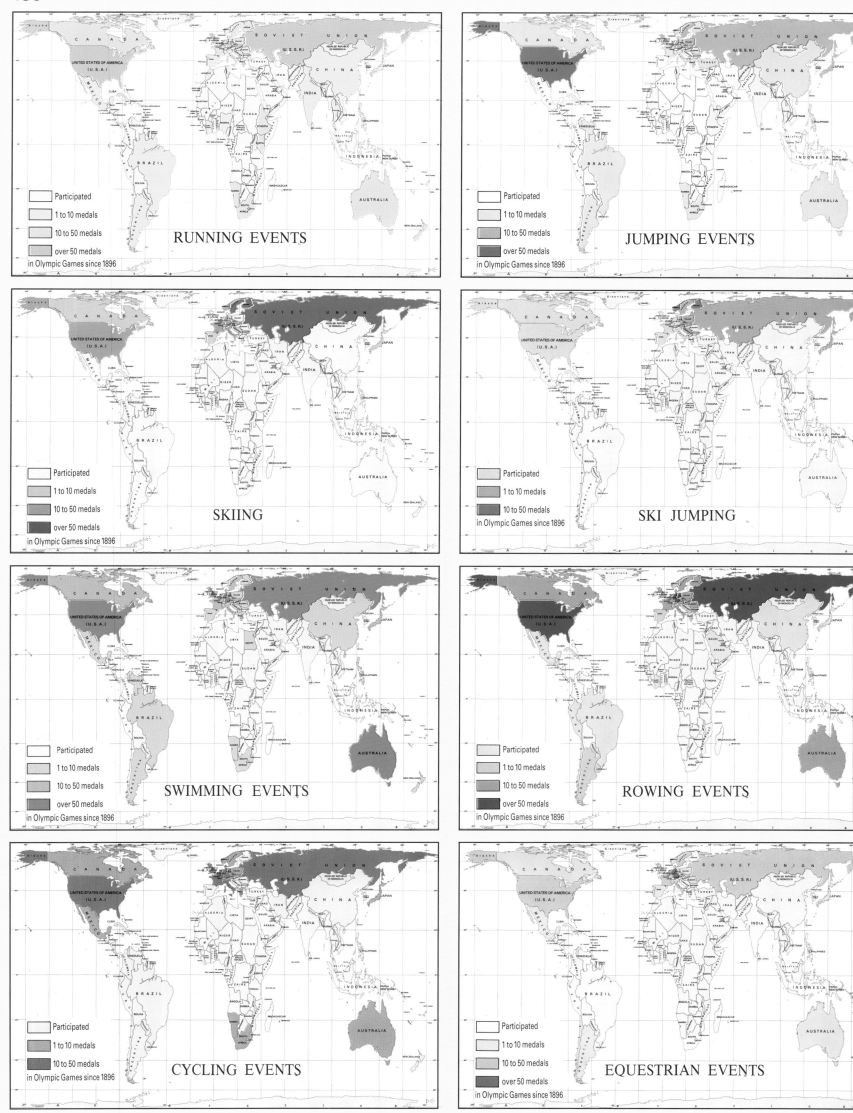

RUNNING EVENTS

Participated
1 to 10 medals
10 to 50 medals
over 50 medals
in Olympic Games since 1896

JUMPING EVENTS

Participated
1 to 10 medals
10 to 50 medals
over 50 medals
in Olympic Games since 1896

SKIING

Participated
1 to 10 medals
10 to 50 medals
over 50 medals
in Olympic Games since 1896

SKI JUMPING

Participated
1 to 10 medals
10 to 50 medals
in Olympic Games since 1896

SWIMMING EVENTS

Participated
1 to 10 medals
10 to 50 medals
over 50 medals
in Olympic Games since 1896

ROWING EVENTS

Participated
1 to 10 medals
10 to 50 medals
over 50 medals
in Olympic Games since 1896

CYCLING EVENTS

Participated
1 to 10 medals
10 to 50 medals
in Olympic Games since 1896

EQUESTRIAN EVENTS

Participated
1 to 10 medals
10 to 50 medals
over 50 medals
in Olympic Games since 1896

SPC

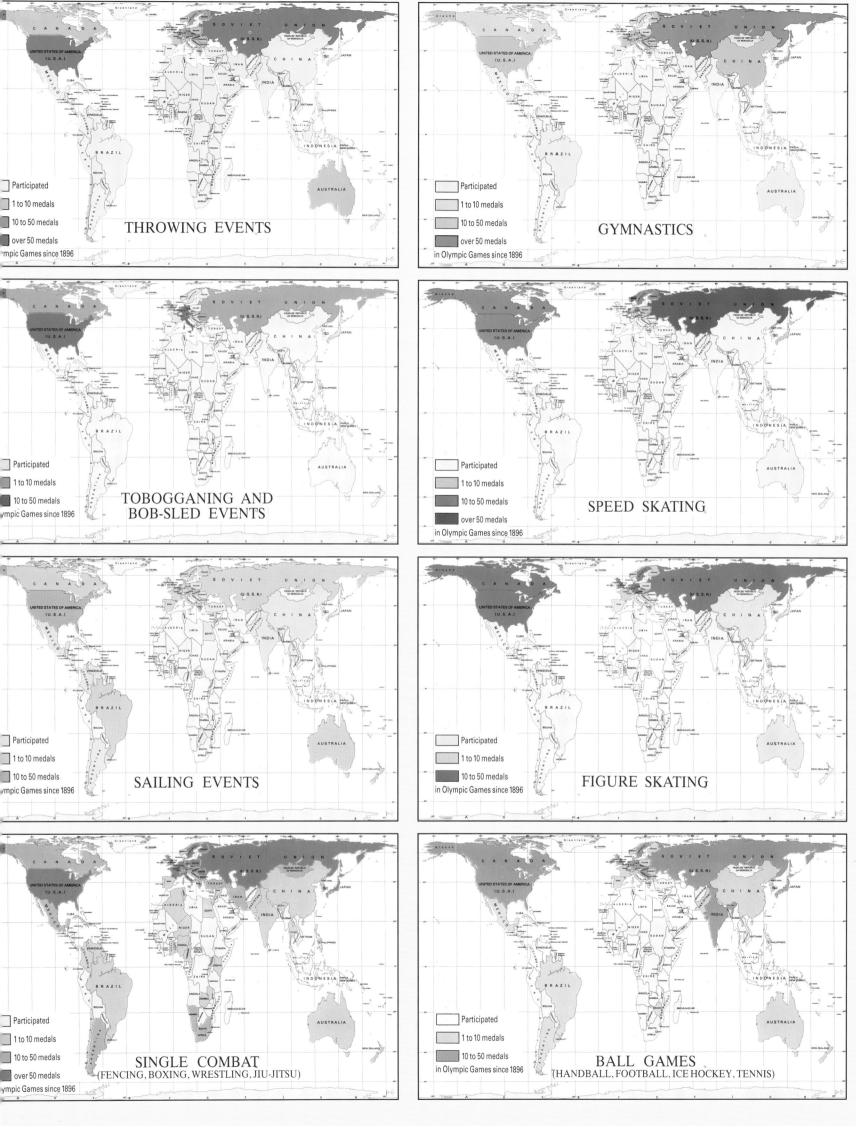

THROWING EVENTS

Participated
1 to 10 medals
10 to 50 medals
over 50 medals
in Olympic Games since 1896

GYMNASTICS

Participated
1 to 10 medals
10 to 50 medals
over 50 medals
in Olympic Games since 1896

TOBOGGANING AND
BOB-SLED EVENTS

Participated
1 to 10 medals
10 to 50 medals
in Olympic Games since 1896

SPEED SKATING

Participated
1 to 10 medals
10 to 50 medals
over 50 medals
in Olympic Games since 1896

SAILING EVENTS

Participated
1 to 10 medals
10 to 50 medals
in Olympic Games since 1896

FIGURE SKATING

Participated
1 to 10 medals
10 to 50 medals
in Olympic Games since 1896

SINGLE COMBAT
(FENCING, BOXING, WRESTLING, JIU-JITSU)

Participated
1 to 10 medals
10 to 50 medals
over 50 medals
in Olympic Games since 1896

BALL GAMES
(HANDBALL, FOOTBALL, ICE HOCKEY, TENNIS)

Participated
1 to 10 medals
10 to 50 medals
in Olympic Games since 1896

T

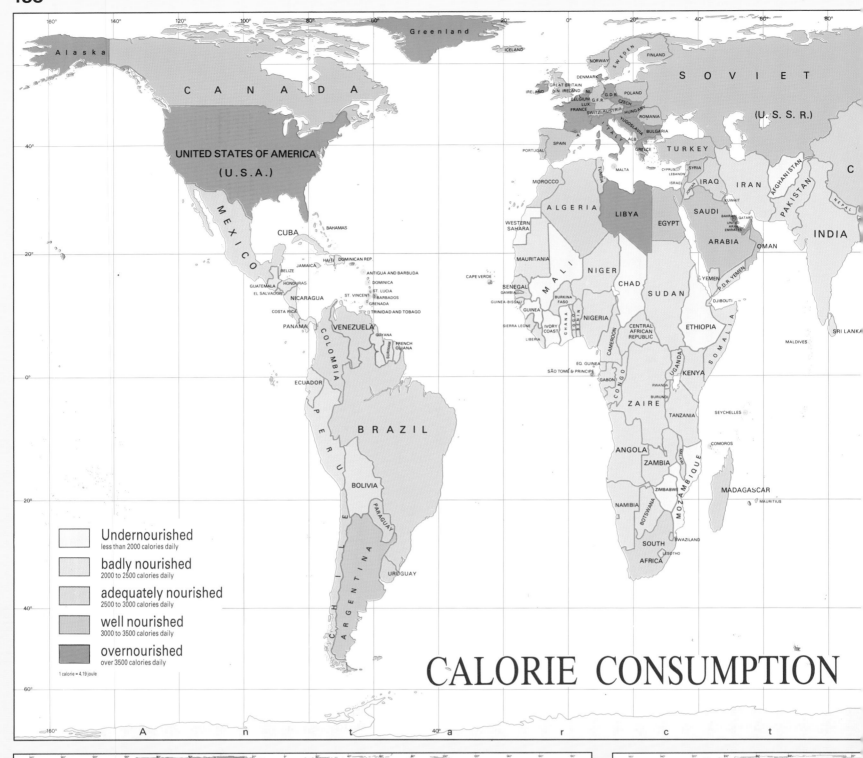

Underncurished
less than 2000 calories daily

badly nourished
2000 to 2500 calories daily

adequately nourished
2500 to 3000 calories daily

well nourished
3000 to 3500 calories daily

overnourished
over 3500 calories daily

1 calorie = 4.19 joule

CALORIE CONSUMPTION

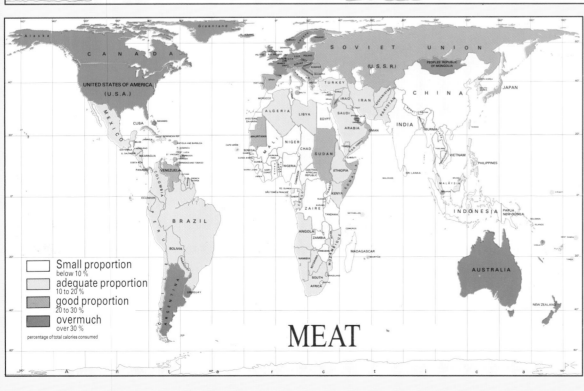

Small proportion
below 10 %

adequate proportion
10 to 20 %

good proportion
20 to 30 %

overmuch
over 30 %

percentage of total calories consumed

MEAT

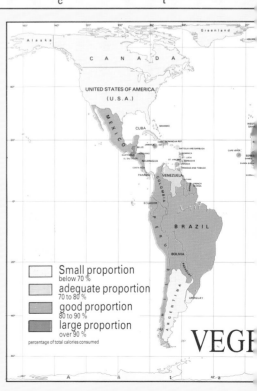

Small proportion
below 70 %

adequate proportion
70 to 80 %

good proportion
80 to 90 %

large proportion
over 90 %

percentage of total calories consumed

VEGE

NUT

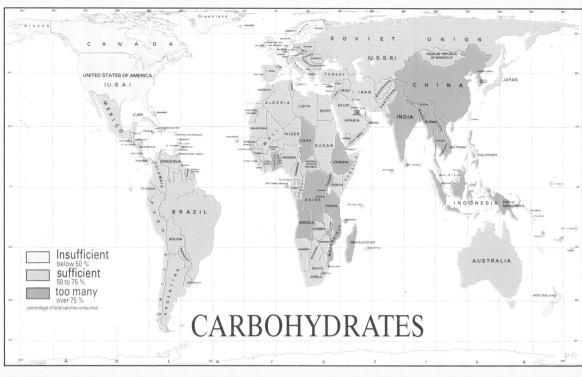

CARBOHYDRATES

	Insufficient
	below 50 %
	sufficient
	50 to 75 %
	too many
	over 75 %

percentage of total calories consumed

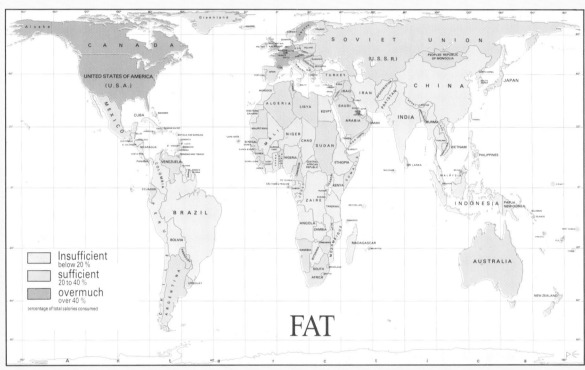

FAT

	Insufficient
	below 20 %
	sufficient
	20 to 40 %
	overmuch
	over 40 %

percentage of total calories consumed

ES AND FRUIT

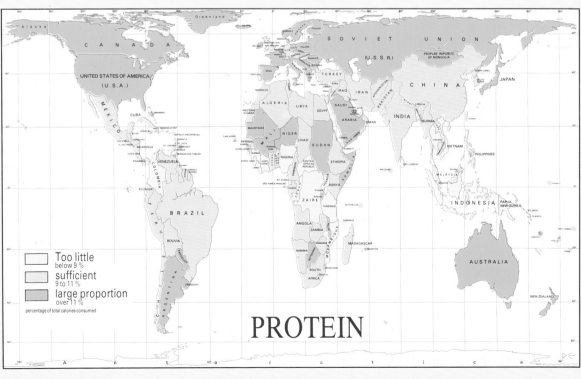

PROTEIN

	Too little
	below 9 %
	sufficient
	9 to 11 %
	large proportion
	over 11 %

percentage of total calories consumed

TION

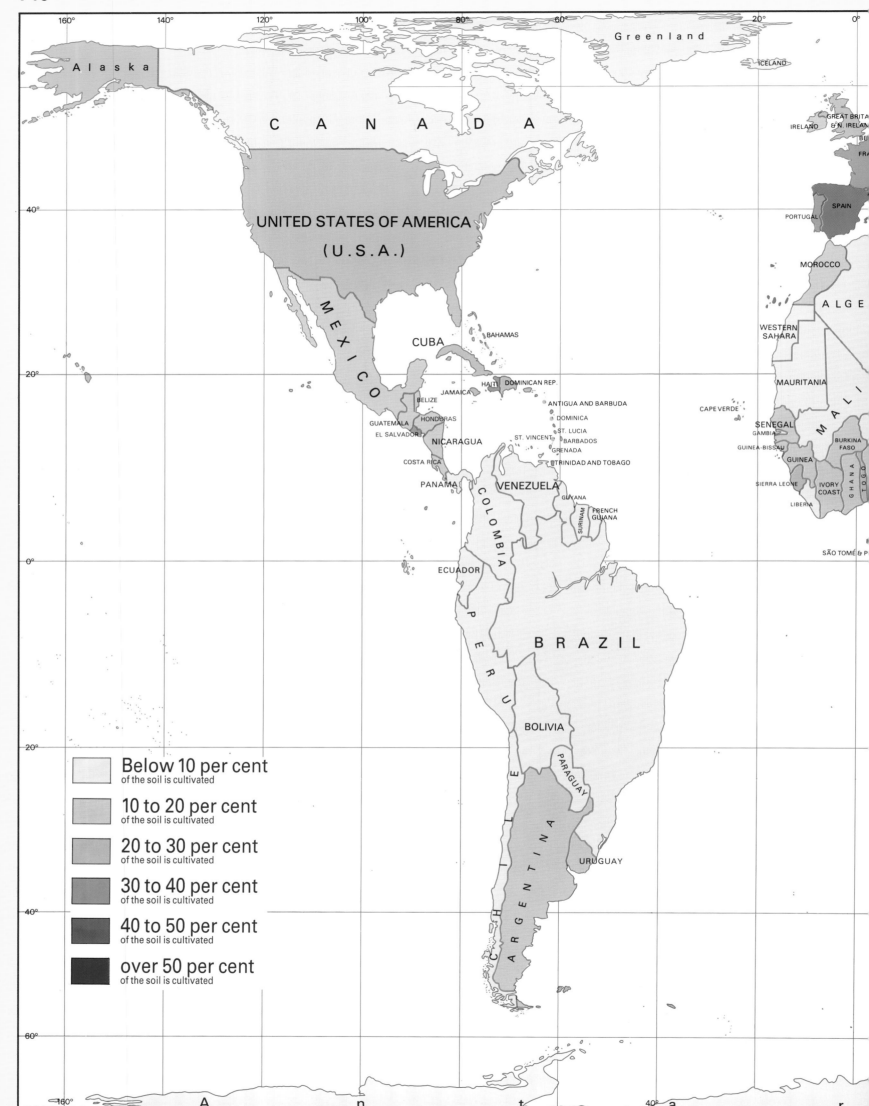

Below 10 per cent
of the soil is cultivated

10 to 20 per cent
of the soil is cultivated

20 to 30 per cent
of the soil is cultivated

30 to 40 per cent
of the soil is cultivated

40 to 50 per cent
of the soil is cultivated

over 50 per cent
of the soil is cultivated

SOIL CULT

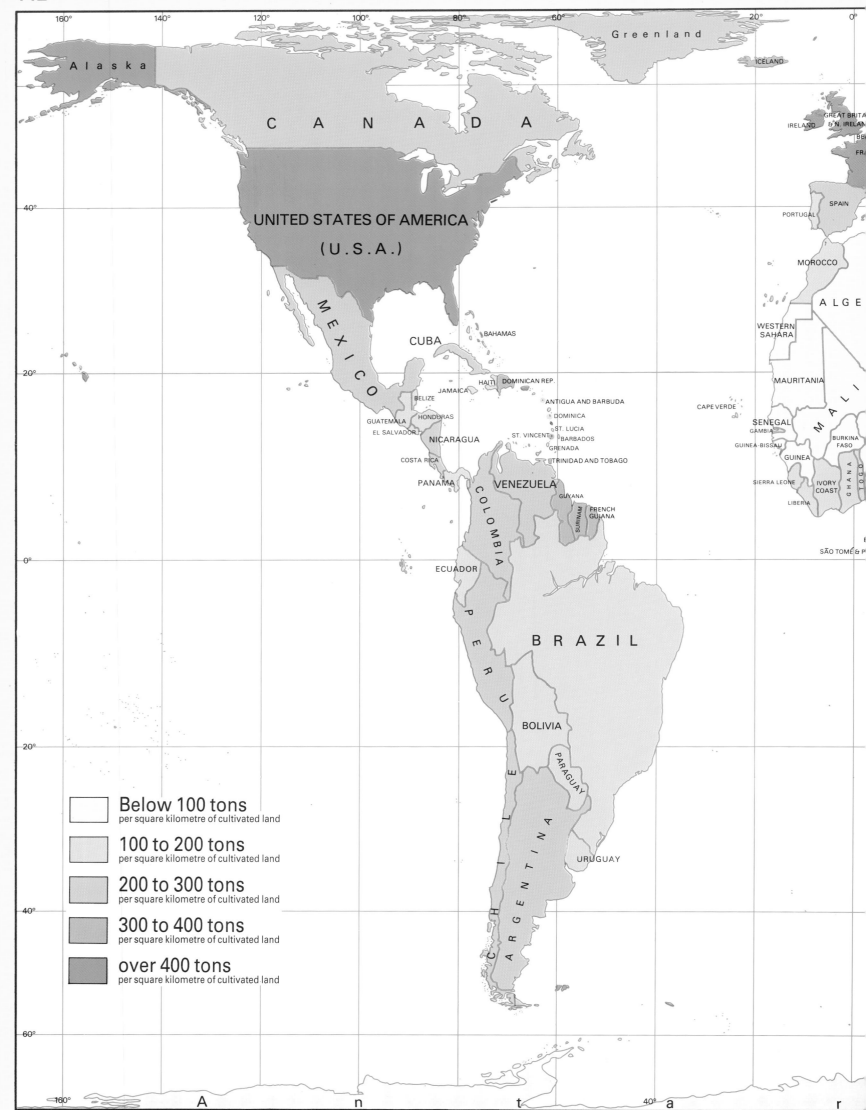

160° 140° 120° 100° 80° 60° 20° 0°

Greenland

ICELAND

Alaska

C A N A D A

GREAT BRITA
IRELAND   & N. IRELAND
                          FRA

40°

UNITED STATES OF AMERICA

(U.S.A.)

SPAIN
PORTUGAL

MOROCCO

M E X I C O

A L G E

WESTERN
SAHARA

CUBA

BAHAMAS

20°

MAURITANIA

M A L I

HAITI   DOMINICAN REP.

JAMAICA

BELIZE   ANTIGUA AND BARBUDA   CAPE VERDE

GUATEMALA   HONDURAS   DOMINICA   SENEGAL

EL SALVADOR   ST. LUCIA   GAMBIA   BURKINA
                                                                   GUINEA-BISSAU   FASO

NICARAGUA   ST. VINCENT BARBADOS   GUINEA

                              GRENADA   SIERRA LEONE   IVORY

COSTA RICA   TRINIDAD AND TOBAGO   COAST   GHANA TOGO

LIBERIA

PANAMA   VENEZUELA

                              GUYANA

0°   COLOMBIA   SURINAM FRENCH   SÃO TOMÉ & P
                                              GUIANA

ECUADOR

P
E
R
U

B R A Z I L

BOLIVIA

20°   PARAGUAY

Below 100 tons
per square kilometre of cultivated land

100 to 200 tons
per square kilometre of cultivated land

C
H
I
L
E
A
R
G
E
N
T
I
N
A

URUGUAY

200 to 300 tons
per square kilometre of cultivated land

300 to 400 tons
per square kilometre of cultivated land

40°

over 400 tons
per square kilometre of cultivated land

60°

160°   A   n   t   40°   a   r

CRO

YIELD

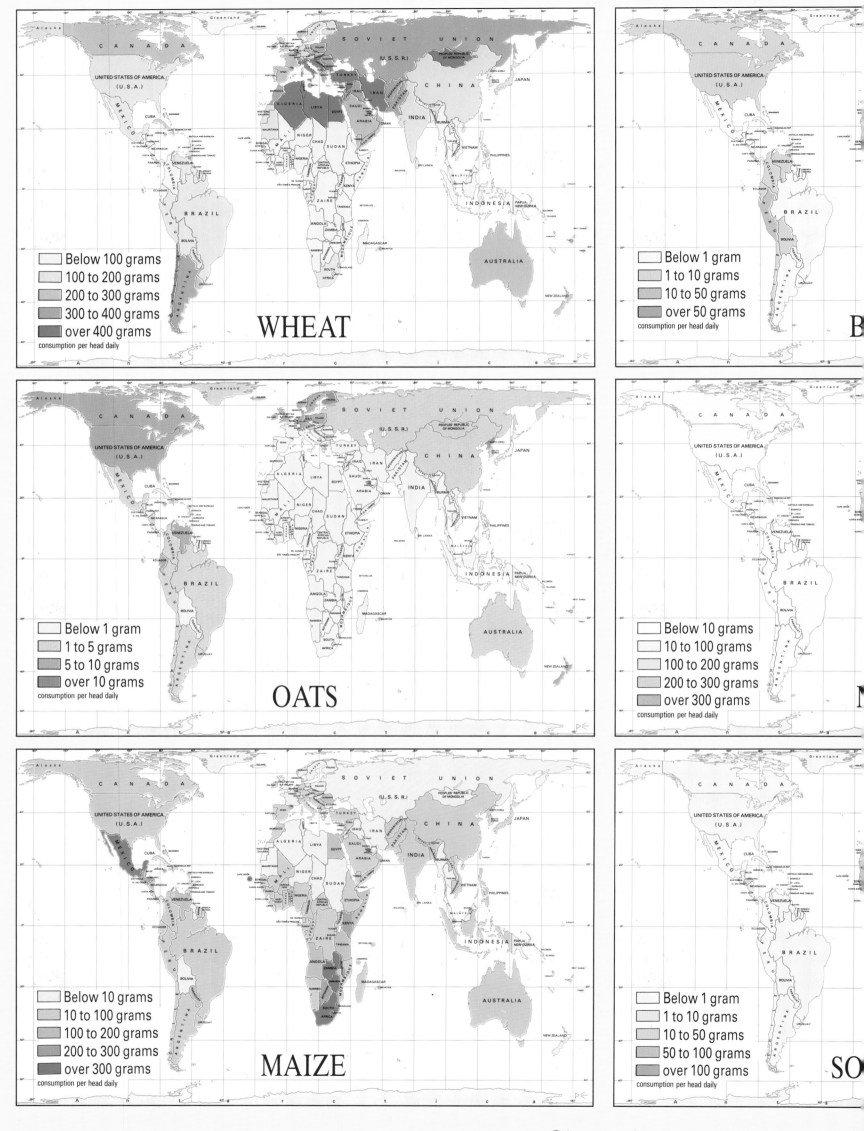

Below 100 grams
100 to 200 grams
200 to 300 grams
300 to 400 grams
over 400 grams
consumption per head daily

WHEAT

Below 1 gram
1 to 10 grams
10 to 50 grams
over 50 grams
consumption per head daily

B

Below 1 gram
1 to 5 grams
5 to 10 grams
over 10 grams
consumption per head daily

OATS

Below 10 grams
10 to 100 grams
100 to 200 grams
200 to 300 grams
over 300 grams
consumption per head daily

M

Below 10 grams
10 to 100 grams
100 to 200 grams
200 to 300 grams
over 300 grams
consumption per head daily

MAIZE

Below 1 gram
1 to 10 grams
10 to 50 grams
50 to 100 grams
over 100 grams
consumption per head daily

SO

STAPLE FO

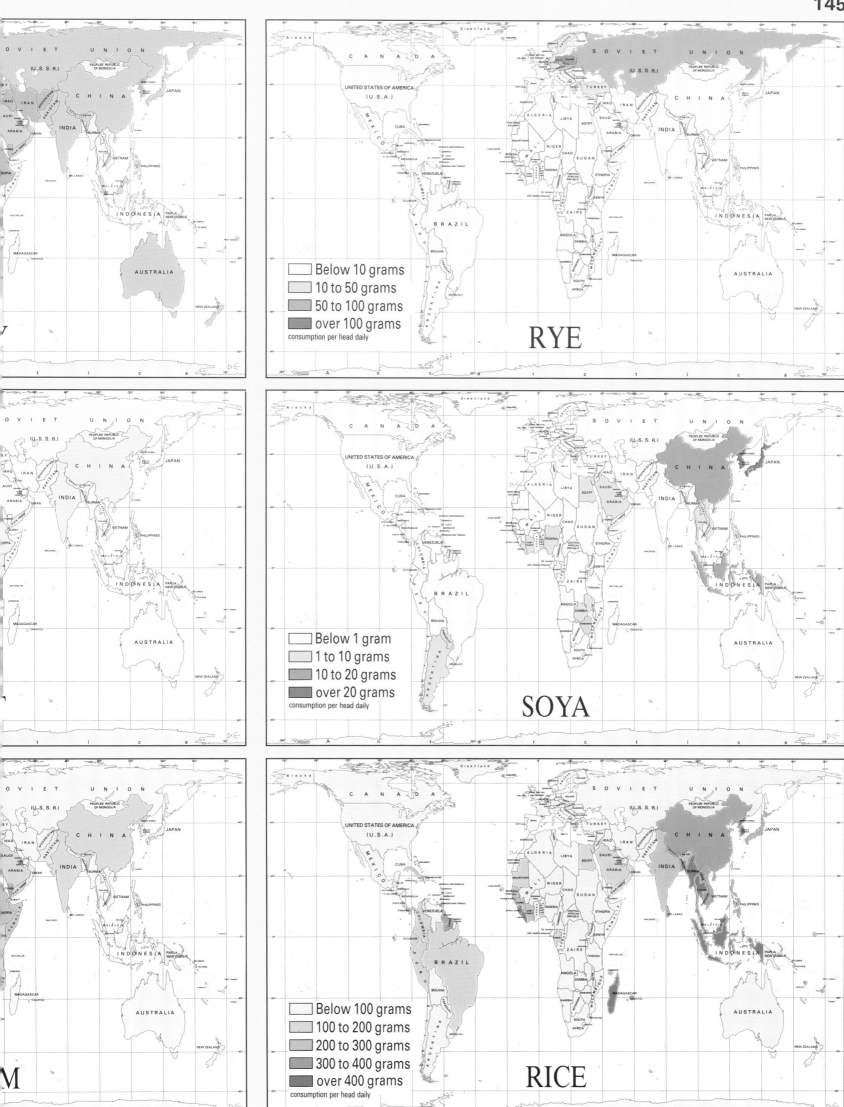

RYE

Below 10 grams
10 to 50 grams
50 to 100 grams
over 100 grams
consumption per head daily

SOYA

Below 1 gram
1 to 10 grams
10 to 20 grams
over 20 grams
consumption per head daily

RICE

Below 100 grams
100 to 200 grams
200 to 300 grams
300 to 400 grams
over 400 grams
consumption per head daily

ODSTUFFS

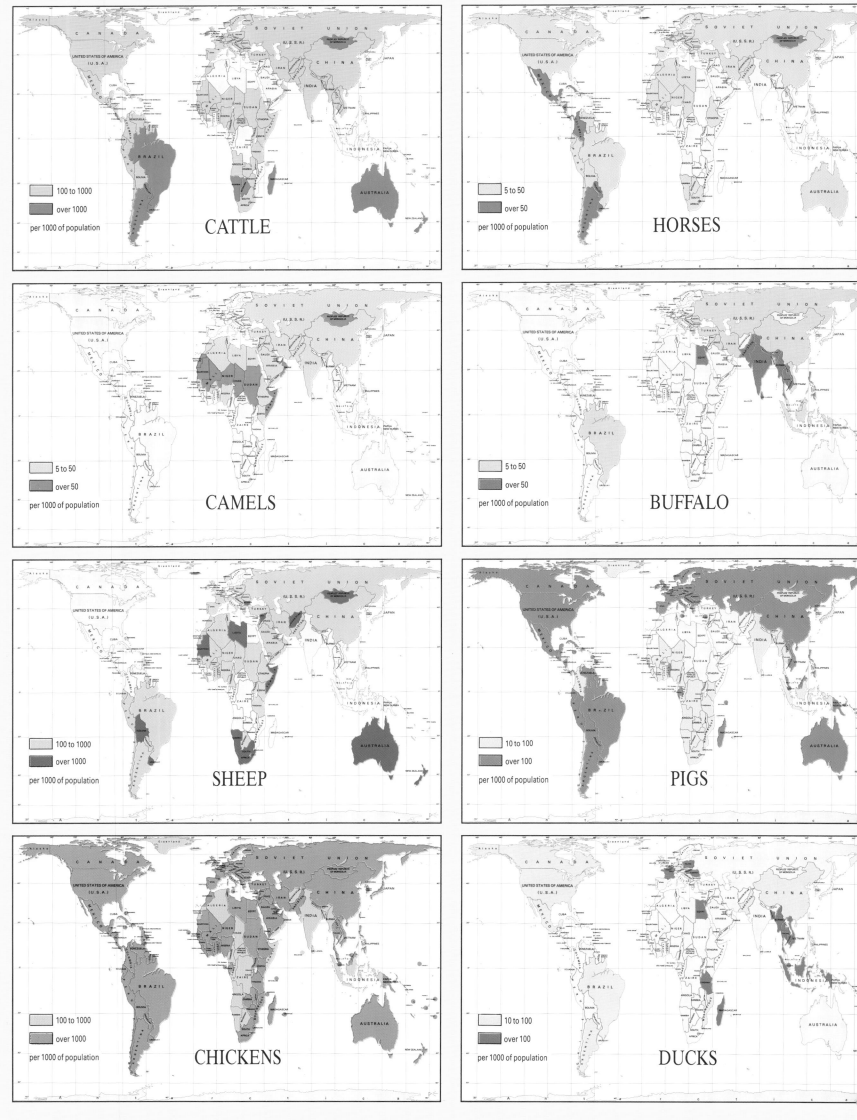

CATTLE

100 to 1000
over 1000
per 1000 of population

HORSES

5 to 50
over 50
per 1000 of population

CAMELS

5 to 50
over 50
per 1000 of population

BUFFALO

5 to 50
over 50
per 1000 of population

SHEEP

100 to 1000
over 1000
per 1000 of population

PIGS

10 to 100
over 100
per 1000 of population

CHICKENS

100 to 1000
over 1000
per 1000 of population

DUCKS

10 to 100
over 100
per 1000 of population

DOMESTI

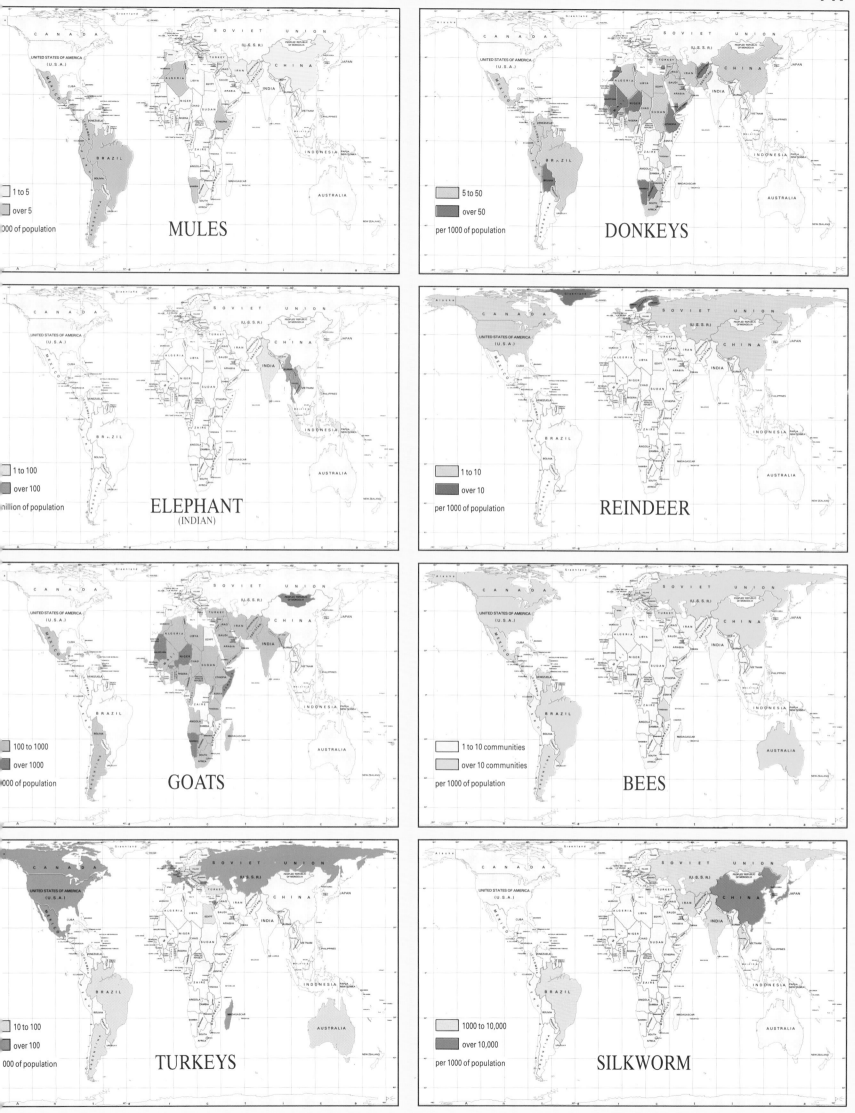

MULES

1 to 5
over 5
000 of population

DONKEYS

5 to 50
over 50
per 1000 of population

ELEPHANT
(INDIAN)

1 to 100
over 100
million of population

REINDEER

1 to 10
over 10
per 1000 of population

GOATS

100 to 1000
over 1000
000 of population

BEES

1 to 10 communities
over 10 communities
per 1000 of population

TURKEYS

10 to 100
over 100
000 of population

SILKWORM

1000 to 10,000
over 10,000
per 1000 of population

ANIMALS

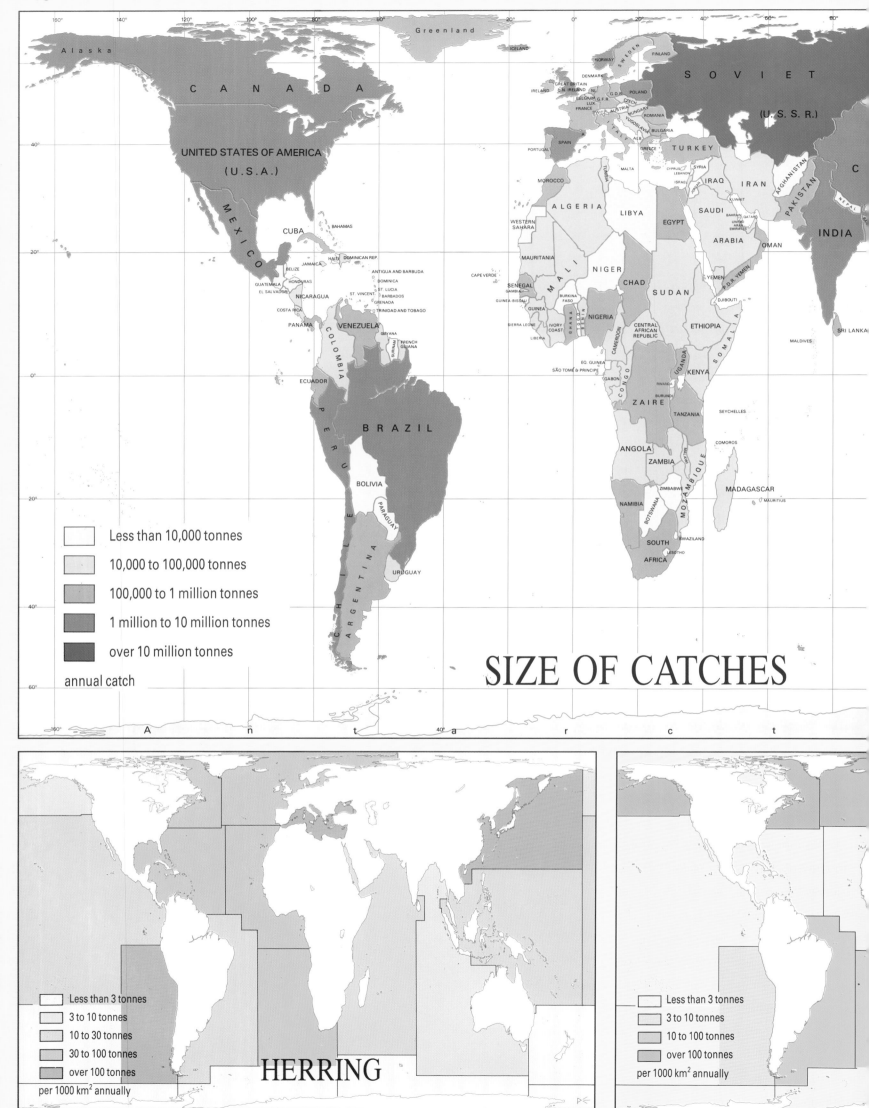

SIZE OF CATCHES

Less than 10,000 tonnes

10,000 to 100,000 tonnes

100,000 to 1 million tonnes

1 million to 10 million tonnes

over 10 million tonnes

annual catch

HERRING

Less than 3 tonnes

3 to 10 tonnes

10 to 30 tonnes

30 to 100 tonnes

over 100 tonnes

per 1000 km² annually

Less than 3 tonnes

3 to 10 tonnes

10 to 100 tonnes

over 100 tonnes

per 1000 km² annually

FISI

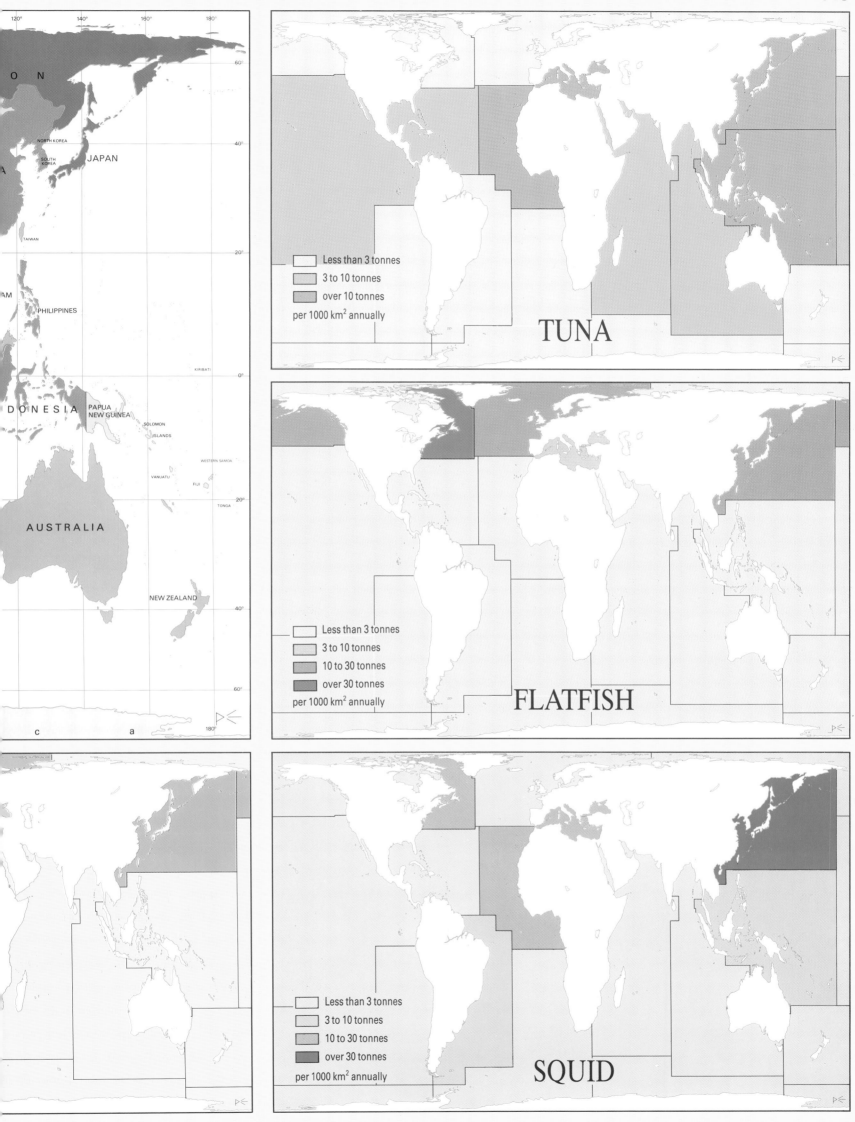

120°   140°   160°   180°   60°
ON
NORTH KOREA
SOUTH KOREA   JAPAN   40°
A
TAIWAN   20°
AM
PHILIPPINES
KIRIBATI   0°
DONESIA   PAPUA
NEW GUINEA
SOLOMON
ISLANDS
WESTERN SAMOA
VANUATU   FIJI   20°
TONGA
AUSTRALIA
NEW ZEALAND   40°
60°
180°
c   a

TUNA

Less than 3 tonnes
3 to 10 tonnes
over 10 tonnes
per 1000 km² annually

FLATFISH

Less than 3 tonnes
3 to 10 tonnes
10 to 30 tonnes
over 30 tonnes
per 1000 km² annually

SQUID

Less than 3 tonnes
3 to 10 tonnes
10 to 30 tonnes
over 30 tonnes
per 1000 km² annually

NG

150

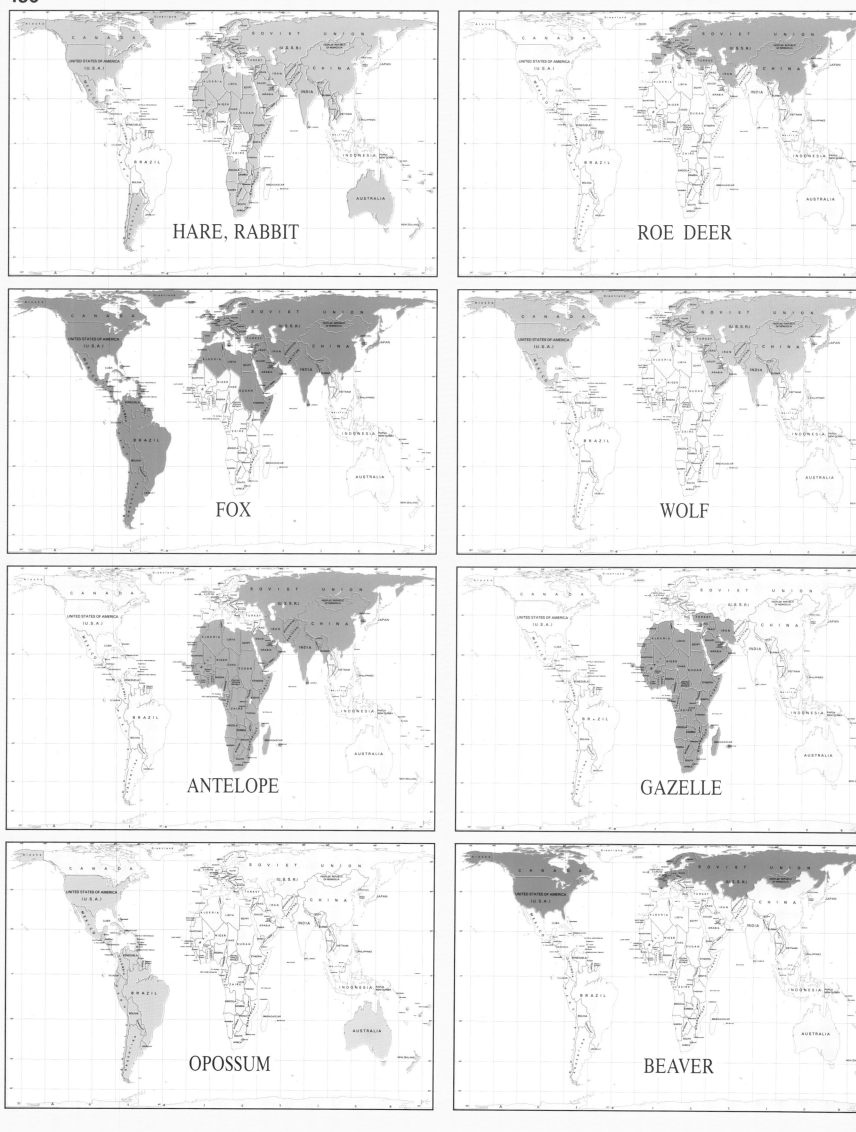

HARE, RABBIT

ROE DEER

FOX

WOLF

ANTELOPE

GAZELLE

OPOSSUM

BEAVER

HUM

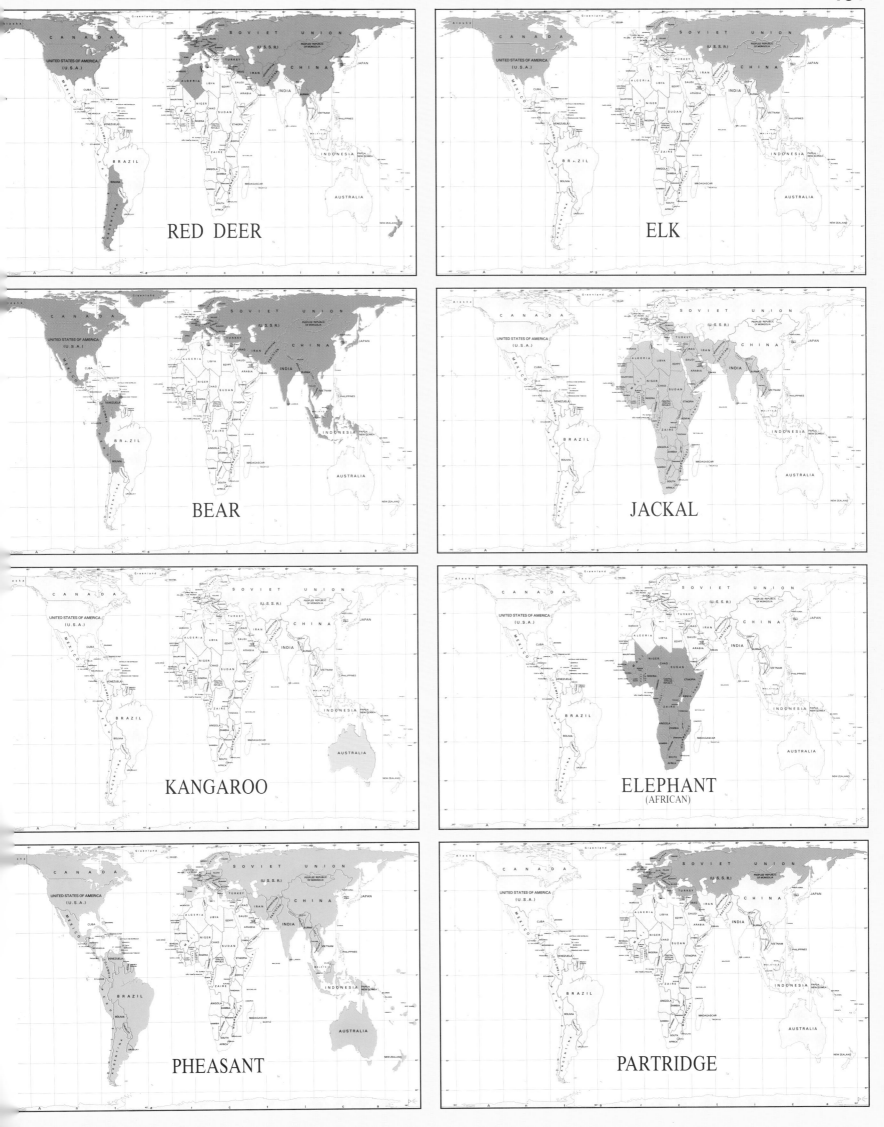

RED DEER

ELK

BEAR

JACKAL

KANGAROO

ELEPHANT
(AFRICAN)

PHEASANT

PARTRIDGE

TING

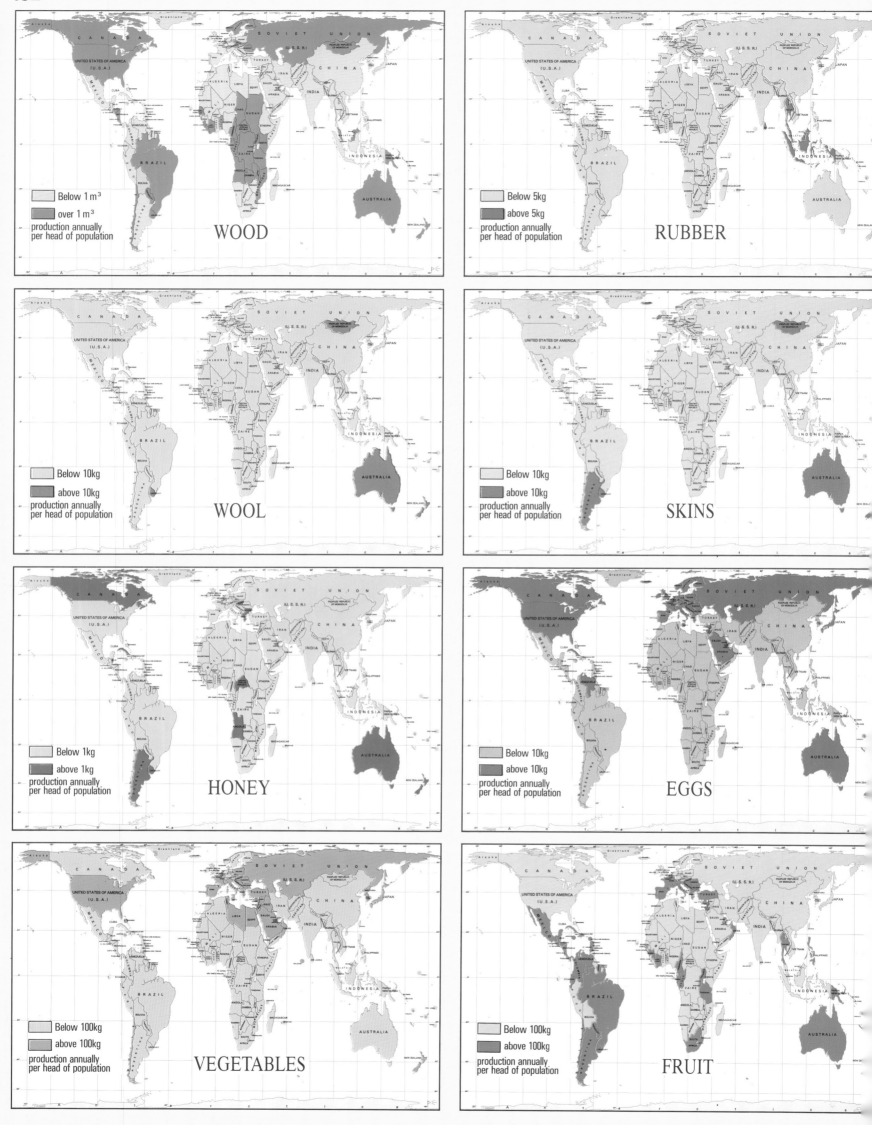

WOOD

Below 1 m³
over 1 m³
production annually
per head of population

RUBBER

Below 5kg
above 5kg
production annually
per head of population

WOOL

Below 10kg
above 10kg
production annually
per head of population

SKINS

Below 10kg
above 10kg
production annually
per head of population

HONEY

Below 1kg
above 1kg
production annually
per head of population

EGGS

Below 10kg
above 10kg
production annually
per head of population

VEGETABLES

Below 100kg
above 100kg
production annually
per head of population

FRUIT

Below 100kg
above 100kg
production annually
per head of population

NATURAL

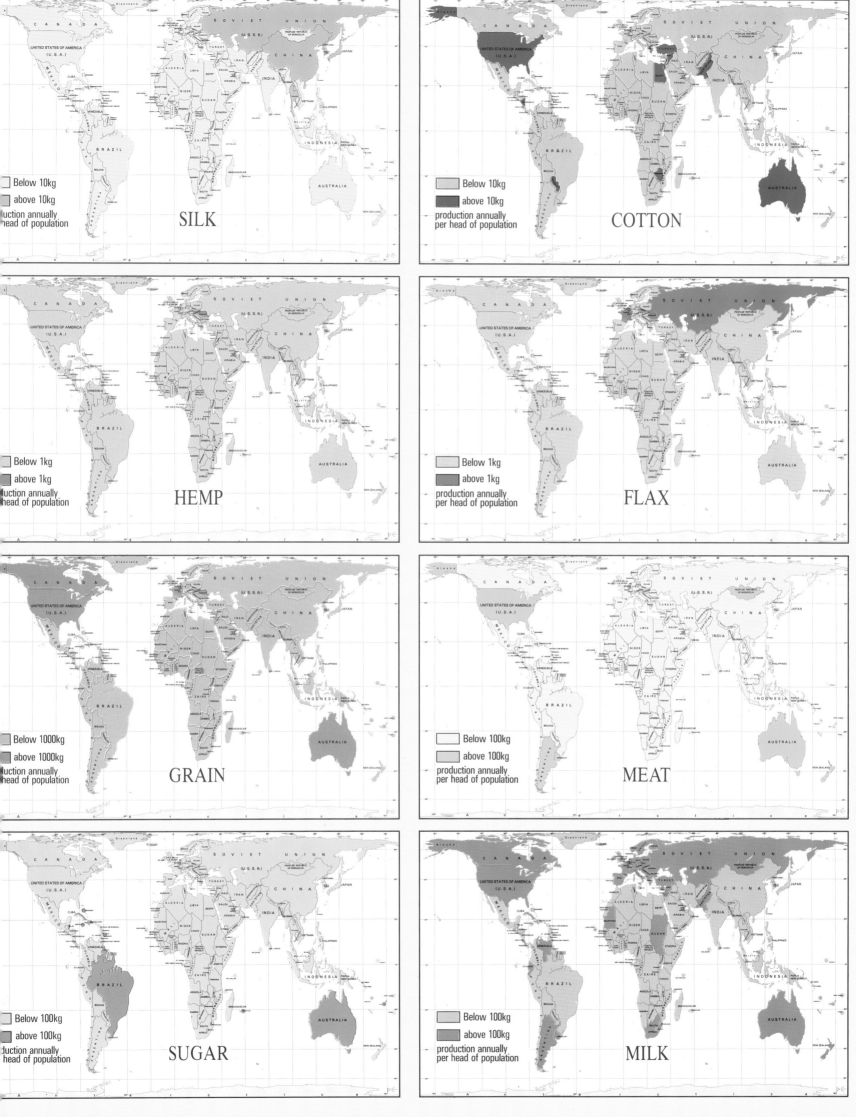

SILK
Below 10kg
above 10kg
...uction annually ...head of population

COTTON
Below 10kg
above 10kg
production annually per head of population

HEMP
Below 1kg
above 1kg
...uction annually ...head of population

FLAX
Below 1kg
above 1kg
production annually per head of population

GRAIN
Below 1000kg
above 1000kg
...uction annually ...head of population

MEAT
Below 100kg
above 100kg
production annually per head of population

SUGAR
Below 100kg
above 100kg
...uction annually ...head of population

MILK
Below 100kg
above 100kg
production annually per head of population

PRODUCTS

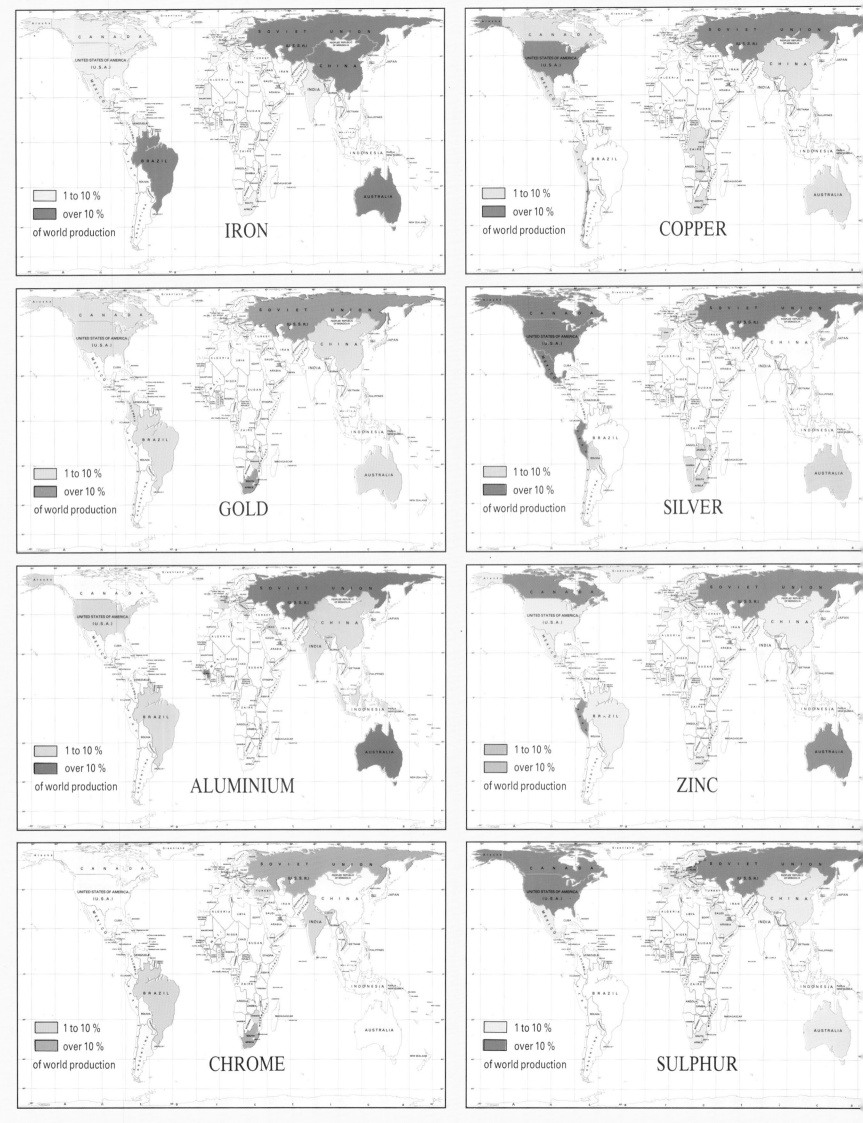

IRON

1 to 10 %
over 10 %
of world production

COPPER

1 to 10 %
over 10 %
of world production

GOLD

1 to 10 %
over 10 %
of world production

SILVER

1 to 10 %
over 10 %
of world production

ALUMINIUM

1 to 10 %
over 10 %
of world production

ZINC

1 to 10 %
over 10 %
of world production

CHROME

1 to 10 %
over 10 %
of world production

SULPHUR

1 to 10 %
over 10 %
of world production

MINERAL

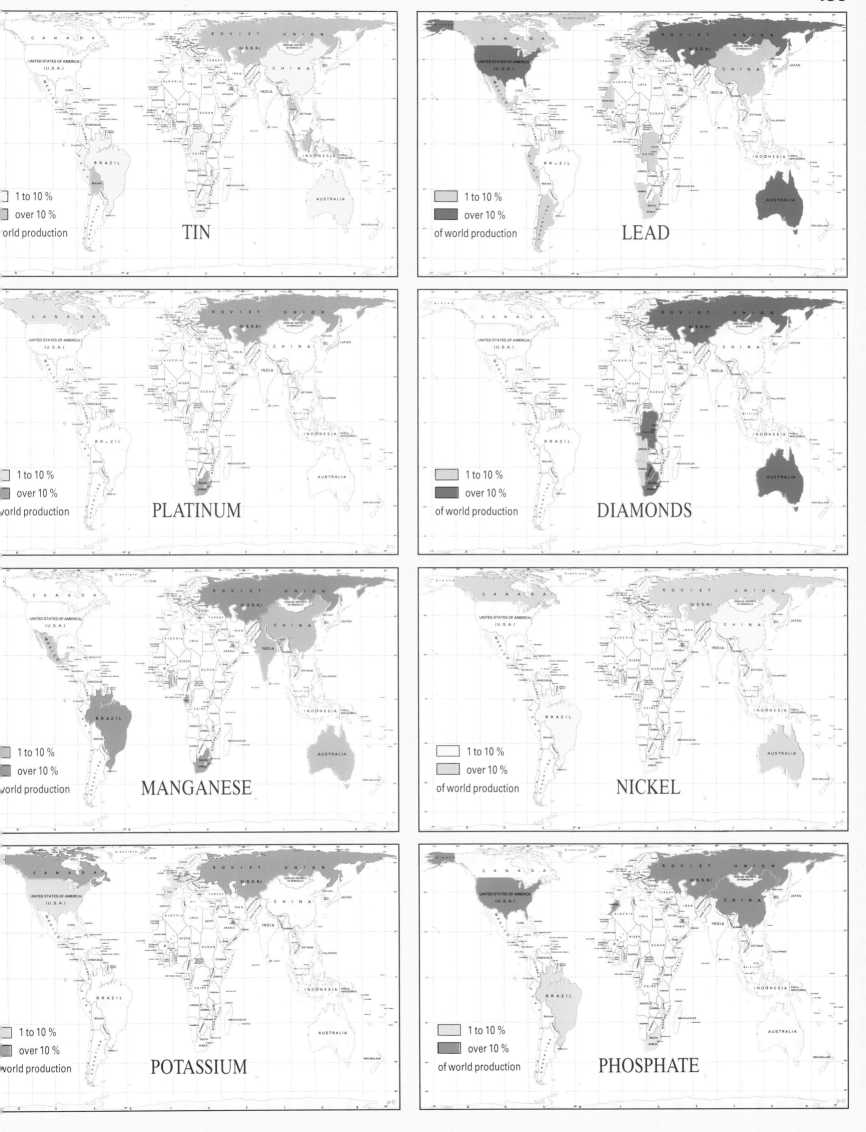

TIN

1 to 10 %
over 10 %
world production

LEAD

1 to 10 %
over 10 %
of world production

PLATINUM

1 to 10 %
over 10 %
world production

DIAMONDS

1 to 10 %
over 10 %
of world production

MANGANESE

1 to 10 %
over 10 %
world production

NICKEL

1 to 10 %
over 10 %
of world production

POTASSIUM

1 to 10 %
over 10 %
world production

PHOSPHATE

1 to 10 %
over 10 %
of world production

RESOURCES

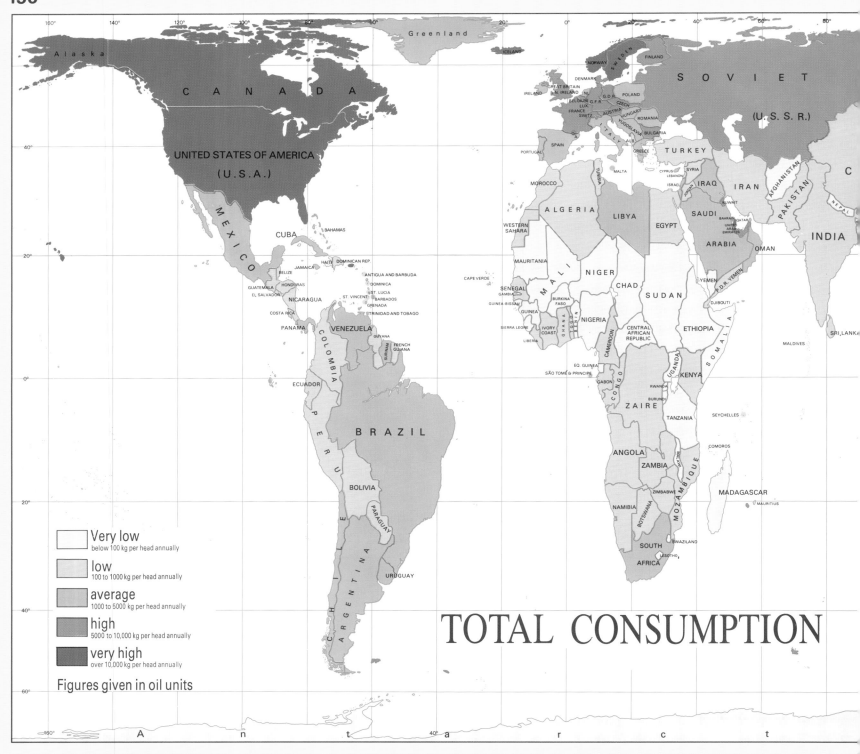

Greenland

Alaska

C A N A D A

UNITED STATES OF AMERICA
(U.S.A.)

M E X I C O

CUBA
BAHAMAS

JAMAICA
HAITI
DOMINICAN REP.
BELIZE
GUATEMALA
HONDURAS
EL SALVADOR
NICARAGUA
ST. LUCIA
ST. VINCENT
BARBADOS
COSTA RICA
GRENADA
TRINIDAD AND TOBAGO
PANAMA
VENEZUELA
GUYANA
COLOMBIA
FRENCH GUIANA
ECUADOR
SURINAM

P E R U

BRAZIL

BOLIVIA

PARAGUAY

CHILE

ARGENTINA

URUGUAY

ICELAND

NORWAY
SWEDEN
FINLAND
DENMARK
GREAT BRITAIN
IRELAND
N. IRELAND
NL
BELGIUM
G.D.R.
POLAND
LUX.
G.F.R.
FRANCE
CZECH
SWITZ.
AUSTRIA
HUNGARY
ROMANIA
YUGOSLAVIA
BULGARIA
ITALY
ALB.
PORTUGAL
SPAIN
GREECE

S O V I E T

(U.S.S.R.)

TURKEY

MALTA
CYPRUS
LEBANON
SYRIA
IRAQ
IRAN
ISRAEL
AFGHANISTAN
PAKISTAN
NEPAL

MOROCCO
TUNISIA
KUWAIT
BAHRAIN QATAR
UNITED ARAB EMIRATES

ALGERIA
LIBYA
EGYPT
SAUDI
ARABIA
OMAN

INDIA

WESTERN SAHARA

MAURITANIA
M A L I
NIGER
CHAD
SUDAN
YEMEN
P.D.R. YEMEN

CAPE VERDE
SENEGAL
GAMBIA
GUINEA-BISSAU
BURKINA FASO
GUINEA
BENIN
NIGERIA
DJIBOUTI
SIERRA LEONE
IVORY COAST
GHANA
TOGO
CENTRAL AFRICAN REPUBLIC
ETHIOPIA
SRI LANKA
LIBERIA
CAMEROON
EQ. GUINEA
SÃO TOMÉ & PRINCIPE
GABON
CONGO
UGANDA
KENYA
S O M A L I A
MALDIVES
RWANDA
ZAIRE
BURUNDI
TANZANIA
SEYCHELLES
ANGOLA
ZAMBIA
MALAWI
COMOROS
MADAGASCAR
MOZAMBIQUE
ZIMBABWE
MAURITIUS
NAMIBIA
BOTSWANA
SWAZILAND
SOUTH
AFRICA
LESOTHO

Very low
below 100 kg per head annually

low
100 to 1000 kg per head annually

average
1000 to 5000 kg per head annually

high
5000 to 10,000 kg per head annually

very high
over 10,000 kg per head annually

Figures given in oil units

TOTAL CONSUMPTION

A   n   t   a   r   c   t

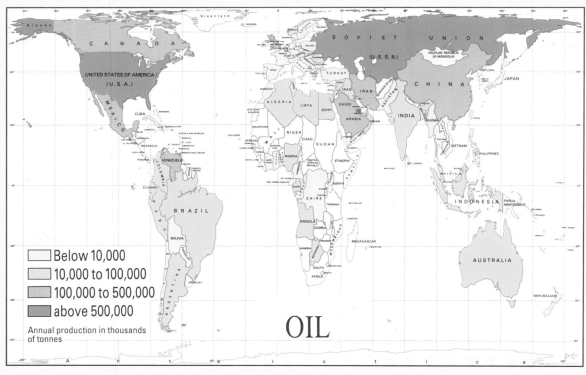

Alaska
Greenland

C A N A D A

UNITED STATES OF AMERICA
(U.S.A.)

M E X I C O

CUBA

VENEZUELA
COLOMBIA

ECUADOR

BRAZIL

BOLIVIA

ARGENTINA

URUGUAY

S O V I E T   U N I O N
(U.S.S.R.)

PEOPLES' REPUBLIC
OF MONGOLIA

JAPAN

TURKEY

MOROCCO
IRAQ
IRAN
ALGERIA
LIBYA
EGYPT
SAUDI
ARABIA

C H I N A

PAKISTAN

INDIA

NIGER
CHAD
SUDAN

BURMA
VIETNAM

SENEGAL
NIGERIA

CENTRAL
AFRICAN
REPUBLIC
ETHIOPIA

PHILIPPINES

SRI LANKA

MALDIVES

ZAIRE
KENYA
TANZANIA

MALAYSIA

INDONESIA

PAPUA
NEW GUINEA

SEYCHELLES

ANGOLA
ZAMBIA

MADAGASCAR

AUSTRALIA

SOUTH
AFRICA

NEW ZEALAND

Below 10,000

10,000 to 100,000

100,000 to 500,000

above 500,000

Annual production in thousands
of tonnes

OIL

A   n   t   a   r   c   t   i   c   a

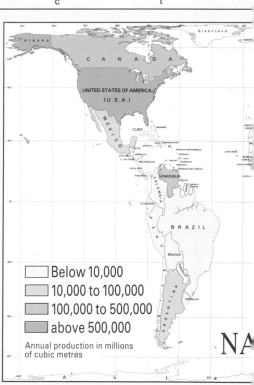

Alaska
Greenland

C A N A D A

UNITED STATES OF AMERICA
(U.S.A.)

M E X I C O

CUBA
DOMINICAN REP.

ANTIGUA AND BARBUDA

NICARAGUA

PANAMA
VENEZUELA
COLOMBIA

CAPE VERDE

ECUADOR

P E R U

BRAZIL

BOLIVIA

ARGENTINA

URUGUAY

WEST

Below 10,000

10,000 to 100,000

100,000 to 500,000

above 500,000

Annual production in millions
of cubic metres

NA

A   n   t   a   r

EN

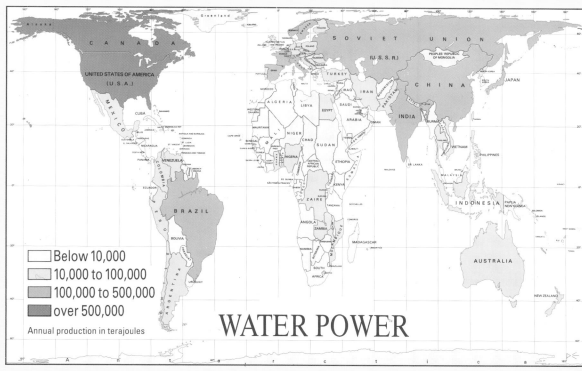

WATER POWER

Below 10,000
10,000 to 100,000
100,000 to 500,000
over 500,000

Annual production in terajoules

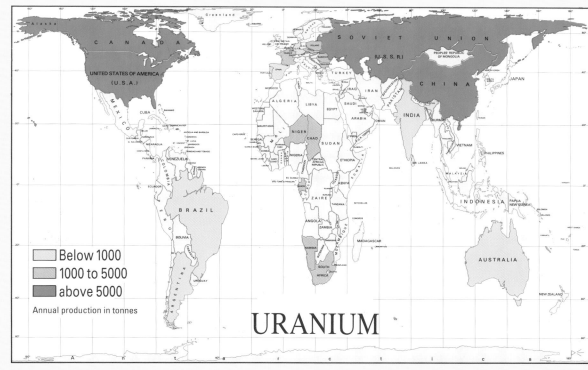

URANIUM

Below 1000
1000 to 5000
above 5000

Annual production in tonnes

L GAS

GY

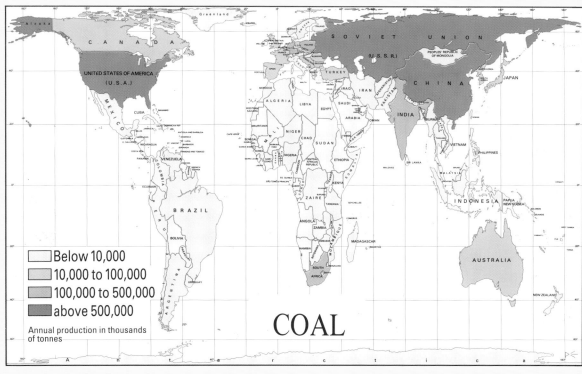

COAL

Below 10,000
10,000 to 100,000
100,000 to 500,000
above 500,000

Annual production in thousands of tonnes

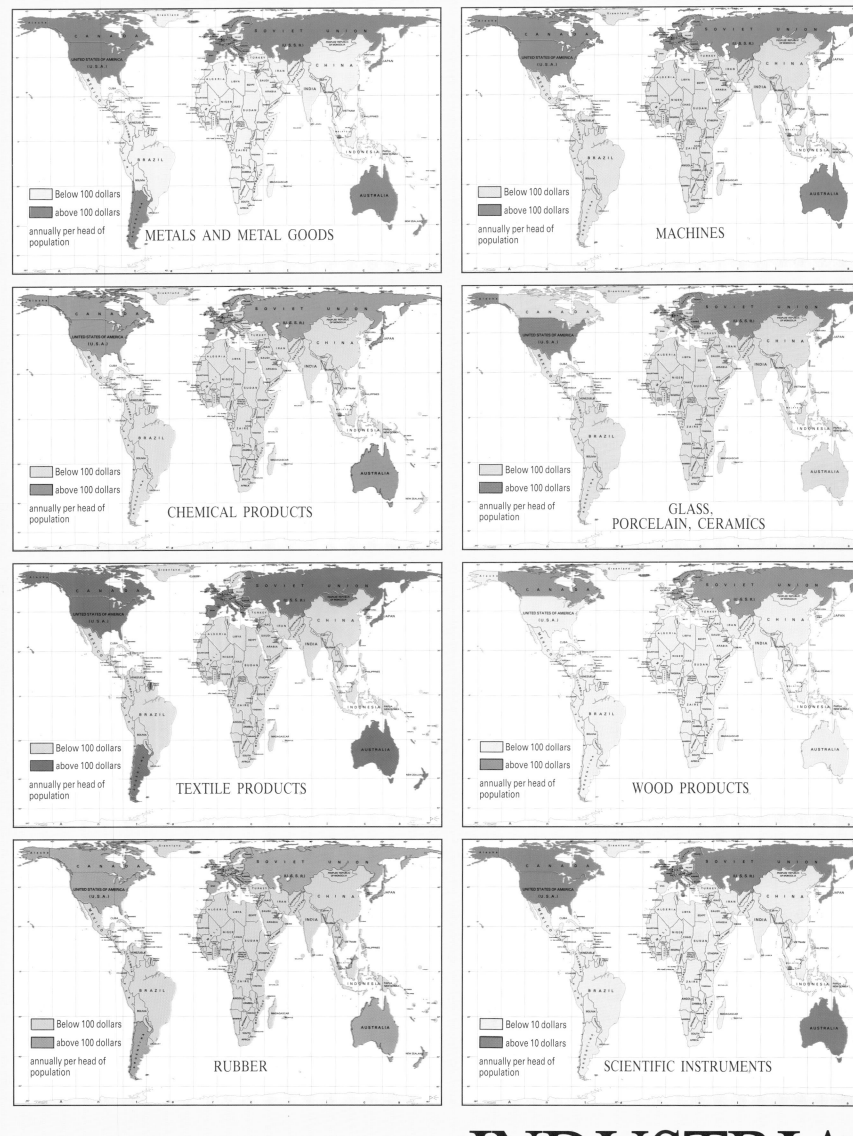

METALS AND METAL GOODS

Below 100 dollars
above 100 dollars
annually per head of population

MACHINES

Below 100 dollars
above 100 dollars
annually per head of population

CHEMICAL PRODUCTS

Below 100 dollars
above 100 dollars
annually per head of population

GLASS, PORCELAIN, CERAMICS

Below 100 dollars
above 100 dollars
annually per head of population

TEXTILE PRODUCTS

Below 100 dollars
above 100 dollars
annually per head of population

WOOD PRODUCTS

Below 100 dollars
above 100 dollars
annually per head of population

RUBBER

Below 100 dollars
above 100 dollars
annually per head of population

SCIENTIFIC INSTRUMENTS

Below 10 dollars
above 10 dollars
annually per head of population

INDUSTRIA

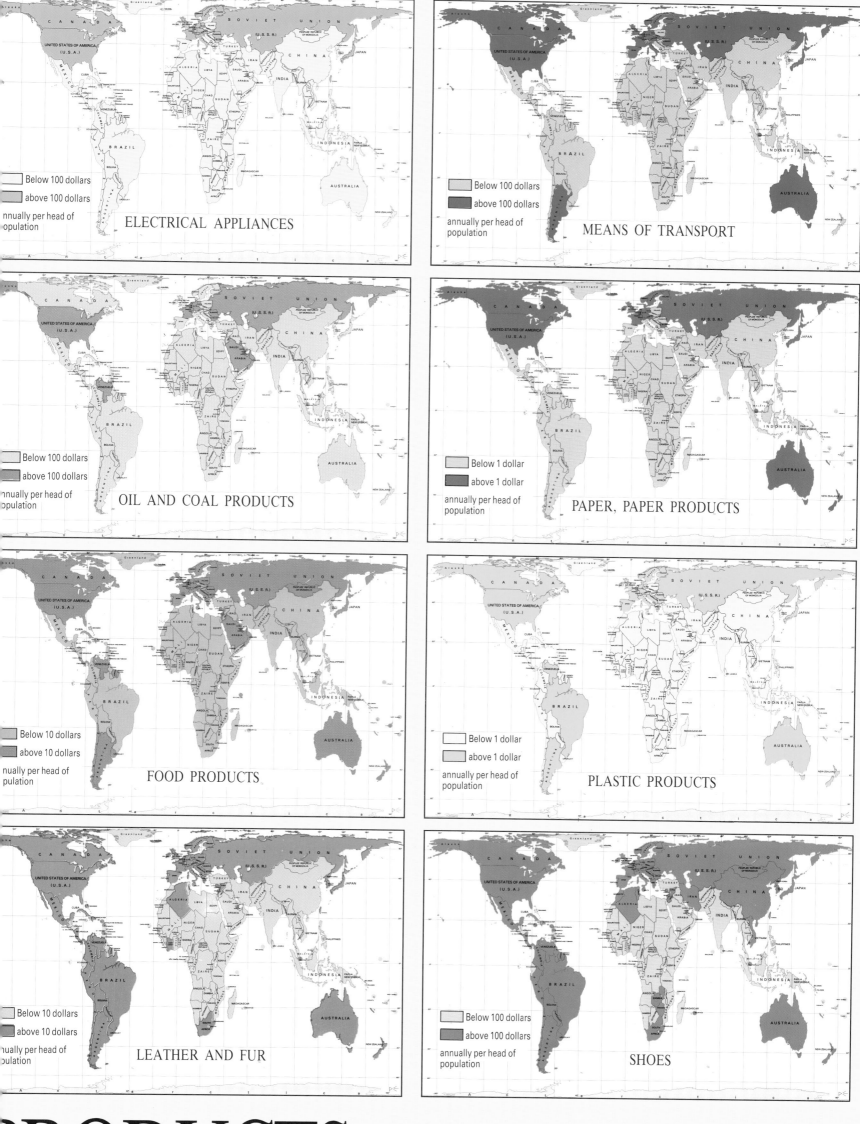

ELECTRICAL APPLIANCES

Below 100 dollars
above 100 dollars
annually per head of population

MEANS OF TRANSPORT

Below 100 dollars
above 100 dollars
annually per head of population

OIL AND COAL PRODUCTS

Below 100 dollars
above 100 dollars
annually per head of population

PAPER, PAPER PRODUCTS

Below 1 dollar
above 1 dollar
annually per head of population

FOOD PRODUCTS

Below 10 dollars
above 10 dollars
annually per head of population

PLASTIC PRODUCTS

Below 1 dollar
above 1 dollar
annually per head of population

LEATHER AND FUR

Below 10 dollars
above 10 dollars
annually per head of population

SHOES

Below 100 dollars
above 100 dollars
annually per head of population

PRODUCTS

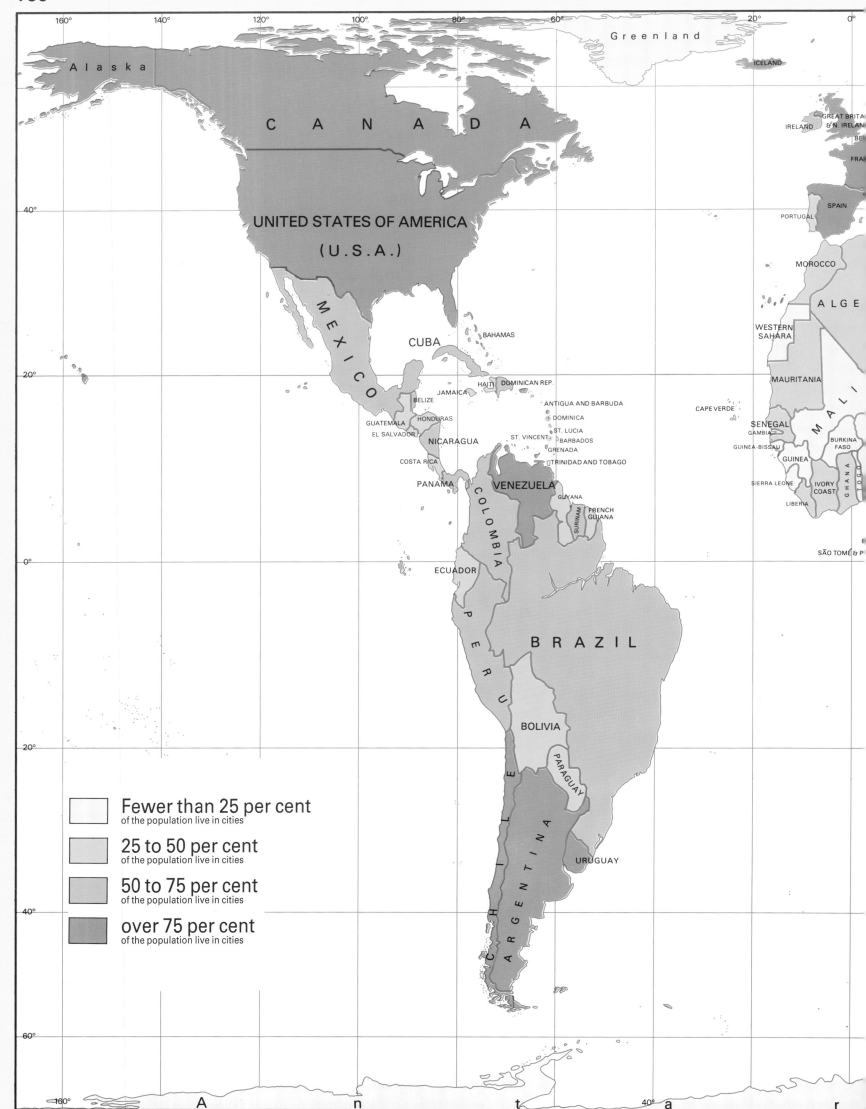

160° 140° 120° 100° 80° 60° 20° 0°

Greenland

Alaska

ICELAND

C A N A D A

IRELAND
GREAT BRITAIN
& N. IRELAND

40°

UNITED STATES OF AMERICA

(U.S.A.)

SPAIN

PORTUGAL

MOROCCO

M E X I C O

A L G E

CUBA

BAHAMAS

20°

WESTERN
SAHARA

MAURITANIA

HAITI
DOMINICAN REP.

M A L I

BELIZE

JAMAICA

ANTIGUA AND BARBUDA

CAPE VERDE

SENEGAL

GUATEMALA
HONDURAS
EL SALVADOR
NICARAGUA

DOMINICA

GAMBIA
BURKINA
FASO

ST. VINCENT
ST. LUCIA
BARBADOS
GRENADA

GUINEA-BISSAU
GUINEA

COSTA RICA

TRINIDAD AND TOBAGO

SIERRA LEONE
IVORY
COAST

PANAMA

VENEZUELA

LIBERIA

0°

COLOMBIA

GUYANA

SURINAM

FRENCH
GUIANA

SÃO TOMÉ & P

ECUADOR

P
E
R
U

B R A Z I L

20°

BOLIVIA

PARAGUAY

C
H
I
L
E

A
R
G
E
N
T
I
N
A

URUGUAY

40°

Fewer than 25 per cent
of the population live in cities

25 to 50 per cent
of the population live in cities

50 to 75 per cent
of the population live in cities

over 75 per cent
of the population live in cities

60°

160° A n t a r

160° 40°

URBAN

SOVIET UNION

(U. S. S. R.)

FINLAND

POLAND

CH

HUNGARY

ROMANIA

GOSLAVIA

BULGARIA

ALB.

GREECE

TURKEY

CYPRUS

LEBANON

SYRIA

ISRAEL

JORDAN

IRAQ

IRAN

AFGHANISTAN

PAKISTAN

KUWAIT

SAUDI

BAHRAIN

QATAR

UNITED

ARAB

EMIRATES

ARABIA

OMAN

EGYPT

YA

YEMEN

P.D.R. YEMEN

AD

SUDAN

DJIBOUTI

CENTRAL

AFRICAN

REPUBLIC

ETHIOPIA

SOMALIA

UGANDA

RWANDA

KENYA

BURUNDI

ZAIRE

TANZANIA

GOLA

ZAMBIA

MALAWI

MOZAMBIQUE

BIA

ZIMBABWE

BOTSWANA

SWAZILAND

SOUTH

AFRICA

LESOTHO

PEOPLES' REPUBLIC
OF MONGOLIA

CHINA

NORTH KOREA

SOUTH
KOREA

JAPAN

NEPAL

BHUTAN

BANGLADESH

INDIA

BURMA

LAOS

TAIWAN

THAILAND

KAMPUCHEA

VIETNAM

PHILIPPINES

SRI LANKA

MALDIVES

BRUNEI

MALAYSIA

SINGAPORE

INDONESIA

PAPUA
NEW GUINEA

KIRIBATI

SOLOMON
ISLANDS

SEYCHELLES

COMOROS

WESTERN SAMOA

VANUATU

FIJI

MADAGASCAR

MAURITIUS

AUSTRALIA

TONGA

NEW ZEALAND

SATION

20° 40° 60° 80° 100° 120° 140° 160° 180°

60° 40° 20° 0° 20° 40° 60°

c   t   i   c   a

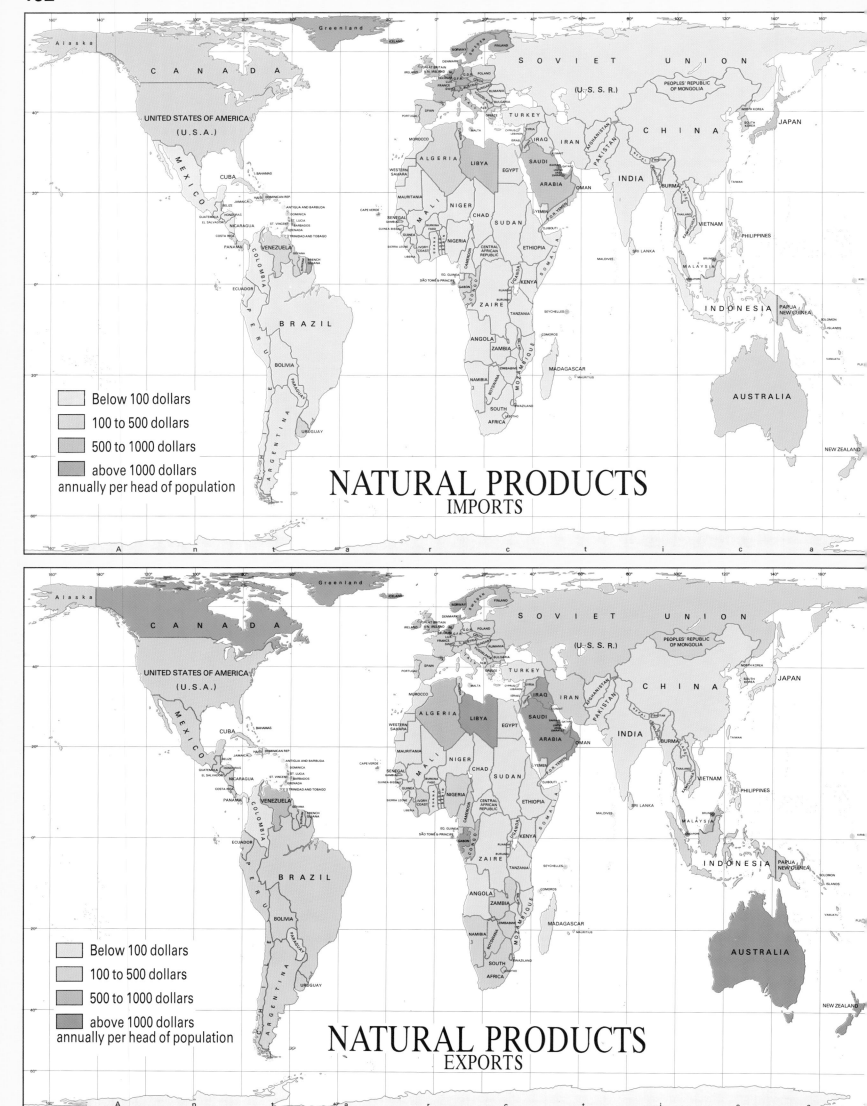

NATURAL PRODUCTS
IMPORTS

- Below 100 dollars
- 100 to 500 dollars
- 500 to 1000 dollars
- above 1000 dollars
annually per head of population

NATURAL PRODUCTS
EXPORTS

- Below 100 dollars
- 100 to 500 dollars
- 500 to 1000 dollars
- above 1000 dollars
annually per head of population

WORLI

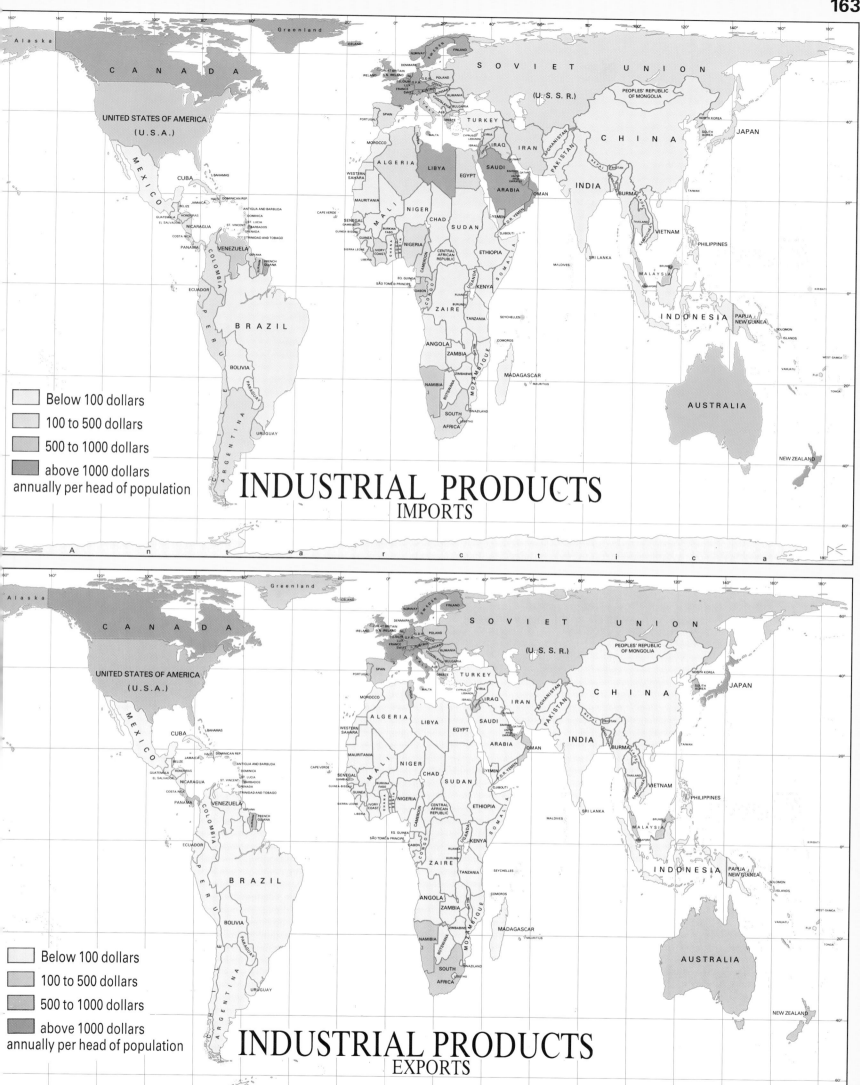

INDUSTRIAL PRODUCTS
IMPORTS

Below 100 dollars
100 to 500 dollars
500 to 1000 dollars
above 1000 dollars
annually per head of population

INDUSTRIAL PRODUCTS
EXPORTS

Below 100 dollars
100 to 500 dollars
500 to 1000 dollars
above 1000 dollars
annually per head of population

TRADE

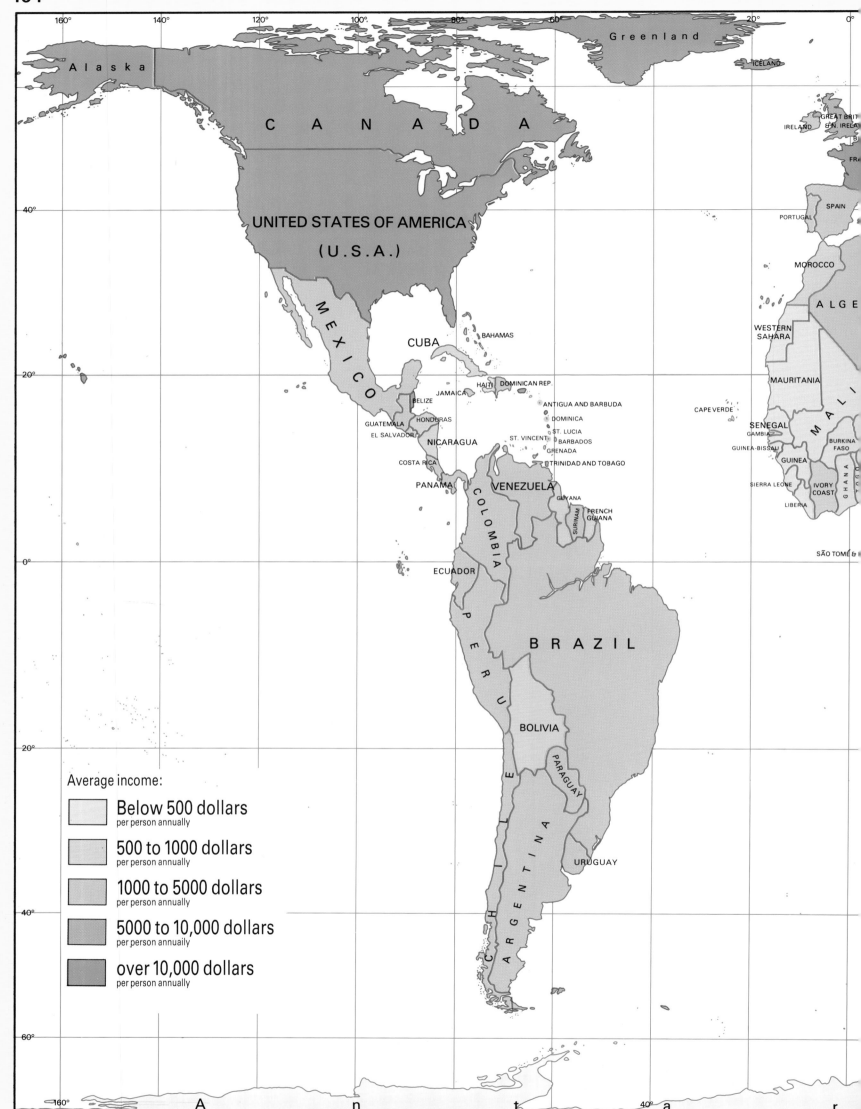

Average income:

Below 500 dollars
per person annually

500 to 1000 dollars
per person annually

1000 to 5000 dollars
per person annually

5000 to 10,000 dollars
per person annually

over 10,000 dollars
per person annually

POOR NATIONS

FINLAND

S O V I E T   U N I O N

(U. S. S. R.)

PEOPLES' REPUBLIC
OF MONGOLIA

ROMANIA

BULGARIA

GREECE

TURKEY

CYPRUS
LEBANON
SYRIA

ISRAEL
JORDAN
IRAQ

KUWAIT

IRAN

AFGHANISTAN

PAKISTAN

CHINA

NORTH KOREA

SOUTH
KOREA

JAPAN

SAUDI

BAHRAIN
QATAR
UNITED
ARAB
EMIRATES

NEPAL

BHUTAN

TAIWAN

EGYPT

ARABIA

OMAN

INDIA

BANGLADESH

BURMA

LAOS

YEMEN

P.D.R. YEMEN

SUDAN

DJIBOUTI

THAILAND

KAMPUCHEA

VIETNAM

PHILIPPINES

CENTRAL
AFRICAN
PUBLIC

ETHIOPIA

SOMALIA

SRI LANKA

MALDIVES

BRUNEI

UGANDA

KENYA

MALAYSIA

RWANDA

BURUNDI

SINGAPORE

KIRIBATI

AIRE

TANZANIA

SEYCHELLES

INDONESIA

PAPUA
NEW GUINEA

SOLOMON
ISLANDS

OLA

ZAMBIA

MALAWI

COMOROS

WESTERN SAMOA

MOZAMBIQUE

VANUATU

FIJI

ZIMBABWE

MADAGASCAR

MAURITIUS

TONGA

BOTSWANA

SWAZILAND

AUSTRALIA

SOUTH
AFRICA

LESOTHO

NEW ZEALAND

c   t   i   c   a

RICH NATIONS

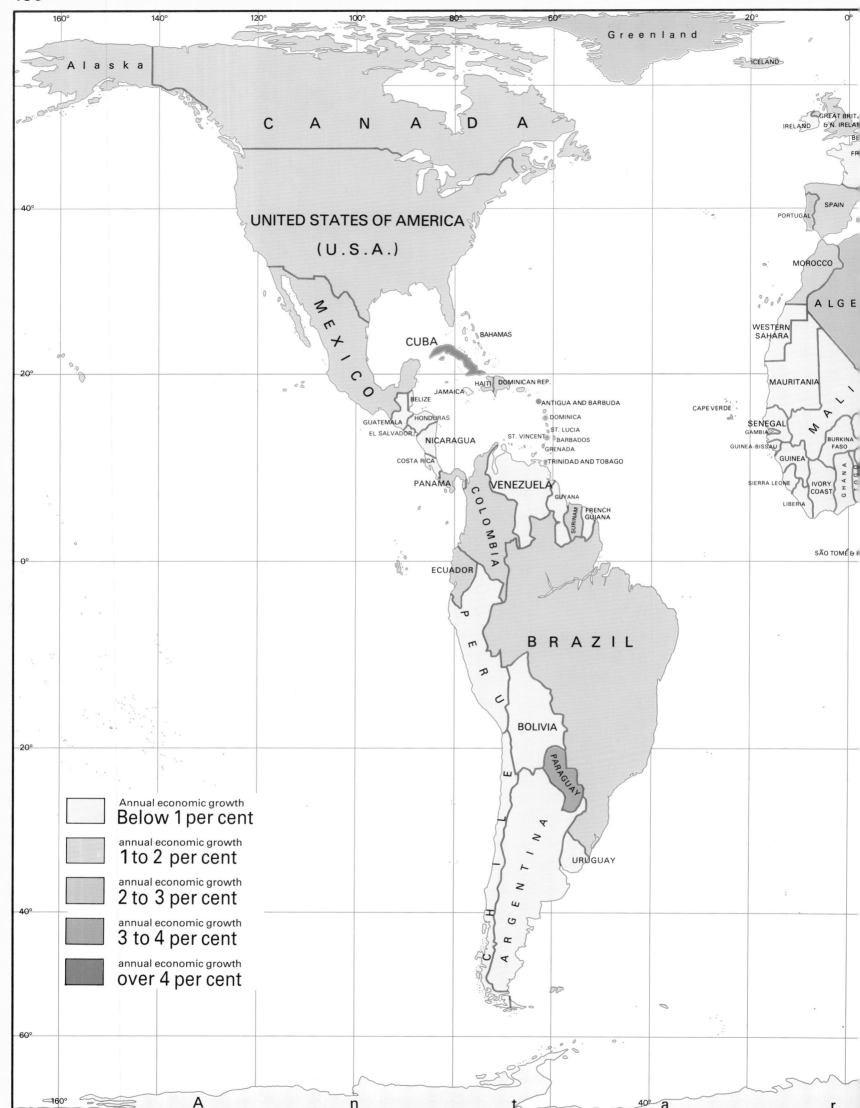

160° 140° 120° 100° 80° 60° 20° 0°

Greenland

Alaska

ICELAND

C A N A D A

IRELAND GREAT BRIT. & N. IRELAND

UNITED STATES OF AMERICA

(U.S.A.)

SPAIN

PORTUGAL

MOROCCO

M E X I C O

ALGE

WESTERN SAHARA

CUBA

BAHAMAS

HAITI DOMINICAN REP.

MAURITANIA

JAMAICA

ANTIGUA AND BARBUDA

BELIZE

CAPE VERDE

M A L I

DOMINICA

SENEGAL

GUATEMALA

HONDURAS

ST. LUCIA

GAMBIA

BURKINA FASO

EL SALVADOR

ST. VINCENT BARBADOS

GUINEA-BISSAU

NICARAGUA

GRENADA

GUINEA

COSTA RICA

TRINIDAD AND TOBAGO

SIERRA LEONE

IVORY COAST

GHANA

PANAMA

VENEZUELA

LIBERIA

GUYANA

COLOMBIA

SURINAM

FRENCH GUIANA

SÃO TOMÉ & P

ECUADOR

P E R U

B R A Z I L

BOLIVIA

PARAGUAY

C H I L E

A R G E N T I N A

URUGUAY

Annual economic growth
Below 1 per cent

annual economic growth
1 to 2 per cent

annual economic growth
2 to 3 per cent

annual economic growth
3 to 4 per cent

annual economic growth
over 4 per cent

A n t a r

ECONOMIC

GROWTH

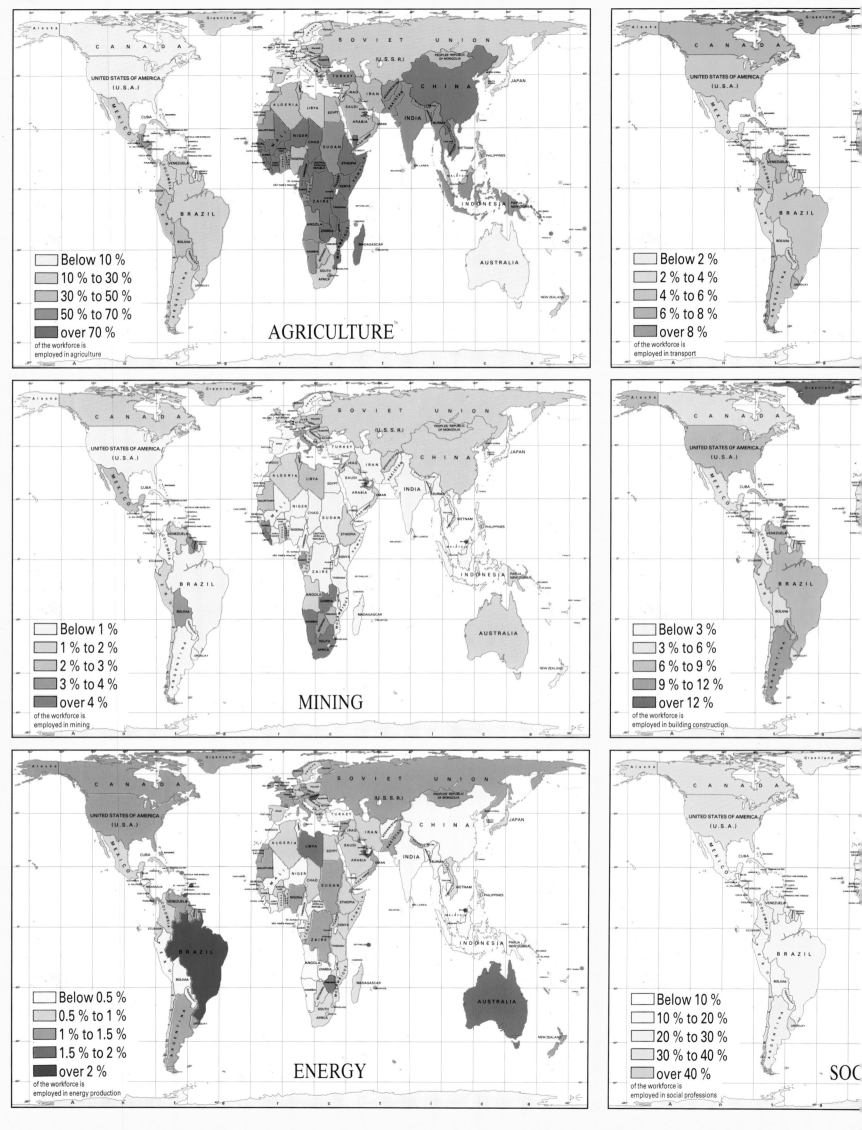

Below 10 %
10 % to 30 %
30 % to 50 %
50 % to 70 %
over 70 %
of the workforce is
employed in agriculture

AGRICULTURE

Below 2 %
2 % to 4 %
4 % to 6 %
6 % to 8 %
over 8 %
of the workforce is
employed in transport

Below 1 %
1 % to 2 %
2 % to 3 %
3 % to 4 %
over 4 %
of the workforce is
employed in mining

MINING

Below 3 %
3 % to 6 %
6 % to 9 %
9 % to 12 %
over 12 %
of the workforce is
employed in building construction

Below 0.5 %
0.5 % to 1 %
1 % to 1.5 %
1.5 % to 2 %
over 2 %
of the workforce is
employed in energy production

ENERGY

Below 10 %
10 % to 20 %
20 % to 30 %
30 % to 40 %
over 40 %
of the workforce is
employed in social professions

SOC

EMPLOYMENT

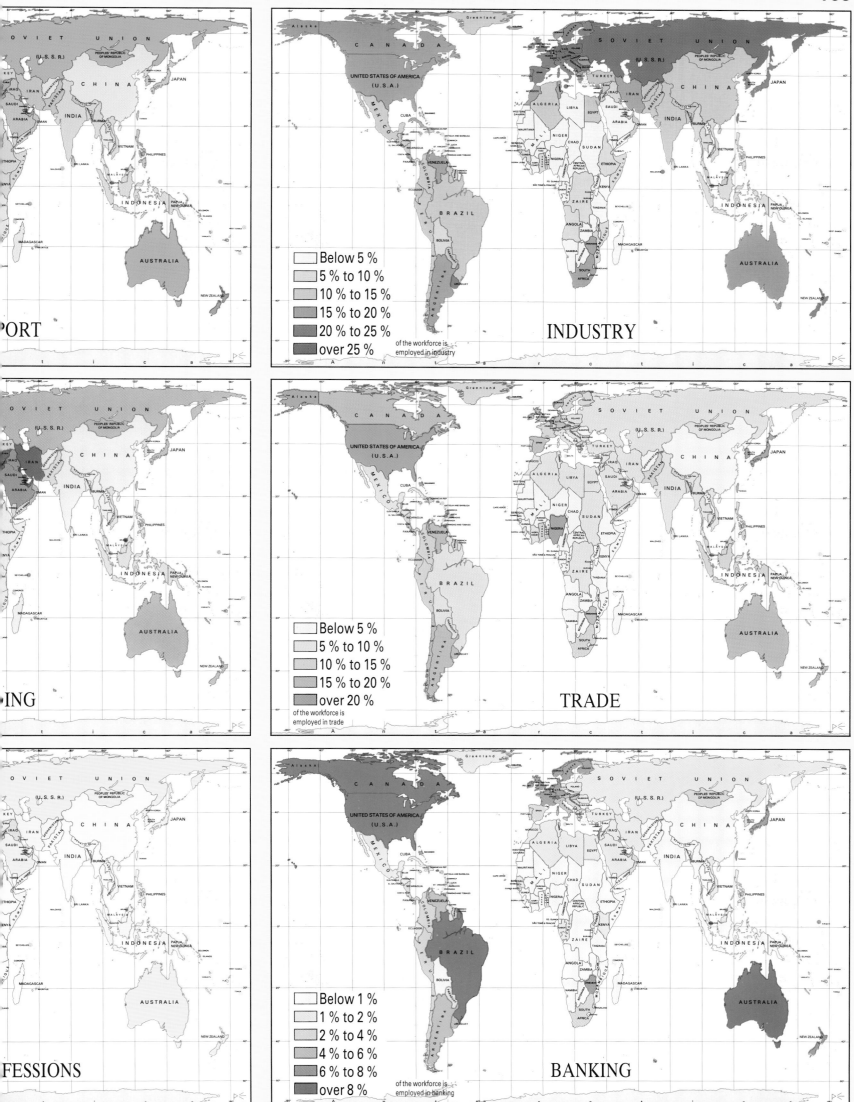

Below 5 %
5 % to 10 %
10 % to 15 %
15 % to 20 %
20 % to 25 %
over 25 %
of the workforce is
employed in industry

INDUSTRY

...PORT

Below 5 %
5 % to 10 %
10 % to 15 %
15 % to 20 %
over 20 %
of the workforce is
employed in trade

TRADE

...ING

Below 1 %
1 % to 2 %
2 % to 4 %
4 % to 6 %
6 % to 8 %
over 8 %
of the workforce is
employed in banking

BANKING

...FESSIONS

STRUCTURE

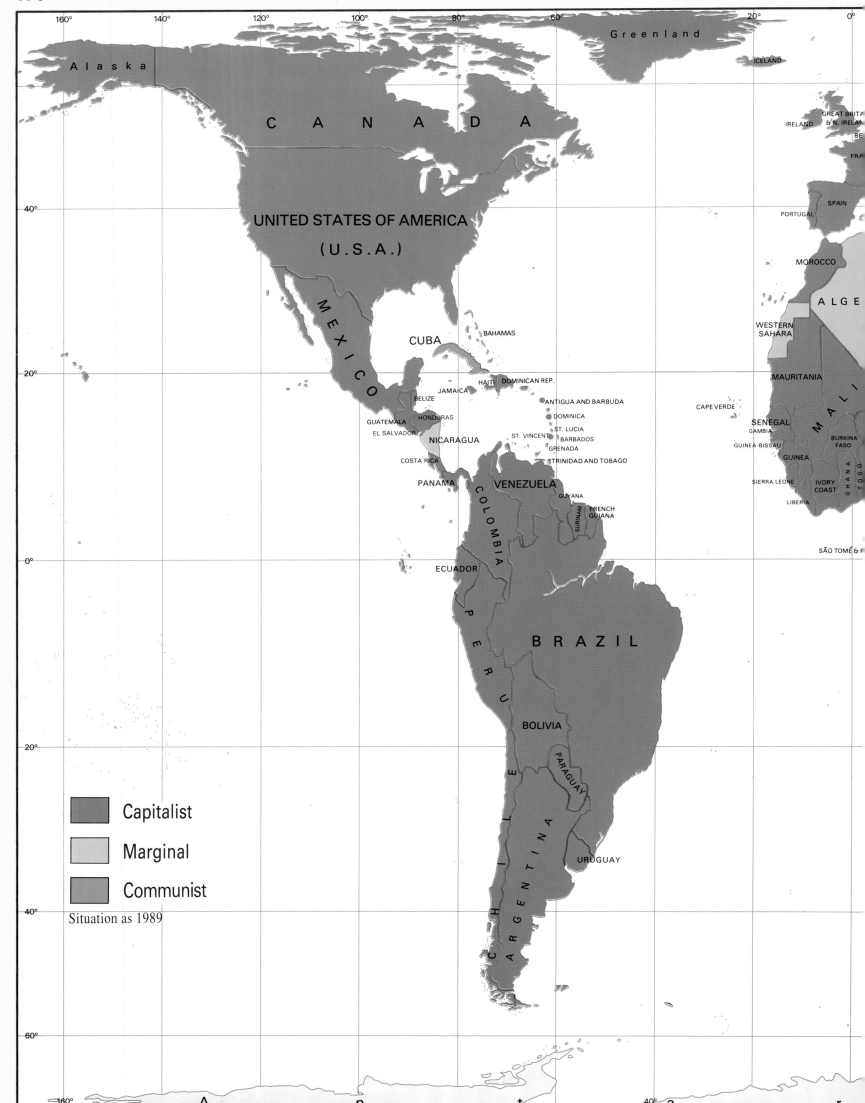

160° 140° 120° 100° 80° 60° 20° 0°

Greenland

Alaska

ICELAND

C A N A D A

GREAT BRITA
IRELAND & N. IRELAN
BE
FRA

40°

UNITED STATES OF AMERICA

(U.S.A.)

PORTUGAL SPAIN

M
E
X
I
C
O

MOROCCO

ALGE

WESTERN
SAHARA

CUBA
BAHAMAS

20°
HAITI DOMINICAN REP.
JAMAICA
BELIZE
GUATEMALA HONDURAS
EL SALVADOR
NICARAGUA

ANTIGUA AND BARBUDA
DOMINICA
ST. LUCIA
ST. VINCENT BARBADOS
GRENADA
TRINIDAD AND TOBAGO

CAPE VERDE

MAURITANIA

M
A
L
I

SENEGAL
GAMBIA
GUINEA-BISSAU
GUINEA

BURKINA
FASO

COSTA RICA
PANAMA

VENEZUELA
GUYANA
SURINAM
FRENCH
GUIANA

SIERRA LEONE

IVORY
COAST

G
H
A
N
A

T
O
G
O

LIBERIA

C
O
L
O
M
B
I
A

SÃO TOMÉ & P

0°
ECUADOR

P
E
R
U

B R A Z I L

BOLIVIA

20°
PARAGUAY

C
H
I
L
E

A
R
G
E
N
T
I
N
A

URUGUAY

40°

Capitalist

Marginal

Communist

Situation as 1989

60°

160° A n t a r 40°

SOCIA

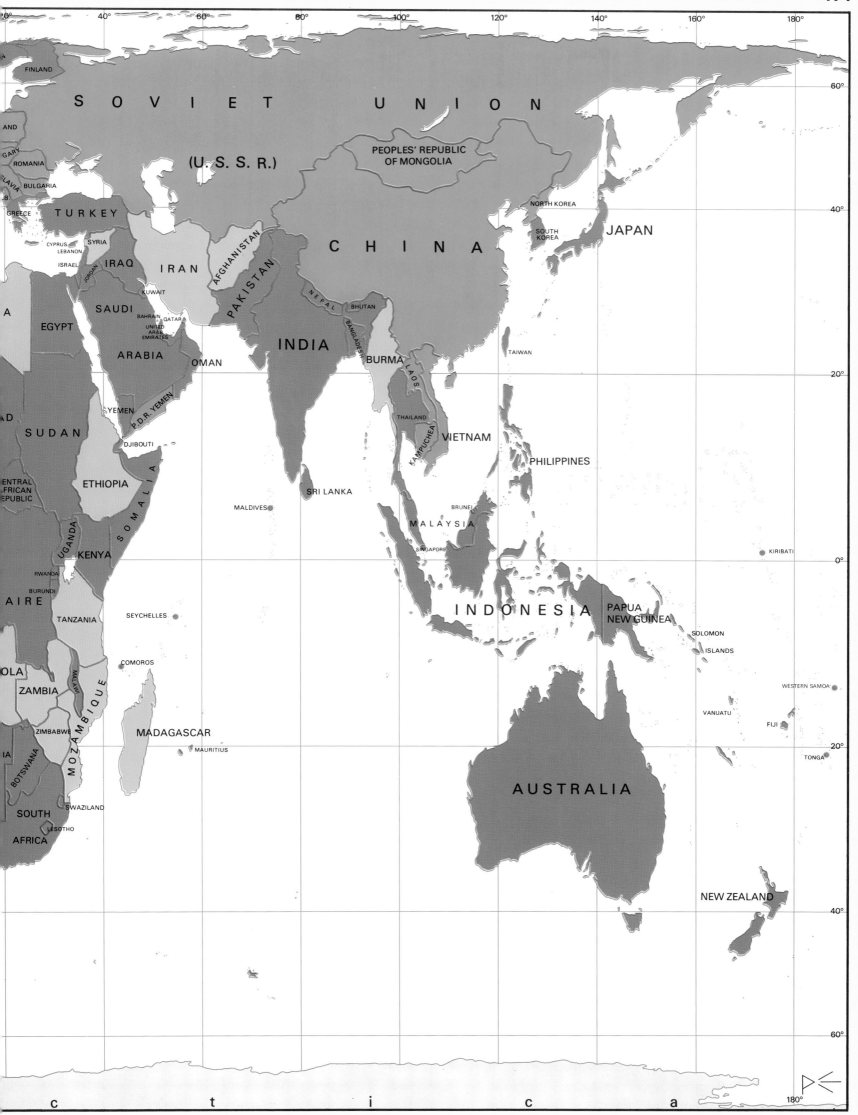

FINLAND

GARY

ROMANIA

LAVIA   BULGARIA

GREECE

AND

A

TURKEY

CYPRUS
LEBANON

ISRAEL

SYRIA

S O V I E T   U N I O N

(U. S. S. R.)

PEOPLES' REPUBLIC
OF MONGOLIA

C H I N A

NORTH KOREA

SOUTH
KOREA

JAPAN

IRAQ

JORDAN

IRAN

AFGHANISTAN

PAKISTAN

NEPAL

BHUTAN

TAIWAN

KUWAIT

EGYPT

SAUDI

BAHRAIN   QATAR

UNITED
ARAB
EMIRATES

ARABIA

OMAN

I N D I A

BANGLADESH

BURMA

LAOS

YEMEN

P.D.R. YEMEN

DJIBOUTI

THAILAND

KAMPUCHEA

VIETNAM

SUDAN

PHILIPPINES

SRI LANKA

CENTRAL
AFRICAN
EPUBLIC

ETHIOPIA

MALDIVES

BRUNEI

MALAYSIA

UGANDA

KENYA

SOMALIA

SINGAPORE

KIRIBATI

RWANDA

BURUNDI

AIRE

TANZANIA

SEYCHELLES

I N D O N E S I A

PAPUA
NEW GUINEA

SOLOMON
ISLANDS

OLA

COMOROS

WESTERN SAMOA

ZAMBIA

MALAWI

MOZAMBIQUE

VANUATU

FIJI

ZIMBABWE

MADAGASCAR

TONGA

IA

BOTSWANA

MAURITIUS

A U S T R A L I A

SOUTH

SWAZILAND

AFRICA

LESOTHO

NEW ZEALAND

40°   60°   80°   100°   120°   140°   160°   180°

60°

40°

20°

0°

20°

40°

60°

180°

c   t   i   c   a

ORDER

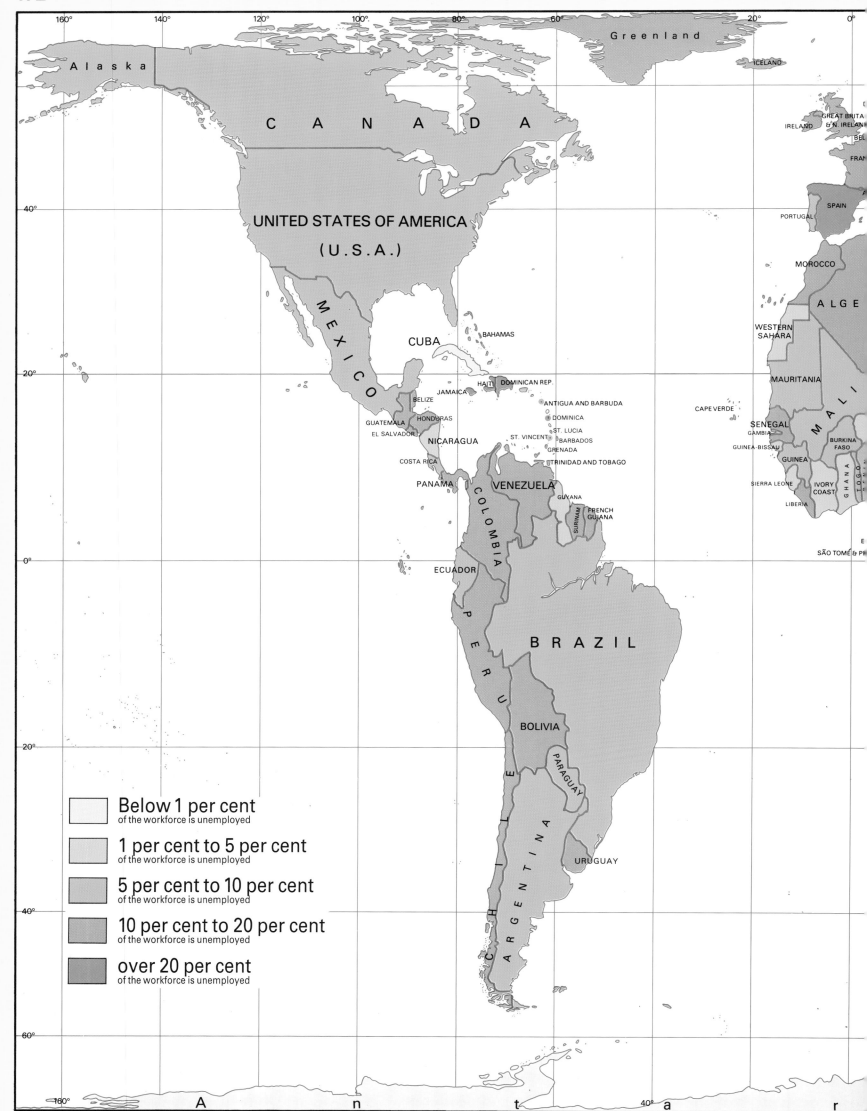

Below 1 per cent
of the workforce is unemployed

1 per cent to 5 per cent
of the workforce is unemployed

5 per cent to 10 per cent
of the workforce is unemployed

10 per cent to 20 per cent
of the workforce is unemployed

over 20 per cent
of the workforce is unemployed

UNEMP

OYMENT

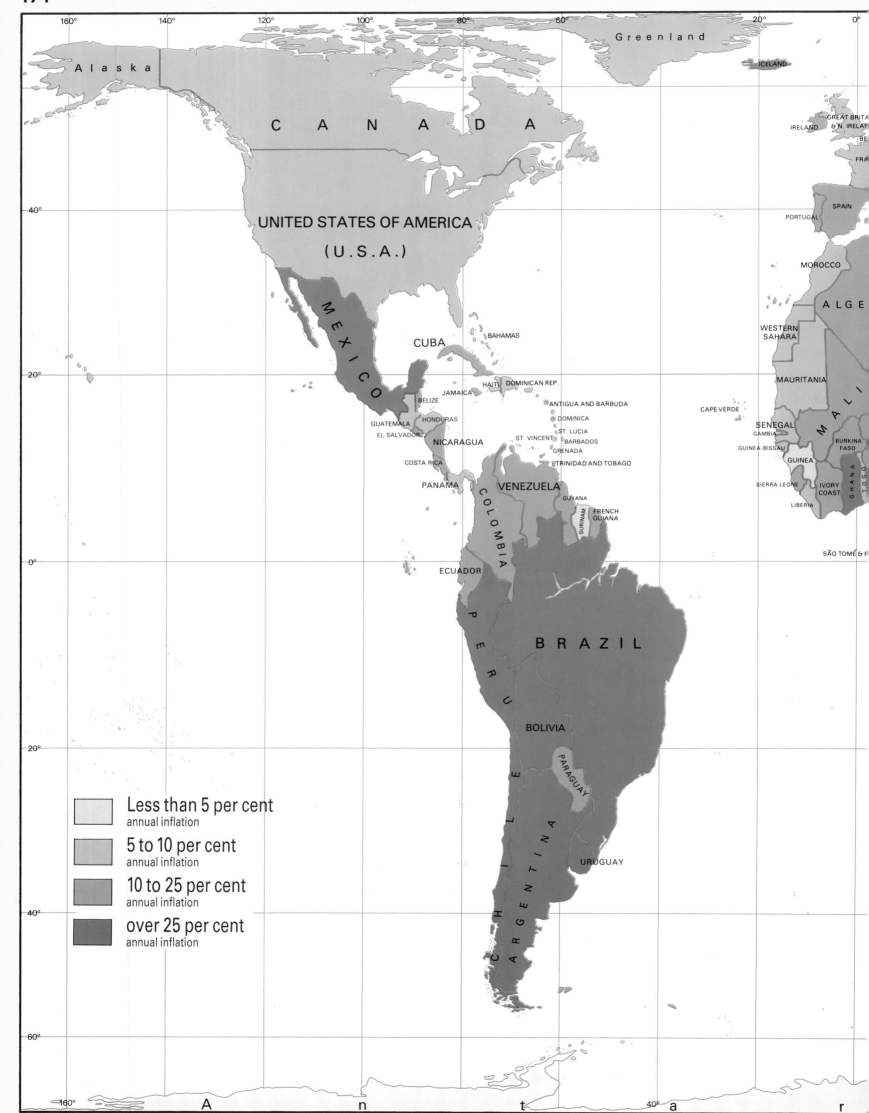

160°   140°   120°   100°   80°   60°   20°   0°

Greenland

Alaska

ICELAND

C A N A D A

GREAT BRITAIN
& N. IRELAND
IRELAND

UNITED STATES OF AMERICA

(U.S.A.)

SPAIN
PORTUGAL

MOROCCO

M E X I C O

ALGE

WESTERN
SAHARA

CUBA

BAHAMAS

MAURITANIA

M A L I

HAITI   DOMINICAN REP.

CAPE VERDE

JAMAICA

BELIZE

ANTIGUA AND BARBUDA

SENEGAL

GUATEMALA
EL SALVADOR

HONDURAS

DOMINICA

GAMBIA

BURKINA
FASO

NICARAGUA

ST. VINCENT

ST. LUCIA
BARBADOS

GUINEA-BISSAU

GUINEA

COSTA RICA

GRENADA

SIERRA LEONE

IVORY
COAST

GHANA

TOGO

PANAMA

VENEZUELA

TRINIDAD AND TOBAGO

LIBERIA

C O L O M B I A

GUYANA

SURINAM

FRENCH
GUIANA

SÃO TOMÉ & P

ECUADOR

P E R U

B R A Z I L

BOLIVIA

PARAGUAY

Less than 5 per cent
annual inflation

5 to 10 per cent
annual inflation

10 to 25 per cent
annual inflation

over 25 per cent
annual inflation

C H I L E

A R G E N T I N A

URUGUAY

40°

20°

0°

20°

40°

60°

160°   A   n   t   40°   a   r

INFLA

S O V I E T   U N I O N

(U.S.S.R.)

FINLAND

ROMANIA
BULGARIA
GREECE
TURKEY
CYPRUS
LEBANON
SYRIA
ISRAEL
JORDAN
IRAQ
IRAN
KUWAIT
BAHRAIN
QATAR
UNITED
ARAB
EMIRATES
OMAN
AFGHANISTAN
PAKISTAN

EGYPT
SAUDI
ARABIA
YEMEN
P.D.R. YEMEN
DJIBOUTI
SUDAN
ETHIOPIA
SOMALIA

PEOPLES' REPUBLIC
OF MONGOLIA

C H I N A

NORTH KOREA
SOUTH
KOREA
JAPAN

NEPAL
BHUTAN
BANGLADESH
INDIA
BURMA
LAOS
THAILAND
KAMPUCHEA
VIETNAM
TAIWAN

PHILIPPINES

SRI LANKA
MALDIVES

BRUNEI
M A L A Y S I A
SINGAPORE
KIRIBATI

CENTRAL
AFRICAN
PUBLIC
UGANDA
KENYA
RWANDA
BURUNDI
AIRE
TANZANIA

SEYCHELLES

I N D O N E S I A
PAPUA
NEW GUINEA
SOLOMON
ISLANDS

WESTERN SAMOA

OLA
ZAMBIA
MALAWI
MOZAMBIQUE
ZIMBABWE
COMOROS
MADAGASCAR
MAURITIUS

VANUATU
FIJI
TONGA

BOTSWANA
SOUTH
SWAZILAND
LESOTHO
AFRICA

A U S T R A L I A

NEW ZEALAND

c   t   i   c   a

ION

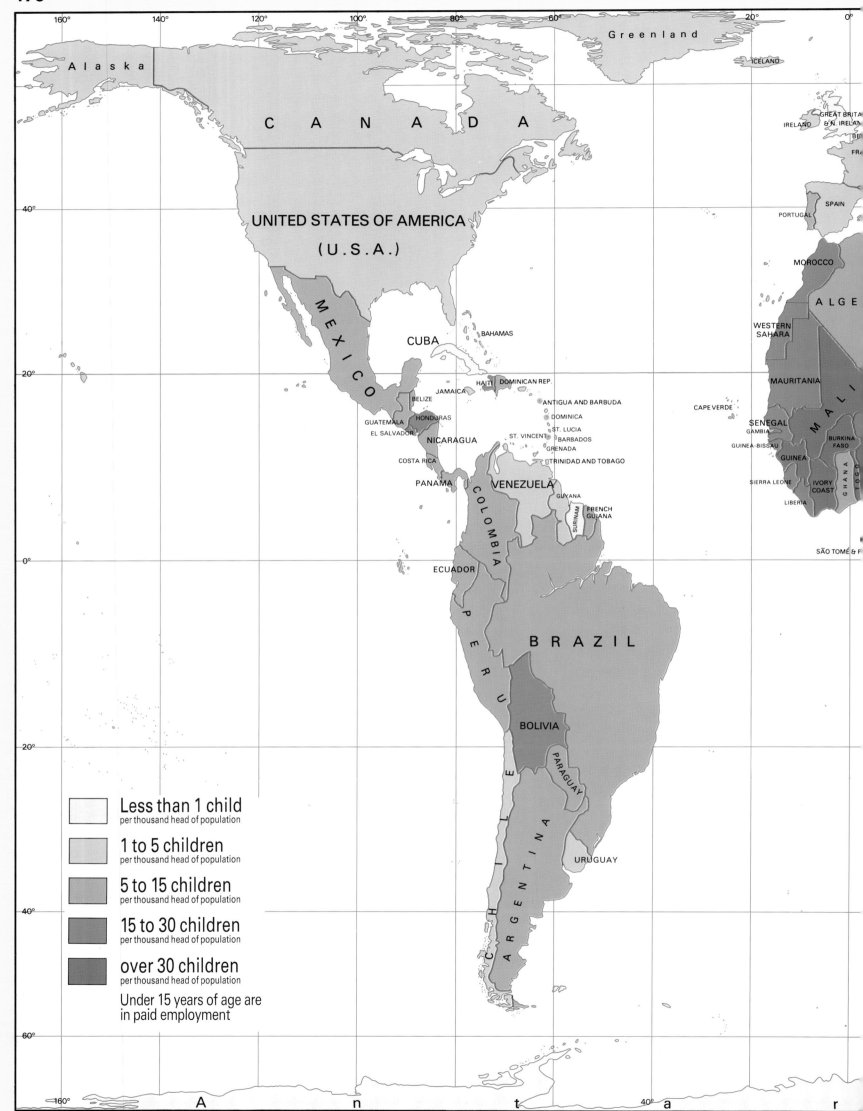

Less than 1 child
per thousand head of population

1 to 5 children
per thousand head of population

5 to 15 children
per thousand head of population

15 to 30 children
per thousand head of population

over 30 children
per thousand head of population

Under 15 years of age are
in paid employment

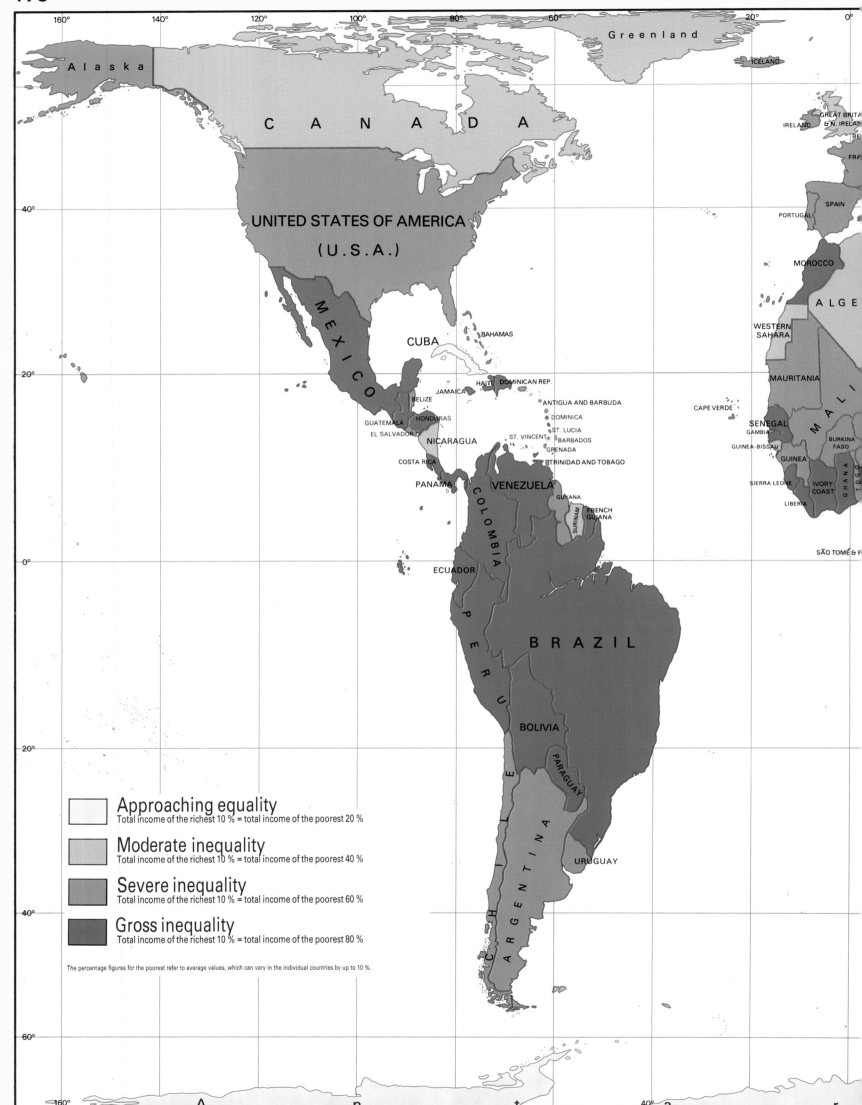

Approaching equality
Total income of the richest 10 % = total income of the poorest 20 %

Moderate inequality
Total income of the richest 10 % = total income of the poorest 40 %

Severe inequality
Total income of the richest 10 % = total income of the poorest 60 %

Gross inequality
Total income of the richest 10 % = total income of the poorest 80 %

The percentage figures for the poorest refer to average values, which can vary in the individual countries by up to 10 %.

FINLAND

POLAND
CH
UNGARY
ROMANIA
YOSLAVIA
BULGARIA
ALB
GREECE

TURKEY

CYPRUS
LEBANON
SYRIA
ISRAEL
JORDAN
IRAQ

IRAN

AFGHANISTAN

PAKISTAN

YA

EGYPT

KUWAIT
BAHRAIN QATAR
UNITED
ARAB
EMIRATES

SAUDI

ARABIA

OMAN

S O V I E T   U N I O N

(U. S. S. R.)

PEOPLES' REPUBLIC
OF MONGOLIA

C H I N A

NORTH KOREA

SOUTH
KOREA

JAPAN

NEPAL
BHUTAN

BANGLADESH

INDIA

BURMA

L A O S

TAIWAN

AD

SUDAN

YEMEN
P.D.R. YEMEN

DJIBOUTI

CENTRAL
AFRICAN
REPUBLIC

ETHIOPIA

S O M A L I A

THAILAND

KAMPUCHEA

VIETNAM

SRI LANKA

MALDIVES

PHILIPPINES

BRUNEI

M A L A Y S I A

SINGAPORE

KIRIBATI

UGANDA

KENYA

RWANDA
BURUNDI

ZAIRE

TANZANIA

SEYCHELLES

I N D O N E S I A

PAPUA
NEW GUINEA

SOLOMON

ISLANDS

GOLA

ZAMBIA

MALAWI

M
O
Z
A
M
B
I
Q
U
E

COMOROS

MADAGASCAR

MAURITIUS

WESTERN SAMOA

VANUATU

FIJI

BIA

ZIMBABWE

BOTSWANA

SWAZILAND

SOUTH

AFRICA

LESOTHO

A U S T R A L I A

TONGA

NEW ZEALAND

c   t   i   c   a

180°

LITY

Low amount of prostitution

medium amount of prostitution

high amount of prostitution

PROST

TION

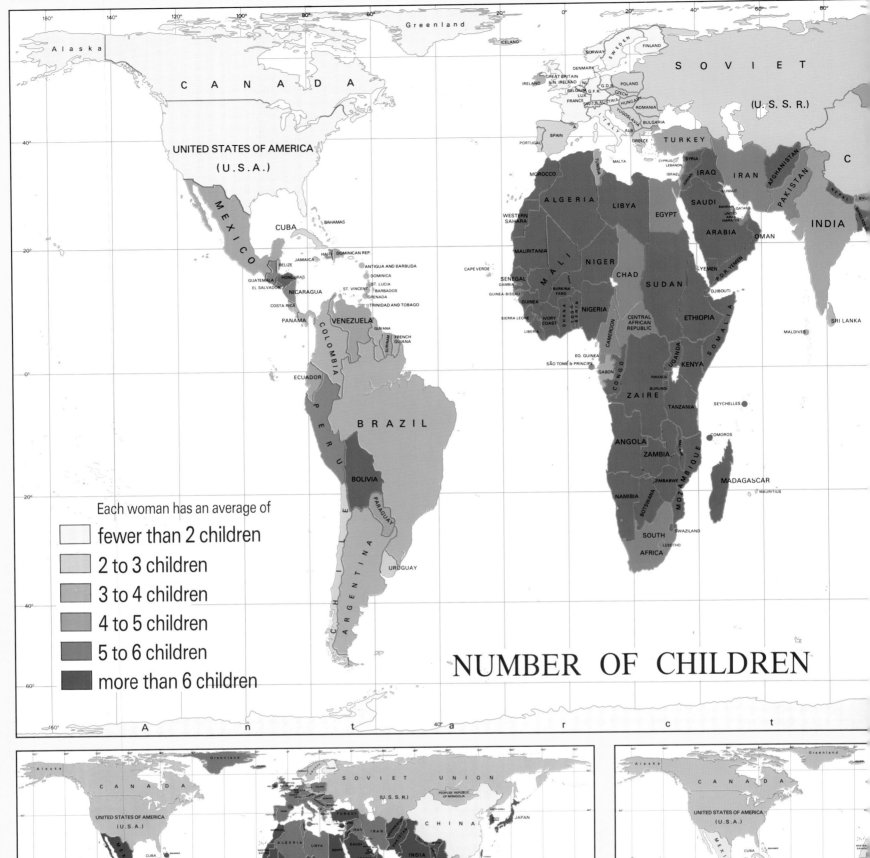

Each woman has an average of

☐ fewer than 2 children
▨ 2 to 3 children
▨ 3 to 4 children
▨ 4 to 5 children
▨ 5 to 6 children
■ more than 6 children

NUMBER OF CHILDREN

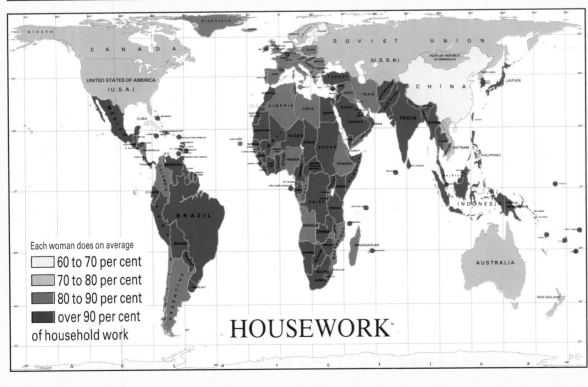

Each woman does on average
☐ 60 to 70 per cent
▨ 70 to 80 per cent
▨ 80 to 90 per cent
■ over 90 per cent
of household work

HOUSEWORK

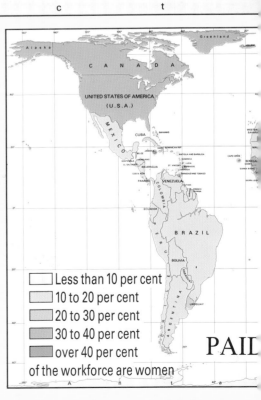

☐ Less than 10 per cent
▨ 10 to 20 per cent
▨ 20 to 30 per cent
▨ 30 to 40 per cent
▨ over 40 per cent
of the workforce are women

PAID

THE STATU

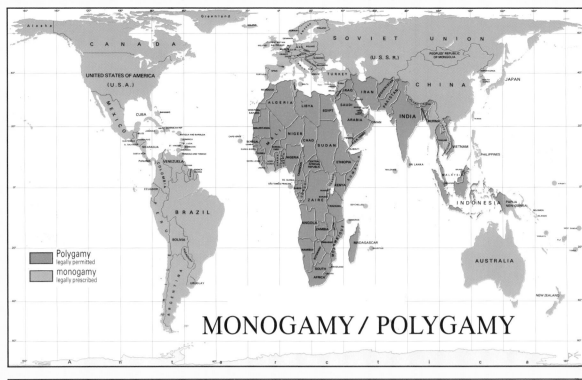

MONOGAMY / POLYGAMY

Polygamy
legally permitted

monogamy
legally prescribed

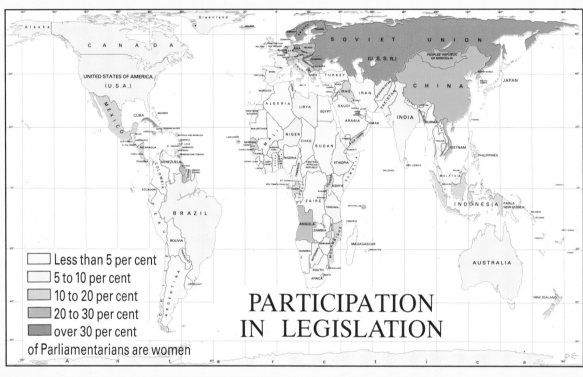

Less than 5 per cent

5 to 10 per cent

10 to 20 per cent

20 to 30 per cent

over 30 per cent

of Parliamentarians are women

PARTICIPATION
IN LEGISLATION

...LOYMENT

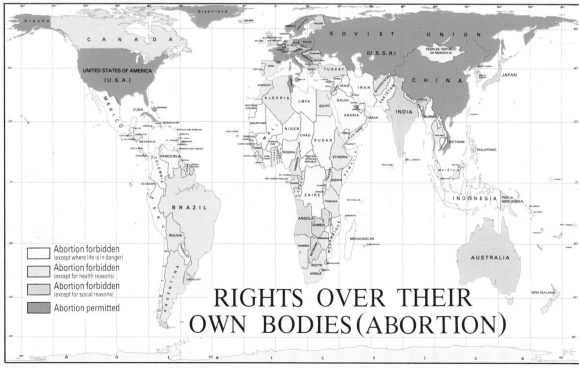

Abortion forbidden
(except where life is in danger)

Abortion forbidden
(except for health reasons)

Abortion forbidden
(except for social reasons)

Abortion permitted

RIGHTS OVER THEIR
OWN BODIES (ABORTION)

OF WOMEN

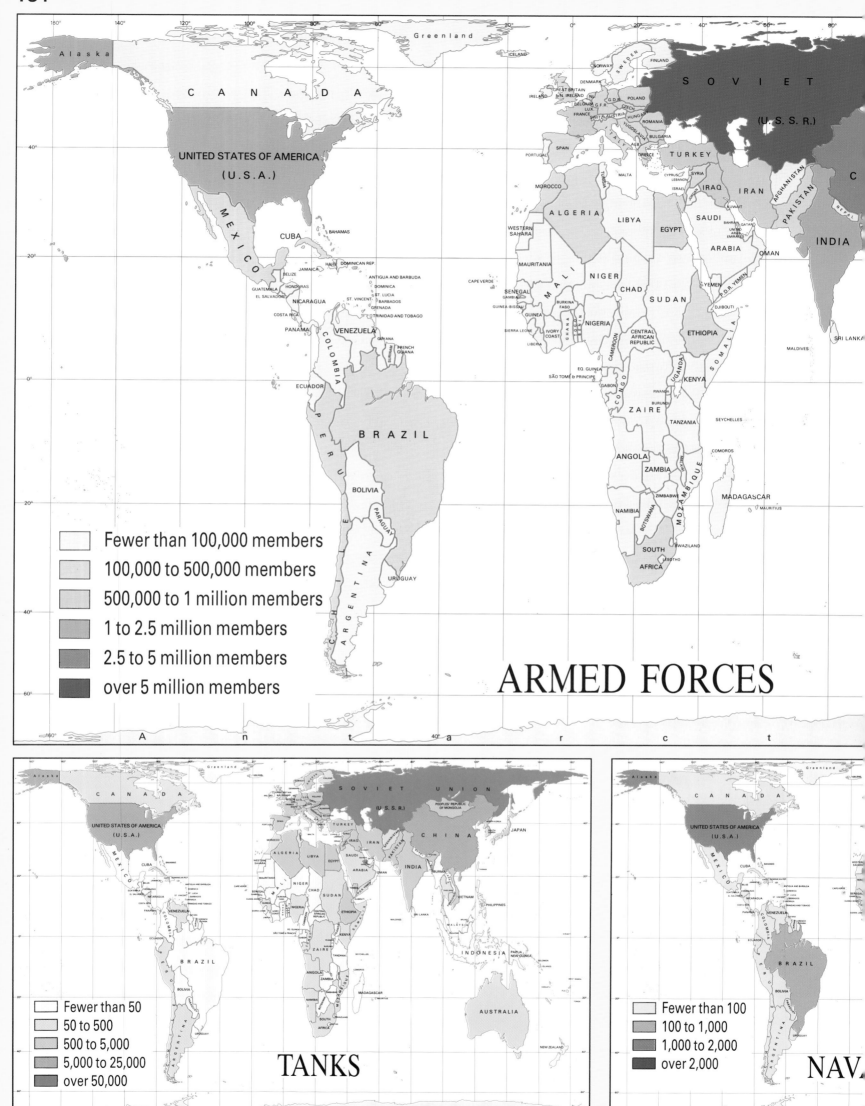

Fewer than 100,000 members
100,000 to 500,000 members
500,000 to 1 million members
1 to 2.5 million members
2.5 to 5 million members
over 5 million members

ARMED FORCES

Fewer than 50
50 to 500
500 to 5,000
5,000 to 25,000
over 50,000

TANKS

Fewer than 100
100 to 1,000
1,000 to 2,000
over 2,000

NAV

RELATIVE MILI

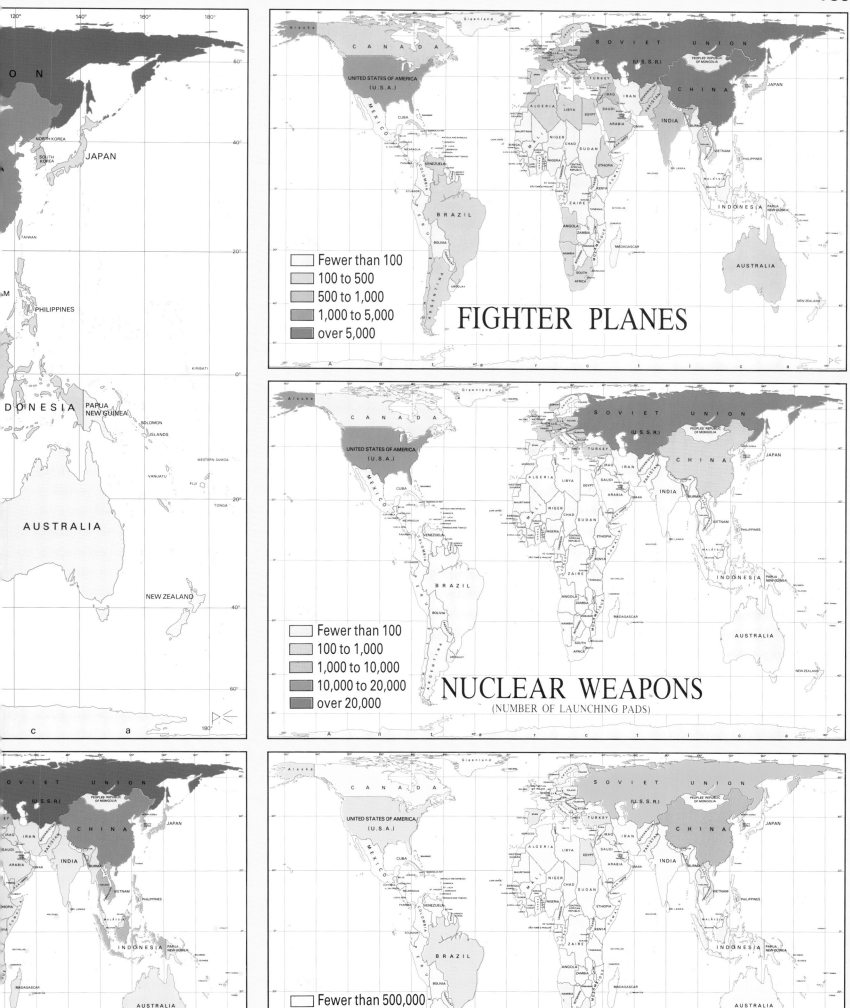

FIGHTER PLANES

Fewer than 100
100 to 500
500 to 1,000
1,000 to 5,000
over 5,000

NUCLEAR WEAPONS
(NUMBER OF LAUNCHING PADS)

Fewer than 100
100 to 1,000
1,000 to 10,000
10,000 to 20,000
over 20,000

RESERVE FORCES
(AUXILIARIES OF ALL KINDS)

Fewer than 500,000
500,000 to 1 million
1 to 5 million
5 to 10 million
over 10 million

ESSELS

RY STRENGTH

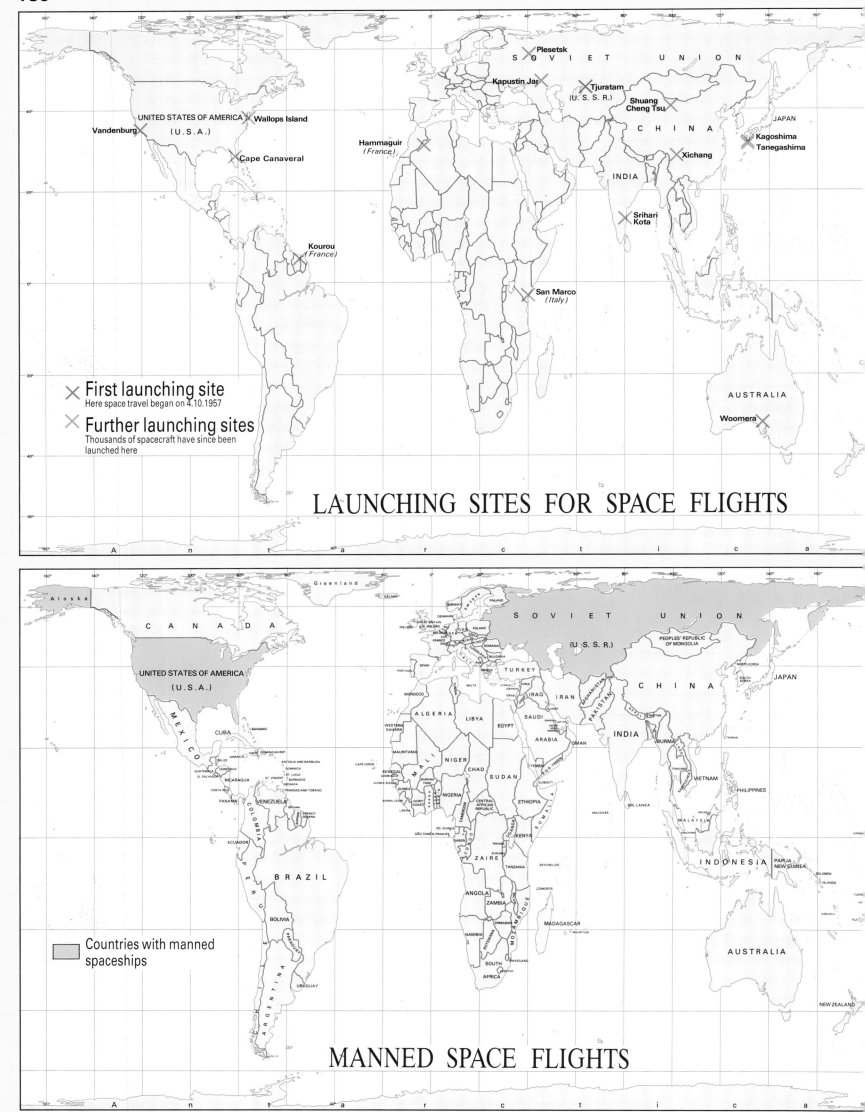

First launching site
Here space travel began on 4.10.1957

Further launching sites
Thousands of spacecraft have since been launched here

LAUNCHING SITES FOR SPACE FLIGHTS

Countries with manned spaceships

MANNED SPACE FLIGHTS

THE CONQU

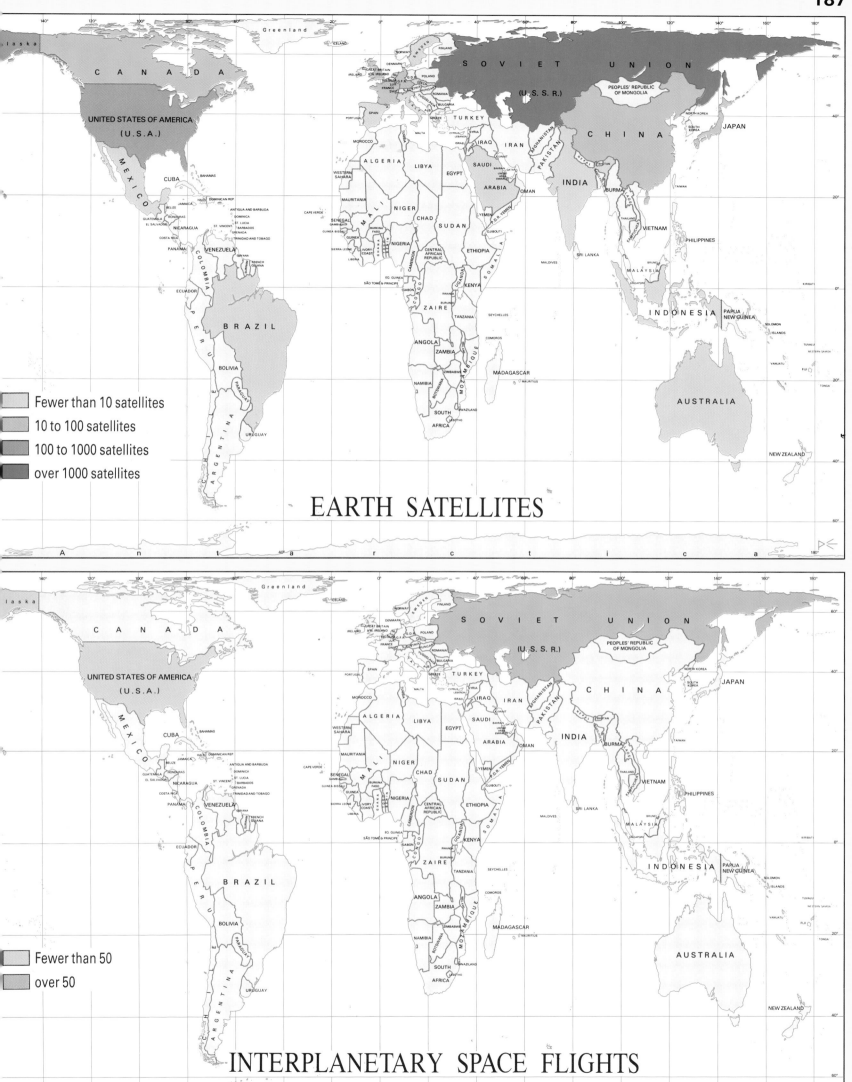

EARTH SATELLITES

Fewer than 10 satellites
10 to 100 satellites
100 to 1000 satellites
over 1000 satellites

INTERPLANETARY SPACE FLIGHTS

Fewer than 50
over 50

T OF SPACE

INDEX

Each name in the index is followed by a page number and a letter. On the page referred to, the letter can be found either at the top or at the bottom of the map frame. In the first case, the place is in the upper half of the map vertically below the letter; otherwise it is on the lower half of the map vertically above the letter.

Names such as countries or oceans which cover a large area on the map are listed with their page number only. However, if they extend over two pages, two page numbers are shown – the left-hand and right-hand page numbers being linked with a dash. Names of countries, oceans, rivers and mountains that extend over more than a double page are listed under each separate page. A dash between two nonconsecutive page numbers means that the place appears on all maps between and including those two pages.

The headwords are in alphabetical order. Names with prefixes like "Saint" or "Bad" can be looked up under the initial letter of the prefix. Place names appear on the maps in their local spelling or a standard transliteration. As well as these spellings, the Index includes all widely-used Anglicised versions of place names. In these cases the Anglicised headword is followed by the local or transliterated spelling in brackets. This indicates that the place name appears on the map, at the reference given, in the form shown in brackets, not in its Anglicised version.

Theodore
Tulsa

Theodore 74 s
Theodore Roosevelt 26 q
The Pas 15 f
Thermaïkos Kólpos 35 s
Thessalonika (Thessaloniki) 35 f
Thessaloniki 35 f
Thief River Falls 15 i
Thiès 40 b
Thika 45 j
Thimphu 61 k
Thingangyun 65 g
Thionville 34 i
Thistle I. 77 e
Thlewiaza 12 z
Thollon 77 m
Thomasville 20 j
Thompson 12 y
Thompson Falls 14 l
Thomson 74 n
Thon Buri 65 j
Thorntonia 73 v
Three Hummock Island 77 x
Three Kings Island 79 g
Three Rivers (Australia) 76 f
Three Rivers (USA) 19 c
Thule (Qânâq) 91 c
Thunder Bay 16 e
Thurso 32 k
Thurston Island 80 m
Thylungra 77 j
Tiancang 57 n
Tiancheng 57 n
Tianguá 27 e
Tianjin 57 x
Tianjun 56 z
Tianlin 62 x
Tianshui 62 k
Tiaret 36 m
Tibati 41 v
Tibé 40 h
Tibesti 37 y
Tibet 61 g
Tiburon 18 f
Tichitt 36 s
Tichla 36 o
Tichvin 50 n
Ticul 19 v
Tidikelt 37 n
Tidjikja 36 q
Tidra, I. 36 n
Tielongtan 61 d
Tien Shan 56
Tientsin (Tianjin) 57 x
Tierra Blanca 19 q
Tierra Colorada 19 o
Tierra del Fuego 30 w
Tiete 29 d
Tieyon 77 c
Tifariti 36 r
Tifton 20 k
Tigieglo 43 t
Tigil' 53 y
Tigre (Peru) 24 k
Tigre (Venezuela) 23 h
Tigris 39 d
Tiguentourine 37 e
Tijuana 18 c
Tikhoretsk 54 e
Tikrit 39 d
Tiksi 52 m
Tilamuta 69 i
Tilemsés 41 d
Tilemsi 36 z
Tillabéri 41 b
Tillamook 14 g
Tillia 41 d
Tilrhemt 34 u
Timané 28 k
Timan Ridge 50 h
Timaru 79 s
Timbaúba 27 v
Timbedgha 40 g
Timber Creek 73 b
Timbouctou 40 l
Timbuktu (Timbouctou) 40 l
Timeiaouine 37 n
Timétrine 36 y
Timia 37 r
Timimoun 36 m
Timiris, Cap 36 n
Timişoara 35 e
Timmins 16 i
Timón 27 q
Timor 69 x
Timor Sea 69 x
Timpton 52 y
Timsah 37 w
Tindouf 36 g
Tiné 42 e
Tinerhir 36 i
Tinfouchy 36 i
Tingo María 24 x
Tingri 61 i
Tinogasta 28 r
Tinos 35 t
Tinrhert, Hamada du 37 e
Tinsukiā 62 d
Tintina 28 u
Tinyay 53 a
Tin Zaouatene 37 o
Tioman 68 h
Tipperary 73 c
Tiracambu, Serra do 27 a
Tirana 35 d
Tiranë (Tirana) 35 d
Tiraspol 35 j
Tirekh 52 m
Tirekhtyakh 53 c
Tirgelir 53 e
Tirgu Mure 35 g
Tirich Mir 60 l
Tiroungoulou 42 e
Tiruchchirappalli 64 f
Tirunelveli 64 t
Tiruntán 24 l
Tirupati 64 h
Tisa 35 d
Tisdale 15 e
Tisisat Falls 43 b
Tit 37 p
Titaf 36 m
Tit-Ary 52 l
Titicaca, Lago 25 o
Titograd 35 c
Titovo Užice 35 d
Titov Veles 35 e
Titule 42 t
Titusville 20 m
Tizimi̇̃n 19 w
Tizi Ouzou 34 v
Tiznit 36 f
Tlacotalpan 19 r
Tlalamabele 49 b
Tlaltenango 18 z
Tlapacoyan 19 q
Tlaxiaco 19 p
Tlemcen 34 s
Tlisen 37 l
Tmed Bu Haschlscha 37 y
Toamasina 47 r
Toba & Kakar Ranges 60 j
Tobago 23 j
Toba, Lake 68 d
Tobelo 67 y
Tobermorey 73 t
Tobermory (Australia) 73 x
Tobermory (Canada) 16 i
Tobi 70 c
Tobo 70 o
Tobol' 55 e
Tobol' (River) 55 d
Tobol'sk 51 n
Tocache Nuevo 24 w
Tocantínia 26 z
Tocantinópolis 26 z
Tocantins 26 z
Tocopilla 28 c
Tocorpuri 28 e
Tocuyo 23 d
Todertang 43 n
Todos Santos (Bolivia) 25 r
Todos Santos (Mexico) 18 u
Toéssé 40 m
Togiak 11 n
Togo 41
Togtoh 57 t
Togyz 55 d
Tok 11 h
Tokar 38 z
Tokko 52 u
Tokko (River) 52 v
Tokoroa 79 v
Toktogul 55 x
Toktogul Reservoir 55 w
Tokuma 53 a
Tokushima 58 y
Tōkyō 59 o
Tolbo Nuur 56 i
Toledo (Brazil) 29 o
Toledo (Philippines) 67 i
Toledo (Spain) 34 q
Toledo (USA) 16 u
Toledo Bend Reservoir 20 d
Tolga 37 c
Toli 56 r
Toliara 47 n
Tolka 51 s
Tolka (River) 51 r
Tolo, Gulf of 69 h
Tolon 52 r
Tolstoy, Cape 53 x
Toluca 19 o
Tol'yatti 54 k
Tolybay 55 d
Tom' 56 g
Tomah 16 q
Tomar 55 l
Tomatlán 18 y
Tombador, Serra do 25 x
Tombigbee 20 h
Tombôco 44 f
Tômbua (Porto Alexandre) 48 e
Tomé-Açu 26 m
Tomi 42 o
Tomini, Gulf of 69 g
Tommot 52 y
Tomo 23 q
Tompo 53 b
Tom Price 72 t
Tom Price, Mount 72 t
Tomra 61 i
Tomsk 51 t
Tomtor 53 a
Tomtor (Cherskogo Mountains) 53 e
Tonalá 19 s
Tonantins 23 r
Tondano 67 w
Tonga 42 k
Tonga (State) 231 z
Tongchuan 62 m
Tongguzbasti 56 q
Tonghae 58 v
Tonghai 62 u
Tonghua 58 f
Tongian Islands 67 u
Tongjiang 58 k
Tongliao 58 e
Tongling 63 f
Tongren 62 h
Tongren (Wu Jiang) 62 m
Tongsa Dzong 61 l
Tongshan 63 d
Tongtian 62 e
Tongtianheyan 62 b
Tongulakh 52 j
Tongxin 57 q
Tongyu 58 e
Tongzi 62 l
Toni 42 v
Tonk 61 o
Tonking 62 w
Tonking, Gulf of 62 y
Tonle Sap 65 m
Tonnel'nyy 57 h
Tonopah 14 x
Tonsina 11 g
Tontantins 25 c
Tonzang 62 p
Toolebuc 73 v
Toompine 77 j
Toora-Chem 56 l
Toowoomba 78 f
Topeka 15 v
Topia 18 k
Topko 53 p
Top Springs 73 c
Torbat-e-Heidariye 60 d
Torbat-e-Jam 60 d
Torbert, Mount 11 d
Torgo 52 u
Torim 18 h
Torino 34 k
Torit 42 y
Torne 33 i
Torngat Mountains 13 y
Tornio 33 i
Toro 28 p
Torodi 41 b
Toro Doum 41 m
Toro, Lago del 30 t
Toronto 16 w
Tororo 42 z
Torrabai 48 f
Torrens Creek 74 o
Torrens, Lake 77 e
Torreón 18 l
Torres Strait 73 k
Tortkuduk 55 k
Tortolas 28 p
Tortosa 34 g
Tortuga 23 f
Torud 39 l
Torun 33 t
Torzhok 50 n
Toson Cengal 56 m
Tostado 28 v
Toteng 48 m
Totma 50 q
Totness 23 z
Totora 28 f
Tottori 58 y
Touba 40 i
Toubkal 36 g
Touboro 41 k
Touggourt 34 w
Tougué 40 e
Toukoto 40 g
Toulépleu 40 u
Toulon 34 j
Toulouse 34 g
Toungoo 62 r
Tours 34 g
Toussoro 42 e
Touws River 48 x
Townsend 15 a
Townsville 74 q
Toxkan 56 o
Toyama 58 z
Toyon-Tirekh 52 m
Tozeur 34 x
Trabzon 54 r
Trail 14 j
Traill er 91 r
Trang 65 v
Transantarctic Mountains 83 v
Trans Canada Highway 16 c
Transhimalaya 61 g
Trapani 34 z
Traralgon 77 y
Trarza 40 c
Travers 79 t
Treinta-y-Tres 31 f
Trelew 30 l
Trenque Lauquen 31 a
Trenton 16 z
Tres Arroyos 31 b
Três Bocas 25 a
Tres Coraçoes 29 h
Tres Isletas 28 w
Tres Lagos 30 u
Tres Marias 29 g
Tres Marias, Islas 18 w
Tres Marias Reservoir 29 g
Tres Puntas, Cabo 30 y
Tres Rios 29 i
Triangulos 19 t
Trichur 64 e
Trier 34 j
Trieste 35 a
Tríkala 35 r
Trincomalee 64 v
Trinidad and Tobago 23 j
Trinidad (Bolivia) 25 s
Trinidad (Colombia) 23 o
Trinidad (Cuba) 20 z
Trinidad (USA) 15 q
Trinity Peninsula 82 t
Tripolis (Greece) 35 s
Tripoli (Tarabulus) (Libya) 37 i
Tripolitania 37 h
Tristan da Cunha 222 y
Trivandrum 64 r
Trobriand or Kiriwina Island 71 r
Trofimovsk 52 l
Troickoje 56 f
Trois Rivières 17 a
Troitsk 55 d
Troitsko-Pechorsk 50 w
Troitskoye 55 a
Trombetas 25 l
Trompsburg 49 n
Tromsö 33 g
Trondheim 33 c
Trondheimsfjord 33 c
Trosh 50 j
Troy 35 u
Troyekurovo 54 e
Troyes 34 i
Troynoy 51 f
Trujillo (Honduras) 20 v
Trujillo (Peru) 24 u
Trujillo (Spain) 34 p
Truk Islands 71 e
Truro 17 f
Tsaratanana Mountains 47 e
Tsau 48 m
Tsavo 45 j
Tsavo National Park 45 k
Tschita 52 r
Tselinograd 55 j
Tsentral'nyy 56 g
Tsévié 41 n
Tshabong 48 z
Tshane 48 l
Tshela 44 e
Tshikapa 44 k
Tshimbalanga 44 z
Tshofa 45 a
Tsholotsho 49 c
Tshuapa 44 l
Tsihombe 47 p
Tsimafana 47 o
Tsimlyanskoye Reservoir 54 g
Tsinan (Jinan) 63 e
Tsingtao (Qingdao) 57 z
Tsiribihina 47 p
Tsiroanomandidy 47 p
Tsitsihar (Qiqihar) 58 f
Tsoe 49 a
Tsugaru-Kaiky 59 b
Tsumeb 48 j
Tsumkwe 48 k
Tsuruga 58 z
Tsushima 58 v
Tswiza 49 f
Tuamotu Archipelago 230 p
Tuan Giao 62 v
Tuangku 65 u
Tuapse 54 r
Tuareg 40 m
Tubaro 29 r
Tubruq 38 c
Tubuai Islands 230 o
Tubutama 18 g
Tuckanarra 76 f
Tucson 18 g
Tucumá 26 x
Tucumcari 15 r
Tucupita 23 i
Tucuruí 26 l
Tuekta 56 f
Tueré 26 k
Tugela 49 r
Tugolukovo 54 f
Tuguegarao 67 g
Tugur 53 p
Tugur (River) 53 o
Tukalan 52 a
Tukangbesi Islands 69 v
Tuktoyaktuk 11 l
Tula 19 o
Tula (USSR) 54 d
Tula Mountains 84 m
Tulancingo 19 p
Tulcán 24 i
Tulcea 35 i
Tuli 49 d
Tuli (River) 49 d
Tulia 15 s
Tulihe 57 m
Tully 74 c
Tulsa 15 v